G. L.

HENRY WHEATON
1785-1848

Da Capo Press Reprints in

AMERICAN CONSTITUTIONAL AND LEGAL HISTORY

GENERAL EDITOR: LEONARD W. LEVY

Claremont Graduate School

HENRY WHEATON
1785-1848

By

ELIZABETH FEASTER BAKER

DA CAPO PRESS • NEW YORK • 1971

HENRY WHEATON

HENRY WHEATON

HENRY WHEATON
1785-1848

By

ELIZABETH FEASTER BAKER

UNIVERSITY OF PENNSYLVANIA PRESS

PHILADELPHIA

1937

The office of a foreign minister is the office of a peacemaker. Diplomacy has been supposed to be a mantle of craft and deceit, but I believe that honor and integrity are the true arts of the diplomatist.

HENRY WHEATON

FOREWORD

HENRY WHEATON ranks as one of the most distinguished of American publicists of the nineteenth century in the field of international law. He began his career as a lawyer in Rhode Island and New York and practised before the Supreme Court of the United States; he founded the *National Advocate* in New York City and edited that paper for three years; he served as Reporter of the Supreme Court of the United States from 1816 to 1827, during the period in which were handed down some of the most important of Chief Justice Marshall's opinions; and he held various official positions in New York. His diplomatic activities as Chargé d'Affaires of the United States in Denmark from 1827 to 1835, and his negotiations with the German Customs Union as United States Minister to Prussia from 1835 to 1846, contributed greatly to the preservation of friendly relations between the United States and Europe. Always working with a quiet mind, richly schooled, Henry Wheaton further promoted the cause of world peace by the publication of his *Elements of International Law* and its companion volume *The History of the Law of Nations.* The distinctions conferred upon him during his lifetime by universities and academies on both sides of the ocean were witnesses of the contemporary recognition of his merits.

Since Henry Wheaton's life as a lawyer, a diplomat, and a publicist overshadowed what might be called his personal relations, this essay is to be considered not as a biography in the modern psychological sense but as an effort to portray the man in his career.

Throughout the preparation of this volume many counselors and friends have given their help and advice. To Professor St. George L. Sioussat especially I am indebted for his suggestion of the subject and for his careful criticism of the entire manuscript. To Professor Edward P. Cheyney I am sincerely grateful for the inspiration given by him to continue in research studies. Without his encouragement this book probably never would have been undertaken. I desire also to express my thanks to Dr. Tyler Dennett for the courteous permission to use the archives in the State Department, and to his assistants Mrs. Natalie Summers and Miss Florence A. Hitchcock for their unfailing help; to the staff of the Manuscript Division of the Library of Congress, and particularly to Dr. Thomas P. Martin for providing convenient access to necessary documents; to Dr. Marie Gerstenfeld, of the University of Vienna, for efficient aid in deciphering the reproductions of official German Documents; to Dr. Alban W. Hoopes and Dr. Margaret McHenry for reading and correcting the manuscript; and to His Honor the Mayor of Providence for permission to have photographed Healy's portrait of Henry Wheaton. To many others who extended courtesies during the progress of the research acknowledgment is due. Among these are the officials of the Massachusetts Historical Society, the New Hampshire Historical Society, the Rhode Island Historical Society, the New York Historical Society, the Pennsylvania Historical Society, the American Philosophical Society, the Boston Athenaeum, the Harvard University Library, the Harvard Law Library, the University of Pennsylvania Library, the University of Pennsylvania Law Library, the Providence Public Library, the Boston Public Library and the New York Public Library. To the staff of the John Hay Library at Brown University especial thanks are extended for the use of the Wheaton papers and books, and to Dr. Henry B. Van Hoesen, Librarian, and Miss Eleanor Leonard for their ready assistance. To all others who in any way contributed to the final accomplishment of this volume I am deeply grateful.

E. F. B.

CONTENTS

ILLUSTRATIONS

PART ONE

A YOUNG AMERICAN

Chapter I

ON THE THRESHOLD OF THE NINETEENTH CENTURY

DURING the course of the last two decades of the eighteenth century sturdy sailing vessels from the eastern coasts of North America began to ply their way to the Orient. Among these the ship *General Washington*, built and owned in Providence, Rhode Island, returned in July 1789 from the first voyage to China made from that port.[1] Thus the growing town entered upon a brief but glorious era of East India trade.[2] The same period witnessed not only this broadening of American commerce to world dimensions but also the evolution of Rhode Island and the other colonies into states in the Union under the Constitution. Likewise, in France, republicanism was about to make its appearance; with Thomas Jefferson, in the rôle of political adviser, aiding Lafayette in the framing of the French Declaration of the Rights of Man.[3] In ideas, then, no less than in commerce, changes were taking place which pointed toward new and radically different trends of thought throughout the young American republic, the old French nation, and the world of international affairs.

In these vital years Henry Wheaton, born in Providence on November 27, 1785, spent his early youth. His ancestor, Robert Wheaton, came from Swansea in Wales to Salem, Massachusetts, in 1636, the same year that Roger Williams started his independent settlement which later became the capital of Rhode Island. In 1645 Robert Wheaton with his wife removed to Rehoboth, Massachusetts, less than ten miles from Providence. In the latter place was born, a little over a century later, Henry Wheaton's father, Seth, the fifth in descent from Robert.[4] His contemporaries saw in him a

3

man of great natural sagacity and of upright and determined character. He had acquired the title of colonel, and during his long business career maintained a distinguished position among his fellow citizens, taking always an active interest in contemporary affairs and improvements. Through the commerce and navigation which played so large a part in the life of the town, he gained a small fortune.[5] Besides his residence and lot on Main Street and his warehouse on Water Street, he owned five and a half acres of farm land on what is now known as Constitution Hill and two and a half acres on Prospect Hill.[6] Eventually he was made president of the Rhode Island branch of the Bank of the United States, the most honorable distinction that could be conferred at that time on a retired merchant.[7]

On August 29, 1784, when Seth Wheaton was in his twenty-fifth year, he married his second cousin, Abigail Wheaton, who was also a descendant of the original immigrant Robert.[8] She was, one reads, a sweet-tempered woman "of strong intellect and of rare delicacy and refinement." [9] With her youngest brother, Dr. Levi Wheaton, Seth and his family were especially congenial. Dr. Wheaton, after studying medicine and graduating from Rhode Island College, acted as surgeon on board a privateer. In the autumn of 1782, his vessel having been captured, he was carried a prisoner to New York and placed on duty in the prison ship *Falmouth*. After the war he lived for a few years at Hudson, New York, and in New York City; then he returned to Providence where he was professor of medicine at Brown University from 1815 to 1828. Eminent as a physician, he earned distinction also as a *littérateur*.[10] Between Dr. Wheaton and his nephew Henry there existed a cordial friendship which played an important part in the development of the boy's outlook on life. Just a few years before his death Henry wrote to his uncle: "I am your debtor in all things, owing to you more of what I am than to all others." [11]

Amid congenial surroundings Henry Wheaton acquired his preliminary education in the Latin school connected with

Rhode Island College. From the time of its removal from Warren to Providence about 1770, the citizens of Providence and the college authorities always endeavored to provide adequate and beautiful buildings for the institution. The first building erected on Prospect Hill was University Hall. The plan or model followed that of Nassau Hall, Princeton, which was then regarded as one of the finest structures of its kind in the country. In the northwest corner room of the lower story of this building was conducted the university grammar or Latin school. Its purpose was to prepare students for entrance to college. The school was under the immediate supervision of the president of the college and the general inspection of the town's school committee.[12]

In 1798, at the age of twelve, Henry graduated from the grammar school and thereupon entered the college. Judged by present standards the preparation seems rather one-sided. The requirements for admission were "the ability to read accurately, construe and parse Cicero's Orations, Virgil's Aeneid, and the Greek testament; also to write Latin grammatically and to know the rules of Vulgar arithmetic."[13]

During Wheaton's undergraduate days the walls of University Hall embraced, besides the Latin school, all the activities of the college—offices, library, recitation rooms, dormitory, and commons. Here the students slept and studied, and here most of them took their meals. Inside the college grounds to the right of this building were the President's house and barn, and, it has been said, "his horse and cow kept the grass down." Apparently the only other structure on the campus was the well-curb around the opening of the well from which the students obtained their supply of water.[14]

Outside the campus, halfway down the steep hill, which at that time led to the waterfront, a building connected with the University had been erected. For many years the First Baptist Church, which had been established in Providence in 1638, formed the basis of a great part of the religious life of Rhode Island. In 1774 the plans for a new Baptist meetinghouse were enlarged so that the edifice would be "for the Public Worship

of Almighty God, and also for holding Commencement in," [15]
and Commencement at Brown has always been held in that
charming old church. The building is of the Christopher Wren
type. The spire, 185 feet high, is a close copy of one of the many
proposed but unused designs of a steeple for St. Martins-in-the-
Fields in London. The bell was made in London and bore at
first the quaint inscription:

> For freedom of conscience the town was first planted.
>   Persuasion, not force, was used by the people:
> This Church is the eldest, and has not recanted,
>   Enjoying and granting bell, temple and steeple.[16]

The bell was rung not only to notify the community when
services were to be held in the church but also every day at sun-
rise, at noon, and at nine o'clock in the evening. This custom
has always been maintained and is still being followed today.

In this environment Wheaton spent his college life. During the greater part of the four years he roomed with John
Whipple, who later became a prominent lawyer in Providence and a member of the Rhode Island general assembly.
Among his other classmates were Henry Bowen, Ferdinand
Ellis, Milton Maxcy, a nephew of the President of the college,
and Richard Waterman.[17]

While Henry was thus spending his early years in Providence, in various sections of the United States other young
Americans with whom he was later to be intimately associated were making ready in their different ways to play their
several parts in the world of action and thought. Among
these were Henry Clay, Daniel Webster, John C. Calhoun,
Lewis Cass, Martin Van Buren, Edward Everett, and George
Bancroft, to mention only a few of his many contemporaries
who were to gain renown.

Young as he was, Wheaton must have found the college
course, as outlined, rather thin and restricted. The only
mention of history in the entire curriculum was made in the
statement for the senior year which comprised "Locke on
the Human Understanding and a review of the authors

PROVIDENCE IN WHEATON'S BOYHOOD

studied in the previous years, with some select parts of history." [18] Henry, however, had an intense love of historical pursuits, and John Whipple has related that Wheaton's intellectual habits differed in a marked degree from every member of his class in this respect.[19] Moreover, he was fortunate in pursuing his studies under the presidency of Jonathan Maxcy, who afterward became the first president of South Carolina College, for he was a man of wonderful eloquence and a rare scholar who encouraged in his students wide reading and a broad outlook on the affairs of life.

This attitude also was emphasized at the college by a literary society known as the "Federal Adelphi." An application had been made in 1789 by the leading men of the college and town for a chapter of the Phi Beta Kappa. The request, although assented to by Yale, was refused by Harvard, much to the indignation of the applicants. As a result the Federal Adelphi was formed and included in its membership many of the prominent men of both the town and state. It played a leading part in the life of the college for many years.[20]

Although Wheaton did not neglect his tasks in classical lore, his passion for historical and general knowledge seemed to absorb him. Much the largest portion of his attention was occupied by a study of the annals of the different nations of ancient and modern times. The story of the experiences of French Republicanism so captivated him and was discussed by him so frequently that his classmates dubbed him "Citizen Wheaton." [21] This devotion to the French was to be a lifelong affection.

He graduated from Rhode Island College in 1802. Commencement at that time was a great annual event in the life of Providence. The whole community and nearly the whole state was interested in it. The town was overrun with strangers. They began to arrive on Monday, and by Tuesday afternoon the stable yards of the Golden Ball Inn, the Montgomery Tavern and other public houses were crowded with square-topped chaises.

On Tuesday evening before it was fairly dark, the college yard was filled with people. Not a light was to be seen at the college windows until the college bell rang, when eight tallow candles at each of the many windows were all lighted together. At the same time a curtain was removed from a box in front of the building exposing the national emblem, the spread eagle, brilliantly illuminated. Then the band of music which the graduates had hired to play at the commencement exercises the next day and which had been gathered on the steps of the building played "Washington's March," "Hail Columbia," and other appropriate selections. At a given signal from the college bell the music ceased, and the lights were extinguished simultaneously. This was the opening scene of commencement.

On Wednesday morning the rising sun was saluted by two of the brass fieldpieces which Burgoyne had surrendered at Saratoga. The great day had arrived. Shortly after nine o'clock the academic procession formed in front of University Hall and proceeded down to the meetinghouse.[22]

There were twenty-eight members in Wheaton's graduating class, and of these, twenty-one took part in the exercises by delivering original orations, dissertations, or poems. The first oration of the day was the salutatory address which was delivered in Latin. Wheaton, who appeared on the program as number nine, made his interest in general knowledge apparent by delivering an intermediate oration entitled "Progress of the Mathematical and Physical Sciences during the Eighteenth Century." [23]

After two or three hours had been spent listening to the first half of the program, the academic procession was formed, and faculty, graduates, undergraduates, and honored visitors went to University Hall for dinner. When everyone had been served, the same formal return was made to the meetinghouse, and two or three more hours were spent listening to the remainder of the exercises. These were brought to a close by the valedictory which also was given in Latin. The next day the Federal Adelphi held its final meeting of the year. Wheaton's college life had been brought to a close.

Long after Wheaton's death, it was written: "If Rhode Island College during the decade of President Maxcy's administration had done nothing else but give this intellect [Henry Wheaton's] a collegiate training, its existence would be amply justified." [24]

Chapter II

EMBARKED ON A PROFESSIONAL CAREER

O F THE twenty-seven youths who graduated with Wheaton in 1802 about half studied law,[1] as did Wheaton himself in compliance with his father's wishes. The trend which his own desire had taken was indicated by his commencement oration, and his inclination, strange as it now seems in the light of his accomplishments, was toward engineering. For three years he pursued his legal studies in the office of Nathaniel Searles, then a prominent attorney in Providence.[2] Since John Whipple had decided to become a lawyer, he and Wheaton frequently studied together. According to Whipple, "For the same reason that while in college Wheaton devoted but a small portion of his mind to the technicalities of language, while a student at law he devoted but little of his time to special pleading." [3] He was more interested in underlying principles and their application. At the age of nineteen he was admitted to the Rhode Island bar.[4] To enable him to acquire additional knowledge and training, his father determined to give him the opportunity of studying and traveling in Europe.

Wheaton sailed from New York in June, 1805. The voyage, protracted by calms and adverse winds, was given a touch of excitement when the vessel was boarded by officers of the British frigates *Topaze* and *Ceres,* which reminded the passengers of the renewed outbreak of war between England and France. This visit brought vividly to Wheaton's attention the belligerent right of search which later was to engage his consideration many times and was to draw upon his best legal power in his enunciation of the principles involved. In this particular instance all on board were treated politely, and they were much interested in the news which the British officers could give them. On the morning of the sixth of July their boat reached the village of St. Nazaire at the mouth of the Loire. After having been detained there three days at quarantine, to which all vessels coming from the States were subjected, Wheaton went by river boat to Paimboeuf. Because of some delay in procuring the verification of his passport, he was prevented from continuing his journey until the next day, but reached Nantes on the evening of the eleventh.[5] During his sojourn in this vicinity he visited Indrêt, an island below the town, to view the national foundry for cannon which was located there and which was said to be the foremost in France.[6] All of the letters written by him to his father from Europe give interesting descriptions of the places he saw and the country through which he passed, touching on many phases of the social, economic, and political life of the people.

While on the road from Nantes to Bordeaux by diligence he stayed overnight at Rochefort. The next morning he took the opportunity of visiting the port, which he was permitted to do by going with his *aubergiste,* who was responsible for him. Here, although it was one of the smallest dockyards the French had, he saw immense supplies of war materials, and, in the course of construction, a ship and several corvettes. He reached Bordeaux on the twenty-sixth, much less fatigued by the journey than he had expected to be.[7]

Upon his arrival he presented himself to M. Pelletreau, to whom he carried letters from friends in New York and into whose family he was received in "the kindest manner." All the friends whom he consulted in New York before sailing and all those with whom he conversed on the subject in France advised him to proceed to some provincial town and reside there a short time before going to Paris so that he might learn more readily to speak French. For this purpose M. Pelletreau recommended Poitiers as a place agreeable, healthy, and peopled by inhabitants who spoke the French language in its utmost purity. It also possessed another very great advantage in that it was the seat of several different courts of first instance and a tribunal of final appeal. Thus he would obtain the opportunity of hearing some of the most eminent advocates in France, which would aid him not only in his desire to increase his knowledge of and fluency in the use of the French language but also in his purpose to pursue the study of law.[8]

For these reasons he decided to proceed immediately to Poitiers where he arrived on Sunday evening, the eighth of August. Through a letter of introduction given to him by M. Pelletreau, he procured the privilege of boarding at a reasonable rate in a private family.

I have the advantages of the instruction of the gentleman of the house, and of the use of his library. I have received every attention from those with whom I have been made acquainted, that can render my situation agreeable and my residence profitable. I have made such progress in the language that I can make known all my wants, and can speak on any common topic of conversation with the aid of explanations, though I do not pretend to say with much propriety or regard to grammatical rules. The attention for which the French are so remarkable in this respect, contributes not a little to my improvement, and I hope with the addition of the period I may spend in Paris to be able to speak with tolerable propriety.[9]

He remained in Poitiers for about two months regularly attending the tribunals and, as he had hoped, hearing some of the foremost lawyers of the country. In later years he always recurred with pleasure to the time spent there. The kindness he experienced from the family in which he lived and the graceful politeness and cheerfulness of the French character gave him ever after a predilection in favor of France.[10]

At the time of Wheaton's residence in France, the *Code Napoléon*, published in 1804, had been in operation for only a year and had not then been rendered into English. Young as he was, he fully appreciated the importance of this great revision of the laws of France and made a translation of the codes into English for publication in the United States; but this was prevented by the accidental destruction of the manuscript by fire.[11]

From Poitiers Henry went to Paris where General John Armstrong, with whom he was later brought into intimate relation, represented the United States. Wheaton not only pursued his study of jurisprudence but also observed the current trends of social and political life and the evidences of a new interest in science and the arts which he found in the city and its environs. This revival was partly due to the influx of art treasures brought to France by Napoleon as a result of the Italian campaigns. While in Paris Wheaton was present at a public sitting of the National Institute at which were distributed the grand prizes in architecture, sculpture, painting, intaglios, and music. Concerning this he wrote, "The effect produced by the enthusiasm excited by these annual rewards of merit must be a great improvement in the fine arts." [12] After having seen everything which he considered worthy of attention, he left for London by way of Rotterdam. To make this journey he was obliged to go through Maestricht and Liege instead of Antwerp—which was the ordinary route—on account of the naval constructions which were going on in that port. At that time this was a regulation applied to all foreigners.[13]

On his arrival in London about the first of November, he called on Mr. Charles Murray with a letter from his uncle, Dr. Levi Wheaton. In reply to Wheaton's request for his advice as to a private family with whom he might board, Mr. Murray invited him to live in his own home. Henry wrote to his father,

Although this was something I had no right to expect, yet the frankness of his manner prevented my refusing his kind offer, which also was not suggested by any hint of my own wishes for the purpose. I find my situation very agreeable here; as, besides the advantage of living in so pleasing a family, I have that of the use of Mr. Murray's books and of his advice and assistance in all the objects of my pursuit.

Fortunately for Wheaton the term of the courts in Westminster Hall began on the fifth of November, just after his arrival, and continued for a month. He was able, therefore, to visit them frequently.[14] What he saw of them inspired in him a respect for their administration of justice. "Learning, purity, and impartiality seem to preside in them," he wrote. "In this my opinion of the English tribunals I do not mean, however, to include the Court of Admiralty, which, though proceeding according to the law of nations, is confessedly under a political direction and governed in its decisions by considerations of state." [15] It is easy to understand how Wheaton with his eager, enquiring mind, full of the zest of youth, felt when he wrote to his father, "I have endeavored to follow your advice as to shunning political discussions, avoiding conversation of that nature when practicable, and silently assenting to the ideas when not. This, however, is not easy to do; almost every important subject of enquiry being more or less connected with politics in the awful times when we live." [16] Wheaton mingled with the prominent men of the day and was often at the house of James Monroe, then our minister in London. He informed his father, on the thirtieth of January,

I saw Mr. Monroe on Sunday last; his family are at Bath; the feeble state of Mrs. Monroe's health preventing her from remaining in town. He informed me that our difficulties with this country would probably be amicably settled; but he was, as you may conclude, totally silent as to the manner or the actual state of the negotiations.[17]

Monroe seems to have taken some pains to converse with Wheaton on the political and social state of Europe. Many years later the latter's daughter, Abby Wheaton, wrote: "Perhaps these conversations contributed to form his taste for diplomatic life." [18]

Not only was the taste for diplomatic life acquired at this

LEVI WHEATON

time, but the broad foundation laid which formed the basis of much of his most valuable work in the future. This is evident from a letter to his father dated the second of March, 1806, four months after his arrival in England, in which he wrote, "The Prize Courts continue in their decrees to manifest a disposition not to recede from those doctrines upon the faith of which they have confiscated so much of our neutral property." He stated further that the judgment of the Court of Appeals had been delivered a few days before by Sir William Grant at considerable length in which the decree of the Admiralty on a continuous voyage was affirmed.[19]

The courts did not claim his entire attention. He attended many of the meetings of the houses of Parliament, studying their methods of procedure in transacting the business brought before them and the questions which were discussed by them. He found the House of Commons a "very confined, unwholesome place." During the proceedings against Henry Dundas, Viscount Melville, resulting from his impeachment for misuse of public funds as first lord of the admiralty, Wheaton heard the arguments of some of the foremost English barristers. He wrote to his father that the trial was "in the highest degree splendid and interesting, being conducted in Westminster Hall in the same manner as Mr. Hastings'." [20]

Having spent over six months in England, he returned to the United States in June 1806 and began the practice of law in Providence, as set forth by the following announcement:

> H. Wheaton informs the Public that he
> has commenced the practice of his
> profession as an Attorney and Counsellor
> at Law.   Office over
> Messrs. Watson & Gladdings Store.[21]

He entered upon his professional life just after the inception of Napoleon's continental system. During the following years both England and France endeavored to embroil the United States in a war each with its respective adversary, as, after England's declaration of war against Denmark in 1807, the United States was practically the only neutral engaged in extensive maritime trade. Henry Wheaton took an active interest in the wrongs which his country was suffering from the depredations of the European belligerents. The *Rhode Island Phoenix,* afterwards the *Rhode Island Patriot,* published many papers of which he was the author, supporting the administrations of Jefferson and of Madison.[22] His political articles also appeared in the *National Intelligencer* and other periodicals, thus establishing his reputation beyond the bounds of Rhode Island. As a result, the first suggestions of a diplomatic career appeared in the proposals of an appointment for him as secretary of legation either to Paris or London.[23]

But international and national affairs were not the only ones which occupied his attention. Both he and his father took an active interest in the affairs of their native state and town. In 1810 they joined with Henry Smith, Thomas Coles, and Christopher Ellery in signing a letter to James Madison, President of the United States, protesting against the appointment recommended by the Governor of Rhode Island of David L. Barnes, district judge, who was a candidate for the office vacated by the death of Mr. Cushing, that of judge of the supreme court.[24]

In the same year Henry Wheaton appeared publicly in connection with an institution politically prominent today. An association by the name of the Tammany Society, or Columbian Order, which derived its name from the Indian Chief Tammany, "whose attachment to liberty was greater than his love of life," was founded for charitable and social purposes about 1788 in New York City in opposition to the Society of the Cincinnati. It was claimed that the latter had aristocratic tendencies.[25] At first most persons of influence and standing in New York and wherever branches were established were members of the Tammany Society as it was not affiliated with any political party. In New York its anniversary, which was held on the twelfth day of May, was regarded as a holiday. Afterwards a large proportion of its

Federalist members were induced to abandon it because of the opposition of President Washington to "self-created societies." It then began to assume a party character leaning to the support of Thomas Jefferson.[26] The association and its branches gradually increased in number.

Thus it was that on July 4, 1810, Henry Wheaton delivered an oration "before the Tammany Society, or Columbian Order, and the Republican Citizens of Providence and its vicinity at the Town-House" to celebrate the anniversary of American independence.[27] The language of the oration was fluent and vigorous. In acknowledging the receipt of a copy, Mr. Jefferson wrote that he rejoiced "over every publication wherein such sentiments are expressed. While these prevail all is safe." [28] Wheaton in the course of this oration referred to the practice of impressment, and indicated how strongly he felt concerning it when he said, "This allusion to impressment reminds us of that foul disgrace to our national reputation, which withers the laurels acquired in the war of our Revolution and almost effaces the glories of its triumphs." [29]

In the following year, 1811, Henry married his cousin Catherine, who was the daughter of Dr. Levi Wheaton, his uncle, friend, and confidant.

Chapter III

A NEW VENTURE

IN THE search for greater professional opportunities than could be secured in Providence, Wheaton moved to New York City in the fall of 1812, with the intention of practising law. On his arrival he found that he was prevented from becoming a member of the New York Bar by the system of apprenticeship or clerkship required in that state. One of the essential conditions of this system, which remained in force until abrogated by the constitution of 1846, was a novitiate of at least three years. This preliminary period could not be dispensed with even in the case of an attorney from another state or in consequence of attainments however extensive.[1] Although greatly disappointed in not being able to gain immediate admission to the bar, he found his affiliation with the Tammany Society in Providence to be the introduction to a literary opportunity in New York.

The measures of Presidents Jefferson and Madison had been supported by *The Columbian*, the paper of the Democratic party in New York. In 1812 the editor, Charles Holt, who was a warm friend of DeWitt Clinton, backed Clinton for President against James Madison. In consequence of this *The Columbian* and Holt gained disfavor at Tammany Hall. To take the place of *The Columbian*, a new paper, *The National Advocate*, was established as the Tammany organ, and of this Henry Wheaton was appointed editor.[2] The first number was issued December 15, 1812. It was published at No. 56 Pine Street at ten dollars per annum for the daily issue and two dollars and fifty cents for the weekly paper. In the original prospectus, it was promised among other things "that this print will never wound the feelings of virtue; never infringe the laws of decorum; and never spare the vices of political turpitude." [3]

About two weeks after the paper had been started, Wheaton wrote to his uncle Dr. Levi Wheaton that he found his task "perfectly pleasant and unmixed as yet with any disagreeable occurrence whatever. I go not to the coffee house —nor to news rooms—nor caucuses—thinking it more dignified to avoid them. The print has yet procured me neither credit, nor discredit—upon any large scale—for in truth I believe its existence is very little known beyond the circle of its subscribers. It is, however, commended by many other papers—and I am happy to add by the most judicious here who have read it." [4] Two months later he wrote, "I am much gratified to find you approve my efforts all of which I assure you are made from the genuine impulse of my heart. My essay on the non-importation was very generally approved of." [5] His well-timed editorials and interesting news items attracted attention, and the circulation of the paper grew steadily, so that it became necessary to move to larger quarters. On March 11, 1813, the announcement appeared that the paper was published at No. 73 Pine Street for N. Phillips, Proprietor.[6]

Henry Wheaton's editorials covered a wide and varied field of contemporary thought and events. Edward Everett paid him a tribute of appreciation by saying that the liabilities and duties created by the war with England "were elucidated by him with the learning of an accomplished publicist and the zeal of a sincere patriot." [7] The paper was sometimes the vehicle of semi-official expositions of national policies, in which he took a great interest. He also occasionally engaged actively in party affairs; as when, with every demonstration of joy, the anniversary of the election of James Madison to the presidency of the United States was celebrated in New York City on the fourth of March. Among the toasts which were drunk was one proposed by Wheaton, "The Navy—the Nation's stay—and hope—and honor." [8]

On July 21, 1813, he completed an editorial review of "An

Oration, delivered July 5, 1813, before the Washington
Benevolent Society" by the Honorable Gouverneur Morris.
Wheaton vindicated the right of expatriation which Morris
had denied.[9] Nine days later, on July 30, appeared an editorial on the subject of impressed seamen and the right of
search.[10] This topic had been discussed previously in the
same columns and was to appear many more times during his
editorship. Judge Story's opinion upon the illegality of
enemy licenses first appeared in Wheaton's paper. The extent
to which such licenses were then used in order to supply the
British armies with provisions attracted great attention to
the subject.[11] Wheaton also came valiantly to the aid of his
friend General Armstrong, then secretary of war, who had
been the representative of the United States in Paris during
Wheaton's visit. He published a statement of the reasons
which had induced Armstrong to remove General Dearborn
from the command of the army and the causes of the failure
of the subsequent campaigns of Generals Wilkinson and
Hampton.[12] After General Armstrong had left the War
Office, the *National Advocate* continued, in opposition to the
popular prejudice excited against the former secretary on
account of the disastrous affair of Washington, to support
and sustain him as "entitled to the gratitude of the nation for
having put out of the way the superannuated generals and
for bringing forward a set of generals who rescued our
country from eternal disgrace." [13] In 1814 Wheaton pointed
out the highly objectionable nature of the Hartford convention held for the purpose of considering the sectional interests of some of the New England states.[14] Many pertinent
topics were discussed by him, such as the matters debated in
Congress, Secretary Monroe's report,[15] and the repeal of the
French Decrees.[16] The current affairs of Europe in general
were kept clearly before his public, and often he translated
and published news and articles contained in the French
papers.[17]

But, even though he was so busily engaged, the real object
he wished to attain—the practice of his profession—was not

forgotten. The delay in gaining admission to the New York
Bar did not prevent him from being retained and appearing
as counsel before the Supreme Court in Washington. He was
present at the February session of the Court in 1814, taking
part in the case of *The Frances*. In writing of this to his uncle,
he gives his first impression of William Pinkney:

> I shall open, and Mr. Dexter and Pinkney will close on our side.
> The latter gentleman is another acquaintance I have made since
> I have been here. He is a most affected piece of stuff—dresses like
> a petit maître—tears a passion to rags, and splits the ears of the
> groundlings with his vehement elocution. However, bating these
> little faults, he is an accomplished advocate, and at times truly
> eloquent. He has imitated the Irish rather than the English bar-
> risters. It is said he will come next year from Baltimore, and cer-
> tainly will make a splendid figure in Congress, debating declama-
> tion would seem to be his forte.[18]

With his pleasing personality, social poise, and literary
ability Wheaton quickly made friends, many of whom had
gained renown and distinction. Among these were Judge
Spencer [19] and Judge Story. From the latter, who had been
appointed associate justice of the Supreme Court of the
United States in 1811, he received the suggestion which resulted in his first book; for in July 1813 the young editor at
the age of twenty-eight commenced an undertaking, to which,
he said,

I have been stimulated by Judge Story, who has flattered me that
I might gain both money and reputation by it. It is to write a digest
of the law of prizes. There is not in our language any such work
of considerable merit of the elementary kind, and it is very much
wanted. It will cost me a great deal of labour, but I hope I shall
be able to overcome the obstacles. You will, therefore, not conclude
me idle, should you not hear from me very often.[20]

In the latter part of August, Mrs. Wheaton wrote to her
father that Henry was going on with his book as rapidly as
could be expected and that he had not been well lately owing
to his constant writing, as "it is very laborious work and

consequently tedious." [21] In September Henry himself wrote to Dr. Wheaton, "I have by no means given up my book, tho' it does not go as fast as I could wish. This has been occasioned by the extreme heat of the season, surpassing almost anything I have ever felt." [22] Over two months later he wrote, "I am working away upon my book as fast as possible, but find the materials accumulate upon me so that I see no end to my labour. The first rough outline being completed will however render the finish easy and pleasant. There is also much perplexity arising from the conflict between the new and the old law of nations which I shall dispose of as well as I can." [23] This took time and on April 16, 1814, he said briefly, "I work hard just now upon 'the book.' " [24]

Although so occupied, in 1814 at the theatre, Anthony Street, New York, he delivered before the different Republican societies another Fourth of July oration to celebrate the anniversary of American independence.[25] Contemporary with this incident, Mrs. Wheaton, who was visiting in Baltimore, wrote to her father, "I was introduced in Philadelphia to M. Duponceau, an advocate of eminence and an author, he lives in great style. He soon with the freedom of a frenchman entered into conversation with me and then launched forth into the highest encomium on Henry and his *paper*, said it was superior to any printed in the country." [26]

Wheaton's talents began to be widely recognized, an evidence of which became manifest when on the twenty-sixth of October, 1814, the appointment of Division Judge Advocate of the Army was unanimously confirmed to him by the United States Senate with cordial expressions of approval.[27]

The year 1815 was a busy one. On January 6 there appeared in the *National Intelligencer* over the signature "Juris Consultus" an article in which Wheaton urged the establishment of a uniform system of bankruptcy laws throughout the United States. In the foreword to the article the *National Intelligencer* said that as it was "from the pen of one of the best writers in the country," it was "entitled to attentive perusal." [28] It was afterwards published in pamphlet form.

In May an article written by Wheaton appeared in the first issue of the *North American Review*.[29] The *North American Review and Miscellaneous Journal* was established and edited by William Tudor, after he had returned from a journey abroad, and apparently was based on a study of the current English periodicals. Tudor's journal contained both reviews and magazine articles. The initial number began with a series of comments on old American books and pamphlets, followed by several brief letters to the editor and two mediocre poems. Then came a thirty-two page notice of Baron de Grimm's *Mémoirs*. "Similar space," it has been recounted, "is given to the Quarterly Review's attack on American manners and morals in its famous review of 'Inchiquin's Letters'—the article using James K. Paulding's contribution to the controversy, 'The United States and England,' as its basis. Thus the North American began in its very first number its participation in the third war with England—the paper war." [30] This review written by Wheaton was a patriotic defense of the literature of the United States against the prejudiced attacks of the British press, which had been holding us up to the derision of Europe because, according to William Beach Lawrence, "in our infancy our literature had not attained the ripeness of adolescence," and "while all our efforts were required for the creation of the necessaries, we were wanting in some of the refinements, which belong to nations where a favored class have the leisure to devote themselves to the elegancies of life." [31]

On April 9, 1815, Wheaton wrote to his wife, "I only wait for some decisions from Washington, to put my book to press. Upon the whole I am pretty well satisfied with it." His book, *A Digest of the Law of Maritime Capture and Prizes*, was at last published, and immediately was well received by the legal profession, although his good friend George Douglass of Washington wrote to him in protest, "I wish with all my heart, that you had printed it on better paper. In the second edition take more care of this complaint to the eye." [32] Judge Story, who was responsible for its inception, commended him by writing, "You have honorably discharged that duty, which every man owes to his profession, and I am persuaded that your labours will ultimately obtain the rewards which learning and talents cannot fail to secure." [33] The book was more than a digest, as Wheaton gave a full analysis of the adjudications of the tribunals of different countries—especially of England and the United States—on questions of prize. This necessarily involved a review of all those debatable points of maritime law which had been the subject of the diplomatic discussions between the two countries. In addition he presented an exposition of the law of nations. It contained a clearer and more accurate view of the English and French edicts against neutral commerce than could be found anywhere else. Richard Rush, who was at that time Attorney-General of the United States, informed Wheaton that he had made the book the basis of a pamphlet entitled *American Jurisprudence*. In concluding his article Rush expressed "an unequivocal opinion" in favor of Wheaton's work, although like Douglass he regretted that its paper and type were not better.[34]

The same year was also to see the publication of another small book by Wheaton. This was a translation from the French language of an exposition written by Lieutenant General Carnot of his political conduct from the first of July, 1814, containing the secret history of the events which had happened at Paris from the return of Napoleon from Elba until his final abdication. Of this exposition Wheaton said it was the work of one of the few men, at once great and good, that the French Revolution had produced. He added a translation of Carnot's speech made before the Tribunate in 1804 against the elevation of Napoleon to the imperial throne.[35]

Just before his *Digest* went to press, Wheaton wrote to his family of another appointment:

You will see that the council have made me Chief Justice of the Marine Court. As there were numerous applications for the office from lawyers, young and old, and as I asked for nothing, I ought perhaps to be flattered with this mark of attention from my friends. It is a respectable situation which will occupy me for two thirds of the year about three hours in the day. The court has jurisdiction of suits for seamen's wages and assault and battery on the high seas. It is worth from 1,000 and 1,500 dolls. according to the quantity of business, and is always held by counsellors of the Supreme Court. I think it will be, like the Judge Advocateship, a useful exercise for me—make me known—and be a stepping stone to the bar.[36]

After receiving his appointment as chief justice of the Marine Court, Wheaton left the *National Advocate* in May 1815. Prior to that date, the war between the United States and Great Britain had been brought to a close by the Treaty of Ghent, which was signed on Christmas Eve of 1814. The battle of New Orleans, which contributed so much to the reputation and popularity of General Jackson, was fought on January 8, 1815, before the news of the treaty had been received. The Congress of Vienna had been in session since September 1814. These events were treated fully in the *National Advocate* during the last part of Henry Wheaton's editorship. The editorials drew from William Pinkney, the attorney-general, an expression of the obligations of all his colleagues for the able support Wheaton had rendered to the Government, with a special commendation of those relating to the treaty, which he said had been done "as well as could be wished." [37]

After resigning from the *National Advocate,* Wheaton entered upon a new venture in Washington.

Chapter IV

HENRY WHEATON AND THE SUPREME COURT

THE city of Washington in 1815 was "a dismal place, where few and unattractive houses were scattered along muddy openings in the forest." At one end of Pennsylvania Avenue was the executive mansion, in the vicinity of which were the residences and shops; at the other end of the sometimes deeply muddy, sometimes very dusty avenue was the capitol. Adjacent to it were some twenty wooden houses. Several of these were boarding houses in which the senators and representatives lived "two and sometimes more men sharing the same bedroom." The city "was a picture of sprawling aimlessness, confusion, inconvenience and utter discomfort." [1] Here Henry Wheaton spent part of every year for the next decade attending the sessions of the Supreme Court of the United States during the days when Chief Justice Marshall laid the foundations of its strength. The opinions expressed by him and his associates and the statement of the cases and the arguments presented before them were put into permanent form and published by the Supreme Court reporter. At that time the office of reporter was regarded as one of honor and importance, commanding almost the same respect as it did when Lord Coke combined the duties of chief justice with those of law reporter. The first reporter of the United States Supreme Court was Alexander J. Dallas, who afterwards became Secretary of the Treasury under President Madison, and the second was William Cranch who at the same time was chief justice of the Circuit Court of the District of Columbia. They both were chosen and appointed by the Supreme Court. They received no salary, depending on

HENRY WHEATON AS A YOUNG MAN

the sale of the *Reports* of the causes decided in the court to recompense them for the effort and investment involved in their publication.[2]

Following Cranch, Henry Wheaton was appointed without salary by the court. As an inducement to undertake the task and attend the terms of the court, the justices agreed to furnish him alone, for his sole benefit, with all writings and memoranda that they made of their decisions to aid him in reporting the cases.[3] Wheaton assumed the office of Supreme Court reporter at the February term, 1816. At that time the judges were John Marshall (the chief justice), Bushrod Washington, William Johnson, Brockholst Livingston, Thomas Todd, Gabriel Duval, and Joseph Story. Richard Rush was the attorney-general.[4] Appearing before the court was a galaxy of renowned lawyers—William Pinkney, Samuel Dexter, Luther Martin, Robert G. Harper, William Wirt, Thomas Addis Emmett, Joseph Hopkinson, William Hunter, Edward Livingston, Charles J. Ingersoll, Henry Clay, and Daniel Webster. In proposing to take up the work, Wheaton submitted a plan, which was approved, calling for a "regular annual publication of the decisions, with good type, and to be neatly printed." [5]

The first volume of Wheaton's *Reports* was published in January, 1817. It immediately met with universal approval. Wheaton later received a complimentary letter from Sir William Scott acknowledging receipt of the first volume, and he also had the gratification of learning in Boston that his reputation was rapidly increasing in that quarter.[6] Webster stated, in his review of this volume, that it clearly demonstrated the learning, industry, and ability of the author and was valuable to the legal profession not only for a faithful account of the decisions of the court but also for the promptitude of its execution. It not only gave the points determined by the court, but also impressed the reasons and motives of the judgments in such a manner as to render their application to future cases easy and practicable.[7] It was while Wheaton was reporter that some of the most notable and fundamental of the court's decisions were made. In the first volume appeared the case of *Martin* vs. *Hunter's Lessee*,[8] which upheld the constitutionality of section 25 of the Judiciary Act of 1789 giving it the power to review and reverse decisions of the state courts where they conflicted with rights guaranteed under the Constitution. This case is the third among those cited by Professor Channing as being the seven leading cases decided by the Supreme Court between 1803 and 1824.[9]

Wheaton greatly added to the value of the volumes by the extent and excellence of his notes. In the preface of the first volume, he said,

Should the annotation contained in this volume be favorably received by the public, the editor will hereafter continue this branch of his labor with a less timid hand, and, in the words of Lord Bacon, make it his aim, "to collect the rules and grounds dispersed throughout the body of the same laws, in order to see more profoundly into the reason for such judgments and ruled cases, and thereby to make more use of them for the decision of other cases more doubtful; so that the uncertainty of the law, which is the principal and most just challenge that is made to the laws of our nation at this time, will, by this new strength laid to the foundation, be somewhat the more settled and correct." Such a commentary seems, indeed, indispensable to the utility of reports of the proceedings in courts of justice. For, as Sir William Jones has observed, "if Law be a science, and really deserves so sublime a name, it must be founded on principles, and claim an exalted rank in the empire of reason." [10]

The commendation and universal approbation which the notes received encouraged him to continue with this phase of the reports. Webster also remarked that in this particular, Wheaton's merits were in a great degree peculiar. No reporter had up to that time inserted so much and so valuable matter of his own. His notes were not dry references to cases—of no merit except as they saved the trouble of research—but an enlightened adaptation, to the case reported, of the principles and rules of other systems of jurisprudence, giving a connected view of decisions on the principal points.[11] In the light of his later activities, it is interesting to note that the appendix of the first volume contained the best illustrations of the law of prizes and the clearest views of that subject that had thus far been offered to the public.[12]

In spite of the acknowledged value of the *Reports* and the cordial reception granted them, the sale of the first volume was so small that Wheaton found it impossible to continue the work under the existing arrangement. He therefore applied to Congress for relief. As a result, a bill giving the reporter of the Supreme Court a salary was reviewed in the Senate in February 1817,[13] and was finally passed on March 3 of the same year.[14] This act recognized the right of the Supreme Court to appoint a reporter, and provided an annual salary of one thousand dollars to be paid on condition that he print and publish the decisions within six months after they were made, and that he deliver eighty copies of each volume to the secretary of state for distribution to the designated government officers.[15]

Besides the *Reports* and his other literary work, Wheaton had published an essay on the *Means of Maintaining the Commercial and Naval Interests of the United States* in which he advocated a navigation act—made necessary by the restrictive policy then existing in Europe—giving special advantages to the vessels of the United States and excluding all foreign sailors from our merchant marine.[16] His professional and literary work had separated him somewhat from political activities, and in October he wrote to his uncle, Dr. Wheaton,

I am, by one means and another, thrown out of the vortex of politics,—and am content that it should be so, for unless we have a Spanish war (the republic being safe) I do not see any public matter sufficiently interesting to excite exertion—and I have long since seen the folly of looking to politics as a trade to get a living by.[17]

His professional activities constantly grew more engrossing. It was not only as a reporter that Wheaton was connected with the Supreme Court; he continued to appear before it in the argument of cases. In his first term as reporter he was counsel for the appellants in the case of the *Antonia Johanna* against Mr. Gaston who represented the defendants.[18] In the February term of 1818, Wheaton came before the court in the capacity of counsel in three cases, two of which had to do with maritime law and one with constitutional law. In one of the former, *United States* vs. *Bevans*—in which was determined the power of the United States over harbors in the different states—he appeared for the United States in opposition to Daniel Webster, who was counsel for the defendant. This was one of the series of far-reaching decisions greatly extending the authority of the Federal Government.[19] At the same time, he had another maritime case under way in which he was associated with William Wirt, who had succeeded Richard Rush as attorney-general on November 13, 1817.[20]

In his second volume Wheaton had continued his notes on prize causes by adding an additional note on the principles and practice in such cases and the President's instructions to private armed vessels. This topic was further enlarged in his third volume where he cited documents on the subject of blockades. In September Webster wrote to Judge Story that he had been at work upon a review of Wheaton's volume of reports and added, "Whatever I write must pass your revision." [21] Later in the month Wheaton wrote to Edward Wheaton, his brother-in-law, "I spent a night at Judge Story's and had a great deal of edifying talk." [22]

The February term of 1819 was a memorable one. It was in this term that the decisions were given in the famous cases *McCulloch* vs. *Maryland* [23] and *Dartmouth College* vs. *Woodward*.[24] Wheaton appeared as counsel in two cases of less importance.[25] In reporting one of them he incorporated extensive notes on the neutrality of the United States in the war between Spain and her colonies.[26]

His continued interest in prize causes is apparent from his correspondence during this term. Early in March he requested the State Department to send him a copy of the prize code established at Buenos Aires to be published in his *Reports* among other extracts from the correspondence of the Department of State with the Spanish minister and the colonial agents. The material was necessary to illustrate some cases of capture decided during that term.[27] This code was translated into English by Wheaton and a copy furnished to John Quincy Adams. The same procedure was followed with the prize code of Chile;[28] both were published in the appendix to his *Reports* for 1819. At the request of the State Department he granted permission for the publication of the translation of the Buenos Aires prize code in the *National Intelligencer*.[29]

In the volume of *Reports* for 1820, Wheaton not only continued his notes on the subject of prize law and on the neutrality of the United States in the war between Spain and her colonies, but also included extensive notes on the act of March 3, 1819, on piracy and on civil law.

In addition to his work along these lines as reporter, he soon published in the *North American Review* a commentary upon the first volume of Mason's *Reports* of cases in the Circuit Court of the United States, for the First Circuit, containing the cases determined in the Districts of New Hampshire, Massachusetts and Rhode Island, in the years 1816, 1817, and 1818.[30] This review by Wheaton of a digest of Judge Story's decisions is really a very carefully prepared and instructive article, valuable as an accurate summary of the law of prize as settled in the courts of the United States during the Revolution and up to the War of 1812.[31]

In July of 1819 he resigned his office of justice of the marine court because a doubt arose concerning the propriety of holding this office concurrently with that of division judge advocate of the Army,[32] although he had so held them for four years.

Meanwhile an event occurred that attracted his attention.

The invasion of Florida by General Jackson in 1818 convinced the Spanish Government that Florida had better be sold before it was seized. Accordingly Spain ceded all its lands east of the Mississippi River, together with its rights to the Oregon country, in return for five million dollars. The treaty between the United States and Spain was signed on February 22, 1819. The following July in a letter to Joshua Bailey to whom Wheaton announced his resignation from the Marine Court he said,

Will you permit me to enquire whether, in case the Spanish treaty should be returned ratified, the appointment of the Commissioners under it will probably be made before this session of Congress, and whether in your candid opinion there is any probability of my being appointed? You may answer these questions in the greatest possible confidence that I shall not breathe the answer to any human being. I am anxious to know what the probability is, on account of some arrangements of professional business which may be modified by your information and advice.[33]

This refers to a readjustment of his professional activities made necessary by his resignation from the Marine Court. The ratification of the treaty, however, was postponed for two years and the appointment of commissioners of course held in abeyance. After resigning as justice of the Marine Court, Wheaton returned to the active practice of his profession, entering into partnership with Elijah Paine at 54 Maiden Lane, New York City.[34]

In September of 1819, when Wheaton was in his thirty-fourth year, his alma mater, Brown University, expressed its recognition of his literary and professional attainments by conferring on him the degree of Doctor of Laws.

The confidence thus shown in his ability was fully justified by future publications. On November 11, 1820, he wrote that he was about to print his *Digest,* "which will be a considerable work, and though a mere compilation, will, I trust, not injure my legal and literary reputation."[35] This book was brought out early in 1821 with the title *A Digest of the Decisions of the Supreme Court of the United States . . . from 1789 to February term 1820, including the cases decided in the Continental Court of Appeals in prize causes, during the war of the Revolution.*[36] In addition to this there were published two reviews by him, both of which appeared in the *North American Review,* one of David Hosack's "A Biographical Memoir of Hugh Williamson . . ."[37] and the other, the report of "The Trial of Robert M. Goodwin, on an indictment of manslaughter, for killing James Staughton, Esq., in Broadway, in the City of New York . . ." by William Sampson, Counsellor at Law.[38] This trial for manslaughter arose from the killing of a counsellor-at-law in an affray growing out of the occurrences of a trial and excited intense interest at the time. The review contains a learned disquisition on the distinctions between the criminal law of the Continent and that of England, especially in reference to the regard which the former paid, in certain offenses, to the intent rather than to the event as constituting the criminality.[39]

But one of the most interesting of his many productions up to this time was "A Discourse on the History of the Science of Public or International Law" delivered before the New York Historical Society on the occasion of its anniversary on December 28, 1820. This was afterwards not only printed in the *Proceedings of the Historical Society* but also brought out in pamphlet form the same year.[40] He received many commendatory letters concerning this address. In one of these John Quincy Adams said,

I have read this discourse with uncommon interest and peculiar delight. It is the production of great reading, profound reflection, a discriminating mind, and a pure taste. I have never read any discourse produced in America relative to the science of public law with so much satisfaction. Had I read such a discourse sixty-five years ago it would have given a different and more respectable cast to my whole life.[41]

Another note of interest was one received from Chancellor Kent who wrote,

Be pleased to accept my thanks for your very interesting and able discourse on the History of International Law, delivered before the Historical Society. There is no person (unless it be our mutual friend and great master of jurisprudence, Judge Story) who could have handled the subject with so much erudition and enlightened judgment. It is a subject very much to my taste, and awakens the deepest interest. Be assured, my dear Sir, that I feel with full force the great obligations we are all under to you, for your professional efforts and illustrious attainments.[42]

Wheaton also availed himself of the opportunity in a review of the publication of Cushing's translation of Pothier on *Maritime Contracts* to aid, according to Lawrence, in making his countrymen acquainted with the merits of that most learned lawyer, by whose introduction to the English bar Sir William Jones deemed that he had, in some measure, paid the debt that every man owes to his profession.[43]

During the 1817 term of the court Mrs. Wheaton made her first visit to Washington and wrote to her father in March, "I am very much pleased with my visit and with the attention which I have received from the people here. H. seems to stand high and has every reason to be satisfied with the place he holds in society here."[44] This opinion is confirmed by a letter written many years later to Abby Wheaton by Theophilus Parsons in which he said that everywhere in the social life of Washington Wheaton was upon the footing not of a received, but of a welcomed guest; that as Supreme Court reporter it might be supposed he would be on terms of intimacy and friendship with the judges of the court and all who practised in it, but that there was something in the character of the friendship that no mere position explained; and that he inspired an equally warm regard in many who never met him in his official duties. Among his many friends were Daniel Webster, who treated him as he might have treated a brother; Sir Stratford Canning, Minister from England;

and M. de Neuville, the French Minister, who at that time "appeared to give tone and character to Washington society," in whose house Wheaton stood on the footing of a confidential friend; Mr. Lowndes of South Carolina, a most wise and excellent man; and lastly and most of all, Chief Justice Marshall.

Parsons further said:

The Chief Justice treated Mr. Wheaton with the fondest regard, and this example would have had its influence had it been necessary; but in fact the best men in Washington were on the most intimate and confidential terms with him. The simple truth is, that universal respect was rendered to him because he deserved it. He was a gentleman; and therefore the same gentleman to all under all circumstances.

No one more enjoyed society, and few sought it more, or were more sought by it. He was,—not perhaps gay,—but eminently cheerful; and his manner was characterized by that forgetfulness of self, which, as in great things, it forms the foundation for the highest excellence, so in the lesser matters of social intercourse it imparts a perpetual charm, and constitutes almost of itself, the essence of all true politeness.

There was with Mr. Wheaton no watching of opportunity to display: no indifference and want of interest when the topics of conversation, or the parties, or other circumstances, made it impossible for him to occupy the foreground; no skillful diversion of the conversation into paths which led to his strongholds, where he might come forth to peculiar advantage. Still less did he—as in this country so many do—play out in society the game of life, by using it only as a means of promoting his personal or professional objects. . . . There was in Mr. Wheaton's demeanor nothing of this: nothing of it in appearance, because nothing of it in fact; cunning of any sort, was a quality of which he had none whatever. Everybody felt and knew this; and therefore everybody met him with a sense of confidence and repose, which of itself would go far in making any person acceptable as a friend or as a mere companion, in a society of which the very surface constantly exhibited the many whirling undercurrents of Washington life. In one word, there was in him nothing of "trick"; but that constant

and perfect suavity which is the spontaneous expression of universal kindness; and an excellent understanding, well and widely cultivated, and always ready to bring forth all its resources, not to
keep himself, but to keep or gratify others with whom he came
into contact, and all this, with no appearance of purpose or design
of any kind; for it was but the natural outpouring of mind and
heart, of one who was open to the widest sympathy, and whose
interest in all persons and things about him was most real and
honest, because he loved nothing so well as to do the good he
could, by word or deed, or little or much, to one, or few, or many.
He was therefore most popular in society. But when we speak of
Mr. Wheaton's social "popularity," we must be careful to use this
word in a higher than its common sense.[45]

Not only did he form enduring friendships with his own
countrymen, but his familiarity with the French language,
laws, and customs led to an intimacy with most of the exiles
whom the downfall of Napoleon had brought to this country.
Count Real, the minister of police under the Empire, Count
Regnault, the most brilliant orator of that time, General
Bernard, General Lallemand, St. Jean d'Angelly, and Prince
Achille Murat—all considered him as a friend, and all found
a kind welcome at his house.[46]

Wheaton, moreover, while in college and during the ensuing years, had studied deeply the works of the great English
theologians.[47] It is not surprising, therefore, to find that he
took an active part in the First Congregational Church in New
York. In November of 1821 the letter of invitation to twenty-
one different churches to assist in the services of the ordination
of the newly elected pastor of the church was signed by Henry
Wheaton and H. D. Sedgewick as the Standing Committee.[48]

After leaving Washington at the termination of the sessions of the court in 1821, Wheaton found in New York that
events were taking place which were to demand his active
interest and ultimately to change the course of his whole life.

PART TWO

A LAWYER IN THE POLITICAL ARENA

Chapter V

THE NEW YORK STATE
CONSTITUTIONAL CONVENTION

IN THE light of Wheaton's interest in constitutional questions and in view of his many literary and judicial achievements in New York, it was natural that his name should be
proposed as one of the delegates to the New York state convention, held in the fall of 1821, to amend and revise the
state constitution of 1777, which had become unpopular,
partly because of the eighteenth-century restrictions on the
right of suffrage.[1]

In the law providing for the election of delegates, the
principle was recognized that whatever restrictions might
exist for ordinary legislation, the whole people had a right to
participate in the formation of their organic law; the convention, therefore, was chosen according to a rule which
would provide as nearly as possible for universal suffrage. All
free males over twenty-one who paid taxes or served in the
militia or in work upon the highways were given the vote
for this election.[2] Many distinguished men of the principal
political parties in the state were elected. The one hundred
and ten delegates of the Democratic or Tammany party were
divided into two sections—a radical group and a conservative
one. Among the former were Daniel D. Tompkins, the vice-
president of the United States, Colonel Samuel Young,
General Erastus Root, and Peter R. Livingston. "These," it
has been written, "led the mad-cap democrats of whom Van
Buren said, 'They thought nothing wise that was not vio-
lent.'"[3] Numbered among the members of the conservative group, who represented the influences of restrained
reform, were Martin Van Buren and Rufus King, both

senators in Congress; Nathan Sanford, the successor of
Chancellor Kent in judicial office and at that time senator;
William Paulding, Jr.; and Henry Wheaton, who was sent
as one of the delegates from the city of New York. From the
"Independent Republicans," a new name for the old Federal-
ist party coined for this occasion, thirteen delegates were
chosen. Among these were Chancellor James Kent and Chief
Justice Ambrose Spencer, both of whom were delegates from
Albany, and also Associate Justice William Van Ness, Elisha
Williams, and J. R. Van Renssalaer.[4] Only three delegates
were elected from the Clintonian-Republican party.

The convention assembled at Albany on August 28, 1821.
At its first meeting Daniel D. Tompkins was elected president, and two days later, on motion of Rufus King, a committee consisting of thirteen members was appointed to
determine how the various questions before the convention
should be brought up for consideration. Their report was
returned on the same day recommending that each subject
should be referred to a separate committee of seven members whose duty it should be to examine and report what
amendments or alterations in their opinion were required
in the part of the constitution thus delegated to them. This
plan was adopted and ten different committees were appointed. As the Tammany party had been successful in obtaining control of the convention, all of the ten chairmen
were of that party except James Tallmadge. He was about to
swerve in his political affiliations and to become openly identi-
fied with it.[5]

In making a revision in the constitution, four principal
objects were to be considered by the members of the convention. These were a change of the appointing power, an extension of the right of suffrage, the abolition of the council
of revision, and an alteration in the judiciary system.[6]
Wheaton, who on every question coming before the convention was to be found on the moderate side of the Democratic
or Bucktail party, was placed on the committee concerned
with the judiciary department.[7]

The judges were involved in the last two mentioned subjects before the convention. The council of revision was
made up of all the judges of the Supreme Court, the chancellor, and the governor. Chancellor Kent, Chief Justice Ambrose Spencer, with Associate Justices Jonas Platt and William
W. Van Ness, as a majority, could veto any law passed by the
Assembly. They had disallowed several bills which had been
enacted to satisfy popular demand, and many people felt that
not only must the council be abolished, but also the justices
should be driven from the bench. When the convention acted
on this question, the council was abolished without a dissenting vote.[8]

As the feeling concerning the judges was so antagonistic, it
became evident early in the discussions of the judiciary committee that there was a definite plan for their dismissal. The
report of the committee proposed certain revisions and
recommended the creation of a Superior Court of Common
Pleas but retained the Court of Chancery and the Supreme
Court. The radical section of the Tammany party was in
favor of destroying the old court by creating an entirely new
one. Appointments to the supreme bench had run until the
judge was sixty years of age. Spencer had four more years to
serve while the youngest, Van Ness, would retain office until
1836. Chancellor Kent, who was fifty-nine, had one more year
in office.[9]

Wheaton was among the conservative group who were
opposed to overturning the Court of Chancery and the
Supreme Court. The decisions of these courts, under the
administration of Chancellor Kent and Judge Spencer, were
universally esteemed; to the more prudent and cautious
delegates in the convention, an entire change seemed to be
altogether too revolutionary and hazardous.[10]

The radical group prevailed and the proposal for the
creation of a new court was accepted.[11] Even then Wheaton
endeavored to save the courts during the lifetime of the presiding judges, Kent and Spencer, by proposing the following
amendment:

But this limitation of the number of the said judges, shall not take effect until their number shall be reduced to three, by death, resignation, the constitutional limitation of their term, or removals from offices; and that until such reduction is made, the said justices shall continue to hold the sittings and circuits in such counties as may be prescribed by law.[12]

This was rejected.

Throughout the entire discussion, with the group who consistently stood together for moderate measures were Kent, Paulding, Sanford, Tallmadge, Van Buren, and Wheaton. Not only were they in accord on the question of the judiciary, but also on many other proposals that came before the convention.[13]

Among the propositions which Wheaton introduced was one which would render it the duty of the legislature to pass general laws on the subject of private corporations and prohibit their establishment by special acts. Though the article proposed by Wheaton was not adopted in 1821, its wisdom was recognized later when the constitution was remodeled in 1846, and it became a portion of the fundamental law of the state.[14]

Another significant proposal was made by Wheaton. "The framers of the constitution," one reads, "realized that democracy and education must make their progress hand in hand, and their generation in New York showed an unexampled interest in the common school." [15] It was Wheaton who submitted a constitutional provision making it the duty of the legislature to cause the cities and towns to raise the sums necessary, in addition to the amounts received from the common school fund, to maintain public schools in every town for the instruction of all the children.[16]

Before the convention closed, Wheaton thus showed he was still imbued with his early Jeffersonian ideals, for "Jefferson's whole theory rested on a 'strong faith in the teachableness of the great mass of the people.' " [17]

Reports from the committees to which had been referred

the different parts of the Constitution were duly made before the Convention, discussed, amended and adopted. The Constitution was finally formulated and on November 10, 1821, the Convention adjourned.[18]

Chapter VI

THE NEW YORK STATE ASSEMBLY

HENRY WHEATON and Martin Van Buren had been working together in harmony throughout the Constitutional Convention, but they soon were to find themselves strenuously opposing each other in both the state and national campaigns for the elections of 1824, during which time a movement for a more complete democracy was beginning.

When the national campaign first started, a great many candidates for the presidency were mentioned, but the number gradually diminished until there were only five who were really in the contest. These were William H. Crawford of Georgia, secretary of the treasury; John Quincy Adams of Massachusetts, secretary of state; Henry Clay of Kentucky, speaker of the House of Representatives; John C. Calhoun of South Carolina, secretary of war; and General Andrew Jackson of Tennessee. DeWitt Clinton, it has been recorded, was the first eminent man in the North who announced a determination to support Jackson, as at the outset it was the prevailing belief that the General could count on the support of only one state—Tennessee; but his military achievements had gained him wide popularity which eventually made him a formidable competitor.[1] The leaders of the Democratic party in New York, among whom were Van Buren and General Erastus Root, supported Crawford, who was expected in all probability to carry Georgia and most of the South.

Calhoun, the youngest of the five, by reason of his strong national rather than sectional tendencies, had won general admiration and confidence and was the favorite candidate of the young men of the country. Certainly he had Wheaton's whole-hearted support. This was expressed by the latter in a letter to his uncle concerning the outlook in the spring of 1823. Wheaton wrote:

We have but little news in our public affairs. All the corrupt intriguers of this state have combined together to forestall the votes of our electors for Crawford and, no doubt, will receive their reward in case of success. I verily believe he is the greatest political manager and least statesmanlike politician this country has yet produced. He neglects the business of his office to attend to the direction of his intrigues which are ramified throughout the Continent. Yet we are very much divided as to who ought to be supported against him. The republicans find it difficult to digest an Adams, and there are great misgivings about Clay. In my opinion Calhoun is worth the whole of them put together. But he is said to be too young.[2]

When Wheaton began to take an active part in the campaign, one of the first things he did was to help counteract the influence of the *National Advocate,* the paper he had started, inasmuch as its editor, Mordecai M. Noah, a forcible and witty writer, now came out decidedly for Crawford. Wheaton and other prominent men thereupon established a new paper called the *New York Patriot,* which was placed under the editorial charge of Charles K. Gardner, who had been one of the assistant postmasters-general. The paper opposed the election of Crawford but, apparently to avoid arousing antagonism, did not definitely give its support to any one of the different candidates until the campaign had reached a later stage.[3]

Although the efforts which were being made to produce an impression among the people unfavorable to Crawford were meeting with apparent success, it soon became certain that if the election of the members of the next legislature was conducted in the usual way, Van Buren and the Albany regency would be able to exert sufficient influence to secure the choice of presidential electors who would vote for Crawford, since at that time the electors were chosen by the two houses of the legislature in joint session.

To prevent such a result, and because a revision of the electoral law had been considered desirable for some time, it was urged that the presidential electors ought now to be chosen by the people. Wheaton became one of the leaders of this plan; in June 1823 the *New York Patriot* opened a campaign for a repeal of the electoral law.[4] Wheaton was in favor of the principle of suffrage involved in such a change in the electorate and therefore urged it strongly at this time because otherwise his candidate, Calhoun, could not carry New York. Calhoun was also interested in such a change. This is evidenced in a letter written by him to M. Stanly in July in which he said,

I rejoice to see that there is a fair prospect to change your mode of choosing electors. Principle and policy require it. I wish to see New York assume her just weight, and this can only be effected by breaking up the machinery by which the political jugglers manage her, and giving the power really and truly to the people.[5]

The agitation found especially strong support among the people in the city of New York. Concerning the list of candidates for the legislature prepared by the nominating committee of Tammany Hall, Henry Wheaton wrote to his uncle,

Our nominating committee have given us a ticket with only two or three of our men on it. My friend Gen. Paulding is one. We shall appeal to the people at the general meeting when the ticket is reported for approbation. If they blow out the candles, and dissolve the meeting in riot and confusion, according to the usual Crawford tactics, we shall make our own ticket, and I doubt not, shall carry it.[6]

When the general meeting was held, determined opposition to most of the candidates became manifest because people suspected that many of them were not in favor of a change in the electorate at the time. Very tumultuous proceedings characterized the meeting. A large portion of those present refused to endorse the nominations of the committee and resolved to support another set of candidates known to be in favor of a repeal of the electoral law. The party which thus sprang into existence called itself the "People's Party." [7] In November a People's ticket for the Assembly was nominated and elected in New York. At the head of this ticket stood the name of Henry Wheaton. Wheaton's principal motive in permitting himself to be elected a member of the Assembly was to aid in Calhoun's campaign for the presidency. General Tallmadge was nominated by the same party in Dutchess county.[8]

The People's party proper did not succeed in electing a majority of the members of the Assembly although many of them were committed in favor of the electoral law. The people had not asked the legislative candidates whom they favored for president; they were confident that they themselves would vote for the electors in 1824.[9]

There was never any doubt concerning Wheaton's attitude. His letters during this period not only state his position but give an interesting account of the events before the opening of the legislature the following January. In the beginning of September he felt that Calhoun's cause was daily improving and that he would ultimately unite all the interests opposed to him and Crawford in New York and Pennsylvania. In writing to Theophilus Parsons about this time he says that Calhoun "holds on to S. Carolina, is growing in N. Carolina, and the moment Gen. J. sees he has no chance, Tennessee, Louisiana and Alabama will come over to him. The whole west is for him, after Clay—and should the latter decline his interest could be transferred to no other. All this *inter nos.*" [10].

That Henry Wheaton had no illusions concerning the real state of affairs and was perfectly well aware of the weakness of his party was clearly stated by him in the latter part of September, when in writing to Dr. Wheaton he said, "Our political crisis is approaching as you will see. I think our new editor lays on his blows well, but the other party excel us in management as much as we do them in discussion and (I hope) in honesty." For Calhoun's candidacy he was still hopeful.

Mr. Calhoun is looming large in every quarter, and I feel more and more hope, of success. I think we may set down North Carolina as certain. In the west, he is second only to Clay, and in some quarters not second to him. In N. England he takes all who leave A., and indeed he seems the natural inheritor of all the other candidates. Gen. Jackson will only yield to him or A. He cannot transfer his interest to A., and therefore the necessary consequence seems to be that Mr. Cn must take his place. In Alabama, Gov. Pickens, who is Mr. Cn's relation and political friend, is elected against Mr. Cd's candidate. Gov. Clark, of Georgia (the same who published the famous pamphlet) writes that it is very doubtful whether Cd will take Georgia. Be this as it may, it is certain that there is a formidable party against him in his own state.[11]

The session of the Assembly to which Wheaton had been elected was to begin its meetings in January extending through the time devoted to the February term of the Supreme Court. This conflict of duties furnished some concern to both Henry Wheaton and his friends, especially as he was being strongly urged to run as speaker of the New York House. The last day of November he wrote confidentially to Daniel Webster,

Let it be understood that I shall be at court until you hear further from me. I shall take all the necessary weapons and I think David Hoffman will be my surrogate. I write to-day to J. C. [John C. Calhoun] as to Speaker. I doubt whether Tallmadge can be got in. Should that be the case I shall perhaps be compelled to run. Is it best? Talk with C. about it as soon as you can, and write me. In that event I shall be obliged to hybernate at Albany, and shall be left at the mercy of the Court and of my enemies. You must talk confidentially to the Chief Justice about it. I will write him an official, and an unofficial letter. DeWitt is playing the fool—but he can do nothing in this state. There are exactly 12 Clintonians in the House—and not more than three who have stood by him in all his turnings and windings— The rest of "the People's" men are Feds. High-minders—Bucktails—and novi homines, "who know not Joseph." [12]

This was followed the next day by another letter to Mr. Webster:

I wrote you and J. C. yesterday about Speaker. But I rec'd last evening from the Judex a letter by which it seems that he is very much alarmed lest an attempt should be made to remove me in the case I am absent any considerable part of the term. If there be any danger, I must not put it out of my power to fly to my post at Washington at any moment. I think of these things. Write me confidentially quo tendit Respublica? Address your letter to Mr. Edward Wheaton, New York, without a frank. It is necessary that I should know the real state of things. This I cannot expect to learn but from yourself, who are a calm and unimpassioned observer. The People are sick to death of Caucuses. Rely on that. Strangle the monster without compunction or remorse.[13]

By the middle of December Wheaton had definitely decided his course. He wrote from New York, "I shall leave here on New Year's day, or the day after at farthest. I have been strongly pressed to run for Speaker, but am resolved not because I do not choose to be deprived of the liberty of going to Washington some time in February." [14] Just before leaving New York he wrote to Dr. Wheaton:

We have nothing in prospect to dampen our spirits. I have no doubt an Anti-Crawford candidate for Speaker will be elected— and that in the course of the Session we shall show strong for Calhoun. He is now decidedly foremost in the race. The idea of a caucus is more and more scouted at Washington, and most certainly Crawford or Clay cannot get on without one, with the people. If the election comes to the House, Clay may stand some chance —but if any candidate is chosen by the Electors, I am firmly persuaded that Cn will be the man. There is no danger of D.W.C. If it were worth while to break a butterfly on a wheel, we could easily demolish him.[15]

But what dire results were to follow from an attempt by someone else to break the butterfly, Wheaton himself was to experience.

The legislature of the state commenced its annual session on January 6, 1824.[16] In his message to the Assembly the Governor was non-committal on the subject of choosing the presidential electors by the people. This attitude was considered by

the public to imply an executive recommendation for the legislature to retain in their own hands the power of appointing
electors.[17]

As soon as the preliminary organization had been completed in the Assembly and before a message had been sent
to the Governor that they were organized, Wheaton on January 6, 1824, gave notice that he would on some future day
ask leave to bring in a bill authorizing the people of the
State of New York to choose the electors of president and
vice-president of the United States.[18] Azariah C. Flagg, who
was the most shrewd and active Crawford man in the assembly
during this session, immediately offered a resolution that the
whole subject of changing the law in respect to the choice of
electors should be referred to a select committee of nine
members.[19]

The introduction of Flagg's resolution at once started a
long and exciting debate. The resolution was vehemently
attacked by Wheaton and other members of the People's party,
and defended with equal warmth by Flagg and several men,
who were friendly to Crawford and Clay. The preponderance
of talent was decidedly with the members who supported the
proposition advocated by the People's party, and they charged
the mover of the resolution with an intention to embarrass
the proceedings of the legislature, to delay action on the subject, and finally to evade or defeat the measure. The resolution
proposed by Flagg was finally adopted.[20]

In pursuance of his previous notice, Wheaton asked for
and obtained leave to bring in a bill entitled "An act to provide for the choice of Electors of President and Vice-President
of the United States by the people of this State." [21] The next
day, Thursday, January 8, 1824, the subject of changing the
mode of choosing electors of president and vice-president was
referred to a committee of nine, of which Wheaton was a
member and Flagg was chairman. All the members of the committee with the exception of Wheaton, and two others were
Crawford men. This gave them a preponderance of six to
three.[22]

That the people were taking an active interest in the changing of the law is evidenced by numerous petitions, such as the one from sundry inhabitants of the town of Minisink in the county of Orange, praying for a passage of a law authorizing an alteration in the mode of choosing presidential electors. This was read and referred to the select committee on that subject, of which committee Flagg was chairman.[23]

Further action on the bill submitted by Wheaton was taken the next day when it was referred to the same committee.[24] The first meeting of this committee was held with open doors, and was attended by many citizens as well as members of the legislature. It soon became apparent that none of the men responsible for forming the committee had a definite proposition to submit for consideration. Wheaton thereupon offered the following motion:

Resolved, as the sense of this committee, that the right of choosing the Electors for President and Vice-President of the United States, ought to be vested in the people of this state, by a law to be passed at the present session of the legislature.

This motion, receiving only one negative vote, was carried in the affirmative. Wheaton then offered the following resolution, *"Resolved,* That such election ought to be by general ticket." Flagg proposed an amendment to add the following words, "and that a majority of all the votes shall be necessary to make a choice."

To insure against delay in having the bill brought again before the House, Wheaton stated that he would not oppose any report the majority of the committee might think fit to make; but that he would bring to the attention of the committee the fact that the proposed amendment probably would defeat the bill, for the constant usage of the state had been to choose by plurality, and if the law were formed as desired by Flagg, the vote of New York would be lost; there would not be time in the thirty-four days preceding the voting to order a new election in case the first did not result in a choice by a majority of all the votes. After some further discussion the committee adjourned without taking definite action on the matter before it.[25]

Wheaton had no illusions as to what was happening. On the fifteenth of the month he wrote to Dr. Wheaton:

The political atmosphere is stormy. You will see by the papers our public doings, but it is necessary to be on the spot and behind the scenes in order to have an adequate notion of the deep game that is playing here. The Junto are resolved to cheat the people out of the appointment of the electors, and looking at the cattle they send here to represent them, there is too much reason to apprehend they may succeed—unless a degree of public excitement is produced in the counties through the denunciations of the Press and of popular meetings adequate to prevent it— The committee have substituted (as you will see) for my bill another scheme which is a mere subterfuge to evade the wishes of the people. I think it must sink them to the depths of perdition, if they should carry it; because the November election brings the state administration again before the people for trial—all of this however *inter nos.* We keep up a good heart, and on the floor of the House can flog them to our hearts content. But it is the midnight caucusing and secret drilling in which they excel us.

I am kept very busy with seeing members, or committees, drawing reports, writing for the newspapers and corresponding with our friends at Washington and New York— But I do not worry so much as at first, and my health is good.

As to men, little has been done among our friends—Crawford's interest in the House would appear very insignificant, if the ballot were given to-morrow— Clay has not more than 14 members who are for him— The rest are either in the market, or for A and Calhoun. I do not think there is much pertinacity for A. But the measure must be secured before we can work with much effect for the Man. The game of the Crawfordites is to whip in the dogs, and accustom them to discipline. Great efforts are making to get up something here that will bolster up the sickly caucus system at Washington. It will come too late, for I take it the patient is on his last legs. Our Gov. is a poor, stupid, dull ass, who permits himself to be used by those corrupt intriguers, and at the same time thinks to preserve the good will of his honest and respectable friends—the men who made him—but he will find himself mistaken.

My private letters, from friends who I am sure would not wilfully deceive me, represent Mr. C.'s prospects in Pennsylvania, North Carolina, and Maryland as very encouraging. If the election goes to the House, his chance is certainly the best of all. On the maturest reflection, I think A is the next best—but whether he has the next best chance, I doubt. There are, in my mind, insuperable objections to Mr. Clay—and upon the whole, I return with intense desire to the man, against whom there is no solid objection, and whom both reason and moral sentiment concur to recommend and support.—But I say little on the subject as yet, not wishing to be considered a zealot, and also considering it necessary to establish an influence before I can do any material good in that way. . . . I dined with Spencer yesterday, who desired to be remembered to you. He keeps aloof from the battle, but I have no doubt is anxious to mingle in it, and will (before the session is over) have considerable influence, which he will exert for Calhoun.[26]

After several meetings of the Committee on the Electoral Law and much discussion, Chairman Flagg reported a bill giving the power of choosing the electors to the people but requiring that the persons elected should have a majority of all the votes.[27] In case no person had such majority, then no election was effected, and no provision was made for a second election in any form. In this shape the bill entitled "An act prescribing the time and manner of choosing Electors of President and Vice-President of the United States" passed on the fourth of February by nearly a unanimous vote, only five members voting against it.[28]

Three days after the passage of the Electoral Bill through the Assembly, Wheaton obtained leave of absence for the remainder of the session.[29] At the time of his departure the fate of the Electoral Bill rested with the Senate, where a long debate concerning it took place. This was brought to a close about the tenth of March by a motion which directed that further consideration of the bill be postponed until the first Monday in November. The motion was carried.[30]

Although Wheaton had obtained' leave of absence during the remainder of the session of the New York State Assembly, he made plans to return at the end of the term of the court, and on March 13, 1824, John Quincy Adams noted in his diary:

> At the office. Mr. R. King came with Mr. Wheaton, who is a member of the New York Legislature, and will leave the city next Tuesday to return to Albany. Wheaton wished to converse with me concerning the Presidential election. His great apprehension appeared to be the rumored coalition between Crawford and myself. I told him what had passed in relation to this subject; the overtures from some of Mr. Crawford's friends, and the answers given by me to them—with which he expressed himself fully satisfied. . . .[31]

Chapter VII

A RETURN TO THE ASSEMBLY

ON THE first of April Wheaton arrived at Albany from Washington and resumed his seat in the Assembly. That Adams was keeping in close touch with affairs in that city is evident from an entry in his *Memoirs* dated April 6 in which he said, "Mr. R. King, Senator from New York, was here; left me with a letter from H. Wheaton, of Albany, of 2nd April, since his return. From that and other letters, nothing decisive can be collected of the dispositions of the New York legislature." [1]

When he reached Albany, Wheaton found existing the general belief that Governor Yates had advised the rejection of the Electoral Bill and would be held responsible. Flagg and some of his colleagues who firmly adhered to Yates insisted that he ought not to be sacrificed for assisting in carrying a party measure into effect. Since Colonel Young was understood to be friendly to a change in the electorate, several of his supporters, who had defended the bill in the Senate, appear at first to have favored the formation of a union with the People's party on behalf of Young. Negotiations were accordingly entered into between them and Wheaton and other members of the People's party whereby it was decided that a state convention should be held and Colonel Young nominated for governor. Before this arrangement could be carried into effect, a caucus of the Democratic members was held wherein it was found that the friends of Governor Yates had to a great extent deserted him. Plans, therefore, were changed. Colonel Young was brought forward as a candidate, and received the nomination by a majority of nearly twenty. General Root was renominated for the office of lieutenant-governor. [2]

The nomination of Colonel Young took the People's party by surprise. On April 7 they also held a meeting and adopted an address protesting against the manner of making nominations by a legislative caucus, and recommending that a convention of delegates, to be chosen by the friends of the Electoral Bill, should be held at Utica on the twenty-first day of September. This movement dissipated completely the hopes entertained by the friends of Colonel Young that he would receive the votes of the People's party, and he was soon after denounced by them for being under the control of the Albany regency.[3]

Before the close of this session of the legislature several active politicians confidently asserted that a desire existed among a number of the leading members of the People's party to nominate DeWitt Clinton as their candidate for governor. Wheaton and others emphatically denied that such a plan existed, and it was generally understood that Tallmadge would be the candidate. But the fears and apprehensions of the Crawford men were not easily allayed, and with a view of preventing the nomination of Clinton—if it were really in contemplation—they concocted a most unjustifiable plan for his removal from the office of canal commissioner. He had discharged the duties of this office faithfully and gratuitously for a number of years; at this time he was president of the board of commissioners, and not a word of complaint had been made imputing to him any official misconduct.[4] On the last day of the session, only a short time before the adjournment of both houses, Bowman, a senator from Monroe County, submitted a resolution for the removal of DeWitt Clinton from the office of canal commissioner. The resolution was acted upon without a moment's delay, and all the senators except three voted in the affirmative.[5] The resolution was then sent to the Assembly.

The plan was formed with the purpose of putting the adherents of the People's party in a dilemma. If they voted against the removal, they would bring down upon their heads the odium of the faction opposed to Clinton—for example, the strong Tammany Hall wing of the Democratic party; on the other hand, if they voted for the resolution they would manifestly lose the support of the Clintonians, who had been acting with them on the electoral law.[6] In the Assembly some little opposition was exhibited to the passage of the resolution, and Cunningham of Montgomery County, who claimed to be neutral in politics, delivered an eloquent and impassioned address against the gross act of proscription and injustice which it contemplated. After a few moments of further debate, the question was put and decided in the affirmative.[7] Thus an attempt was made "to break the butterfly on the wheel," with far different results from those intended.

Concerning the resolution Wheaton wrote to Rufus King,

The Senate sent us this morning a vote to remove DeWitt Clinton as a Canal Commissioner, just as we were on the point of adjourning. This was a contrivance of the faction to fix on us the imputation of partiality to him. They believed we would vote against it. But they were much mortified to find that the most conspicuous members on our side of the House voted for the Resolution. The gun missed fire, as many of their own men voted against it.[8]

Both Wheaton and Tallmadge voted for the removal. They also were taken and were intended to be taken by surprise, but it was the most unfortunate vote ever given by General Tallmadge; because had he not so voted, he would undoubtedly have been the next governor of the state of New York with the consent and support of the whole Clintonian party.[9] The consequences for Wheaton were just as disastrous, as will appear later. The legislature then adjourned on April 12, 1824, to the first Monday in November.[10]

In reference to this action against Clinton, Van Buren in his autobiography said,

Mr. Clinton was removed by a vote of the legislature, on the last day of the session (April 12, 1824), without notice or specific complaint. It has been truly said that this removal "operated like an electric shock upon the whole community." It secured to Mr.

Clinton a full measure of what he had never before possessed—
the sympathy of the people. The friends of Mr. Adams, generally,
in the legislature and their leaders Wheaton and Tallmadge
(James) voted for the removal, but we had the majority—the motion came from our side—and ours was the responsibility.[11]

The public indignation over the failure of the legislature
to pass the electoral bill had meanwhile not abated, and
hope still existed that the reform might be accomplished. In
various parts of the state, in public meetings, in the columns
of the newspapers, in private letters from prominent men to
the Governor, the demand went forth for an extra session of
the legislature. Yates, at first hesitating but at length convinced of the strength of the public demand, issued the
necessary call.[12]

With the keenest interest the people awaited the approaching extra session, many believing that under the circumstances the legislature would not dare to refuse to adopt the
Governor's recommendations. In spite of the slow methods
of travel, crowds hastened to Albany to watch the proceedings. A correspondent wrote to his paper in New York City
that visitors were thronging into the capital "from all points
of the compass and from all sects in politics." He further
stated that the steamboats from New York City in the course
of some three days landed from one thousand to two thousand
passengers, and loaded stages and vehicles came in from all
quarters. "All the public houses are overrun, vast numbers
are quartered upon private families, and many being unable
to obtain lodgings on any terms, were compelled to take
stages for Troy." [13]

When the legislature met on August third, the galleries and
lobbies were crowded to overflowing. Again the party that
was endeavoring to check the movement did not dare meet
the question squarely by arguing against the principle of a
popular choice of electors. On the contrary, the opponents of
the new electoral law hid their real motives behind the pretext that the call for an extra session was unconstitutional,
and therefore they moved that the legislature should im-

mediately adjourn. Azariah C. Flagg, the same member of
the Assembly who had acted as chairman of the committee of
nine, now urged that the House should adjourn without
taking any action. But the Assembly insisted upon debating
the question.[14]

Wheaton and Tallmadge again led the discussions for a
reform of the state's electoral methods, as they had during
the debates of the preceding winter. On the twenty-first of
August Wheaton wrote to his uncle, "I enclose you my
speech in the Legislature, and have also sent a copy by mail
to father." [15]

While the debate was proceeding in the Assembly a resolution was received from the Senate, which had passed a motion on the second day of the session declaring the call of the
legislature unconstitutional and demanding immediate adjournment. But the Assembly, unwilling to accept this resolution from the Senate similar to the one introduced into the
house by Flagg, passed a motion declaring it expedient to
enact a law at that session giving the choice of electors to
the people. The Senate could not be moved; and its presiding
officer, Erastus Root, refused to entertain the resolution of
the Assembly, stating that since the Senate had decided that
the call of the legislature was unconstitutional, it would be
out of order to proceed with any business whatever. The
Senate sustained the ruling of its presiding officer, and the
House then also consented to adjourn.[16] The last chance of
changing the electoral law had now been lost.

After the adjournment of the legislature, everyone waited
with intense anxiety for the Utica Convention.[17] This convention was a natural and logical development of the movement represented by the new state constitution, which had
broadened the suffrage and extended popular control over
the state government by greatly increasing the number of
elective officers. The change had proved most salutary, and
a nominating convention would simply widen still further
the extent of popular control.[18]

Many of the political and personal friends of Clinton began to urge his nomination, while others doubted the advisability of doing so. The People's party, at the head of which stood Tallmadge, Wheaton, and others, were against Clinton. But they had no man whose standing would warrant them to bring him forward as governor except Tallmadge, who was a connection of the Clinton family. For many years he had been a Clintonian. As such he had been elected a member of Congress; but at the convention of 1821 he had claimed to be of the other party. In the winter of 1824 he had been universally the favorite candidate of the Clintonian party for governor. But his vote on the removal of Clinton from the office of canal commissioner had changed that partiality into a feeling of the most bitter hostility.[19]

"Such was the personal resentment entertained against him," according to Hammond, "that the Clintonians would much more willingly have supported Henry Wheaton, who had, from the time of the establishment of the *National Advocate,* to the time of his vote for the removal of Clinton, steadily, and I may add, bitterly opposed him." [20] Wheaton's opposition to Clinton had begun when the latter, although avowedly a Republican, had permitted himself to be the candidate of the Federalists for the presidency in opposition to Madison, at which time the *National Advocate* had been established to oppose him.

Had the People's party been able to offer some other man of equal standing and talents with Tallmadge, a majority of the Clintonian party no doubt would have yielded him their support. Clinton's attitude towards both Wheaton and Tallmadge is clearly shown in his letters of this time. Referring to the Utica Convention Clinton wrote, "The appointment of Wheaton as a delegate is a barefaced insult and must be met as such. Tallmadge can scarcely get a vote in his own county; he is the prince of rascals, if Wheaton does not exceed him." [21]

The Utica Convention contained an assemblage of many distinguished men, but when organized, it was soon found to consist of a large majority of members who were favorable to Clinton rather than Tallmadge.[22]

The People's party in the convention, finding it was impossible to nominate Tallmadge, proposed John W. Taylor of Saratoga, late speaker of the United States House of Representatives, who was known as a Clintonian. A majority of the Clintonian members manifested a disposition to accede to this proposition; but Viele, a delegate from Saratoga, produced a letter from Taylor positively declining a nomination. Thus this compromise failed.[23]

On the twenty-second of September DeWitt Clinton was nominated governor by a large majority, and James Tallmadge was unanimously nominated lieutenant governor. Before it adjourned, the convention resolved that legislative caucuses were improper and that justices of the peace ought to be selected by the people. Both these resolutions were in accordance with the public sentiment at that period.[24] It also appointed a "corresponding committee," or what we should call a campaign committee, and issued an address similar to modern party platforms.[25]

As soon as it was declared in convention that DeWitt Clinton had been nominated, Coffin, the vice-president, Wheaton, the rest of the New York delegation, and most of the members who belonged to the People's party seceded in a body from the convention and formed another meeting of which Coffin was made chairman and Todd, of New York, secretary. But as they were committed against both Young and Clinton, the only thing they could do was to publish a protest against the nomination of the latter and resolve that they would support Tallmadge as lieutenant-governor. Their only real accomplishment was to banish all suspicion of a secret understanding between the Clintonians and the People's party.

The result of the election was a decisive defeat for the Regency party. Clinton was elected governor by over 16,000 majority, and Tallmadge lieutenant-governor by over 33,000 majority.[26] New York has witnessed many exciting political campaigns, but few probably have been more warmly contested than the struggle of 1824.[27] The final vote of New York in the presidential election of that year stood twenty-six for Adams, five for Crawford, four for Clay, and one for Jackson.[28]

The real importance of the campaign of 1824 in New York, it has been stated,

. . . lies not so much in the intrigues of the Albany Regency to save the state for Crawford as in the movement for a popular choice of the Presidential electors, in the revolt against the legislative caucus, and in the permanent establishment of the nominating convention as a method of making state nominations. These were not isolated movements unrelated to the political progress of other states; they were parts of that political evolution which was changing the democratic theory of the early republic into democratic practice.[29]

In each of these significant movements Henry Wheaton was one of the leaders. In appreciation of the services which he had rendered, Adams wrote to him in November 1824, "Your share in the legislative labors of the year have been great and conspicuous. I trust it has been introductory for you to movements on a yet wider field; and observe with pleasure your name among those of the candidates for a seat in the United States Senate." [30] And in congratulating him on the results of his labors, Calhoun wrote,

Never, in this country, has there been a more important political contest. The whole train of future events depended on the result. The part which you have individually taken has been important and honorable to you, and will, I trust, be held in remembrance to your advantage. You have acted under circumstances of great complication, and of relations apparently contradictory, and if you have erred at all on any point such error may be traced to a firm and virtuous tone of character.[31]

Chapter VIII

BACK TO WASHINGTON

A<small>FTER</small> reaching Washington in time for the term of court
in 1824, Wheaton had written to his uncle:

I have been pretty much confined to my law concerns since I
came here—I have suffered no inconvenience whatever from my
absence, nor any (that I can perceive) from the earnest part I have
taken in the dissensions of the time. Mr. Adams and Mr. Clay
have treated me with special attention, and the anti-Crawford
and anti-Caucus party in Congress are so much the strongest
both in weight of character and numbers, that a man loses nothing of estimation or favor here by being considered as opposed
to the Radical faction— We have the interesting question of the
constitutionality of the state Insolvent Laws before the court,
and I, yesterday, argued against them, "to great acceptance."
Mr. Clay is to follow today on the opposite side, and Webster
brings up the rear in reply.—

The President has been a good deal indisposed since my arrival. I have only seen him once, which was at the Drawing
Room on Wednesday Evening— He asked me about the Albany
campaign in a smiling manner, which evidently showed that he
is with us.

I drank tea with Mr. Eddy [of Providence] last evening. I have
said, and shall say nothing to him, respecting the Caucus. It is past,
and cannot be helped—but what could have induced him to attend
I cannot imagine.—

I think the Court will sit a fortnight longer, as I have other
Causes to attend to, besides my office business, I shall stay it out.[1]

Although he had been engaged so busily with the affairs of
New York State and the national campaign, Wheaton had
not neglected his professional engagements. His volume of
Supreme Court *Reports* for 1822 had been written and pub-

lished, and in the following year he had appeared before the court as counsellor in two cases.[2] Besides the volume of *Reports* for this term in which he included an extensive note on the civil law, he published in 1823 *An Abridgment of the Law of Nisi Prius, by William Selwyn, Esq., of Lincoln's Inn, Barrister at Law; with Notes and References to the Decisions of the Courts of this Country.*[3] Edward Everett said in his review of this book that the author had "fulfilled the duties of an editor in a manner which will detract nothing from his established reputation."[4] By inserting into the text of this volume the principles extracted from thirteen hundred American cases, Wheaton had made apparent his learning in the old common law.[5] This knowledge appeared also in his review of Theron Metcalf's edition of Yelverton's *Reports.*[6]

By this time his reputation as reporter, counsel, and author had been thoroughly established; and when Brockholst Livingston, an associate judge of the Supreme Court of the United States, died in the early part of 1823, Wheaton's name was among those considered as a candidate for the vacancy caused by his death.

That he was desirous of securing the judgeship and made some effort to obtain it is evident from his correspondence at this time.[7] It is certain, also, that his name was mentioned in connection with this vacancy. In July Calhoun wrote to M. Stanly, "You say nothing of the vacant place on the Bench. Who ought to fill it? Spencer, Kent, Van Ness, Wheaton, Edwards and Sanford are named. What would be the effect of making the selection of either of those gentlemen? The subject is an important one in my point of view. I consider the office as the highest, excepting the Chief Magistrate, under our system."[8] Wheaton was to be disappointed in this possibility; the president finally appointed Smith Thompson, who had been chief justice of the state of New York and at that time was secretary of the navy.[9]

In preparation for the term of the Supreme Court to be held in 1824, Wheaton wrote from New York to Daniel

Webster that he had intended to communicate with him before, but had been prevented by ill health and a variety of avocations, that he enclosed briefs in three cases, which would be reached the first week of the term, and that in a few days he would forward the papers in another case with a brief which would save Webster the trouble of all research as to the law.[10]

Wheaton was able to secure leave of absence from the Assembly, reaching Washington in time to argue the cases himself. The first one took but a short time; [11] the second, *Ogden* vs. *Saunders,* proved to be more formidable, since it introduced the question concerning the validity of bankruptcy laws passed by the various states. Ever since 1815 both Wheaton and Webster had strongly advocated the passage of a national bankruptcy act by Congress; in this case they contended that the Constitution did not permit individual states to legislate upon the subject. Against them appeared Henry Clay, David B. Ogden, and Charles G. Haines. The Supreme Court was divided in its opinion; it adjourned without a decision.[12] Wheaton also had the opportunity of reporting one of the causes of outstanding interest which was argued during this term, *Osborn* vs. *Bank of the United States.*[13] This case was very similar to that of *McCulloch* vs. *Maryland.* It had arisen from the attempt of the state of Ohio to drive the Bank of the United States outside its borders, and the decision upheld the opinion that the act of a state legislature taxing it was unconstitutional.[14]

Realizing how significant the success of steamboat operation would be to transportation, Wheaton published separately in October 1824, the report of *The Case of Gibbons against Ogden,*[15] involving the constitutionality of the laws of the state of New York which granted to Livingston and Fulton the exclusive navigation of its waters by steamboat.[16] The opinion in this case put an end to the steamboat monopoly in New York and has been denominated as the first great "trust" decision in our history.[17]

Another activity which was to make this winter memorable

was an address which Wheaton delivered at the opening of the New York Athenaeum on the fourteenth of December.[18] In this discourse he took a rapid survey of what had been accomplished in American literature; and presented an interesting view of the intellectual prospects of the country by pointing out the connection between the principles on which the ancient republics were founded and the rapid growth of the arts and sciences to which they gave encouragement and by tracing analogies and causes in a manner which indicated deep reflection on the nature, spirit, and tendencies of our government.[19] Madison spoke of it as an "elegant address, . . . a specimen of judicious and interesting observations." [20]

In 1825 and 1826, Wheaton appeared in several cases before the Supreme Court.[21] In the term of 1827 he acted as counsellor in seven cases. In one of these he was associated with Edward Livingston in representing the appellants who were connected with his old friend General Armstrong.[22] Armstrong had named his son after Thaddeus Kosciuszko, an interesting figure in American history. Kosciuszko, just before his departure from the United States in May, 1798, had placed a fund in the hands of Thomas Jefferson and executed a will whereby he directed that, should he make no other testamentary disposition of his property in the United States, Jefferson was to employ the whole of it in purchasing Negroes and giving them liberty in his name, giving them an education in trade or other directions, having them instructed for their new condition in the duties of morality and their duty as citizens, and doing whatever might make them happy and useful. He made Jefferson executor of his will.

About the twenty-eighth of June, 1806, Kosciuszko executed another will in which he stated that he was "formerly an officer in the United States of America, in their revolutionary war against Great Britain, and a native of Liloane, in Poland, at present residing in Paris." In this will he directed that the sum of $3,704 should be "delivered over to the full enjoyment and use of Kosciuszko Armstrong, the son of General Armstrong, Minister Plenipotentiary of the

said United States at Paris"; and he authorized Jefferson to
reserve this sum in trust for that special purpose. It appeared,
however, that Kosciuszko, before his death, had disposed of
the greater part of his fortune in favor of several other people in Europe. Wheaton was unable to secure action favorable
to his client, Kosciuszko Armstrong; the Supreme Court side-
stepped the case nicely by referring it to the proper probate
court.[23]

In three other cases of this same term Wheaton was associated with Webster.[24] One of these was the famous *Ogden*
vs. *Saunders* case which had originated with Wheaton. This
case had first been argued in the February term of the court
in 1824, and was continued for advisement both in 1825 and
1826. It was again argued in 1827 in connection with several
other causes involving the general question of the validity
of the state bankruptcy or insolvency law. Webster and
Wheaton argued against the validity of the state law; and
the attorney-general, William Wirt, Edward Livingston,
David B. Ogden, Walter Jones, and William Sampson represented the plaintiff. The court on February 18 at last rendered an opinion adverse to Wheaton's client by a vote of
four to three, with Chief Justice Marshall dissenting.[25]

In three cases argued in this term Wheaton appeared as
counsel against Webster. In one he was associated with
Attorney-General William Wirt for the plaintiff against
Webster and Berrien for the defendants; [26] in another Webster and Bliss appeared for the plaintiff, and Whipple and
Wheaton for the defendant; [27] in the third David B. Ogden
and Wheaton appeared for the plaintiffs-in-error, and Webster and Bliss for the defendants-in-error.[28] In each of these
causes the verdict was in favor of the side on which Wheaton
appeared.

In the meantime in 1826 Wheaton brought to a conclusion an undertaking begun by him three years before. This
was a biography of William Pinkney, a task to which
Wheaton was attracted by the international aspect of Pinkney's activities both in his argument of cases before the Su-

preme Court and in his diplomatic functions. On the sixth
of September, 1823, Wheaton wrote to Theophilus Parsons
of Taunton, Massachusetts,

You formerly promised me that you would sketch some account
of what you saw of Mr. Pinkney at St. Petersburg and during his
last illness. You will very much oblige me if you would put on
paper your recollections of him. I shall publish such of his
speeches, etc. as I can collect, and wish to prefix a short biographical account. I want your views of his prominent points of character and of his attainments and what he told you as to his early
education and discipline. I indulge the hope that you will render
me this service, and I assure you that I cannot receive a greater
favor at your hands. I am sure that it would not occupy much of
your time. But do not fear making it too long. I shall be glad to
get it in the course of a fortnight, as I wish to collect all my materials before I begin to write.[29]

The collecting of the materials covered a much longer period
of time than Wheaton had anticipated.

In the latter part of September 1823 he asked President
Madison to allow him to publish some of Madison's private
correspondence with Pinkney, and to favor him with personal
recollections of the man.[30] Madison replied about two weeks
later that he would supply Wheaton with any correspondence
which he might have to fill any chasms. He also said that
Pinkney's letters did equal honor to his penetration and
patriotism during his diplomatic service in Great Britain.[31]
About this time the People's party was being formed, and
Wheaton was elected a member of the legislature, so his reply
was delayed until New Year's day when he requested Madison to lend him all of Pinkney's letters, for in his proposed
work he intended to do justice to Madison's administration
and his resistance to the exorbitant pretensions of Great
Britain in 1812.[32] Over a year later he returned these letters,
from which he had made the necessary extracts, and asked
if Madison would supply him with copies of his own letters
to Pinkney as necessary links in the chain of correspondence.[33]
A month later Madison complied with this request.[34]

In his introductory sketch of Wheaton's life Lawrence says,

If this enterprise had had no other effect than to elicit from President Madison two letters, explanatory of the events connected with the adoption of our restrictive system, and of the immediate circumstances that caused the declaration of war, at the time that it occurred, it would have been the means of adding valuable materials to history.[35]

In the first of these Madison wrote that the President was unofficially possessed of the Order in Council of November 11, 1807, when the message to Congress of December 11, recommending an embargo, was sent; and this fact is corroborated by a note to him from Jefferson confirming his recollections. He also vindicated the efficiency of the restrictive measures by referring to the fact that the repeal of the obnoxious British orders, which had taken place on the twenty-third of June, 1812, had been induced by the influence of the manufacturers before it was known in Europe that war had been actually declared by us. In the second letter Madison stated that the declaration of war was recommended in consequence of the peremptory statement of Lord Castlereagh, made officially through the minister at Washington, that the British orders would not be repealed without a repeal of internal measures of France which did not violate our neutral rights.

The cause of the war lay, therefore, entirely on the British side. Had the repeal of the orders been substituted for the declaration that they would not be repealed, or had they been repealed but a few weeks sooner, our declaration of war, proceeding from that cause, would have been stayed; and negotiations on the subject of impressment, the other great cause, would have been pursued with fresh vigor and hopes, under the auspices of success in the case of the Orders in Council.[36]

Since the letters of Madison did not contain the whole story, in November of 1825 Wheaton received from Monroe, who had been the colleague of Pinkney in the negotiations at London in 1806 and his associate in the cabinet of President Madison, the correspondence which had been interchanged between the latter and Pinkney.[37] Also at Wheaton's request, he received from Monroe explanations of the correspondence between him and Pinkney concerning the treaty negotiations with England in 1806.[38] Pinkney had been a member of the joint British and American commission under the treaty of 1794 and Wheaton included in his biography the opinions delivered by Pinkney on the questions of international law, involved in the various reclamations before the commission.[39]

In writing of Pinkney, Wheaton discussed also a question later of interest to him. In 1816, after the Commercial Convention with England had been concluded, the question was raised whether it was necessary to pass a bill to make the revenue laws of the United States conform to the treaty stipulations. The view held by Pinkney and his argument were set forth in detail by Wheaton.[40]

On July 26, 1826, Wheaton sent to Madison a copy of his publication which appeared with the title *Some Account of the Life, Writings, and Speeches of William Pinkney*.[41] A very interesting commentary on this work by Dr. Greenwood was published in the *North American Review*.[42]

The term of 1827 was the last in which Wheaton was present either as counsellor before the Supreme Court of the United States or as a reporter of the causes tried under its jurisdiction. In the meantime, between the terms of court, Wheaton had been engaged in several other activities.

Chapter IX

ONE OF THE REVISERS OF THE NEW YORK STATE LAWS

HENRY WHEATON and John Duer had been members of the constitutional convention of 1821; its proceedings show they usually voted on the same side of the various questions which came up for consideration. Another of their contemporaries, Benjamin F. Butler, at that time was a member of the Albany regency, whose activities Wheaton so strongly opposed while a delegate to the New York state assembly. Duer, Butler, and General Erastus Root had been appointed by the legislature of the state of New York to revise the statutes of that commonwealth. In January 1825 they presented a plan to the legislature by which they sought authorization to replace the mass of disconnected statutes by a new and complete system of fundamental law. Duer and Butler suggested that Wheaton should replace General Root who had resigned because he was not in sympathy with their plans. On April 2, 1825, the bill authorizing the execution of this new proposal and appointing Henry Wheaton one of the revisers was finally passed. It allowed two years for the completion of the work.[1]

William Allen Butler, grandson of Benjamin F. Butler, in his account of the revisers states:

In the correspondence of the Revisers in my possession there is no trace of any considerable work done by Mr. Wheaton in conjunction with his colleagues, although his name appears with theirs, appended to the Reviser's reports to the legislatures of 1826 and 1827. He prepared one or two of the earlier chapters, but, probably, besides this did little more than to concur in the action of his associates. But, at the outset, he gave to their plan his hearty assent.[2]

Butler claims that Wheaton was engrossed with his duties as reporter and with the completion of his volume of reports; that Duer was taken up with his professional engagements in New York and that the latter wrote on June 10, 1826, to Butler, stating these interruptions, and closed by saying: "I am resolved to be proud of your labors, as I cannot exult in my own. The truth is (and we both agree) that you are worth a dozen such lazy fellows as Wheaton and myself." [3]

There is evidence that Wheaton did play a more active rôle. It would seem that he had lost no time in preparing with his usual thoroughness to make a distinct contribution to the revision, for he furnished the *North American Review* for April of that year with an extensive notice of a French publication which covered seven divisions: three concerning the civil code; two upon the criminal code; one on the code of commerce; and the seventh covering "The five Codes with Notes and Treaties in order to serve as a Complete Course of French Law for the use of Students in Law, and for all Classes of Cultivated Citizens." [4] It is again perhaps significant in connection with his work as reviser that a year later appeared a review written by Wheaton of Gulean C. Verplanck's "Essay on the Doctrine of Contracts; being an Inquiry how Contracts are affected in Law and Morals, by Concealment, Error or Inadequate Price," [5] in which Wheaton made his readers acquainted with what he terms in a letter to his co-worker, Butler, "Verplanck's beautiful speculation on the theory of the Law of Contracts, as to price," and in which he contends for absolute equality in contracts, as binding *foro conscientiae*. [6] Again on March 13, 1827, John Quincy Adams noted in his *Memoirs* that one of the reasons given by Wheaton for delay in accepting an appointment to office is "to finish a volume of the revised Statute Book of New York, upon which he is occupied." [7] Later, while in England, Wheaton during a conversation with Jeremy Bentham seems to have claimed credit for a considerable part in the work; [8] he was not a man to make such a claim when it had not been earned. It well may be,

(No. 103)

Berlin, 27 March, 1839

Sir,

I have the honour to enclose a printed Copy of Mr Zea Bermudez' Memoir on the Spanish Succession referred to in my No. 101.

Mr Zea left here on the 23d. on his way to Vienna, where he proposes to continue his efforts to procure the recognition of Isabella II. by the Powers which have hitherto sustained Don Carlos. He has certainly made a considerable impression here in favour of the cause he pleads, — although Prussia is not disposed to take the initiative in a question in which she has hitherto followed the lead of Austria —

I have the honour to be, with the highest consideration & respect, Sir, your obedient Servant,

Henry Wheaton

The Hon. John Forsyth
Secretary of State

WHEATON'S HANDWRITING

therefore, that Wheaton actually performed more work in the revision than has usually been accredited to him.

While no letters or memoranda by him were included in the papers of the revision, one important document was found which by a few words of endorsement in his handwriting established the authorship and the date of the first written plan of the entire work. This paper was endorsed, *"Projet* of General Plan of Revision handed in by Mr. Butler, May 11, 1825." [9] As William Allen Butler said in 1889 before the New York Bar Association,

Probably Wheaton alone of the New York lawyers of his day would have thought of designating as a *"projet"* a word which his habits of study, as a civilian and a publicist, suggested to him as best descriptive of such novel and far-reaching propositions. In this term, and in the marginal suggestions which he made, we find one of those incidental traits which reveal, by a casual touch, the individual character and distinct personality of the writer. It would doubtless have been a pleasing anticipation, could he have foreseen that the few words of endorsement traced by his hand on the discolored manuscript now first produced, after the lapse of more than threescore years, before a body of lawyers in the chief city of the nation, would identify the earliest recorded effort at a written system of governmental statute law for an English-speaking people.[10]

In March 1827 Wheaton resigned as one of the revisers. In his letter of resignation, quoted by Lawrence, Wheaton himself stated definitely that he had done considerable work in connection with the revision. He wrote,

I cannot refrain from expressing the grateful sense I feel at the proof of confidence which has been reposed in me by the legislature of this State, in associating my name with a work of such magnitude and interest. There is, in my view, no public employment of more permanent dignity and importance; and though considerations, not necessary to be adverted to, have induced me, after mature deliberation, to relinquish it, I feel very great regret in quitting a work, in which I have labored with a zeal disproportionate to my faculties, and which I deem closely connected with the reputation and prosperity of the State of New York.[11]

Chapter X

THE AFTERMATH

IN THE meantime, as a result of his steadily growing reputation in the legal profession and also as a result of his political activities, Wheaton's name was mentioned in connection with several different offices. John Quincy Adams noted in his *Memoirs* on the nineteenth of January, 1825, "I had called at General Brown's office on going to mine, to return him a letter from Ambrose Spencer to him, recommending H. Wheaton for a mission to South America, which Brown had sent me to read, and which had been in the President's possession." [1] And again in February, Mr. Adams wrote, "Judge Thompson, to speak again for H. Wheaton, who is willing to go as Chargé d'Affaires to the Netherlands." [2]

Another suggestion was in connection with Mexico. After the resignation in 1824 of Ninian Edwards of Illinois as envoy to that country, the diplomatic post remained open. The delay lengthened, and the number of candidates for the vacancy increased. The most prominent were George M. Dallas, who had been urged when Edwards was appointed and who later was vice-president, Henry Wheaton, Thomas H. Benton, and William H. Harrison. [3]

Concerning one of the proposals made at this time, Wheaton wrote to his wife:

I think you will agree with me in thinking that what I am promised is better than a second rate diplomatic appointment—especially as I shall not discontinue my connexion with the Court here. Mr. A. is a cold-blooded, and I will not say, heartless, being —but something very like it. He seems to have no sympathy but with such icy things as Alex. Everett. I went yesterday to see Mr. Monroe who is a striking illustration of the vanity of all political greatness. He will find it not very easy to go from here unmolested by his creditors. Yet he invited me very cheerfully to visit him in the country, and gave me a Paper containing an account of his claims, etc. which I sent to Mr. Douglass, and would have you read as a curiosity. The old man makes no secret of his dissatisfaction with Mr. A's arrangements as to the cabinet, asked me if Mr. A. had consulted me, on my answering in the negative— "Nor me; Sir," said he. In the meantime they are fretting at Mr. A's because they cannot have immediate possession of "the house." But they will not have to wait long.[4]

The only reason for Wheaton's desire to obtain a suitable office was the small returns which he was receiving for his brilliant services. That he regretted this state of affairs is evidenced by a note written in 1826 to Daniel Webster, "If it were not absolutely necessary to me, you should not find my name on the list of office seekers. If I could live over again the years that are past, those who are in power should not know me in that character." [5]

But notwithstanding the worth and value of Wheaton's labors and the general recognition of his professional attainments, he was to be deprived of any reward which he might have received for his active support of Calhoun and Adams in the New York State Assembly. As a result of the unfortunate vote against DeWitt Clinton which had been forced upon him, and of the divisions which had resulted therefrom in the People's party, Wheaton was defeated in election to the House of Representatives for which he was nominated in the city of New York.[6] Moreover he was disappointed in one of his ambitions when his name was again unsuccessfully proposed to fill a vacancy on the bench of the Supreme Court of the United States, caused by the death at the beginning of the February term of 1826 of Associate Justice Todd, who had been absent on account of illness the entire previous term. The vacancy was not filled until May 9, 1826, when Robert Trimble was appointed to begin his duties in February 1827.[7]

Wheaton also failed to secure an appointment to the bench

in New York state. On the ninth of October, 1826, Edward Everett wrote,

I duly received your favor of the 23 inst., on the subject of the judicial vacancy in your state. I sought the first opp'y agreeably to your wishes of conversing with the Pres't on the subject of the way you desired. The Pres't of course made no comparisons either as to the claims or the prospects of different candidates, but observed to me that as an immediate appt. was not necessary he tho't the vacancy might not be filled at present nor till he had had an opp'y to meet the H. of Dept. at Washington. In the course of last winter I heard yr. name mentioned by Mr. Clay and Mr. Adams in such a manner as yr. best friends wd. be pleased with. With regard to this place, if you wish it, I hope you will be called to it, but must own I think the floor of Congress yr. sphere and that you ought to do nothing to prevent yr. friends from making the proper efforts to place you there.[8]

But Wheaton was destined never to reach Congress, for in the beginning of March, 1827, he received the appointment of chargé d'affaires to Denmark,[9] and on March 13 John Quincy Adams, then President of the United States, noted in his *Memoirs,*

Mr. Wheaton came to tender his thanks for the appointment of Chargé d'Affaires to Denmark, though seeking time—three or four months—to consider it; to publish the volume of his reports containing the present term of the Supreme Court; to finish a volume of the revised Statute Book of New York, upon which he is occupied; and to consult his father, who is far advanced in years and may perhaps object to his leaving the country. I told him that the time of his departure might be accommodated to his own convenience.[10]

Five days later he wrote,

Mr. Henry Wheaton called upon me, to converse again upon his contemplated mission as Chargé d'Affaires to Denmark. He has yet to obtain the consent of his father, but hopes it will not be withheld. He has read the previous correspondence upon the claims and I advised him to see and confer with Mr. Connell at Philadelphia. He goes for New York tomorrow.[11]

None of Wheaton's friends were particularly enthusiastic about this appointment; they felt he was worthy of a more important post. In June Jonathan Russell wrote to him,

I had after I first heard of your appointment . . . been continually on the point of writing you mainly to speak of your mission and to say that after having sent Richard Rush to London you ought not to have been commissioned to Copenhagen. In what I have said of Copenhagen I merely meant that the treatment (reward) due to merit entitled you to a more distinguished and arduous trust. Still Copenhagen is an honorable post and you will find it quite as agreeable as a court shackled with more fastidious etiquette.[12]

Wheaton himself wrote to Monroe, "I have, after much deliberation, concluded to accept the mission to Denmark, spontaneously conferred on me by Mr. Adams, upon the ground that it will certainly contribute to my health, and that possibly I may do some good in that country."[13]

A long commentary by Wheaton on a French work was published in the *American Quarterly Review* for June 1827. In this article he described the wonder and importance of Champollion's discovery of the key to the Egyptian hieroglyphics, and the conclusions derived therefrom.[14] Thus, before his departure from the United States, Wheaton gave an indication of the increase in the sphere of his interests which he was to experience in Europe.

Chapter XI

COPENHAGEN

O N Sunday evening, the first of July, 1827, Wheaton and his family embarked from New York on a sailing vessel which took twenty-seven days to cross the Atlantic Ocean, so that they did not arrive at Cowes on the Isle of Wight until noon of the twenty-eighth. From Cowes they proceeded to London.[1]

It had been twenty-one years since Wheaton had resided in England as a student, and during that time the world had seen many changes from which had issued the growth and struggle of nationalism, democracy, and imperialism characteristic of the nineteenth century. Foreign relations had been the dominant factor in the life of America during this period. Napoleon I had run his course, involving not only all Europe but the United States as well. A new world had been inaugurated by the Treaty of Ghent and the settlements of the Congress of Vienna, and within this new world far-reaching accomplishments had been effected by new inventions, which were to result in rapid advances in the development of industry, transportation, and communication.

These same years witnessed the renaissance of the study and interpretation of history and civilization in the European universities.[2] With many of the scholars thus engaged Wheaton was to be associated intimately; with some of them such as Eichhorn and Savigny in Germany, Guizot and Thiers in France, Mackintosh and Bowring in England, and Everett and Bancroft in the United States, in the dual capacity of publicist and diplomat. To this new conception of historical study and its social aspect Wheaton soon added a significant contribution.

He found London wonderfully improved. He was fortunate, as he had been previously, in the time of his arrival, reaching there just before the courts of equity closed and after the assizes had commenced, so that he again had an opportunity of observing them. What he saw, strange to say, confirmed his former impression that an American court of justice was a "much more orderly and dignified scene than even those high Tribunals surrounded with all their pomp and paraphernalia." [3] But he found them very interesting and enjoyed meeting the new lord chancellor, the master of the rolls, and the vice-chancellor.

While in England he renewed old friendships and formed many new ones. Among these was his association with Dr. Bowring, who afterwards became Sir John Bowring, and who at that time was distinguished for his contributions to English literature.[4] He later took a prominent place in the parliamentary history of England and in its East Indian diplomacy. According to Jared Sparks, Bowring resided with Jeremy Bentham,[5] another friend to whom Wheaton became particularly attached. Bentham was one of the foremost leaders in the cause of legal reform, to which Wheaton's own attention had been so recently directed. He apparently often entertained Wheaton, Lawrence has written, "at those dinners which, never extending beyond a single guest, were literally tête-à-tête, and which were the sole occasions that Mr. Bentham devoted to conversation on the great topics that occupied his mind." Wheaton found Bentham "a charming old man, less dogmatical than he had expected, who criticized the specimens of the New York *Revised Laws* that had been sent to him, in a tone of great politeness, expressing himself satisfied with what the revisers had done, as far as they had attempted to go." [6]

After leaving England and traveling by way of Hamburg and Lübeck, Wheaton and his family proceeded to Denmark.[7] On his arrival in Copenhagen on the nineteenth of September, the new chargé sent a note to the minister of foreign affairs, Count Schimmelmann, requesting an audience. He received an answer the next day, arranging an appointment for him at the latter's country home. There, on the twenty-first,[8] he delivered to him his letter of credence.[9] Count Schimmelmann, who was a venerable statesman over eighty years old and had been in the public service more than fifty years, proposed to present Wheaton to the King and Queen, stating that it would be most convenient to do so before the reviews commenced, which would be on the thirtieth.[10] He spoke of the King's paternal character, adding *"mais il a été malheureux.* Both he and the King of Saxony, the most virtuous sovereigns in Europe, have been despoiled of their dominions."[11]

Four days later Wheaton received a note from Count Schimmelmann informing him that Their Majesties wished to receive him the next day. Accordingly he was introduced to the King, Frederick VI, at his palace in town.[12] The government of Denmark was at that time absolute. Concerning the King, Wheaton wrote,

The king's character for *bonté* is uncontested. He enters into all the minutiae of government, which, is no very hard task in a little kingdom like this. But he is anything but a *roi fainéant.* The army is his hobby. The peasantry, though no longer serfs, are subject to military duty; every farmer's son, of mature age, being liable to serve six years. In the towns, all must serve in some corps; either the regular troops, or the burger guard, or fire companies. In short, Denmark is Prussia in miniature. The king gives audience to all his subjects every Monday, when every man, woman or child may present a memorial to him in person, or speak to him.[13]

After his presentation to the King, Wheaton went to the Château of Fredericksberg and had the honor of an audience with the Queen.[14] The next day he attended a conference at Count Schimmelmann's and made various diplomatic calls,[15] and two days later "the corps diplomatique" returned his visits.[16] His diplomatic career had begun.

A week after his arrival Wheaton had written to his father

that he had taken the second story, completely furnished down to the minutest article, of a house in a pleasant and convenient part of the town. For this he was to pay seventy pounds until the twentieth of April, which he said was "moving time" there.[17] When moving time came, a change was made. Many years later Wheaton's daughter described the house then occupied and the city of Copenhagen as it appeared at that time. The latter, she wrote, had fine palaces, a military and a naval academy, admirable hospitals, an extensive public library, a valuable collection of northern antiquities, a good gallery of pictures, and fine public walks. The house occupied by Wheaton was situated on the Strandvei, a road which ran along the shore of the Baltic to the Dye-Hange, a fine park well stocked with deer. Wheaton's home, which was sometimes called the West India House and which was known also as the Lantern, the Queen told him, because it had many windows, stood at some distance from the road with a green lawn before it. It was surrounded by lilacs, laburnums, and beech trees. From the windows of the house might be seen the blue waves of the Baltic studded with sails, and in clear weather the opposite coast of Sweden was discernible. The road was enlivened

. . . by the brilliant equipages of the Royal family and nobility, by the Holstein-wagons, long span carriages which contain ten persons, two only being seated abreast, and much used for parties of pleasure, and by the women from the neighboring fishing villages, with their green petticoats and red bodices, carrying large baskets of fish to the city.[18]

The life at the court in Copenhagen was socially pleasant. On the Queen's birthday, the twenty-eighth of October, Mrs. Wheaton was presented to Her Majesty by Mrs. Wynn, the wife of the British minister at Copenhagen, and in the evening she was at court with her husband attending a ball and supper.[19] A few days later Wheaton, together with Colonel Cordova and Prince Palazola, dined with Prince Christian,[20] a cousin of the King and heir presumptive to the crown; and on the seventeenth he went with Count Waga to call on Prince Christian to see his collections.[21] But it was not long before this phase of Wheaton's life was temporarily stopped.

On Prince Ferdinand's birthday, the twenty-second of November, Wheaton was at court in the evening attending a ball and supper. Mrs. Wheaton, however, did not go. She remained at the bedside of her brother Edward, who had accompanied Wheaton's family to Copenhagen.[22] He always had been delicate and was unable to survive the change in climate. His illness proved fatal two months later.[23]

In the meantime, Wheaton had received letters which informed him that his father had died on the twenty-sixth of October.[24] On February twenty-third he noted in his diary, "Have been nowhere and seen nobody for four weeks." [25]

There was, moreover, an aspect of affairs in Denmark which greatly affected the negotiations entrusted to him. The condition of the country at the end of the European war is best told in Wheaton's own words when writing to the Secretary of State, Henry Clay:

Indeed you can hardly have an adequate notion how this country was impoverished by the war brought upon it by the unjust aggressions of England, and followed by the dismemberment of the Kingdom at the peace. If they had remained neutral, their commerce and navigation must have sensibly declined at the latter epoch. But when we consider that they lost at a single blow their navigation and all their capital engaged in commerce; that they made immense pecuniary sacrifices to the faithful observance of their alliance with France; that the Kingdom with its diminished territory, population, and resources is now staggering under a debt of 50,000,000 dollars, we cannot wonder at their reluctance to enter into new engagements. They have had no means of replacing the capital thus lost. France, after repeated evasions, has at last peremptorily refused to repay them a debt of the most sacred character, being for supplies furnished the French troops beyond the stipulations of the alliance. This is their true condition, although the King is a man of very simple habits, and observes a most praiseworthy economy in his household, and in other respects except the Army which has been his hobby from his youth. But the former condition of the kingdom has entailed upon him a numerous pension list, and the burthen of supporting establishments quite disproportionate to its diminished resources.[26]

So Wheaton could readily understand why in his discussions with him concerning the relations between the United States and Denmark, Count Schimmelmann continually stressed the plea of poverty.

But Wheaton was to find, as Jonathan Russell in a farewell note had written to him, that the court of Denmark was not only socially pleasant but the country "had intellectually in herself and her dependencies a vast fund of enjoyment." [27]

Chapter XII

WRITINGS ABOUT SCANDINAVIAN HISTORY AND LITERATURE

Not only did Denmark with its dependencies evoke Wheaton's interest, but the whole of Scandinavia was to prove a source of enjoyment for him. Less than a month after his arrival in Copenhagen he noted in his diary that he had dined with Mr. Peder Pederson. Pederson later became minister to the United States. There were also in the company some members of the diplomatic corps and several Danish counsellors of conference; among them was Professor Schlegel, who appeared to Wheaton to be a man of extensive learning in his profession. They talked together a great deal about jurisprudence.[1] Wheaton found that he was an "assessor" in the high court, and at the same time head of the Law Faculty in the Royal University of Copenhagen; that he was author of the book on the case of the Swedish convoy, which had been published in 1799 against Sir William Scott's celebrated judgment in the case; and that he had written in Danish on the history of legislation.[2] Jared Sparks has described Schlegel as "a small man, quick in his motions, of a light, flush complexion, and apparently more than fifty years old." He was a bachelor and lived in more style than Sparks was prepared to see in the house of a German professor.[3]

A few days later Wheaton dined at Count Schimmelmann's with the two Professors Gersted, Professor Reinhard, Bishop Munter, and the renowned poet of Denmark, Oehlenschläger, who later made him the subject of some complimentary verses.[4] Many friendships were formed by Wheaton with the leading literary men in Denmark. Concerning them he wrote, "There are some men who are unknown, if not in the rest of Europe, at least with us, that deserve to be known; and in general, the attainments of their savans are much more profound in what they pretend to a knowledge of, than with us; and I suspect generally, even in England, they do not go to work so doggedly and so perseveringly." [5]

Wheaton himself apparently at once became actively engaged in his literary pursuits, and before the following June he had acquired sufficient proficiency in the use of the Danish language to furnish the *American Quarterly Review* of that month with a review of four publications by the Danish philologist Erasmus Rask.[6] Of Rask he said: "The vast attainments of the learned editor of these publications, who is still a young man, will perhaps be rather appalling to our more languid and moderate students." [7] Although Wheaton's article is entitled "Scandinavian Literature," it covered a wider field than the title indicated, but, even so, it is not much more than a review of the works mentioned therein. Besides discussing the general significance of the Scandinavian nations and languages, and listing the important sagas then published, Wheaton gave a brief description of Rask's travels and particularly of his interest in and purchase of a valuable collection of manuscripts relative to the Zend-Avesta, or institutes of Zoroaster. Furthermore, he discussed the proposal of Professor Rasmus Nyerup to establish a national museum of antiquities and the collections of this museum. He also noted the contents of the Royal and University libraries, mentioning especially the manuscripts in their possession.[8] The last of the four books listed for comment is related to Wheaton's previous review of Champollion's work in French, and is a treatise on the chronology of ancient Egypt.

Wheaton's contributions to the *North American Review* were always received gratefully by the editor, Edward Everett, who wrote in August that an article on the "Public Law in Denmark" had been received too late for the July number of the magazine but that it led "the van" for October. This paper, which was primarily a notice of the work of Professor Schlegel,[9] explained the institutions of Denmark—the *lex regia,* which regulated the succession to the throne and conferred on the king the whole executive and legislative power, and the assembly, the *Höieste Rett,* which limited the theoretical despotism of the monarchy. In it Wheaton also described the political connection of Denmark with the duchies of Schleswig, Holstein, and Lauenburg—a subject which several years afterward menaced the peace of Europe.[10] In December of 1828 a long review appeared in the *American Quarterly Review* of Georges-Bernard Depping's interesting history entitled *Histoire des Expéditions Maritimes des Normands, et de leur établissement en France au dixième siècle,*[11] a work which was acclaimed in 1822 by the Royal Academy of Inscriptions and Belles Lettres.[12] This book no doubt was a great stimulus to Wheaton in his own studies. These three reviews were followed in January of 1829 by one concerning Pars III of *Edda Saemunder hins Fórda* by Professor Finn Magnüssen and the first part of E. G. Geijer's *Svea-Rikes Häfder.*[13] This was really an essay entitled "Scandinavian Mythology, Poetry and History." In this the sources of the materials for the early history of the Gothic and Teutonic kingdoms of Norway, Sweden, and Denmark are indicated; [14] and as Benson has stated, "compelling snatches of early Scandinavian history—manners, customs, religion, runes and institutions" are given. Brief translations of several songs are provided, and paraphrased accounts of them are included.[15]

The varied researches of the Danish scholars continued to attract Wheaton's attention. In the *North American Review* for October he again commented on the contribution by his friend, Erasmus Rask, to the study of Egyptian antiquities. In this review Wheaton also discussed the analysis of Egyptian mythology by J. C. Prichard, and reverted to the deciphering of the Egyptian hieroglyphics through the discoveries of Champollion.[16]

In 1830 appeared two reviews by Wheaton in the *North American Review*—a brief one on Professor J. F. Schlegel's *Hin forna Lögbok Islendinga,* under the title of the *Ancient Laws of Iceland,* and a notice of Professor Erasmus Rask's

*Danish Grammar, adapted to the Use of Englishmen, with
Extracts and Dialogue.*[17]

Wheaton was thoroughly enjoying his studies in Scandinavian history and literature. His writings were attracting many readers by their enthusiasm and by opening an entirely new field of knowledge. As has been well stated, "He had become a pioneer in introducing a carefully compiled account of Scandinavia, and more particularly medieval Scandinavia, to both American and European readers."[18] His intellectual attainments were quickly recognized. In the United States, on the nomination of Robert Walsh, Jr., Peter S. Du Ponceau, and Joseph Hopkinson, he was elected in 1829 a member of the American Philosophical Society. The recommendation was based on his profound researches into the literature and antiquities of the northern kingdoms of Europe as well as his various publications on legal and literary subjects before he had left the United States.[19] Two Danish authors also were elected members in the same year —Christian Rafn and Erasmus Rask, the latter upon the suggestion of Du Ponceau and Wheaton.[20] The Alpha Chapter of Phi Beta Kappa was established at Brown University in July 1830. At a meeting held August 14 the first members were elected. Among the group of alumni chosen for membership was Henry Wheaton. He and John Whipple were the only men of the class of 1802 so honored.[21] In Denmark on Professor Schlegel's nomination, Wheaton was elected a member of the Scandinavian Society at an extraordinary meeting held in March of 1830 for that purpose. In writing to him about it Professor Schlegel said, "Tous les membres reconnurent votre mérite et le *zèle* avec lequel vous avez travaillé à répandre la connaissance des ouvrages Danois et de l'ancienne littérature du Nord dans les États-Unis d'Amérique."[22] The following November he was elected a member of the Icelandic Literary Society. In the note informing him of the election Professor Rask said it was due to the recognition of "his knowledge of the Northern History, his proficiency in the language, and his zeal in promoting the literature of Scandinavia." [23]

A review of two publications, the first a new edition of John Josias Conybeare's *Illustrations of Anglo-Saxon Poetry* and the other an English translation of Rask's *Grammar of the Anglo-Saxon Tongue,* appeared in the *North American Review* of October 1831. This article entitled "Anglo-Saxon Language and Literature" [24] was really an essay of some twenty-five pages comparing the Anglo-Saxon and Old Icelandic languages and literatures and dealing largely with Scandinavian material.

In a letter to his uncle in June of 1831 Wheaton said, "I am now very busy publishing my Northern History, which will not make me rich, but will be I hope not disadvantageous in another point of view." [25] By this book, which was published in both England and America with the title *History of the Northmen or Danes and Normans, from the earliest times to the Conquest of England by William of Normandy,* some idea of the extent of the author's investigations in the history, mythology, and jurisprudence of Scandinavia was made known to the world. It received instant commendation from reviewers in the periodicals not only in the United States, but also in England and on the Continent.

Wheaton here showed his trend toward modern historical writing by giving numerous, detailed footnotes from which can be derived a bibliography of his sources, both ancient and modern. It is apparent, moreover, that he had endeavored to include in his research all material pertinent to his subject. The list of the authorities he used is a long one and includes among the moderns not only Danish writers but also French and English. He stated in his preface that the ancient Icelandic sagas were "the most authentic and valuable historical monuments of early transactions possessed by any European nation," and that they had been "illustrated with a diligence and critical skill that may fairly be said to be unrivalled by the antiquarian labours of any other country." [26] He further explained that his aim in writing the book had been "to seize the principal points in the progress of society and manners in this remote period, which have been either entirely passed over or barely glanced at by the national historians of France and England, but which throw a strong and clear light upon the affairs of Europe during the Middle Ages and illustrate the formation of the great monarchies now constituting some of its leading states." [27] The significance of the Northmen in history appealed to him in its relation not only to Europe but also to the early history of America. He expressed the belief that the Northmen had discovered the North American continent, and in this connection later wrote to Dr. Wheaton that he thought he had clearly proved that Dighton Rock was one of the places where they had landed.[28] Since this was near Providence, he believed that the discovery would be of interest to Rhode Islanders.

In France his book was reviewed in the *Revue de Droit Français et Étranger*,[29] and in England in the *London Athenaeum*,[30] the *Westminster Review*,[31] and the *Monthly Review*,[32] which closed by saying, "Mr. Wheaton, after giving a succinct account of the establishment of the Normans in France, concludes his history with the battle of Hastings, whereby they also obtained a permanent footing in England, thus presenting us, in a single, compact, and well-digested volume, details which hitherto could only have been gathered, with much labor, from a great variety of sources." [33] Other countries paid some attention to it also. In America it was most favorably received.

Long reviews appeared in the *American Quarterly Review*,[34] the *American Monthly Review*,[35] and the *North American Review*.[36] The last, the longest of them all, was written by Washington Irving. His review, the only one contributed by him to this periodical, is very interesting and enlightening and is well worth reading even today. The article in the *American Monthly Review* stressed the discovery of Vinland in which Wheaton was so much interested.

Another study by Wheaton appeared as a review of the publication in 1830 by Dr. Peter Erasmus Müller, Bishop of Sioelland, entitled "Critisk Undersögelse af Saxos Histories, etc." This article which was inserted in the *Foreign Quarterly Review,* was really an essay on the Danish constitution.[37]

Other publications by Wheaton concerning Scandinavia appeared after his departure from Denmark. These will be discussed in a later chapter. But it was perfectly apparent that no opportunity was lost by him to obtain a knowledge of the language, traditions, and institutions of the country to which he was accredited. This sincere interest gained him many friends at the Danish court and secured official consideration and coöperation in the diplomatic negotiations with which he was entrusted.

Chapter XIII

THE TREATY OF INDEMNITY

THE special subject confided to Wheaton was the negotiation of a satisfactory arrangement between the United States and Denmark by which the claims of the American citizens against that country for the injuries committed on their commerce during the European war would be indemnified.

The extent and importance of the contacts which existed between the two countries perhaps required that there should have been a representative at the court of the king of Denmark at an earlier period; but considerations of economy by the United States Government had delayed the appointment. Wheaton was well aware of the history of the relations between the two countries prior to his appointment.[1] A brief survey of these is necessary to understand the problem he faced.

As mentioned before, after England's declaration of war against Denmark in 1807, the United States was practically the only neutral engaged in extensive maritime trade. While carrying on its accustomed and lawful trade in the Baltic Sea in the years 1809, 1810, and 1811, the United States found its navigation suddenly interrupted on various pretexts by the commissioned cruisers of Denmark, a power with which it had always cultivated the most friendly relations, and from which no such interruptions were expected, because Denmark had always shown the greatest respect for the rights of neutral commerce.[2] The amount of property of which American citizens were unjustly deprived by these aggressions was very great, and the interruptions of the lawful trade of the

United States in the Baltic were very numerous and highly vexatious.[3]

Early in the year 1811 the President of the United States, James Madison, determined on a special mission to Denmark to arrest the progress of the capture and condemnation of the vessels of the United States, activities then threatening the total destruction of its trade in the Baltic and adjacent seas, and to demand indemnity for the past. George W. Erving, selected for the service, proceeded to Copenhagen. His mission was attended with only partial success. He was able to prevail on the Danish Government to repress some irregularities and to check the condemnation of most of the vessels of the United States the cases for which were then pending or vessels which had been captured and brought into port after his arrival; but he could not procure satisfaction in cases of erroneous or unjust condemnation by the Danish tribunals, for the decrees were held to be irreversible.[4]

Upon the termination of Erving's mission in June of 1812, he left John M. Forbes as an agent of American claims, in which character the latter was recognized by the Danish Government. His efforts were unavailing. In the fall of 1818 George W. Campbell, who had been appointed minister of the United States at St. Petersburg, stopped at Copenhagen on his way to that capital and in an interview with Rosenkrantz, minister of foreign affairs, stated that, although not instructed to renew the discussion of the claims at that time, he had been charged to say to him, that the United States, entertaining the strongest conviction of their justice, could not abandon the claims.[5]

Seven years later, because nothing had been done about them, Christopher Hughes, who had been appointed chargé d'affaires of the United States to the Netherlands, was directed to call at Copenhagen on his way from Stockholm and to repeat the demand for satisfaction of the American claims. Accordingly, in the execution of this duty on August 5, 1825, he presented a note to Count Schimmelmann, the Danish minister of foreign affairs, urging anew the payment of the indemnity which had been so long delayed. On the seventeenth of the same month he received an answer which insisted on the irreversible character of the sentences of the High Court of Admirals. Hughes, in a despatch addressed to the secretary of state giving an account of his mission, says that the general result of his observations during his short stay of eighteen days was that there did exist a disposition to go into an examination of the claims, but that "the owners of the claims must consent to forget, in a great measure, their justice, and to take up the subject on the more liberal principle of compromise." [6]

On the twenty-sixth day of April, 1826, a general convention of friendship, commerce, and navigation was signed between the United States and Denmark.[7] This treaty and the great value of the commercial intercourse between the two countries in addition to the unsatisfied claims of indemnity convinced President Adams that a longer delay in instituting a permanent mission to Denmark was not advisable,[8] and for that office Wheaton was chosen.

At the time of the signing of the treaty, a note was addressed by the secretary of state to Peder Pederson, the Danish representative in the United States, in which the statement was made that it would have been satisfactory to the Government of the United States if the Danish official had been charged with instructions in the negotiation to treat of the indemnities due to its citizens. But as he had had no instructions to that effect, the secretary of state had been directed, before proceeding to the signature of the treaty, explicitly to declare that the omission to provide for these indemnities was not to be interpreted as a waiver or abandonment of them by the United States Government, which, on the contrary, was firmly resolved to persevere in the pursuit of them until they should be finally arranged upon principles of equity and justice.[9]

The new chargé was to convince the Danish Government of the injustice of longer persisting in withholding indemnity, especially since the commercial convention of 1826 had shown the liberal spirit of the United States towards that country. No determination had been made of the method by which such an arrangement could be consummated.

Adams preferred that it should be by a board of commissioners which would ascertain the amount due to American citizens. This board might also be authorized to decide any claims of Danish subjects against the Government of the United States. But even so, he felt that the method of ascertaining the amount was less important than the object of procuring the indemnity itself. In the instructions given to Wheaton, it was stated that if he should find his efforts unavailing to get a board established, he was then authorized to say that the Government of the United States would agree upon a basis formed on the principle of a compromise and would accept a gross sum as a complete discharge of all the claims. He also was instructed to request the Danish Government to state the sum which it would be willing to pay, and to communicate its decision to the State Department.

As a further evidence of the friendly disposition of the United States to accommodate Denmark, Wheaton was authorized to propose receiving whatever sum might be awarded by the board of commissioners or might be accepted by way of compromise in Danish stock bearing such interest and reimbursable at such time as might enable the holders thereof to sell it at par in the money markets of London, Paris, Amsterdam, or Copenhagen.

Any arrangement, however, whether through a board of commissioners or by compromise, was to be considered as distinct from and not comprehending the claim for the cargoes of the ships *Fair Trader* and *Minerva Smyth* and the brig *Ariel,* detained at Kiel during the year 1812. John Connell, of Philadelphia, had been the agent of the owners of those cargoes and had been long endeavoring to obtain indemnity for the losses then incurred. He was engaged in the prosecution of that object in 1825 and obtained from Count Schimmelmann assurances which authorized the belief that redress would be at last effected. It was understood that Con-

nell would shortly proceed to Denmark for the same purpose; and Wheaton was directed to give him such official aid
and coöperation as might appear to him best adapted to the
accomplishment of Connell's agency.[10]

Connell was not only the agent of the claimants for these
ships, but he also represented many other claimants, among
whom were the Baltimore Insurance Company,[11] Daniel W.
Coxe of Philadelphia, and Stephen Girard, a friend of Connell. He arrived in Copenhagen a few days after Wheaton
reached that city. Wheaton at once addressed a note to Count
Schimmelmann concerning these cases and had subsequent
conferences with him. Schimmelmann hardly denied the
justice of the claims, but his principal object seemed to be to
reduce the demands to their minimum, insisting with much
emphasis upon the poverty of the treasury of Denmark.

Count Schimmelmann repeatedly assured Wheaton that
the official report to the King concerning the various claims
was favorable in its general features. Both in written notes
and verbal conferences Wheaton urged the rendering of a
final decision. Ultimately Count Schimmelmann sent for
Connell (who had not before seen the Minister), and after
some protestations as to his own disposition that justice
should be done, in which Wheaton had no doubt he was
sincere, desired Connell to name the smallest sum which he
would take and give a release to the Danish Government. He
mentioned 100,000 Spanish dollars; but Count Schimmelmann having advised him not to exceed 75,000 dollars (as the
King would not go beyond that), a compromise was finally
reached between them by which it was agreed that Connell
should receive 230,000 marks banco of Hamburg (equal to
about 76,000 dollars) in full satisfaction of the claims.[12]

The matter having been thus arranged between the minister and the agent and attorney for the claimants, Wheaton
did not hesitate to express his satisfaction at what had been
done, at the same time saying nothing from which Count
Schimmelmann had a right to infer that the United States
could be induced to desist from prosecuting its other claims.

The actual loss sustained by the parties represented by Connell could not, Wheaton felt, be justly estimated at more than $100,000, taking into view the enhanced price of the commodities in consequence of the edict; and even including the gain which they would have made in the exchange at that time on the remittance of the proceeds to England, the loss could not exceed $150,000. One computation made the compromise equivalent to three-fourths and the other to one-half the actual loss sustained by the claimants, who were about forty in number, including insurance corporations and persons claiming in a representative character.[13]

The arrangement between Count Schimmelmann and Connell was sanctioned by the King. Connell received the amount of the stipulated indemnity in government bills which he had converted into cash, and by the fourth of March, 1828, was on the way home.[14]

By this time Wheaton had become convinced that a compromise to receive a gross sum in payment of the other claims was the only mode of adjustment which could be consummated. The circumstances tending to diminish the hope of ultimate success in respect to the remaining claims were: first, the impoverishment of the kingdom and the embarrassments in its finances consequent upon the calamitous events of the war; second, the failure of the United States to obtain justice for similar aggressions from France and her vassal states; and third, the impression which prevailed in Denmark that the claimants had not strength enough in public opinion to induce Congress to pledge the legislative support to such measures as the executive might think it expedient to adopt in order to compel a redress of the injuries involved. Wheaton felt that the first difficulty, the only one he could control, might perhaps be obviated by reducing the demands of the United States to their minimum and accommodating them to the convenience of the Danish Government both as to the time and manner of payment.[15]

On July 28, 1828, Wheaton wrote to Clay that Count Schimmelmann on account of illness and his age had turned the preliminary discussions over to Count de Reedtz with the proviso that Wheaton could take the matter up with him personally whenever he so desired. Wheaton, also in his despatch, covered the whole discussion of the principles of the claims to that date and the bases on which both he and Count Schimmelmann had rested their arguments.[16]

Meanwhile, negotiations had been taking place between the Government of the United States and that of Russia respecting the cases of the American ships *Commerce* and *Hector,* captured by a Russian squadron in the Mediterranean in 1807. A summary of these negotiations was published in the *National Intelligencer* of June 1828. The knowledge that these claims were under discussion caused delay; Count Schimmelmann requested the Russian legation to write to their court for detailed information respecting the circumstances of these cases. Wheaton also wrote to Henry Middleton, our minister in Russia, on the same subject. Upon receipt of the desired information from Russia, Baron Nicolay, the Russian minister residing in Copenhagen, who had manifested a very friendly interest in whatever concerned the United States, communicated the contents of the papers to Wheaton before he sent them to Count Schimmelmann.[17]

Frederick VI had consistently taken the position that the decisions of the Danish tribunals could not be reversed, and therefore he was not liable for indemnity. From the outset of the negotiations Wheaton on the other hand had argued that though the decisions of the courts of the capturing nation had the effect of closing forever all private controversy between the captors and the captured, they could not be held to do so as between nations; but that on the contrary, the right of a foreign government to demand redress against an illegal capture only arose after the failure to obtain justice, in ordinary course, from the courts. What the United States demanded of Denmark was not a judicial revision and reversal of the sentences pronounced by the Danish tribunals, but the indemnity to which the American citizens were entitled in consequence of the denial of justice by the prize courts, and of the responsibility thus incurred by the Danish Government for the acts of its cruisers and tribunals.

It appeared by the documents received from Russia that in one of the cases, the *Hector,* there had been no regular sentence of condemnation; but since the other, the *Commerce,* had been carried into Corfu, a port then in possession of the Russians, and since Count Nesselrode had not stated the contrary in his report to the Emperor, it was fairly to be inferred that this vessel with her cargo had been regularly condemned by a competent prize court. It was, therefore, a case precisely in point upon the question of the conclusiveness of admiralty sentences between nation and nation, one in which the Emperor of Russia had made reparation, notwithstanding the sentence of his tribunals affirming the capture, for the injury complained of by the citizens of the United States. This supported Wheaton's contention, and at last convinced the King that some compromise should be made. A further delay took place in the progress of the negotiations on account of the festivities connected with the marriage of the King's daughter to the son of Prince Christian, and also of other circumstances over which, Wheaton had reason to believe, Count Schimmelmann had no control.[18]

On January 12, 1829, Wheaton was notified that the Danish king had appointed Count Schimmelmann jointly with De Stemann, minister of justice, as commissioners to negotiate the claims with him.[19] At the end of the month Wheaton could only say,

They have manifested an invincible repugnance to the project of a mixed commission, and, though not unwilling to negotiate upon the basis of a compromise, have not hinted at any sum, which, in my judgment, the Government of the United States, taking into view the condition of the country, and the impossibility of obtaining a full satisfaction, would be willing to receive as a partial indemnity to our injured citizens.[20]

John Connell, the agent of most of the claimants, again arrived in Copenhagen on the first of July with despatches from the State Department [21] in which Van Buren had written to Wheaton concerning the compromise to be arranged:

With regard to the sum which the President is willing should be accepted from the Danish Government as a full and entire indemnification for the claims of our citizens, you are already acquainted with his views upon this point, and he relies with confidence upon your knowledge of circumstances, your zeal and patriotism, for procuring, through the exercise of a sound discretion on your part, in behalf of the just and important interests involved, a satisfactory arrangement. He is the more anxious on this score, because it has been found impossible for me, from my recent assumption of the duties of this department, to make him acquainted with it in all its details, or to have become sufficiently so myself, to enable him to authorize or warrant me giving more precise instructions on the occasion. [22]

Wheaton consistently refused to accept a compromise which he deemed inadequate. By the middle of October he had had various informal conferences with Count Schimmelmann besides several formal and official meetings with the Danish commissioners, and the protocols from these conferences were sent to the State Department. Connell returned to the United States in December, leaving the matter entirely in the hands of Wheaton. By January 9, 1830, there was "no present prospect of any beneficial result of the negotiations." [23]

Wheaton continued to urge the consummation of a settlement of the claims and, in accordance with the instructions received, informed the commissioners "in earnest and respectful terms, that the present Executive of the United States will not be wanting in all suitable exertions to make good" the formal declaration at the time of the signing of the convention of 1826 that "the Government of the United States was firmly resolved to persevere in the pursuit of them [the claims] 'until they should be finally arranged upon principles of equity and justice.' " [24]

The consistently firm attitude taken by Wheaton, the

justice of the arguments presented by him, and the cordial relations which existed between him and the Danish officials finally produced results. On the twenty-seventh of March, 1830, Wheaton wrote to Secretary of State Van Buren that he had at last agreed with the Danish commissioners upon the articles of a convention of indemnities which would be signed the next day. The principal basis of the treaty was a renunciation on both sides of all claims for captures, seizures, and condemnations and an assurance of the payment of 650,000 Spanish dollars to the United States for the use of the American claimants. He felt that the sum was the utmost he could obtain and that nothing would have been gained by longer delay. Further delay also would have rendered quite improbable the conclusion of the treaty in time to be laid, as the President desired, before the Senate then in session.[25]

In accordance with the instructions he had received after the convention had been signed, Wheaton sent it by special courier to Louis McLane, the United States minister in London, for prompt despatch to the United States. The amount agreed to be paid by the Danish Government in addition to the renunciation of all claims of Danish subjects was considerably more than the minimum which he had been authorized to accept. The sum to be paid under the convention, together with that received in 1827–28 on account of the seizures at Kiel, and the Danish claims on the United States amounting to about $50,000, then renounced, made altogether an amount exceeding three quarters of a million. Considering the diminished resources of Denmark exhausted by the war, Wheaton hoped this would be considered as a tolerable salvage from the damage incurred. The time and manner of payment were regulated with the view of avoiding any addition to the permanent public debt of Denmark, an addition to which the King would not consent. Before signing the treaty, Wheaton ascertained that the credit of the commissioners of the sinking fund, by whom the obligations for the second and third payments were to be issued, was perfectly good, and that the obligations could be cashed upon delivery at a reasonable discount either in Copenhagen or at Hamburg.[26]

The fifth article was proposed by the Danish commissioners and is significant of the obstacles surmounted by Wheaton in concluding a convention acceptable to both parties. The article stated:

> The intention of the two High Contracting Parties being solely to terminate definitely and irrevocably all the claims, which have hitherto been preferred, they expressly declare, that the present Convention is only applicable to the cases therein mentioned, and having no other object, can never hereafter be invoked, by one party or the other, as a precedent or rule for the future.[27]

As Wheaton's object was to obtain practical redress for past injuries and not to assert any particular doctrines of the law of nations for future application, he did not very strenuously oppose the insertion of this stipulation which was made a *sine qua non* by the Danish commissioners.[28] As Lawrence has pointed out, Laurent Basile Hautefeuille, at that time one of the foremost French writers on international law, noticed the remarkable character of the transaction which, although it accorded an indemnity, left the two claimants just where they were as to contested principles.[29]

The respective ratifications of the convention were exchanged at Washington on June 5.[30] Wheaton was instructed not only to take measures to secure the collection of all the prize papers relating to the claims under discussion, but also to receive personally the payments of the installments due from the Danish Government and to negotiate for their exchange.[31]

In May 1833, the *Washington Globe* published a list showing the result of every claim presented to the board of commissioners under the treaty with Denmark. The full amount awarded in all cases was $2,154,425. The sum actually payable was $670,654.70.[32]

But the convention had more far-reaching results than just

the payment of the Danish claims, for it was the pioneer of the subsequent conventions with France and Naples.[33] Wheaton had commenced in 1829 a correspondence with William C. Rives at Paris upon the subject of the claims of the United States, and his despatches to the secretary of state which had a bearing upon some of the questions Rives would have to discuss with the French Government were sent to him open in order that he might have an opportunity to read them before they were transmitted. Wheaton found that the line of argument pursued in his counter declaration was approved by Rives.[34]

On March 27, the day before the treaty was signed, Wheaton again wrote to Rives in the hope that he might be able to make the treaty with Denmark available for some good purpose with France.[35] That the French negotiators were interested in Wheaton's treaty is apparent from a note which one of them sent to Rives requesting a copy of the Danish convention that the French commissioners might peruse it.[36] The arrangement finally made with France on July 4, 1831, was used as a precedent in the subsequent negotiations with the Neapolitan Government.[37] From the treaties with France and Naples millions were obtained for the citizens of the United States, and "our right to redress was established for violations of neutral commerce, the sole palliation of which was the illegal acts of the opposing belligerents. And, in these last cases, it was also shown that, as long as a nation maintains the forms of external sovereignty, neither a change in the reigning dynasty, nor a plea for the preponderating influence of a powerful ally, can relieve it from its accountability to foreign states." [38]

As stipulated in the treaty, the Danish indemnity was to be paid in three installments. The negotiations concerning them required Wheaton's presence in England, so he was thereby afforded an opportunity of renewing old friendships and forming new ones. In the meantime he was in Paris during the July Revolution of 1830.

Chapter XIV

VISITS TO FRANCE AND ENGLAND

ON THE first of June, 1829, Wheaton had written to Secretary of State Van Buren asking leave of absence from his post in Copenhagen for four months during the ensuing fall. The reasons given for this request were the need of the settlement of his father's estate, of which he was one of the executors; his own private concerns, which required his presence at home; and the state of the health of his family, which necessitated their return to the United States.[1] The request was granted, but the negotiations entrusted to Wheaton were not concluded until the end of the following March, so that his departure with his family from Copenhagen was postponed until the first of May, 1830.[2]

On the way to Paris Wheaton stopped at The Hague for a few days. This was a short time before the movement which severed the two portions of the kingdom of the Netherlands, and, after he had attended the deliberations of the states-general, Wheaton wrote that the kingdom was far from being united. He was received cordially by the minister of foreign affairs, Baron Verstolk, and presented to the King by William P. Preble, who represented the United States at that court. The King of the Netherlands had been chosen arbiter between Great Britain and the United States in the controversy over the northeastern boundary. Preble was from Maine. He therefore was very much interested in securing the best terms possible and was over-active in his efforts to influence the decision concerning the boundary line. From the information Wheaton could collect from him and from the diplomatic circles at The Hague, the general belief seemed to be that the cause of the United States would receive favorable consideration.[3]

From The Hague Wheaton proceeded with his family to France. The letters which he received after reaching Paris removed the necessity of his return to the United States. He therefore sent his family to America without him and after embarking them at Le Havre, he returned to Paris. By the end of May he had been consulted by Rives several times concerning the question of the French indemnities.[4]

Wheaton was in Paris at the time of the French Revolution of 1830. A few days before the outbreak Lafayette had invited him to his country home, Lagrange. Immediately after this visit Wheaton had dined at the Danish minister's with the Marquis de Barbé-Marbois, who was then almost ninety years old and who, besides having experienced various vicissitudes in the French Revolution of 1789, had been employed in eminent posts both under the Empire and the government of the Restoration. He had been in America as secretary of the French legation during the struggle for the independence of the colonies. In 1803 he was one of the French negotiators of the Louisiana Purchase, and later had written a history of the cession.[5] A review by Wheaton of the French edition of this work had been published by the *North American Review* in April 1829, and just a year later Wheaton had reviewed the English translation of the same book.[6]

During this memorable summer Wheaton made the acquaintance of Louis Philippe, to whom he was presented by Lafayette, and he saw the former take the oath to the charter. Congeniality of pursuits brought association with Guizot, Thiers, and the other distinguished men of the Orléans dynasty, who besides their official rank had attained eminence in the literary world. With the Duc de Broglie he was on terms of the most friendly intercourse, also with the historian Mignet, the Perpetual Secretary of the Institute for the Class of Moral and Political Sciences, and with most of the other celebrities whose society contributed so much at that time to the intellectual attractions of Paris.[7]

After reaching Boston, Mrs. Wheaton wrote to her father,

To-day I had the plea⌐re to get a letter from Henry of the 31st. Aug., he was still in Paris where he was detained by the disturbance in the Netherlands, but he seems not to be in haste to quit Paris, he says "I dined yesterday with Pazzo di Borgo, the Russian ambassador, who is the first diplomat in Europe in point of talents and address, he was very polite and I had a long and interesting conversation with him upon the state of France which he is very capable of appreciating as he has resided here ever since the restoration of the Bourbons in 1814, he agrees with everybody else as to the inevitable folly of the race, which can only be compared to the infatuation of the Stuarts." He appears to feel a little lonely.[8]

That Henry Wheaton had hoped to be transferred to another post or, failing to secure a transfer, had planned to return home is evident. When his family sailed for America in the spring of 1830, all his household goods were sent with them. His intention also is indicated in the letters which he himself wrote [9] and in the correspondence of his friends. As early as the first of December 1829, Christopher Hughes had written from Brussels to Samuel Smith in Baltimore that Connell had told him he believed Wheaton would not remain long at Copenhagen.[10] But for various reasons Wheaton determined to return to his post in Denmark, there to await the further orders of the President.[11] In this connection Rives wrote to Van Buren from Paris in September of 1830 that Wheaton was about to return to Copenhagen, but with rather a heavy heart, for he did not find that position a very agreeable one. He suggested that Wheaton might be sent to Naples to revive the prosecution of our claims there, as his success at Copenhagen argued well his diplomatic ability.[12]

Two months later in a letter to his uncle Wheaton himself said,

I am very glad to find you entirely approve of my resolution of continuing at my post to await the tide. There is certainly nothing very inviting in the prospect of our American politics—and probably my public services will be more firmly appreciated if I remain abroad a little while longer than if I were to be tossed once more on that tempestuous sea. I hear from other quarters a confirmation of what you say about the satisfaction with which my doings have been received. I shall try to wait with patience the result. In the meantime I endeavor to relieve what, with some would be the ennui of banishment, by reading and scribbling. For myself I can truly say I do not know what it is, as proceeding from a want of occupation, though I certainly feel in this lonely life some moments of depression which I cannot master entirely. I can say with Mr. Jefferson that my temperament is sanguine. I try, at least, to look on the bright side of things.[13]

He was, however, to have his banishment at least mitigated as a result of his treaty of indemnity, which stipulated that the first payment by Denmark should fall due on March 31, 1831, the second on September 30 of the same year, and the third a year later.[14] In accordance with these terms Wheaton received on the first date mentioned the bill of exchange for the first payment and the two obligations for the second and third payments. He had received instructions from Van Buren to go to England to superintend in person the negotiation of the bill by Baring Brothers and Company, the bankers of the United States at London, so that the parties interested might receive the benefit of as full a measure of indemnity as could be secured.[15] After having deposited the obligations for safe keeping at Copenhagen, Wheaton left for London the first of April. The payment of the bill was finally made on the twenty-third of May.[16]

Among the statesmen with whom Wheaton was particularly friendly on this and other occasions when he visited the British capital were Lord Aberdeen, Lord John Russell, Sir Robert Peel, and Lord Palmerston, and especially the Marquis of Lansdowne. With Sir James Mackintosh he was well acquainted.[17]

He also renewed his friendship with many of the most noted literary men in England, with Mr. and Mrs. Austin and others of fame, and with the historians Sir Francis Palgrave and Henry Hallam. He was on terms of intimate association with

Nassau William Senior, the eminent jurist and political economist, who later by his able paper in the *Edinburgh Review* helped to place Wheaton's merits as a publicist properly before the world.[18] Wheaton's own prestige was greatly enhanced during this visit by the publication of his *History of the Northmen.*[19]

Likewise as a learned jurisconsult he was requested to furnish answers to the queries of the common-law commission then in session, who were occupied with the same investigations to which his own attention had been directed when he was a commissioner at New York.[20]

Meanwhile, in the interim between his return to Copenhagen from Paris and his mission to England, Wheaton had been seriously ill for several weeks, and after reaching London wrote for his family to join him. To avoid worrying them he had said nothing about it at the time, but he wrote to Dr. Wheaton that he was not willing to pass another winter in Europe alone.[21] Remaining in his post at Copenhagen depended on his own inclination,[22] but he still hoped that a desirable appointment would be forthcoming. The last of June he wrote to his sister, Mrs. Lyman, that Mr. McLane had sailed for New York to take his seat in the cabinet, that he had been very civil, even friendly to him, and that he had expressed his conviction that Wheaton would be employed in some other quarter as soon as there should be an opening.[23] Hoping for a desirable change within a short time, he returned to Copenhagen with his family who had joined him in London about the middle of July.[24]

Wheaton was also made responsible for the collection of the remaining two obligations assumed by Denmark. In conformity with the instructions from the State Department,[25] he received the payment of the second installment on the thirtieth of September, 1831. He then opened correspondence with Baring Brothers about realizing the amount of the bill of exchange in London and remitted the bill directly to them with directions to negotiate it on the most advantageous terms they could obtain for the claimants.[26] For the collection of the third installment, in 1832, he was instructed to go to England and negotiate for the payment of the bill as he had done for the first payment.[27]

Mrs. Wheaton accompanied him on this trip. They reached Hamburg before the middle of September[28] and embarked by a steam packet for London on the fifth of October in the expectation of reaching that city on the seventh, but because of a very heavy gale they were compelled, after having been exposed to extreme peril, to put into the port of Lowestoft near Yarmouth on the tenth. They therefore did not reach town until the twelfth.[29] The transaction was completed by the twenty-eighth, so their stay in London was a brief one. They proceeded from that city to Hamburg and returned to Copenhagen overland by way of Brussels and the Rhine. The season was so far advanced as to render the navigation of the North Sea extremely uncomfortable and even dangerous;[30] indeed the vessel on which Wheaton's heavy baggage was transported from London to Copenhagen was wrecked on the coast of Jutland, and the greater part of the ship's lading was lost or badly damaged by which he was a "very considerable loser."[31] They finally reached Copenhagen on the first of December.[32] A year later Wheaton was to take another boisterous sea trip, but meanwhile during his mission to Denmark his attention had been given to various subjects of national and international interest.

Chapter XV

OTHER DIPLOMATIC NEGOTIATIONS

SHORTLY after Wheaton's arrival in Copenhagen he was brought into more direct activity in connection with several matters of vital interest to the United States.

One of these was the trade with the West Indies. This was a leading topic of discussion between the United States and Great Britain at that time. The conditions proposed by England to powers having colonial possessions were much more favorable than those offered to the United States. These powers, in order to participate in the British West Indian trade, were only required to grant to British ships the same privileges of trading with their colonies as Great Britain granted to their ships in trading with the British possessions abroad; whereas it was made a condition that the United States, since it had no colonies, should place the commerce and navigation of Great Britain and of her possessions abroad upon the footing of the most favored nation.[1] The refusal of the United States to comply with this proposal led to the temporary interruption of its intercourse with the West Indies.

By the middle of November 1827, Count Schimmelmann had frequently mentioned to Wheaton confidentially that Denmark, though repeatedly urged by England to give its adherence to the terms of the act of Parliament of 1825 relating to the colonial trade, refused to do so, not knowing what might be the consequence if it gave the English this direct trade to Europe and fearing that such an absolute reciprocity might be very injurious to their navigation.[2]

They were anxious, however, to maintain their trade with the United States, and Wheaton's services were more directly required in the beginning of the year 1830. The governor-general of the Danish colonies, Von Scholten, had visited Washington on his way to Copenhagen and was the bearer of a letter of introduction to Wheaton, which James A. Hamilton, then acting secretary of state, had given him by directions from the President. In this letter Wheaton was requested to confer with the Governor-General. The latter also had been referred to him for the same purpose by Count Schimmelmann. They had several interesting conversations on the subject of the commercial relations of the United States with the Danish West Indies. Count Schimmelmann then sent for Wheaton whom he informed that he was engaged in framing an official note to him relating to the additional duty on rum imposed by the tariff act of Congress of 1828, a duty which had had an injurious effect upon the trade between the Danish West Indies and the United States. Schimmelmann also alluded in general terms to the other points which had formed the matter of informal conversations with Von Scholten, viz., the United States consulate at St. Thomas and the encouragement which the escape of fugitive slaves from the Danish islands too often received from the negligence or connivance of the shipmasters of the United States; but he did not state that Denmark was prepared to make any formal complaints on those latter heads. Wheaton answered these suggestions in general terms, reiterating the friendly disposition of the United States towards Denmark.[3]

In April Wheaton wrote to Van Buren that it was the intention of the Danish Government to send Von Scholten on a special mission to the United States to obtain some arrangement mutually beneficial to both by which a maximum of duties might be fixed on each side to liberate the commerce from its then embarrassed state.[4] On the same day Wheaton received from Count Schimmelmann a letter asking for a modification of the duties on the produce of the Danish islands.[5] In the following January Van Buren wrote to Wheaton that he was enclosing copies of the correspondence which had taken place between the State Department and Major General Von Scholten, for he felt that it was due to

the frankness and liberality with which the latter had opened
the negotiation and which had characterized every stage of
it, that Wheaton should explain with equal candor the motives which compelled the President to decline the propositions which had been made. At the request of General Von
Scholten the correspondence had been laid before Congress
by the President, who had expressed himself willing to co-
operate with the legislative branch of the Government in
any measure which it might deem expedient to adopt toward
the fulfillment of the Danish king's wishes.[6] Wheaton informed Van Buren that he believed the Danish minister,
De Stemann, was fully satisfied that the President could not
have taken any other course than the one he had adopted.[7]
As far as Wheaton was concerned, the matter was closed
when on June 18, 1833, he sent to the State Department a
translation of the ordinance of the Danish king regulating
trade with the West Indies.[8] This, in accordance with
Wheaton's recommendation, was sent to the *Globe* for publication.[9]

In connection with one phase of the conversations between
Wheaton and Von Scholten—the slaves in the Danish West
Indies—it is interesting to note, in view of his later activities
in Paris, that Wheaton sent to the State Department a copy
of a treaty, signed July 26, 1834, by which Denmark acceded
to the conventions, dated November 30, 1831, and March 22,
1833, between England and France for the suppression of
the slave trade.[10] The situation in which the Danish West
India colonies were then placed by the measures of the British Parliament for the emancipation of the slaves in the
British colonies had called the attention of Denmark to the
subject not with the view of adopting any similar measure
but in order to mitigate the condition of the Negroes in so
far as might be consistent with the rights of property and the
safety of the colonists. For this purpose the King had named
a commission to consider the subject. The commission had
reported a set of regulations or rather instructions to the

governor-general of the Danish West India Islands by which very extensive discretionary powers were given to that officer to frame and execute such regulations in the islands as might, in his judgment, tend to promote the object in view. These instructions were based upon the leading principles—first, that any slave should be permitted to buy his freedom, whenever he was able to do so from the fruits of his labor, during the intervals allowed him to earn money; second, that any slave who was discontented with his master and could find a purchaser who was willing to buy him might in that way change masters.[11] Wheaton informed the State Department that these instructions had been given to Von Scholten and that he had left Copenhagen for the purpose of returning to the West Indies and carrying them into effect in order to avoid, if possible, the disastrous consequences which were apprehended from the example of the very hazardous experiment then being undertaken in the neighboring British colonies.[12]

Another question pending at that time in the United States was in reference to the northeastern boundary line. The commissioners, who had been appointed under provisions of the Treaty of Ghent to determine this boundary, had been unable to agree, and in 1827 a special convention had been signed submitting the dispute to arbitration. At the time of the selection of an arbiter, the first choice of the United States was Emperor Nicholas of Russia; the King of Denmark was the sovereign next preferred. Lawrence maintained that it could not be "doubted that the knowledge possessed at Washington of the superior fitness of the Minister at Copenhagen, to conduct the conference on our part, was among the motives for placing Denmark second on the list." [13]

The King of the Netherlands, who was finally chosen, decided upon an arbitrary division of the territory. Concerning this decision, which had caused surprise, Wheaton wrote to Van Buren:

Count Schimmelmann had also sent to me for perusal a very long despatch from Baron Selby, the Danish Minister at The Hague, respecting the Arbitration between us and Great Britain as to the eastern boundary of the Union, with a Copy of the Award pronounced by the Sovereign arbitrator.—The terms of the Royal decision seem to have surprised the Danish Minister, and he expresses his opinion of Mr. Preble's protest as being suited to the occasion and quite temperate and dignified.—Indeed I should infer from a single reading of the despatch which was all I was favored with, that such was the general impression at the Hague. Indeed when I was there last summer, a decision favorable to our pretentions, at least upon the main point, was very generally expected by the members of the corps diplomatique resident at that Capital.[14]

The matter of governmental quarantines by which the commercial interests in the United States were affected was closely followed by Wheaton. In August 1831 the *Globe* published an extract taken from one of Wheaton's despatches: [15]

Strict Quarantine Regulations are established at Copenhagen to exclude the Cholera Morbus, some vessels coming from the upper Baltic ports have passed Elsineur without being allowed to communicate with the shore, and an Ordinance has been published at Berlin declaring all bills of health granted in Prussia, Poland, and Gallicia a nullity, and subjecting all vessels and travellers coming from those countries to a strict Quarantine. These measures are the result of the terror which this formidable disease excites in Western Europe.[16]

Wheaton kept his Government informed of the various regulations enforced from time to time and the several changes made. He was successful in obtaining some modifications of the quarantine regulations on vessels from America. The regulations were, in 1831–32, very strictly enforced on account of the cholera and the decision of Denmark was particularly important since that country acted as the sanitary police for the several Baltic states.[17]

He also successfully obtained some reimbursement of overcharges on vessels that had passed the Sound during the summer of 1831. The Baltic would be a closed sea if it were not for the three narrow straits which by their continuation through the Cattegat and the Skagerak connect it with the North Sea and the Atlantic Ocean. The Little Belt between Jutland and the island of Fuenen is too shallow to be of much use to navigation. The Great Belt between Fuenen and Zealand does not run in a favorable direction for ships bound for the eastern Baltic ports. Consequently, the Sound between Zealand and Sweden has always been the main entrance to the Baltic.[18] For centuries Denmark had claimed the privilege of collecting dues from vessels passing through the Sound.

The sanitary commission at Elsinore in 1831 thought proper to impose on each vessel that stopped there an extraordinary quarantine duty in addition to the Sound dues. The Danish King sanctioned the measures of the sanitary police but ordered on the third of August that vessels ought not to pay more than the Sound dues, that the levying of extraordinary quarantine duties should cease in the future, and that restitution should be made of the sums already received on this account.[19]

In May of 1832 Wheaton sent to the Secretary of State a chart, plan, and description of the new quarantine ground established by the Danish Government at the entrance of the Great Belt.[20] The next month he wrote that there was cholera in the duchies of Schleswig-Holstein and Lauenburg; that Sweden had previously declared all the Danish dominions suspected and then had declared Holstein infected and had enforced against it the strictest quarantine regulations; but that it was believed the measures had been adopted rather with a view to the prevention of smuggling than from any belief in their efficacy in excluding the communciation of the cholera.[21] Ports in the Baltic were then quite free from the dread disease.

On the first of September, however, he wrote that cholera had broken out in Lübeck, Rostock, and several other places on the southern coast of the Baltic, and that apparently the

quarantine regulations were useless.[22] He also sent a translation in his own handwriting of the Danish ordinance on the
subject of these regulations [23] and later corresponded with
William Wilkins, envoy of the United States at St. Petersburg,
respecting the quarantine on vessels bound up the Baltic.[24]
This related principally to vessels coming from what were
called infected places in the West Indies bound to the Russian and neighboring ports. Wheaton had several conversations with Baron Nicolay, the Russian minister at Copenhagen, who received from Count Nesselrode a despatch which
had been written in consequence of Wilkins' representations
to the Vice-Chancellor.[25]

Baron Nicolay read to Wheaton Count Nesselrode's despatch, from which he gathered that the Russian court was
disposed to promote the wishes of the United States in miti-
gating the inconvenience suffered by its trade in so far as
was consistent with the paramount object of executing the
quarantine system, which they believed to be necessary to
secure the ports of Russia from infection. The Russian Minister was also cordially disposed to coöperate with Wheaton
for the same object, in so far as might be consistent with his
duty to his own Government.

With this view they both communicated with the Department of Foreign Affairs in Copenhagen in order to ascertain
to what extent the inconveniences to their commerce, complained of by the parties interested, were to be attributed to
the inevitable consequences of the quarantine system itself,
and how far to the want of efficient means in its execution
and operation. The Danish Government also manifested a
disposition to correct any abuses which might have crept
into the administration of the system.[26]

As to the principles of the quarantine system, which would
open a wide field for discussion, Wheaton felt that any representations which the United States might think fit to make
respecting it would be most advantageously addressed to
the Russian court. Denmark had undertaken to establish and
maintain the quarantine regulations not for its own sanitary

security but for that of Russia and the other states bordering on the Baltic Sea. It could not, therefore, reasonably object to any relaxation of it which might receive the assent of the other powers.[27] During the same month in which Wheaton wrote that he and Baron Nicolay were thus coöperating, he received his transfer to another post, and the matter was temporarily dropped.

Chapter XVI

CONTEMPORARY EVENTS OUTLINED
IN DESPATCHES

ONE of his friends, commenting on the indefatigability of Wheaton's labor, said that he seemed to derive the same enjoyment from his work as another might from lighter diversions.[1] The truth of this belief is evidenced by the diversity of the subjects covered in detail in his private and diplomatic correspondence.

Many times information sent by Wheaton to the Secretary of State was transmitted to the other departments of the Government; things such as a chart of the Cattegat with a drawing and detailed description of a floating light stationed there, which were turned over to the Navy Department.[2]

In November 1829 he wrote to Clay that he had been collecting, concerning the commerce of Denmark and its regulations, information which he soon would send to him, since the statement communicated to the United States Congress in 1819 (with the aid of such materials as the Government then had) and published in the book entitled *Commercial Digest* was very incorrect even in respect to the actual condition of things at that period, and had become still more so by alterations since made.[3]

A few days before his death, which occurred February 9, 1831, Count Schimmelmann confidentially communicated to Wheaton the royal rescript addressed to the German chancery. This rescript was considered the first step toward the establishment of a free constitutional government in Denmark.[4] Wheaton's despatches contain an interesting and continuous history, much too long to be given in detail, of the constitutional movements in Denmark and the duchies of

Holstein and Schleswig and of their relation to contemporary events.[5]

In view of his later activities in Paris it should be noticed that as early as December 1827 he appreciated the true position of Turkey when, after the battle of Navarino in which the Turco-Egyptian squadron was destroyed by the combined fleets of the allies, he wrote:

I think we have only, as yet, the opening scene of a great drama, which is to be enacted in the Eastern world; and how the dénouement is to be brought about without a partition of the Ottoman Empire, I am at a loss to conjecture. The general impression in the diplomatic circles here is that the affairs of the East will terminate in a pacific manner, the Porte being now convinced that the allies are in earnest, and all the powers having so strong an interest in preventing the further territorial aggrandizement of Russia.[6]

Denmark had just concluded, under the mediation of Russia, a treaty with the Porte. This provided for the free navigation of the Black Sea upon terms similar to those granted to Sweden by the treaty of May 28, 1827. "But," Wheaton wrote, "Sweden obtained her treaty without the intervention of Russia, believing it to be rather injurious than useful, the Turks still regarding the Swedes as Anti-Muscovites." [7] He discussed in detail the policy of the Russian cabinet, the principles of the two parties which contended for power within its Government, and the attitude of Russia toward Turkey and Poland.[8]

While he was in Denmark, Wheaton commented at length upon many aspects of European affairs, especially between 1831 and 1835.[9] In the summer of 1832, he informed the Secretary of State that Lord Durham had arrived in Copenhagen on his way to St. Petersburg; that Durham's connection with Earl Grey and the present English cabinet and his high standing in Parliament was attracting an unusual degree of interest toward the objects of his mission; that doubtless the primary object was to endeavor to cut short the Belgic question which had become more entangled than ever since the pretended ratification of the treaty of November 15 by Russia, Austria, and Prussia; that the King of Holland, relying upon the refusal of these three powers to concur or even to acquiesce in any measure of coercion against him, still calculating on what the chapter of accidents might produce in his favor, continued to resist more obstinately than ever the decisions of the London conference; and that it was supposed the British cabinet at last suspected that his pertinacity was secretly encouraged by Russia. Wheaton further said that the affairs of Poland would also probably engage a share of Lord Durham's attention.[10]

Of the conditions in Germany and the Germanic Confederation he had much to say. His discussions of this subject will be given in fuller detail in a subsequent chapter. But in the light of his further experience it is interesting to note that he wrote:

It is difficult to conceive that so intellectual and highly cultivated a nation as the people of North Germany can be long kept in the state of pupilage to which they have been hitherto condemned in the Prussian dominions, or how the existence of constitutional Governments in Hanover and the other smaller States can be compatible with the prolongation of such a state of things in the Prussian monarchy. In the meantime a rather sharp correspondence has recently taken place between the Austrian and British cabinets respecting the inquisitorial repressive policy adopted by the former in the affairs of the Confederation, and the influence of Great Britain is exerted, so far as it may be through the connexion with Hanover, to counteract this policy, and at the same time embarrass the efforts of Prussia to draw the smaller states within the group of her peculiar commercial system and consequently of her political influence.[11]

While these movements were taking place in Europe, the United States was having troubles of its own in connection with the dissension aroused by the tariff of 1832, and in the attempt to arrive at an amicable compromise. Wheaton informed the Secretary of State that

The attention of the friends of free government in Europe is now faced with intense interest on American affairs. The firm but prudent measures adopted by the President to assert the legitimate authority of the central government, without trespassing on the just rights of the States, are universally approved of; and the hope is indulged that our people may have the wisdom and virtue to avoid the rock, on which every preceding federative Government has been wrecked, and which must prove equally fatal to our domestic happiness and external consideration as a nation.[12]

Just six months later Wheaton was on his way home to the United States on a matter connected with his private affairs which had been causing him much concern and anxiety for some time.

Chapter XVII

WHEATON VS PETERS

To understand why Wheaton crossed the ocean so late in the season for sailing vessels, it is necessary to review some of the activities in which his successor as Supreme Court reporter had engaged just after entering on the duties of this office. Upon Wheaton's resignation, Richard Peters of Philadelphia, a friend of Judge Hopkinson of the same city, had been appointed to fill the position.

In June of 1828, Peters sent out from Philadelphia a circular entitled "Proposals for publishing, by subscription, the cases decided in the Supreme Court of the United States, from its origination to the close of January Term, 1827." The circular stated that on account of the heavy expense of the original volumes, about $180, there were few copies in some parts of the country. Therefore, he planned to issue in six volumes, at a cost not to exceed thirty-six dollars, a set of books to be known as *Peters' Condensed Reports,* in which would be contained all of the decisions of the Supreme Court to be found in the twenty-five volumes previously published —four volumes by Dallas, nine volumes by Cranch, and twelve volumes by Wheaton. His own regular series of reports, then just beginning, would continue the *Condensed Reports.* He would in this way have in his own hands a complete series of reports from the establishment of the Supreme Court to date. The circular closed with the statement that the proposed work would "increase the demand for the original reports, as their superior merits and accuracy will, by its means, become more generally known." [1]

Judge Cranch immediately informed Peters that he would insist on his legal rights because he was still out of pocket

$1,000 for the publication of his last three volumes. A protest was written in September 1828 by Donaldson, who was the publisher of all of Wheaton's *Reports,* except the first volume, and to this Donaldson had also obtained the rights. The seriousness of the situation was stated by him in his letter. He wrote:

I readily anticipate . . . that you will not issue such a work, the effect of which would be to me literally ruinous on a large amount of property I have vested in the work, which I have been endeavoring to accumulate from my labor and care of twelve years; likewise the injury that would be done to my absent friend Henry Wheaton, Esquire, by such a publication, and the result of which would be to deprive him and his family of the pecuniary reward due to his professional labors of twelve years.[2]

On receiving the circular, Wheaton was at once fully aware of how serious the results of such a publication would be to him. In November of the same year he wrote to Daniel Webster:

I perceive that my successor Mr. Peters has issued proposals for publishing by subscription "the cases decided in the Supreme Court of the United States from its organization to the close of January Term, 1827."

This attempt has very much surprised me, and I cannot help thinking that he has not duly considered the injury such a publication would do to me. It would in fact nearly, if not quite, destroy the sale of the volumes published by me from 1816 to 1827. I should, therefore, be much obliged to you, if you think fit, to remonstrate with him on the subject. I have looked forward to the publication of a second edition in order to realize the fruits of my labor, but this expectation will be entirely defeated should Mr. Peters persist in his design. In that case, I shall feel it to be my duty to protect my property by legal measures. Indeed I have already given contingent instructions to that effect, but not to be executed until amicable remonstrances have been first tried.

Will you mention to Judges Story and Thompson that I have long since written them.[3]

Nevertheless Peters went ahead with the publication of the *Condensed Reports,* issuing in 1830 volumes 1 and 2, containing the reports of Dallas and Cranch, and in February 1831 volume 3, which besides the eighth and ninth volumes of Cranch contained the first volume of Wheaton's *Reports.* The edition numbered 1,500 copies, and 900 were sold by subscription before the date of publication. Judge Cranch took no steps to ascertain his legal rights through judicial proceedings, but Donaldson took action as soon as volume 3, containing the cases from the first volume of Wheaton, was issued. He threatened to prosecute Halstead, a bookseller of New York, if he sold the volume. This produced a new circular from Peters in the form of a letter to his publisher, John Grigg, March 2, 1831, in which he offered to "indemnify and save harmless from all costs and damages all who publish or sell this work." His determination to proceed with the publication was repeated, and there was now added to his former statement that the judicial opinions were not susceptible of copyright the new claim that "there does not exist a copyright, legally secured, to any one volume of Mr. Wheaton's Reports." He asserted that neither Wheaton nor his publishers had complied with the statutes for securing copyrights. "Peters derived considerable satisfaction by announcing in this same circular that on March 1, 1831, Congress by a joint resolution had authorized the purchase of seventy copies of his *Condensed Reports*." [4]

In May 1831 Donaldson filed a bill in equity praying an injunction to prevent the further printing, publication, and sale of Volume III of the *Condensed Reports;* asking for an accounting and payment of what might be due Wheaton; and petitioning for further relief. The injunction was granted, and in July Wheaton wrote to Webster, "I am involved in a law suit with Richard Peters in the Circuit Court at Washington. I request you to consider yourself as retained for me in the latter court, and will take care that your fee is sent you in due season." [5]

In September Peters and his publisher moved to dissolve

the injunction. After argument the court, being divided, denied the motion and continued the cause until final hearing.[6] In December, Paine, the former partner of Wheaton, also wrote to Webster engaging his services for Wheaton.

The cause was heard in the Circuit Court in January 1833, the title of the case being *Wheaton and Donaldson* vs. *Peters and Grigg* (Federal Cases, No. 17,486). Judge Baldwin on account of illness was absent from court during the entire trial, and Justice Hopkinson, sitting in the Circuit Court, held that Wheaton had not taken the steps necessary under the statutes and that no common-law copyright existed in the United States. He therefore dissolved the injunction and dismissed the bill January 9, 1833. An appeal to the United States Supreme Court was immediately entered.[7]

According to Wheaton's own statement, if it had not been for the disastrous effect such termination of the proceedings would have had on Donaldson's fortunes, he would not have proceeded with the case.

For certainly I would never have sacrificed the last farthing of my paternal inheritance, and made a winter's voyage across the Atlantic on my own account, knowing as I did that Hopkinson had corresponded with S. [Judge Story] about the case, and that the latter had agreed to confirm above what the former should decide below, and that H. had taken advantage of Judge Baldwin's absence from illness to dissolve the injunction.[8]

The dissolving of the injunction destroyed all hope of any future financial return from his labor of twelve years.

Nevertheless, on June 1, 1833, Wheaton wrote to Secretary of State McLane requesting leave of absence.[9] This was cordially granted,[10] and by the middle of October he was in London on his way to the United States.[11] After "a boisterous passage of thirty-two days in the Packet Ship *Roscoe* from Liverpool," he arrived in New York on the twenty-sixth of November, expecting to reach Washington about the middle of December.[12]

After the removal of the injunction Peters had proceeded

with the publication of the *Condensed Reports* and issued the sixth and last volume in January, 1834. The case on appeal came on for hearing in the January term, 1834. On the bench were Chief Justice Marshall and Justices Story, Duval, McLean, Thompson, and Baldwin. The attorneys for the complainants were Daniel Webster and Elijah Paine; and for the defendants, Thomas Sergeant and J. R. Ingersoll. "The arena was prepared, all the principals were on hand, and now began a combat which taxed to the utmost the intellectual capacities and legal knowledge of the contestants." [13]

Neither the intricacies of the argument nor the varying opinions of the judges can be followed here. "The case takes its place with the great English copyright cases which were fully discussed by Counsel and Court." [14] Wheaton and Donaldson asserted their right on two grounds: first, under the common law; and second, under the act of Congress. The decision of the court given by McLean stated that no right of copy exists under the common law in the United States. Justices Thompson and Baldwin dissented on this point. The Chief Justice and Justices Story, Duval and McLean agreed that whatever rights the complainants possessed must have accrued under the acts of Congress, and since they were left in doubt after the examination of the evidence whether there had been a substantial compliance with every legal requisite, the case was remanded to the Circuit Court for a further trial, by a jury, of the issue of facts.[15] With this conclusion Justices Thompson and Baldwin disagreed but for different reasons. As the decree of the Circuit Court had been made during the absence of Judge Baldwin, it is interesting to note that Justices Thompson and Baldwin both believed that the decree of the court below should be reversed, the injunction made perpetual, and an accounting directed.

It might appear that the decision of the majority still held out some hope for the complainants provided they could show that they had a statutory claim to copyright; but it was not the fact, because the court was "unanimously of opinion, that no reporter has, or can have any copyright, in the written opinions delivered by this court; and that the judges thereof cannot confer on any reporter any such right." Thus was settled at once and for all time in the United States the question of literary property in the written opinions of courts.[16] The decision reduced the claim of Wheaton merely to a copyright in the marginal notes and arguments of counsel, dependent on affirmative proof of the technical performance of certain specified requirements, of which the public offices in those days afforded but imperfect means of furnishing the evidence.[17] The case as reported by Peters fills 108 pages,[18] and in an appendix he reprinted the opinions given by Judge Hopkinson in the Circuit Court. In addition, he issued a report of the case in separate form which he dedicated to Chief Justice Marshall.[19]

Although the long friendship which had existed between Judge Story and Wheaton was forever destroyed,[20] Wheaton wrote after the decision:

I have seen my judges. The old Chief Justice received me with fraternal frankness. What a green old age! I have also had the pleasure of meeting many old friends of the bar with cordial greeting. They are one and all against Peters, crying out that his conduct has been shameful. But he bears it off with brazen impudence . . . I don't envy him his feelings.[21]

The contemporary opinion of the action Peters had taken was expressed by Lawrence:

It is seldom that among literary men questions arise rendering necessary a reference to the technical provisions of the copyright act, and among publishers, even in cases for which the law does not provide, there is a respect generally paid to priority of possession. It was reserved for a counsellor at law, vested with the confidence of the highest tribunal of the country, in the absence, in a foreign land, of a professional brother, to whose voluntary resignation he owed his place, to disregard all these honorable obligations.[22]

For Wheaton the decision in the case was financially disastrous. After the settlement and division of his father's estate, the amount received by him had been only about eight thousand dollars.[23] The expenses of the case had practically dissipated this legacy, and besides, he lost all the reward to which he was justified after his twelve years of arduous work on the reports. To use his own words: "Justice will never be done me—it never can—the lapse of time is wearing out the copyright. It cannot be renewed unless I publish a new edition within the term—and that is out of the question." If the opinion of Justices Thompson and Baldwin had held, that the decree of the court below, which had been rendered during Judge Baldwin's absence, should be reversed and an accounting directed, "I might have published new editions of each volume as the right successively expired, and should have been in the possession of a regular and annual income of at least 2,000 dollars from this source for many years to come. Such is the extent of the mischief done by the reckless partiality of prevaricating judges." [24]

Judge Story, in a letter to Chancellor Kent, who felt that Wheaton's "imposing" brief should have received a decision written either by the Chief Justice or by Story himself, replied:

I am sorry for the controversy between Mr. Wheaton and Peters, and did all I could to prevent a public discussion of the delicate subject of copyright. . . . The strict construction of the statute of Congress we adopted with vast reluctance, but after turning it fully and freely to our minds, the majority of the court did not see how they could give any other construction to it. I wish Congress would make some additional provision on the subject to protect authors, of whom I think no one more meritorious than Mr. Wheaton. You, as a Judge, have frequently had occasion to know how many bitter cups we are not at liberty to pass by . . . .[25]

The irreparable loss which Wheaton and his family experienced in being denied the fruits of his labor of twelve years explains perhaps the violence of his language when he wrote to his sister, Eliza some time later. To her he said in part:

Even though the quibbles of the law be against me (and I have never yet met with a lawyer on this or the other side of the Atlantic who thought so) how can the court justify it to their own moral sense to continue as the recorder of their judgments the accessory in such an iniquitous spoliation. Can it be accounted for on any other supposition than that of Webster "that he has something in writing" under the hand of one of their learned Bench which, if made public, would condemn him to infamy? —and to avoid which he would sacrifice my interests and the property given to me by the Judges in the Reports of their Decisions, and ruin an unfortunate tradesman who confided in their right to dispose of a copyright which they are now made to declare they have no power to transfer to any man? But it will perhaps be asked how it happened that such an upright man as Ch. Justice Marshall came to concur in this iniquitous sentence? I answer that he never studied the cause, and I have the highest authority for this assertion. He pinned his faith on the sleeve of his prevaricating brother, believing that, if the latter had any leaning it was toward me on the friendship the hypocrite once professed—and which doubtless still continued to pour into that venerable man's ear.[26]

At the time, the decision of the court was seriously questioned by some of the leading American authorities. In July of 1834 Wheaton wrote from London to Chancellor Kent: "I beg leave to repeat to you my thanks for your kind sympathy with the unjust and illiberal manner in which I was treated in the Copy Right Case which Mr. Paine has reported. I have not met a single English lawyer that does not concur with you in your opinion." [27] Later he wrote from Berlin:

The most extraordinary part of the business is—that I cannot get inserted in any of our periodicals a fair and decent criticism of the report of my Case—interesting to literary men as a question of literary property—in America I mean—whilst in England the Reviews have no hesitation in examining it freely. Even in this country, where there is a censorship of the Press, there would not be the least hesitation in discussing in any of the Law Journals the legal merits of the Judgment of the highest Courts where

Justice is administered in the King's name. All this is, to me quite inexplicable.[28]

The case as published by Peters was reviewed extensively abroad. The consensus of opinion was that expressed by the writer in the *London Westminster Review,* which begins:

This work contains a report of a very interesting case, determined in the highest American court of Justice, respecting the law of literary property. The matter is of common concern to all who live by literature, both in this country and in America; and the decision in question seems to leave the law in America even in a more unsatisfactory and uncertain state than under the administration of justice in England.[29]

But Wheaton's visit to America was not entirely full of unpleasant circumstances. He had no reason to be dissatisfied with his reception after an absence of more than six years. He was received with a warm welcome by his old friends, and he made many new ones.[30]

On arriving in New York, he was invited by a committee of the most influential citizens, at the head of which was the mayor of the city, as "a mark of their respects for his successful efforts, as a scholar and diplomatist, to sustain the reputation and interests of the country abroad," to partake of a public dinner.[31]

He was also requested by the New York Law Institute to pronounce a discourse before them at their anniversary in May 1834. Engagements at Washington prevented the delivery of the address which was, however, prepared and subsequently published.[32] Some account of this will be given in the next chapter.

On the twenty-eighth of the month Wheaton and Edward Livingston, who at that time was United States Minister to France, were elected members of the American Antiquarian Society.[33]

Wheaton's leave of absence had been extended by the President for four months.[34] At its expiration he started on his journey back to Copenhagen in the latter part of June.

He was in London in July and reached his destination on the tenth of August, 1834.[35]

Before leaving Denmark on his visit to the United States, he had received from Count Raczynski, the minister from Prussia at the Danish court, a communication which his Government had directed him to deliver to the American chargé d'affaires with a view to its transmission to Washington. In it was conveyed the wish that diplomatic intercourse might be established between the United States and Prussia, and that Wheaton, whose reputation was already established there, should be sent to Berlin.[36]

At the request of President Jackson for views concerning the proposed transfer, James Buchanan expressed his approval and said that during his residence in St. Petersburg he had had frequent opportunities of learning the character and standing of Wheaton at Copenhagen and that it was but justice to say they were such as would make a decided impression in favor both of Wheaton himself and his country. Baron Nicolay, the Russian minister at the court, told Buchanan there was no member of the diplomatic corps who stood higher in public esteem. Wheaton's character as an author, Buchanan was inclined to believe, was more justly appreciated abroad than in the United States and would be the best introduction he could have at Berlin. "Besides," Buchanan wrote, "he is well acquainted with German literature, and speaks the German language—two great recommendations among a people so proud of their origin as the Germans." [37]

This appointment was made the following spring when he was commissioned as chargé d'affaires to Prussia by President Jackson.[38]

PART FOUR

ENVOY EXTRAORDINARY AND MINISTER PLENIPOTENTIARY TO GERMANY

Chapter XVIII

THE GERMAN CUSTOMS UNION

EVER watchful of the commercial interests of the United States to which his instructions had called his particular attention, Wheaton was enthusiastic with regard to the economic future of Germany. Six months after his arrival in Berlin he wrote to the secretary of state:

Whoever looks at the vast extent of Germany stretching from the Baltic to the Adriatic, and from the Rhine to the undefined frontiers peopled by the Slavonic nations to the east; whoever contemplates the immense variety of its soils, climate and productions; the patient and curious industry of its ingenious people; and whoever considers how little the development of all these bounties of Providence has been hitherto favored by the different Governments which have swayed its beautiful lands, must be convinced that their agricultural, manufacturing, and commercial industry are capable of vast augmentations; that they offer to every nation, and especially to the United States, exchanges of increasing value, elements of trade not yet explored and inexhaustible sources of wealth and prosperity from the cultivation of friendly relations based on the solid foundation of reciprocal justice.[1]

When Wheaton reached his post, the Prussian minister of foreign affairs was Johann Peter Friedrich Ancillon, the descendant of a Huguenot family, which, after the revocation of the Edict of Nantes, had sought an asylum in Germany. He was even better known as a philosophical writer and historian than as a statesman.[2]

Wheaton soon found, however, that concerning ordinary affairs of state the king, Frederick William III, was guided not by his Minister of Foreign Affairs but by the advice of two of his oldest ministers and intimate friends, Prince Wittgenstein and Count Lottum. Furthermore, in cases of difficulty, both as to matters of foreign policy and even with regard to the affairs of his own kingdom, he consulted Prince Metternich, the minister of Austria, the great rival of Prussia, whom he was in the habit of seeing almost every year at the baths of Toplitz. He seldom saw and hardly ever transacted business with his other ministers.[3]

To Ancillon, Wheaton announced his arrival by a note; a slight illness which had detained him in Copenhagen prevented him from immediately calling upon the Minister.[4] In reply to his note, Ancillon informed Wheaton that the King was about to leave for his annual visit to Toplitz. The formal presentation of the new Chargé's credentials was, therefore, postponed until fall. Concerning the meeting at Toplitz in the summer of 1835 Wheaton later wrote:

Nothing important, it is believed, took place at the conference. The three sovereigns of Austria, Russia, and Prussia probably merely renewed their pledges of mutual coöperation against the revolutionary principle, without any specific engagement to support these pledges by force of arms. The useless and lavish expenditure of the camp at Kalish is unpopular in both Russia and Prussia. Have reason to believe King of Prussia regrets it. The almost exclusive attention of Prince Metternich is now given to the objects of securing his own influence over the infirm, diseased mind of his Imperial master, of appeasing the growing discontent in Hungary and Transylvania, and of asserting the Austrian dominion in the Italian peninsula. Under these circumstances, it is probable that this sagacious minister, who may now be regarded as the real sovereign of the Austrian Monarchy, as he has long been the soul of the Northern alliance, will be less disposed than ever to enter upon any crusade against the revolutionary principles on which the new governments of Western Europe profess to be founded and which he is satisfied with excluding from his dominions and the confederated States of Germany by measures of internal police rather than of armed intervention in the affairs of others.[5]

In view of the King's absence and the consequent lack of pressing business from the first of July until the first of September, Wheaton decided to make a tour of the Prussian Rhine provinces which by the Congress of Vienna had been severed from France and annexed to the Prussian monarchy. For the outside world there were three great approaches to the interior of the Prussian dominions; one, by the Oder River through Stettin and its outpost of Swinemunde; another, by the River Elbe through Hamburg; and the third, by the Rhine through Holland and Belgium. Wheaton had acquired knowledge pertaining to the Elbe and the Oder in frequent visits to Hamburg and in his recent journey through Pomerania. Notwithstanding his illness he had stopped two days at Stettin for the purpose of examining the commercial resources of that place; but he felt that the condition of the Westphalian and Rhenish provinces, which were separated from the other Prussian dominions by the intermediate independent states of Hanover, Brunswick, and Hesse-Cassel, required more particular examination. This was especially desirable in the light of the regulations which had been established in 1831 by the treaty between the different riparian states of the Rhine, regulations which were intended to carry out the stipulations for the free navigation of that river as laid down by the Congress of Vienna, the delay in the complete execution of which had been resisted by the King of Holland.[6]

Ancillon, to whom Wheaton mentioned this projected journey, highly approved of it, and gave him letters of introduction to the different Prussian authorities on the Rhine for the purpose of facilitating his inquiries. He left Berlin about the first of July and proceeded by way of Lübeck, Hamburg, and Hanover to the Prussian provinces of Westphalia and the Rhine. In the course of this tour, he gathered a great deal of useful information respecting the commercial and other resources of the provinces and of the intermediate states including the kingdom of Hanover, the electorate of Hesse-Cassel, and the grand duchies of Nassau, Hesse-Darmstadt, and Baden.[7]

At the end of July he arrived at Carlsruhe, the capital of Baden, where he found the local diet of the grand duchy in session, deliberating upon the legislative details necessary to carry into effect the accession of that state to the Prussian commercial union, the Deutsche Zollverein.[8]

Early in August he left there and, crossing the Rhine at Strassburg, proceeded to Paris where he remained a few days. During this time he seized the opportunity to ascertain from authentic sources the progress which had been made in revising the French tariff. This tariff, which was essentially prohibitive in its features, was under reconsideration to bring it in closer accord with the more liberal commercial system which had recently been adopted by the British legislature. Wheaton found that the investigations already made by the commissioners named by the governments of France and Great Britain, and the more recent inquiry set on foot by the French minister of commerce into the present state and conditions of the different branches of industry in France, had encountered at every step deep-rooted prejudices and interests too powerfully represented in the chambers to be suddenly overcome or directly attacked.

From Paris he journeyed to Brussels where he witnessed "a very interesting exhibition of the various products of the manufacturing industry of Belgium, reflecting great honour upon the skill, enterprise and taste of this industrious people which only want a more extensive market to give full development to its national wealth." [9]

Pursuing his journey through Belgium, he again entered the Prussian Rhenish provinces, recrossed the Rhine at Cologne, and proceeded to Elberfeldt, a considerable manufacturing center of that part of Prussia. The trade on the Rhine had increased vastly since the removal of the obstructions to the navigation of that river by the treaty of 1831 among the different riparian states.

From Elberfeldt he traveled through the Prussian province

of Westphalia to Bremen, the shipping port of which had been recently improved at a great expense. Bremen at that time carried on a very flourishing and lucrative direct trade with the United States. It communicated with Hamburg by an excellent highway and with the interior of Germany by the Weser, which was already navigated by steamboats. The communication between these points was soon to be improved by means of railroads.[10]

From Bremen Wheaton returned directly to Hamburg, reaching that city about the twentieth of September, and completed his journey by arriving at Berlin about the middle of October.

He had explored thoroughly the western provinces of Prussia, studying their commercial resources and relations with the bordering countries of France and Belgium, and at the same time had visited all the Hanseatic towns and some of the principal states connected with the German League; examined all the great outlets of German commerce on the Oder, the Elbe, the Weser, and the Rhine; put himself in personal communication with the United States consuls at Stettin, Hamburg, Bremen, Elberfeldt, and Frankfort; and thus gathered a mass of information which would be useful in the performance of his official duties.

During this long journey, he had found repeated occasions to ascertain the disposition of the different German states to enter into arrangements with the Government of the United States, by which their mutual commercial and international relations might be placed on a more permanent and secure footing. On his return to Berlin he immediately applied himself to carry into execution the instructions on this head by sounding the different diplomatic agents representing those states at the Prussian court.[11]

The instructions received by Wheaton from Secretary of State Forsyth covered mainly two matters. The first was the question of the Elsinore Sound dues, with special reference to the quarantine regulations, with which Wheaton, while in Copenhagen, had been much concerned; the second was in regard to the removal of the obstructions imposed on emigration by the existence of the *droit d'aubaine et de détraction.*[12] By the latter, a duty of not less than 10 per cent was levied on the sales of property effected by those who were about to leave their native country. The *droit d'aubaine* amounted to a similar tax on all property which might accrue to emigrants to the United States on the death of relatives at home.

There were three groups of states with which Wheaton's activities were connected. These were the Deutsche Zollverein, or the German Customs Union; the Steuerverein, composed of Hanover, Oldenburg, Brunswick, and Schaumburg-Lippe; [13] and the states which had not acceded to these two nor formed any special commercial union among themselves. This last included the Hanseatic cities of Lübeck, Hamburg, and Bremen; the duchies of Holstein and Lauenburg, which belonged to the king of Denmark; and the grand duchies of Mecklenburg-Schwerin and Mecklenburg-Strelitz.[14] The history of the formation of the German Customs Union subsequent to the Congress of Vienna in 1815 is so well known that it need not be given here. Whatever details may be necessary to clarify the activities of Wheaton in his diplomatic relations with the Zollverein will be narrated later in their proper place. The accompanying map may be of interest as giving a view of the geographical extent of the Zollverein in 1835, with the population of the several states respectively included in the commercial union.[15]

By the end of November Wheaton had been corresponding with his friend in England, Dr. Bowring, about the Prussian system; he had made an informal inquiry relative to the basis upon which the German commercial confederacy would be disposed to treat with the United States, and he had become well informed of the conditions relating to the Prussian duties on tobacco and rice. The German newspapers were beginning to be interested in his mission, and on November twenty-fifth he enclosed in his despatch a paragraph from one of them.[16] The controversies between the

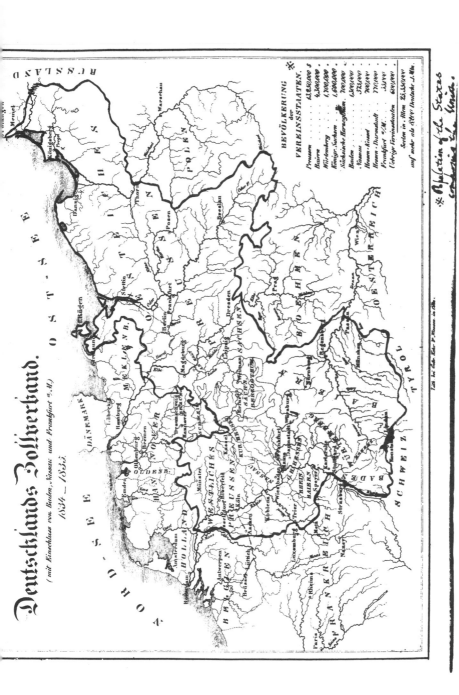

THE ZOLLVEREIN

United States and France resulting from the non-payment of the indemnity due the former was attracting wide attention at that time, especially in respect to the events which might follow should an open break between the two countries occur. This was a subject of discussion both in the official correspondence of the day and in the press in touching upon the relations of the United States with other countries. Unusual interest, therefore, was aroused by the suggestion of negotiations between the United States and the Zollverein.

In the newspaper, *Allegemeines Organ für Handel—und Gewerbe des In—und Auslandes und damit Verwandte Gegenstande,* published in Cologne by C. C. Becher, formerly vice-president of the Rhine West Indian Company, was an article of the twenty-ninth of November entitled "Commercial Treaty between the U. S. and the Zollverein." This stated that the editors were authorized to declare that the United States consul residing at Elberfeldt had received instructions which made it his duty to communicate to Mr. Wheaton, Chargé d'Affaires at Berlin, all propositions made on the part of merchants and manufacturers with a view to the development of commercial relations, and that such propositions would be received and attended to by Mr. Wheaton with the greatest cheerfulness. The article further stated that all would find in this gentleman every possible desire to further by his support the development of the mutual relations of America and Germany.[17]

The Department of Foreign Affairs of Prussia immediately received inquiries from the various states of the Zollverein relating to the background of this announcement.[18] Other German newspapers also had published articles referring to the proposed negotiations. All of these comments of the German press were forwarded by Wheaton to his Government. Enclosing a translation of an extract from a commercial newspaper printed at Stettin, called the *Boisen-Nachrichten der Ost-see,* Wheaton wrote, "Although founded on groundless conjecture, they do good by exciting public attention in Germany to the subject of foreign trade, and eliciting the truth

by provoking discussions." [19] The attitude of the Department
of Foreign Affairs of Prussia was that such enunciations as
expressed in the article would create suspicion and appre-
hension in other members of the Zollverein against Prussia,
and that the publication of the alleged preliminaries was a
mistake. They therefore notified the bureau of censorship
not to allow without special authority the printing of articles
which dealt with negotiations between Prussia and any government outside of Germany.[20]

Of these publications the newspapers in the United States
did not fail to take note. In the *Washington Globe* of July
20, 1836, for example, appeared an article entitled "Treaty
of Commerce: Between the United States of North America
and the States comprised in the Prussian Customs League."
This article referred to one in the *Allegemeines Organ* of
Cologne, which had called upon all chambers of commerce
in the German cities to look into the commercial relations
between Germany and North America, and to make propositions to their respective governments. The *Globe* expressed
the hope that this would be attended by beneficial results,
and further stated, "It will not be easy to find, for the negotiation of an advantageous commercial treaty, a more favorable moment, since the happiest disposition is evinced on all
sides for the foundation of one based upon liberal principles." [21] But this optimism proved to be illusory.

Chapter XIX

THE *ELEMENTS OF INTERNATIONAL LAW*

CONCURRENTLY with his diplomatic activities Wheaton had been engaged in an undertaking, the results of which were published early in 1836. From the beginning of his career Henry Wheaton's attention had been given to questions of international import. As a student in Europe he was brought into contact with the problems resulting from the Napoleonic wars on the continent; as an editor of the *National Advocate* he had discussed the questions involved in the War of 1812 between the United States and Great Britain, the Treaty of Ghent, and the Congress of Vienna; as a reporter and counsellor before the Supreme Court he had cited, studied in detail and taken an active part in many cases covering various phases of international relations; as a publicist he had issued his digests of cases, written reviews of diverse law publications, and noted the trend of the conferences of Aix-la-Chapelle, Troppau, Laibach, and Verona; and as a diplomat he had been in the midst of the revolutions of 1830 in Europe, had had intimate knowledge of the Conference of London and the establishment of Belgian neutrality, had investigated carefully the questions involved in the negotiations and settlement of the Danish indemnity, and had studied in detail the various questions of international relations discussed in his despatches. All of these happenings he said formed

. . . a portion of the human history abounding in fearful transgressions of that law of nations which is supposed to be founded on the higher sanction of the natural law, (more properly called

145

the law of God,) and at the same time rich in instructive discussions in cabinets, courts of justice, and legislative assemblies, respecting the nature and extent of the obligations between independent societies of men called States.[1]

As a result of this experience and interest Wheaton attempted "to collect the rules and principles which govern, or are supposed to govern, the conduct of States, in their mutual intercourse in peace and in war," [2] and on January 1, 1836, just after he had passed his fiftieth birthday, he wrote the preface to the first edition of a publication which was more comprehensive in scope and more far-reaching in results than anything he had previously undertaken—The *Elements of International Law.*[3]

The object of the author as stated in the preface was to compile an elementary work for the use of persons engaged in diplomatic and other forms of public life rather than for mere technical lawyers, although he ventured to hope that it might not be found entirely useless even to the latter.[4] He also said,

The principal aim of the Author has been to glean from these sources the general principles which may fairly be considered to have received the assent of most civilized and Christian nations, if not as invariable rules of conduct, at least as rules which they cannot disregard without general obloquy and the hazard of provoking the hostility of other communities who may be injured by their violation.[5]

Wheaton's book was divided into four parts: the first dealing with the definition, sources, and subjects of international law; the second, with the absolute international rights of states; the third, with the international rights of states in their pacific relations; and the fourth, with the international rights of states in their hostile relations. He derived his definition of international law from Madison and stated it thus:

International Law, as understood among civilized nations, may be defined as consisting of those rules of conduct which rea-

son deduced, as consonant to justice, from the nature of the society, existing among independent nations; with such definitions
and modifications as may be established by general consent.[6]

Wheaton gave six sources from which international law
could be derived: text writers of authority, showing what is
the approved usage of nations or the general opinion respecting their mutual conduct with the definitions and modifications introduced by general consent; treaties of peace,
alliance, and commerce declaring, modifying, or defining the
preëxisting international law; ordinances of particular states,
prescribing rules for the conduct of their commissioned
cruisers and prize tribunals; the adjudications of international tribunals, such as boards of arbitration and courts
of prize; the written opinions of official jurists, given confidentially to their own governments; and the history of
wars, negotiations, treaties of peace, and other transactions
relating to the public intercourse of nations.[7] All of these
six sources were used largely by Wheaton in his work. He
was thoroughly familiar with the writers on the law of nations from the earliest time.

He stated clearly the differences in the theories of the
leaders of the seventeenth century such as the Dutch scholar,
the "Father of the Law of Nations," Hugo Grotius; the English jurist, Richard Zouche; and the German professor,
Samuel Pufendorf. From them arose respectively the three
different schools of writers on the law of nations: the "Eclec-
tic" or "Grotians," the "Historical" or "Positivists," and the
"Philosophical" or "Naturalists." [8]

In his discussions Wheaton showed an equal familiarity
with the writers of the eighteenth century. Among the latter
he referred continually to the famous Dutch jurist, Corne-
lius van Bynkershoek, and the German professors, Johann
Jakob Moser and Georg Friedrich von Martens, of the Positivists; to the English admiralty judge, Sir Leoline Jenkins,
the English professor, Thomas Rutherforth, and the learned
French translator and commentator, Jean Barbeyrac, of the

Naturalists; and to the German philosopher, Christian Friedrich von Wolf, and the Swiss publicist, Emerich de Vattel,
of the Grotians. Many other writers of the eighteenth century
were discussed in detail by him.

He was well versed in the work of the foremost of his contemporaries of the nineteenth century, with most of whom
he was personally acquainted both in Europe and in the
United States. Space permits the mention of only a few in
each country with whom he associated and corresponded. In
Germany there were Johann Ludwig Klüber, who may be
called a Positivist, and August Wilhelm Heffter, who, although of the same school, does not absolutely deny the law
of nature. Wheaton later reviewed his work in the *Revue de
Droit Français et Étranger* and regarded him as being one
of the leading public jurists of the day. In France there were
Laurent Basile Hautefeuille and Theodore Ortolan. The
latter's work also was reviewed by Wheaton in the same
periodical. In England there were Sir William Scott (Lord
Stowell), the founder of British maritime jurisprudence, Sir
James Mackintosh, Jeremy Bentham, and William Oke Manning. In the United States from the beginning of his professional career Wheaton had been associated with, among
others, James Kent, Joseph Story, Edward Livingston, and
Peter S. Du Ponceau. The latter was known as a jurist as
well as a philologist, and the importance of his annotations
of Bynkershoek was cited by Wheaton.

Wheaton's *Elements* at once attracted the attention of the
whole of Europe as well as the United States. For the first
time the principles underlying international law were
brought together in a book written in English. The publication was received with favor by its reviewers in England,
France, Germany, and the United States. Long articles about
it appeared in the *Monthly Review* in London,[9] *The Revue
Étrangère et Française de Législation et d'Économie* in
France,[10] and the *North American Review* in the United
States.[11] The last-named notice was written by Alexander H.
Everett. The book was recognized by all as a standard treat-

ise, and the French periodical recommended the work strongly and urged its immediate translation. The French review did justice to the frankness with which Wheaton had met the discussion of new and interesting matters on which his predecessors had maintained silence, particularly "on that delicate question, the right of intervention by one power in the affairs of another," which Wheaton had elsewhere declared to be an "undefined and undefinable exception to the mutual independence of nations." [12]

Enough has been said here to show the eminent position Wheaton had gained among the scholars of Europe. As Lawrence has stated, "The 'Elements' do not purport to be an inquiry into what the law of nations ought to be independently of their usage, but what that law is, as recognized by the practice of nations." [13] And therein rests the real value of Wheaton's work, for, it has been written, "He translated the ideal dreams of philosophers to a practical science." [14]

Wheaton may be called a Grotian. During the latter part of the nineteenth and the beginning of the twentieth centuries the writers on international law were increasingly historical and positive, and the school of the Positivists became almost predominant, especially in England. But many of the more recent writers tend to the belief that the rigid elimination of the law of nature from international law has not been conducive to the development of that science and, to quote one of them, now urge that

International Law may, without losing its character as a legal science, be fittingly reinforced and fertilised by recourse to rules of justice, equity, and general principles of law, it being immaterial whether those rules are defined as a Law of Nature in the sense used by Grotius, or a modern Law of Nature with variable contents; and that recourse to such rules is a frequent feature of the practice of States, especially as evidenced in arbitration conventions and judicial awards of arbitral tribunals.[15]

Wheaton's choice of the middle course would seem to be justified by modern tendencies.

Besides this achievement, which placed Wheaton among the foremost of the contemporary authorities on international law, two other publications which also appeared in this year showed the catholicity of his interests. A revision of his *Life of William Pinkney* was published in Volume VI in the Library of American Biography edited by Jared Sparks.[16] A notice of it appeared in the *North American Review*, which after referring to the commentary in that periodical of the former publication, continued:

Having treated the subject of Mr. Pinkney's life and genius at such length before, we have nothing now to say, except that Mr. Wheaton, in his preparation of the present sketch, has manifested his characteristic good sense and good taste, and made a valuable contribution to our means of convenient access to an acquaintance with an illustrious man.[17]

There also appeared in the *Foreign Quarterly Review* a notice by Wheaton of Count Raczynski's first volume *De l'Art Moderne en Allemagne*, published in Paris in 1836 and in Berlin with the title *Die neuere Deutsche Kunst*.[18] This was much more than a review; it was really an article on modern painting in Germany.

As in Copenhagen Wheaton had lost no time in becoming acquainted with the literary and intellectual life of Denmark and Scandinavia, so in Berlin he immediately produced proofs of kindred activities. Nevertheless these did not interfere with his official duties, and he made every effort to care for the diplomatic engagements entrusted to him. Mrs. Wheaton wrote to her father: "Berlin presents many advantages but to enjoy them all one must have money! There is an Opera, a German and French Theatre all open every night. We have invitations for every evening in the week regularly. The play comes out at 9 o'clock so that the fashionables go first to the Theatre, and then to the soiree, when there is dancing, playing cards and supper, but for all this I am not out sometimes for ten days together." [19]

Chapter XX

ACCREDITED AS ENVOY

JUST before the close of the last session of Congress under President Jackson, an appropriation was made for the outfit and salary of a full minister to Prussia instead of the salary of a chargé d'affaires. A new nomination for Berlin therefore became necessary.[1] Although Van Buren, the incoming President, and Wheaton had been on opposite sides during the campaign of 1824, for both the state and the federal elections, it will be remembered they previously had been in accord on every question during the New York constitutional assembly; and Van Buren undoubtedly had been aware of the work done by Wheaton as one of the revisers of the New York constitution. Subsequent to that, cordial relations had always existed between them while the former was secretary of state and the latter was negotiating successfully the treaty of indemnity between the United States and Denmark. Following this, when Van Buren was minister of the United States at London, he had had full opportunity to know the eminent position Wheaton had attained in literary and diplomatic circles. The *Elements of International Law*, which had just been published, had attracted the attention of Attorney-General Benjamin F. Butler both because of the direct connection between the subject and his duties, and also because of the friendship which existed between him and Wheaton, who often spoke of Butler as "our excellent friend."

In the interchange of sentiment which took place between Van Buren and Butler even before the former had entered on his duties, Butler urged Van Buren to disregard the clamors of politicians and while rendering justice to an experienced public officer, to do an act which would confer lasting honor on his administration. He set forth that in addition to his other merits Wheaton alone, of all those who from the commencement of the Government of the United States had been employed in its diplomacy, had made a permanent contribution to the science of international law; that he had unusual personal qualifications; and that he had performed eminent services in the negotiation of the Danish treaty. "All the respectable and intelligent portion of the community," he declared, "all whose good opinions are worth possessing will, at once, sanction your course, and all parties will soon approve of it." [2] In this advice Butler was earnestly seconded by the retiring President, who had transferred Wheaton from Copenhagen to Berlin.

Wheaton first received information of his appointment as envoy from the newspapers and from private sources. In a cordial letter of thanks to Van Buren for this proof of his confidence, he expressed his wish to contribute to the success of the new administration and promised to exert his best faculties to give effect to Van Buren's "sound maxim of desiring 'commercial relations on equal terms,' being ever willing to give a fair 'equivalent for advantages received.' " [3]

Before the letter of credence reached Berlin in May 1837, the foreign minister, Ancillon, had died. According to the etiquette observed at the Prussian court, Wheaton could not be presented to the King in his new capacity until a new minister of foreign affairs had been appointed. Baron de Werther, Prussian envoy at Paris, was at last named to succeed Ancillon but did not arrive at Berlin until the tenth of June, nor did he take over the direction of the affairs of the department until a fortnight later. After he had assumed office, Werther told Wheaton that, since the King was then occupied with the preparations for his annual journey to Toplitz, it would be more convenient to receive the latter on His Majesty's return to the capital in August. Under these circumstances, and especially as Werther was to accompany the King, Wheaton thought he could not better employ the interval than by making a third journey to the Prussian,

Westphalian, and Rhine provinces [4] and to Belgium, for the purpose of adding to the stock of information acquired in his former tour of 1835 and in a similar journey which he had taken in the summer of 1836. During those years he had gathered information relating to the commercial resources of these countries and their communications with the North Sea.[5]

Wheaton traveled from Berlin through the province of Brandenburg, which he had not before explored, crossing the Elbe at Magdeburg to Cassel, the capital of the electorate of Hesse,[6] and extended his journey through Belgium. At Brussels he received every aid in his inquiries from the Belgian ministers of foreign affairs, commerce, and public works, as well as from De, Behr, their chargé d'affaires in the United States, then at home on leave of absence. Wheaton went on as far as Antwerp for the purpose of making some inquiries as to the commercial advantages of that port in comparison with the ports of Holland and France as channels for the trade of the United States with Germany. He found the members of the Belgian Government were well disposed to cultivate friendly relations with the United States and to facilitate its direct commercial intercourse with Belgium and, through that kingdom, with the interior of Germany by means of the chain of railroads which were being constructed from Antwerp to the Rhine.[7]

From Belgium Wheaton returned to Berlin to present his credentials as envoy and to carry out the instructions he had received from the State Department. With the letter Forsyth had included a copy of the report of the select committee of the House of Representatives on the high rates of duty and the restrictions imposed by foreign governments upon tobacco from the United States. Again Wheaton was specially instructed to collect carefully all the information within his reach concerning the tobacco duties.[8]

On the tour just completed, in passing through the different intermediate provinces of Prussia, Wheaton had already collected a good deal of information bearing upon the question of a reduction of the duties on American tobacco. He also had noted the intimate connection between the commercial interests of the United States and those of the Rhenish provinces, the manufacturers of which, in their diminished exports, were experiencing the effects of the monetary crisis then prevailing in England and America.[9] Wheaton reported to Van Buren from Aix-la-Chapelle about the middle of July, 1837:

I wrote our excellent friend Mr. Butler on the 17th inst. a few crude thoughts upon our commercial and financial crisis which I hope has at last reached its height. If our enterprising but reckless countrymen could learn a lesson of prudence and moderation from their present "distress" it would be well. But I fear it will be vain to expect it, and that we shall be every few years, at uncertain intervals, exposed to similar shocks arising from overtrading, over-speculating or gambling, and over-banking. It seems to me the only way of checking the former, is to apply adequate checks to the latter. This cannot be done by the State Governments, or at least not by them alone, since they are the authors of all mischief in chartering so many local Banks with the power of flooding the country with paper money. There must be some central power invented and applied for the regulation of the currency, which has fallen into disorder by the States usurping (in effect) the coinage power of Congress. If the constitutional objections to the incorporation of a National Bank could be overcome in the opinion of the President and People, perhaps the best means would be the creation of such a Bank in which the power of discounting and that of deciding on the quantity of paper to be issued should be separated, and the latter conferred exclusively on Government directors. As this cannot be done, resort must be had to the acknowledged constitutional powers of the Federal Government to determine in what medium the taxes and debts due to that government shall be paid, and in what medium its disbursements shall be made. It appears to me that the fair exertion of the Power by the creation of Treasury Notes redeemable in gold and silver would be adequate to regulate the currency. But there may be difficulties in the way of this project, either intrinsic, or arising out of party combinations, the extent of which I cannot duly estimate.[10]

Chapter XXI

COMMERCIAL RELATIONS WITH
THE ZOLLVEREIN

FROM his extensive travels through the German states and minute study of their various activities, Henry Wheaton had come to the conclusion that eventually Hanover, the other members of the Steuerverein, and the Hanseatic towns would be included within the Zollverein. As early as 1835 he had written, "The Hanseatic Towns will certainly not surrender their independence without a struggle, in which they would be countenanced by Great Britain. But statesmen must be watchful of possible and probable contingencies, as well as of certainties." [1] His study of international relations, and his early grasp of the changes which would result in transportation and communication from the introduction of steamships and railroads influenced his attitude in the negotiations concerning the adjustment of the commercial relations between the United States, the Zollverein, and the other German states.

Prior to May 1836, by mutual agreement, the discussions of these relations had been conducted orally between Wheaton and Ancillon. But under date of May 27, 1836, at the request of the latter, Wheaton presented his proposals in writing. In this communication he stated that he had been authorized by his Government to ascertain whether or not Prussia and the other states associated with it in the German Commercial Union were disposed to conclude a treaty of commerce with the United States upon the basis of the broad principles of reciprocity similar to those in the then existing treaty between the United States and Russia, with such modifications and additional stipulations as the peculiar nature and objects of the Commercial Union of Germany might render desirable.[2] In reply to this proposal Ancillon expressed readiness to negotiate, though remarking that the existing treaties were perfectly satisfactory. He also stated that he would notify the other members of the Zollverein.[3]

The Department of Foreign Affairs in Berlin wrote to the Prussian representatives in the several states of the Zollverein, setting forth Wheaton's proposal. This communication ended by stating that they were requested to notify the different governments about his preliminary conversations and notes, and that, although they would probably have to wait for further proposals from the United States, still they ought to consider the possibility of making certain propositions themselves. If they shared this opinion, they were to send in such material. The letter further stated that in Wheaton's note reference was made to the treaty of the United States with Russia of December 1822, which ought to serve as the basis of a treaty between Prussia and the United States, but that at close examination it absolutely corresponded with the already existing convention and did not contain anything which tended to extend the commercial relations between the two countries. The Foreign Office stated it would notify its minister resident in the United States, Baron von Roenne, of the negotiations and ask his opinion concerning the means by which mutual commercial relations could be fostered; his thorough knowledge of American conditions would help to indicate on what products from Prussia and the Zollverein imported to the United States new arrangements could be made without offense to existing principles. The various states were to be informed of Roenne's answer.[4] A letter covering all the above proposals and suggestions was despatched to Roenne in the United States.[5]

Over a month later, but evidently before receiving the above letter, Roenne wrote to the Department of Foreign Affairs in Prussia that after numerous articles had been spread through the papers in the United States (articles taken apparently from German, English, and French newspapers) about the proposed new treaty, he had seen Forsyth and had asked him if it were true that such instructions had been sent to Wheaton. Forsyth answered that a treaty already existed between the United States and Prussia. Roenne agreed to this, but also questioned whether or not, since the United States had reciprocal treaties with all the seaport states, it had further interest in the products after they had been brought into the harbors. Forsyth replied that the task of Wheaton was to find out what influence the German Zollverein had on the trade of the United States and then to make his recommendations to the latter. Roenne also noted that another article had been published, which apparently had been taken from a German newspaper, concerning the question of a commercial treaty.[6]

About two weeks later Roenne answered the communication received by him from the Prussian Foreign Office. His opinion was that, considering the principle of not favoring any special nation, such a treaty would not improve prevailing conditions. It might be well for the other members of the Zollverein to join the existing treaty between Prussia and the United States. But as it chiefly concerned navigation, they would not be interested in it; and even if they were, they could enjoy the same privileges in accordance with the acts of Congress of May 24, 1828. He suggested having the present treaty extended for a number of years, because the principle of reciprocity had many opponents in the United States.[7] In general his opinion was that commercial advantages were less likely to be achieved by treaties than through legislation, and efforts in this direction, i. e., for reduction of tariffs, though in very general terms, would favor the Prussian commerce. He thought that it was most important to maintain the existing privileges and not to lose them.[8]

In the meantime replies received by the Prussian foreign office from the representatives of the various German states indicated an attitude favorable to the negotiation of a commercial treaty between the Zollverein and the United States, but also expressed the desire to wait for further proposals from the American representative.[9]

Wheaton had been raised to the position of envoy in the latter part of March 1837. The following June Forsyth wrote to him that the importance of tobacco as a staple commodity of the United States, in the exportation of which a very large class of its citizens was interested, had made the Government desire from the earliest period to procure a repeal or modification of the extraordinary burdens and restrictions which had been imposed upon the importation of that article by the different countries of Europe. This subject had been urged upon the attention of Congress at its last session [10] by a meeting of tobacco planters from different parts of the country, and by the general assembly of the state of Maryland. A resolution had been passed by the House of Representatives that the President be requested to instruct the ministers and other representatives of the country in France, England, Russia, Prussia, Holland, and Germany to negotiate with the respective governments to which they were accredited for a modification of these duties and restrictions. Also it was resolved that the President be requested to appoint special agents to negotiate with the governments of those countries into which tobacco was imported under similar restrictions if those countries had no accredited representatives from the United States.

The large quantity of tobacco consumed in the various states of Germany; the nature and extent of the restrictions to which that commodity was there subject, especially upon its introduction into the interior; the strong disposition which many of the German states had recently shown to cultivate and extend their commercial intercourse with foreign nations; the friendly relations which subsisted between the United States and those governments—all these factors united in directing attention to Germany as a field in which immediate and vigorous exertion should be made to obtain a relaxation of the duties then imposed upon tobacco. This action, it was firmly believed, would be conducive to the interests of all parties. Forsyth said in writing to Wheaton that his situation afforded him great advantages for the promotion of this object in respect not only to Prussia, but also to all the states which composed the German Zollverein as well as those which were included in the Hanoverian Union, and that in regard to those and to such others as might be within the sphere of his influence, the President relied upon his efforts for the accomplishment of so desirable a result. Forsyth wrote:

Your first duty will be to collect the most thorough and accurate information possible, respecting the cultivation, the importation, and the consumption of tobacco within the respective states; and to assist you in the labor, Mr. Joshua Dodge, who has been for some time Consul of the United States at Bremen, has been appointed by the President a Special Agent, to be employed under your direction in traveling through the several parts of Germany to which your attention has been directed, (with the exception of Prussia), for the purpose of gathering intelligence on the subject and performing such other services as you may deem useful in preparing the way for future operations. The information which you may thus obtain, as well as that which you may derive from other sources, you will communicate to this Department. You will receive further and full instructions on the information communicated if they should be deemed necessary.[11]

Wheaton's efforts, therefore, according to the instructions received by him, were to be directed to at least two principal subjects of commercial intercourse between the two countries —the reduction of import duties by Germany on staple productions of the United States and the consummation of a treaty of commerce and navigation.

Before the receipt of the instructions concerning Dodge, Louis Marke, the consul of the United States at Ostend, who had long been familiarly acquainted with the commerce of Germany and had particular connections at Munich, offered to proceed to that city with the view of ascertaining the disposition of the Bavarian Government in respect to a reduction of the duties on tobacco. Not being aware that the appointment of a special agent relating to this subject had been made, Wheaton accepted his offer. Marke gave Wheaton reason to hope that he had made an impression favorable to the views of the United States upon the minds both of the Bavarian King and his principal minister, who at that time was Prince Wallenstein, charged with the department of commercial affairs. With Wheaton's approbation Marke also had translated into the German language and published in the *Franconian Mercury,* with a preface, the report of the committee of the House of Representatives on the subject of the tobacco trade. A number of extra copies were struck off for distribution.[12]

Joshua Dodge arrived in Berlin in September 1837. The need of such a special agent in Germany was questionable. Wheaton had traveled extensively and had spared no effort to accumulate all necessary information concerning the states of Germany, including Hanover and the other members of the Steuerverein, and the Hanse towns. Moreover, the sending of special agents where an accredited minister is already installed is always of doubtful expediency.

In pursuance of the directions received by him from the Secretary of State, Wheaton, after relating to Dodge in full the desires of the State Department as communicated to him, instructed the latter to travel in a leisurely manner through all the countries of Germany except the Austrian dominions, and carefully examine everything connected with the cultivation, manufacture, and trade of tobacco; to communicate to him, from time to time, the results of the inquiry, including everything relating to any one state in one report, carefully digested, with marginal notes for more convenient and easy reference. He was to visit the different seaports and interior commercial and manufacturing towns as well as the capitals or respective residences of the governments. Wheaton furnished him with official letters of introduction to the ministers of commerce and of foreign affairs of the respective states which he might visit. In his intercourse with them it was to be one of the objects of Dodge's mission to endeavor to ascertain the practicability of obtaining a reduction of the heavy duties and other burdens imposed on American tobacco in the different countries of Germany. Wheaton concluded his instructions to Dodge by stating:

Although it is not within the particular scope of your instructions to extend your inquiries beyond the subject of tobacco, I cannot but strongly recommend your attention to the commercial resources of Germany in general, and the means they afford of furnishing commercial exchanges with the United States. The information you may gather on these subjects cannot fail to promote the common prosperity of our beloved country, and may be very useful in the course of the negotiations confided to the mission here. Your long experience in trade, and in the duties of the consular office, will afford you great facilities in making such inquiries, and your zeal and perseverance in fulfilling the objects of the government, are confidently relied upon by the department. The order to be observed in your different tours is left to your own discretion; but, for the particular reasons which have been suggested in conversation, I would recommend that you should visit Hanover, and the States associated with her in a separate union of commerce and customs.[13]

With these instructions Wheaton enclosed a detailed statement of the particular points upon which it was most important that intelligence should be obtained concerning tobacco of whatever description or origin.[14]

Dodge, after examining the tobacco and other manufactures of Berlin, set off on October 24, 1837, for Hanover by way of Magdeburg. At Wheaton's request the Hanoverian minister at Berlin furnished him with letters of introduction to official persons at Hanover, and Wheaton also applied to the minister of foreign affairs, Baron de Werther, requesting him to cause the necessary orders to be given to the Prussian authorities in the different provinces of the monarchy to facilitate Dodge's researches.[15]

The press of Germany, France, England, and the United

States took note of the proposed negotiations. The *Allgemeine Zeitung* of December the seventh stated that

The propositions made by the United States for a treaty of commerce with the German Commercial Union, have produced a great sensation, not only on account of the great advantages which they offer, but inasmuch as they are the first fruits we gather from commercial liberty, and they show the importance we have acquired among commercial nations. The Americans prove by these propositions, that they are more prompt than other nations in seeing to their interests, and more skillful in profiting by them.

Most of the Paris papers published an account which had appeared in the *Augsburg Gazette*. The *Moniteur de Commerce* considered it probable that such a proposition had been made, and remarked that a treaty of commerce and reciprocity appeared to be the natural consequence of the geographical position of the two countries.[16]

In December 1837 Wheaton prepared an article and had it published on the twenty-third of that month in a German newspaper, the *Berliner Spernicher Gazette*,[17] which had a wide circulation and had the reputation of being the only paper the Prussian King read.[18] The article was written to sound out the way to an official discussion of the tobacco question. The American Minister took measures to have the article inserted in various gazettes published in the different states of the Commercial Union with the object of diffusing information on the subject and exciting public attention to the importance of the tobacco trade which furnished one of the principal means of paying for the German manufactures, wines, and other products exported to the United States.[19]

After Dodge had completed his examination of Hanover with the intermediate provinces of Prussia, Wheaton in March of 1838 directed him to proceed to Carlsruhe, the capital of Baden, and thence through Stuttgart, the capital of Württemberg, to Munich, the capital of Bavaria, and afterwards to join him at Dresden to attend the congress of the Zollverein to be held during the summer of 1838. He furnished him with letters of introduction to the governments of these different states through their ministers residing at Berlin, and gave him particular instructions as to the objects to which his attention ought to be especially directed during this tour.[20]

Wheaton, meanwhile, informed Baron de Werther that he had received full power with the necessary instructions [21] for the negotiation of a treaty of navigation and commerce between the United States and the Zollverein upon the basis of the most complete reciprocity.[22]

In April, in reply to a note from Werther inviting a frank and full communication of the views and wishes of the United States, Wheaton reviewed the subject of the commercial intercourse between the two countries at some length and combined this statement with a discussion of the question of the tobacco duties, which formed the principal obstacle to the extension of the trade of the United States in Germany. His object in presenting remonstrances on the subject in a written form at such an early period in the negotiations was to enable the Prussian Government to give instructions respecting it to their commissioner at the commercial congress soon to be held at Dresden, where the question would have to be examined with a view to all its bearings upon the trade, finances, and political objects of the Zollverein.[23]

Wheaton could arrange to go to Dresden since a Secretary to the Legation in the person of Theodore S. Fay had arrived in Berlin. At his own request Fay had been sent by Forsyth from the post of secretary to the Minister in London, Andrew Stevenson, because he was unable to agree with Stevenson. He was received cordially by Wheaton, who had been a friend of his father.[24] Wheaton reached Dresden on the twentieth of June, 1838, and met Dodge, who had already arrived. They found the deputies of the German Commercial and Customs Association still occupied with the subject of a uniform currency, the establishment of which had been one of the original objects of the Union, one which had been attended with great practical difficulties. In the meantime, the commissioners appointed to attend the annual congress for the purpose of considering the subjects connected with the tariff and the execution of the fiscal regulations of the association having arrived, the congress was constituted in due form on the twenty-fifth of June. It consisted of deputies from the kingdoms of Prussia, Bavaria, Württemberg, and Saxony, the electorate of Hesse, the grand duchies of Hesse and Baden, the duchy of Nassau, the Thuringian Union, and the free city of Frankfort-on-the-Main. Altogether these represented a population of over twenty-five and a half million people. There were also a number of other smaller states in the Prussian territory, called enclaves, which were represented by Prussia.

In order to bring the business of the United States regularly before the congress, Wheaton prepared a memoir in French and communicated the same through De Zeschen, minister of finances, charged with the portfolio of foreign affairs to the King of Saxony, the state presiding over the congress at Dresden. At the same time he had the memoir printed in order to furnish copies for the use of the members. He also transmitted a copy of it to Baron de Werther at Berlin and handed other copies to the Prussian and Bavarian envoys at the court of Saxony, the only ministers from any of the Zollverein states resident there.[25]

This memoir was prepared from data and calculations furnished by Joshua Dodge or taken from statistical works of authority together with the information which Wheaton had gathered in the different journeys made by him in the various parts of Germany during the previous three years. It discussed principally the duties levied by the Zollverein upon the importation of tobacco and rice from the United States. But an attempt was made to explain fully, by a reference to facts as well as to general principles, the importance to the Germanic Confederacy of its trade with the United States and the advantages which would accrue from the introduction of a liberal policy.[26]

A confidential despatch gives an account of Wheaton's interview with the King of Saxony, Frederick Augustus, with whom he dined on the sixth of July at Pilnitz. He relates that the King, who was extremely well informed on all matters connected with the public administration, turned the conversation to the subject of our negotiations with the commercial association and stated that Saxony had no particular interest in the question of the proposed reduction of the duties on American tobacco, either as to revenue or the cultivation of the native plant. The King admitted that it had a deep interest in the preservation of a vast and increasing market for German manufactures. At the same time he did not disguise from Wheaton the difficulties the United States must expect to encounter in endeavoring to reconcile so many conflicting interests as were involved in any change of the tariff then existing. Wheaton further said that the King's remarks had been conveyed in the kindest and most conciliatory terms towards the United States, with the resources of which he was perfectly acquainted. For its welfare he had expressed the warmest interest, with an earnest desire to cultivate the most amicable relations.[27] A few days later Wheaton wrote:

I availed myself of a short interval of leisure, afforded by the printing of a second memoir, which I intend to present to the Commercial Congress at Dresden, to visit Toplitz, in order to pay my respects to the King of Prussia, who is taking the baths here, where he was yesterday joined by the Archduke Francis (brother to the Emperor of Austria, and heir presumptive to the imperial crown), accompanied by Prince Metternich and a numerous suite.

Count Nesselrode and Baron de Werther are also here, with their respective chanceries; and it is probable that the public affairs of Germany, and of Europe in general, will engage more or less of the attention of the representatives of the three great military monarchies who are here assembled.

I had, yesterday, a conversation of some length with the Archduke Francis (who is a member of the council called in conference, by which the Government of the Austrian Empire is administered), and with Prince Metternich (the real sovereign of that empire), both of whom appeared to me to attach great importance to the extension of the direct commercial intercourse between the United States and Austria. I did not fail to seize the occasion for intimating, that the main obstacle which had hitherto restricted that intercourse to a much less amount of exchanges than might have been expected from the great value and variety of the productions of the two countries, adapted for exportation to each other, was to be found in the great inequality between their respective tariffs; and, especially the discouragements created by the monopolies, lengthened quarantine, lengthened guaranties, and other pernicious restraints on trade existing in the Austrian dominions. I insisted, principally, on the Government monopoly of the trade and manufacture of tobacco as being almost equivalent to a prohibition of our tobaccos, only a small quantity of which is annually purchased by the Austrian regie at Bremen, to mix with the Hungarian and other native tobaccos.[28]

While at Toplitz, Wheaton also received detailed information concerning the commercial arrangements which had shortly before been consummated between Austria and Great Britain, a result of the activities of John Macgregor, who for some years had been traveling through Europe collecting information for the Government of Great Britain.[29] In 1836 he had attended the Zollverein conference at Munich and had begun to report on the commercial situation in Germany and the effects of the Zollverein tariff on English trade. He had discussed the question of a treaty between Great Britain and the Zollverein informally with Kuhne, the Prussian commissioner, but had found that formal negotiations must be carried on at Berlin and that a *sine qua non* was a reduction of corn duties. While in Munich, he had come into touch with the Austrian chargé d'affaires and as a result had gone to Vienna. After prolonged negotiations between the two governments, a commercial treaty was finally signed on July 3, 1838.[30] The innovations in trade regulations introduced by this treaty, which formed a precedent for subsequent conventions, will be discussed later in connection with Wheaton's negotiations.

On his return to Dresden Wheaton issued his second memoir. In conversation with him, the Saxon minister of finance expressed the conviction that the duties on rice would be more easily reduced than those on tobacco.[31] Wheaton also forwarded to the State Department information which he had received from Macgregor and notes from Macgregor's report respecting the commercial and financial resources of Austria. He expected the report would be read in Parliament.[32]

Having made every effort which he thought advisable at that time in the interests of the United States and deeming his presence no longer necessary at Dresden, Wheaton returned to Berlin on the twenty-third of July, leaving Dodge with instructions to observe and report the progress of the congress.

After his return he had a conversation with Baron de Werther respecting the subject of the pending negotiations. The latter seemed disposed to encourage the expectation that the duties then levied on rice might be diminished; but as to tobacco, he anticipated greater difficulties. His main objection seemed to be that the classification of the tobaccos according to their qualities and origins, a classification proposed by Wheaton, would be an innovation upon their financial system, which imposed the duty upon every kind of commodity by the weight without regard to the quality, origin, or value. This simple and uniform rule had been adopted for the sake of convenience and for a guard against frauds. Werther seemed to think there would be no practical means of discriminating between different sorts of tobacco if those frauds and invasions which might deplete the revenue to an unforeseen extent, were to be prevented. However, he assured Wheaton that the subject should be fully examined with the sincerest desire to gratify the wishes of the United States, if it could be done without too much risk to their financial system.

Wheaton learned secretly that Roenne had written from the United States to the Government at Berlin not to reduce duties on tobacco at that time but to suspend the whole question, for there was no danger of retaliation on German manufactures by the United States, because its tariff would not be revised until 1842 and because only five or six states, which were not enough to carry a measure of retaliation, were interested.[33]

On the presentation of a memoir on the duties upon Belgian manufactured leather to the congress at Dresden by M. Beaulieu, chargé d'affaires of Belgium, the congress declined to take up the subject of their relations with any foreign power except the United States,[34] and as Lawrence has said,

The favor which was accorded to his [Wheaton's] representations may be ascribed to the personal consideration which he commanded, and to the opportunities which his familiarity with the language of the members, as well as his thorough knowledge of the matters which he discussed, afforded him. By the Ministers of State, as well as by their sovereigns, he was everywhere received as the honored representative of a great and powerful nation.[35]

The activities of Wheaton at the congress were alluded to in the report of a select committee of the House of Representatives in the United States, to which had been referred the part of the President's message relating to the tobacco trade. Upon their request, the State Department had granted them access to all despatches dealing with that commodity. Special attention had been given to Wheaton's communications. On February 25, 1839, the report of this committee was submitted by its chairman Daniel Jenifer of Maryland, who in 1841 was appointed minister to Vienna at the special request of the planters. The committee said that they could not omit "to notice the very able argumentative memoir presented to the Congress of Deputies of the German Commercial and Customs' Association assembled at Dresden in June last by our zealous and talented minister, Henry

Wheaton, in which paper he takes an enlarged view of the policy which should be adopted in relation to the products of the Southern States and submits a project for the consideration of Congress"; an extract of this was inserted.[36]

About the middle of December Wheaton had a short conversation with Count Alversleben, Prussian minister of finance, in which the latter stated that his department had been engaged in examining the representations made by Wheaton at Dresden on the subject of the duties levied by the states of the Zollverein on rice and tobacco; that the result of the examination had led to the conclusion that the duties on rice might be safely diminished without affecting the revenue; but that it was plain that a reduction in the duties on tobacco would not be attended with a corresponding increase in the consumption of that article. He also added that the production of the native plant must be protected or the planters would require the abolition of the excise duty which was then levied on the tobacco raised in Prussia and other parts of Germany.[37]

The conclusions of the conferences at Dresden were not officially made known until the protocol of the congress had been reported to the respective governments composing the commercial association. The report was favorable to a reduction of the duties on rice. These duties were to be reduced not in favor of North American rice exclusively, but in favor of the same article, the growth of whatever country, without any demands for new special equivalent concessions on the part of the United States Government.[38] The question of the tobacco duties with remarks by the deputies upon the difficulties which might attend any change in the manner of levying duties was referred to the next session of congress, which was to be held in June 1839.[39] The report was confirmed by the respective governments.

Wheaton, therefore, had been successful on one item under discussion, having secured a reduction of the duties on rice.

Chapter XXII

TREATY WITH HANOVER

O N November 11, 1835, soon after his arrival in Berlin, Wheaton had asked whether the State Department would consider it expedient to negotiate treaties of commerce with those states which had not yet acceded to the Prussian commercial system, thereby endeavoring to secure for the commerce of the United States a free access to the various ports of Germany on the North and Baltic seas.[1]

A glance at the map shows that the countries included within the Zollverein had no seaports except the Prussian ports in the Baltic—Königsberg, Danzig, Stettin, and Stralsund. The external communications of Prussia via these ports were very much impeded by the long and tedious navigation necessary to reach them through the Cattegat, the burden of the duties exacted by Denmark on the passage of the Sound, and the circumstance of their being frozen up or rendered inaccessible by the increased danger and difficulty of winter navigation. A large part of the external commerce of the Union, therefore, was carried on through the Hanseatic towns and the countries of Hanover, Holland, Belgium, and Austria by means of the artificial communications which connected the Elbe, the Weser, the Ems, the Rhine, and the Danube with the interior of Germany.[2]

The terms of the existing association of customs between the kingdom of Hanover, the grand duchy of Oldenburg, the duchy of Brunswick, and the principality of Schaumburg-Lippe, known as the Steuerverein, subjected goods imported into any of these states to uniform duties; these once paid, the articles circulated freely within their territories.

The population of the Steuerverein totaled over two million and a quarter people. Besides the usual agricultural and mineral productions of North Germany, Hanover and the states associated with her manufactured many articles intended for exportation. The duties on the staple products of the United States such as cotton, tobacco, and rice were very low and were not likely to be increased. The duties on raw tobacco especially were not more than one-fifth as high as the duties imposed in Prussia and the other German states associated with Prussia in the Zollverein.[3]

The principal seaport of the kingdom of Hanover was Emden, which formerly had carried on a considerable foreign commerce when the province of East Friesland had belonged to Prussia and as long as the Prussian flag had enjoyed the privileges and advantages of neutrality during the wars of the American and French revolutions.

The Hanse towns, especially the ports of Hamburg and Bremen, as Wheaton stated, played a very important part in the commercial relations of the United States with the German states. Situated near the mouths of the Elbe and the Weser, these towns were not only those through which the greater part of the imports and exports of Hanover were made but also those through which a very large portion of the transatlantic commerce of Germany was carried on. With Lübeck the United States had little or no direct intercourse; it is situated on the Baltic and it served principally as an entrepôt for the overland trade between the two seas.[4]

Wheaton knew that as Bremen was an enclave in Hanover, it was vitally interested in the continued separation of Hanover from the Zollverein. He argued that should Hanover join the Union, the Steuerverein would be dissolved and Bremen would be insulated and compelled to accede also. The Hanseatic League being thus broken up, the accession of Hamburg would necessarily take place, and that of Mecklenburg-Schwerin and Holstein would soon follow.[5] He therefore felt that commercial relations with Hanover were especially important. He believed that even the smaller states of Mecklenburg-Schwerin and Oldenburg ought not to be neglected, for their ports might become of great commercial importance in some future crisis of the struggle which was then going on between the British-Hanoverian and Prussian-German systems.[6]

Another subject analogous to the Sound dues, which will be treated in a later chapter, received Wheaton's continued attention in connection with Hanover. This was the payment of the duties levied by the Hanoverian Government at Stade on the goods of all nations passing the Elbe except those goods belonging to citizens of Hamburg. The origin of these duties was said to be founded on a title going back to a grant from the Emperor Conrad in 1038, and they had not been abolished by the Congress of Vienna nor included in the provisions in relation to the rivers of Germany, because they were considered sea and not river tolls. Some idea of their importance to the United States may be gathered from the fact that in the three years 1834, 1835, and 1836, one hundred and forty-five American vessels passing up the Elbe paid large duties on their cargoes.[7] It was not only the mere amount of the duties collected at Stade that operated as an injurious restraint on the free navigation of the Elbe, affecting the commerce of the United States as well as that of other nations, but also the attendant vexations and delays that were causes of continual complaint. In point of strict right this tax rested on the ground of prescription only, it being manifestly contrary to the letter and spirit of the treaty of Vienna relating to the free navigation of the great rivers. Wheaton believed that if the efforts of Prussia had been properly seconded by Austria at the time of the subsequent negotiations between the different riparian states of the Elbe to carry into effect those stipulations, it was probable that this tribute would have been totally suppressed. By 1836 it was believed that its abolition could be effected only by making some compensation to the kingdom of Hanover for the loss of this ancient revenue. Wheaton felt that in any negotiations with Hanover efforts should be made to secure abolition of these duties as applied to American commerce.[8]

Baron Mauchhausen, the minister of Hanover at the Prussian court, discussed with Wheaton the question of a commercial treaty, and expressed the strong desire of his Government to enter without delay upon the negotiations, which it was willing should be conducted at Berlin.[9]

Wheaton was given full power for this purpose, and he was also empowered to include the grand duchy of Oldenburg, the duchy of Brunswick, and any other state that might join the commercial and customs union formed by them. He was also to keep in view and use every exertion to obtain a modification of the duties upon American tobacco. He was to assume for the basis of the convention the treaty with Prussia as proposed by the Hanoverian minister with the important difference, however, that no stipulation should be inserted placing the vessels of Hanover and of the states that might be joined in the treaty and their cargoes, engaged in the indirect trade to the United States, upon the footing of American vessels and their cargoes. In that respect he was to be guided by the treaty of 1815 between the United States and Great Britain.[10]

The latter part of these instructions was modified somewhat after further correspondence between Wheaton and the State Department; in March of 1838 Wheaton wrote to President Van Buren that "the Hanoverians may at any time (though they do not seem to be aware of it) entitle themselves, under the act of 1828, to bring to the United States, not only their own produce, but that of *any other foreign country,* in Hanoverian vessels." [11] Forsyth instructed him in May of 1838 that he might stipulate that the vessels of both Hanover and Oldenburg should be permitted to bring into the United States the produce or manufactures of any of the countries of Germany. For this privilege the United States must have, as the only equivalent Hanover and Oldenburg could give, the privilege of carrying all articles grown or manufactured in this continent and the West India Islands.[12]

The negotiation of a commercial treaty was suspended for over a year by the unsettled state of affairs in Hanover, a condition resulting from the decree of the King annulling the constitution of 1833.[13] After this agitation had been quieted,[14] Sieur Auguste de Berger received from Hanover full power to negotiate on the subject of the commercial relations with the United States and to conclude a treaty. The Hanoverian Government had previously declined to negotiate conjointly with Mecklenburg-Schwerin and Oldenburg as at first proposed. After several conferences between Berger and Wheaton the articles of a treaty had been agreed upon when an unexpected difficulty arose.

The instructions received by Wheaton authorized him to take the treaty of the United States with Prussia as the basis of the proposed negotiation. He therefore made no objection to inserting an article in the same terms as the ninth article of that treaty, providing (as was done in most commercial treaties) that if either party should thereafter grant to any other nation any particular favor in navigation or commerce, the same should immediately become common to the other party freely where freely granted or on yielding the same compensation where the grant was conditional. Berger proposed to amend the article so that Hanover would on giving the same equivalents secure the same privileges as to the indirect trade which had been granted to Prussia and the Hanse towns by the existing treaties of the United States with those states—these concessions to continue until due notice of termination of the treaties should be given by either party.

Wheaton declared he was not authorized to accede to such a stipulation; but Berger declared that it was a *sine qua non* with his Government that Hanover should be put on the same footing with any other German state in any commercial arrangement the United States might thereafter make or prolong with such a state. Wheaton concluded to accept this stipulation and to ask for further instructions on that point.

A *projet* of a treaty as agreed upon by Berger and Wheaton was sent by the latter to Forsyth with the stipulation under discussion included as article six.[15] The proposed treaty received the sanction of the President but at the same time

Forsyth set forth the interpretation which the United States would place upon the article in question.[16] After further negotiation between the two ministers, the Hanoverian Government agreed to suppress this article which they had originally proposed.

The Stade toll, some adjustment of which was at first intended to be included in the negotiation, was left by the convention just where it had been before, so that the United States was at liberty to negotiate for its suppression at any time. Wheaton had also ascertained that the duties on the importation of raw tobacco into Hanover were already as low as could reasonably be desired, and since there was no probability of their being increased, although the Hanoverian Government was unwilling to agree not to raise them without an equivalent, he deemed it inexpedient to urge their reduction, especially as he could offer no such equivalent stipulation on the part of the United States.[17]

The different articles having been agreed upon, the convention was signed on the twentieth of May, 1840,[18] and ratified by the Senate of the United States on the fifteenth of July. Ratifications were exchanged the following November.[19]

The convention was based upon the same principles of reciprocity as the existing treaty between the United States and Prussia, with the important difference that the indirect trade which might be carried on under the respective flags of the two contracting parties was confined on the one side to the carrying in vessels of the United States of articles the growth, produce, and manufacture of the American continent and the West India Islands, and in the Hanoverian vessels of articles the growth, produce, and manufacture of the different countries of Germany.

The privileges of navigation granted by the treaty were also confined by the second paragraph of the second article to such vessels as were built within the territories of the respective contracting parties, or lawfully condemned as prize of war, or adjudged to be forfeited for a breach of the municipal laws of either party, and belonging wholly to their citizens or subjects respectively, and of which the master, officers, and two-thirds of the crew should consist of citizens or subjects of the country to which the vessel belonged. Wheaton hoped that this stipulation might be of some use in preventing the fraudulent abuse of the flag to cover the navigation of other powers not privileged by treaty.[20]

On the conclusion of the treaty Wheaton wrote,

The participation of the United States in this commerce on terms of reciprocity will now be secured by treaties with Denmark, Prussia, the Hanseatic Towns, Hanover, and the Netherlands, placing their navigation and commerce on a footing with the national navigation and commerce in all the ports of the North Sea from the mouths of the Rhine to Tonnigen, and of the Baltic from Nemel to Kiel, excepting those of Oldenburg and Mecklenburg-Schwerin in which it still rests on the President's proclamation issued under the acts of 1824 and 1826.[21]

Chapter XXIII

TOBACCO DUTIES

A REDUCTION of the duties on rice had been granted by the states composing the Zollverein, but they would not consider making such an arrangement in connection with the importation of tobacco; they sought to derive from the proposed reductions some concessions in favor of their produce and manufactures.

In answer to the specific inquiry made by Baron de Werther whether in return for a reduction of the tobacco duties he could offer any additional concessions on the part of the United States in favor of the industry of the Zollverein, Wheaton frankly declared that he was not at that time empowered to make any such offer, being merely authorized to receive such a proposal and transmit it to his Government for consideration. It would be necessary for Prussia to specify definitely what in its opinion were the articles, the produce and manufacture of Germany which were then charged with excessively high duties in the ports of the United States. At the same time Wheaton stated that it was his duty to declare that if he rightly comprehended the nature of the concessions alluded to by Baron de Werther as implying a formal stipulation of any preferences in the ports of the United States for the productions of the Zollverein over similar articles imported from other countries, he could not consistently with his instructions encourage the hope that any such proposal would be favorably listened to by the American Government.[1]

The next congress of the Zollverein met in Berlin from the sixteenth of June to the end of September, 1839. Very few alterations were made in the tariff of customs and none which was important to the trade of the United States. The question of the duties on tobacco was suspended as a result of Wheaton's request for a specific statement concerning the duties of which they felt they had reason to complain.[2]

There were, however, two occurrences of interest to Wheaton. Dodge had just returned from a tour in Baden, Hesse-Darmstadt, and the Prussian Rhine provinces, intending to remain in Berlin during the session of the congress; [3] but shortly after his arrival his mission was terminated by a letter from Forsyth stating that the President deemed the information already collected sufficient for the object the Government had in view and directing him to return to Bremen to resume his duties there as consul.[4] Therefore Dodge departed from the vicinity of Berlin, much to Wheaton's relief.

Also Wheaton had the unexpected pleasure of renewing his friendship with Dr. Bowring, who, as British commercial commissioner, had come to Berlin [5] to attend the congress. His purpose was to ascertain the possibility of making advantageous arrangements for Great Britain with the German league by a reciprocal diminution of duties whenever it should be in the power of England to offer an equivalent in both a considerable reduction of its timber duties and an essential modification of the British corn laws, or in either of these reductions. Since a new arrangement between Great Britain and the Zollverein might affect his own activities in Germany, Wheaton, through his friendship with Bowring, kept in close touch with the negotiations.[6] But a treaty between the two countries was not consummated at that time.

As adjustment in the commercial relations between the United States and the Zollverein had been held in abeyance until the next congress, which was not to meet for a year, Wheaton left Berlin the latter part of October [7] to visit Paris, where his family had been residing since the preceding May on account of his younger daughter's health.[8] His usual participation in contemporary events wherever he might happen to be was curtailed, since it was during this visit that he experienced one of the deepest sorrows of his life; for his eldest child, his son Henri Edward, a delicate lad of great intellectual promise, contracted scarlet fever. This illness proved fatal within three days.

On Wheaton's return to Berlin he found that no answer had been made to his note requesting a specific statement of the articles upon which the German states desired to have a reduction of import duties into the United States. He anticipated that duties might be imposed during the session of the United States congress in 1840–41 on the importation of silks, linens, and other industrial products with the view of countervailing the duties imposed on its staple productions in different European countries. For this reason Wheaton transmitted another note to the Prussian minister of foreign affairs calling upon the Zollverein to say what reductions they were willing to make in the duties then levied by them on the tobacco of the United States in return for equivalent reductions by the latter on the duties imposed in the United States upon the productions and manufactures of the Association.

By this time Wheaton had arrived at the conclusion that it would be possible to favor the productions and manufactures of any particular country which might relax in its impositions upon the staples of the United States without any infraction by the latter of existing reciprocity treaties with other foreign powers, because of the qualification (". . . freely, where it is freely granted to such other nation, or on yielding the same compensation when the grant is conditional" 9) which always accompanied the stipulation contained in these treaties that any particular favor granted to one nation should become common to the other party.

Matters were now to become somewhat more complicated by the return of Joshua Dodge upon the scene. In October 1840 Wheaton had been informed by Forsyth that at the last session of Congress in Washington an appropriation had been made for a special agent to attend to the interests of the tobacco trade of the United States with Europe. As the President believed that the ends in view could be best promoted in the different countries of Germany, Joshua Dodge had been appointed the special agent and directed to proceed to Berlin. The appointment was limited to one year from September 21, 1840. He was to report to Wheaton for instructions with regard to the measures which he was to pursue.[10] Wheaton had heard nothing from him directly after an absence of more than a year until he arrived in Berlin in December of 1840. Dodge told him that Forsyth had refused to give him any instructions, for the Secretary of State was altogether opposed to a renewal of the agency, deeming it unnecessary and inexpedient.

During the absence of Dodge, Wheaton had learned from others that he had returned to the United States from Bremen and had been very busy at Washington during the session of Congress, 1839–40, in agitating the question of the tobacco duties with a view to his own reappointment as agent. Wheaton had also understood from the newspapers, and had been informed from other sources, that Dodge had caused himself to be "puffed" in the papers as having been the instrument for effecting great things in favor of the trade of the United States with Germany, and that he had taken credit to himself in this respect at Wheaton's expense. The latter was quite as much at a loss as Forsyth what assignment to give Dodge, and therefore referred him to his former instructions. Dodge remained in Berlin the whole winter.[11]

In the meantime, the congress of the Zollverein met in Berlin in November, 1840. Their deliberations were almost exclusively confined to the important question of the renewal and revision of the fundamental treaty of union, which would expire by its own limitation on the first of January, 1842. Upon the main question of renewal there was hardly a doubt in any quarter, as the confederated states found they were reaping immense advantages from the Association in point of revenue, freedom of internal trade, protection to national industry, simplicity and uniformity of custom-house regulations, and a gradual approximation to a uniformity of coins, weights, and measures. Prussia had participated in those advantages and also had gained in political influence, but it desired some readjustment in the distribution of the revenues, since it had suffered a considerable diminution in the amount of its receipts under the system then in force.[12]

Wheaton did not fail to avail himself of the opportunity afforded by the congress to impress upon the deputies the importance and urgency of the Association's yielding to the demand of the United States for a reduction of the duties on raw tobacco. But they did not appear willing to believe that the United States was in earnest in its menaces of retaliation by laying countervailing duties on the importation of the products of the Association into the country, and were besides too much engrossed with their own domestic arrangements to pay much attention, at that moment, to what concerned their external relations.[13]

In a note to Baron de Werther, Wheaton again asked the single question whether or not the Prussian Government and its commercial allies were willing to make any, and if so what, diminution in the tobacco duties in return for an equivalent reduction of the duties which were levied, or might be imposed before the negotiations were closed, on the importation of its products into the United States.

He concluded this note by earnestly requesting that a subject so important to the mutual interests of the two countries might be reconsidered by the Zollverein with a view to ascertaining whether some means could not be devised of reconciling the conflicting views which had hitherto prevented the complete development of those commercial relations which natural circumstances ought to render so beneficial to both nations and which it was the ardent desire of the American Government to enlarge by removing all the existing obstacles to their improvement.[14]

Wheaton enclosed with this note a long letter addressed to him by Dodge in reply to Baron de Werther, who had written to Wheaton pointing out what he claimed were errors in statements made August 31, 1839, by Dodge in his report to Wheaton. In the enclosed letter Dodge refuted point by point the assertions made by Werther.[15]

While the congress was still in session, a convention of commerce and navigation was signed in London on March 2 between Great Britain and the Zollverein.[16] As we shall see later, the stipulations in this treaty concerning sugar and rice and the ports to be considered as Prussian Baltic ports eventually had a decided effect on Wheaton's negotiations.

The treaty, which was studied with great interest by Wheaton, had been negotiated as a result of the Anglo-Austrian commercial treaty of July 3, 1838, by the second article of which Great Britain promised to give most-favored-nation treatment to Austrian goods "exported through the Northern outlet of the Elbe and the Eastern outlet of the Danube." This was a new type of clause in such treaties, since it applied to exports through territory not actually Austrian and was not made legal until 1840, when by an order in council, "Ports which are the most natural and convenient shipping ports of States within whose dominions they are not situated may, in certain cases, be treated as the national ports of those states for all purposes of British navigation regulations." [17] The fourth article authorized Austrian vessels to fill up with cargo at Turkish-Danubian ports and so carry the produce of a third country into England.

Wheaton learned that Baron von Bülow, the Prussian minister in London, immediately sought to obtain a similar concession for all vessels under the Prussian flag or any other flag of the Association sailing for British ports from the mouths of any of the rivers of Germany and Holland between the Elbe and the Scheldt, inclusive.[18] But in the treaty finally concluded between Great Britain and the Zollverein, the Scheldt was not included, the concession being for all the ports between the Elbe and the Meuse, inclusive.

It should be borne in mind that Prussia had no seaports on the North Sea and that the other German states which had joined with her in the Customs Association had no seaports at all, most of their foreign trade being carried on through the Hanse towns and Holland. This concession from Great Britain, Wheaton held, was not only a great advantage to the Prussian shipping interest but also of considerable advantage to the general commercial interests of the Association. The latter had no equivalent to offer to Great Britain except a stipulation that the British might continue to import sugar and rice on the same terms as the most favored nation; as no nation was favored or was likely to be favored in this respect by the tariff of the Association, this was in fact a mere nominal equivalent made use of in order to give the forms of a convention to this further relaxation of the British Navigation Laws.[19]

The congress of the Zollverein adjourned in May 1841, after agreeing to renew the Treaty of Union for twelve years from January 1, 1842, with little or no alteration except indemnity to be granted to Prussia to recompense it in part for the diminution in its revenues. No measures were taken for the reduction of tobacco duties.[20]

After becoming convinced in April that the tobacco duties would not be changed, Wheaton wrote to Webster suggesting the expediency of the President's making some allusion in his message, on the opening of the ensuing session of Congress, to the relations of the United States with the Zollverein. This subject had never been mentioned in any of the President's messages, and Wheaton felt that his efforts to extend the commercial intercourse of the United States with Germany had not only never been noticed by the previous executives in America, but that Forsyth in particular had positively discouraged those well-meant efforts by every means in his power. The reduction of the duty on rice had been attended with a considerable increase of its importation. Since this increased consumption had brought a corresponding increase of revenue, Wheaton hoped that the Association might be encouraged by the success of that experiment to reduce the duty on raw tobacco. He believed that an intimation in the President's message of an assurance that the same liberal view which had prompted a reduction of the duties on rice on the part of Prussia and her commercial allies might induce them to adopt a similar reduction of the duties on tobacco, would have a conciliatory and favorable effect on the councils of the Association. He brought this suggestion to a conclusion by saying, "You need not be reminded of the importance of these topics to the agricultural interests of our southern and western states, and to the commercial and shipping interests of the whole Union. It is with this view that the above suggestion is respectfully submitted to your better judgment." [21]

At an extra session of the Congress of the United States in May, a report from Secretary of State Webster respecting the commercial relations with the Zollverein and the Danish Sound dues, was laid before the two houses with the President's message. The materials from which it was compiled had been furnished by the despatches of Henry Wheaton. In this report the suggestion was distinctly made of entering into commercial treaties with the German states with a view to the extension of trade with them and to the abrogation of the taxes in the character of *droit d'aubaine* and *droit de détraction* which existed in many of them.[22]

Wheaton expressed satisfaction with Webster's report; he also suggested the advisability of sending to him a full power to negotiate a treaty of navigation and commerce between the two countries.[23]

Another matter had been giving Wheaton much concern for some time. At the end of May he was reluctantly compelled in self-defense and in justice to the public interests to write privately and confidentially to Webster concerning Dodge's agency. Dodge had remained in Berlin until after the middle of April, when he had set off on a tour of South Germany. For six weeks Wheaton had heard nothing from him. He did not know whether Dodge had made any reports or other communications to the State Department.

During the time Dodge was in Berlin, the Prussian authorities frequently stated to Wheaton that Dodge's manner was

extremely discourteous and even offensive, and the tone of
menace assumed by this subordinate agent, who had not even
a letter of credence to any government, appeared to them
very extraordinary. They were also unable to understand
what object could be promoted by having him again travel
through the different German states associated with the Zollverein; he had no power to treat with any of them, the Prussian Government possessed full powers to treat on the part
of its allies, the United States had a minister in Berlin in-
vested with a similar full power on its part, and it had already received all the information it could desire respecting
the cultivation and trade in their bearings upon the question of the duties. Wheaton was unable to explain these circumstances, and at the same time he felt it necessary to be
very reserved in his replies to their remarks on account of
the delicacy to be observed in speaking to the members of
a foreign government of the conduct of an agent of his own.
But he felt at liberty to say to Webster, in confidence, that
he considered the presence of Dodge in Germany worse than
useless and hoped that when his present commission expired
in September it would not be renewed. "At the same time,"
Wheaton wrote, "I should be extremely sorry to prevent his
being employed in another quarter, or to do him an injury
in any respect, although he has been entirely wanting towards
me in manifesting a proper sense of the services I have rendered him, of the uniform kindness I have shown him, and
of my constant disposition to render full justice to whatever
merits he may possess." [24] Wheaton felt that he had "had
quite enough of agents, who are rather an embarrassment
than a help."

Before the receipt of this despatch Webster had written to
Wheaton that a communication had been received from
Dodge containing his report No. 1 on the subject of tobacco
and urging that the tobacco agency which would expire in
September should be extended indefinitely. Webster asked
Wheaton to send his views on the subject.[25] As a result of the
combined opinion of the President, the Secretary of State,

and Wheaton, the term of Dodge's agency was not extended.[26]

The following May Baron von Roenne, in a report sent by him from the United States to the Foreign Office in Berlin, stated that he had had occasion to show to the State Department the mistakes made in Dodge's reports; that Dodge had left a few days before for Vienna, though he wished to be sent again to Berlin; that Webster, who saw through the futility of the tobacco agency in Germany, had consulted him (Roenne) confidentially in the matter and so the Zollverein had gotten rid of Dodge; that Webster and the President would have liked to abolish this agency altogether but did not dare to arouse the ire of the planters; that it was, therefore, decided to send Dodge to Jenifer in Vienna, "whose creature he is," but then he was most strictly advised not to assume any diplomatic character, but only to collect materials on the tobacco question and refer them to Jenifer.[27]

The negotiations concerning the contemplated treaty between the United States and the Zollverein remained suspended during the summer of 1841 and the following winter while Wheaton was in Paris.

Chapter XXIV

PARIS
1841–1842

WHEATON desired to have his children educated in France and felt that their mother should be near them, so his family had been living in Paris since 1839. He had given up his house in Berlin and taken an apartment for himself.[1] Under these conditions he visited Paris as often as he could, whenever his absence from Germany would not interfere with his official duties. Such an opportunity occurred in the fall of 1841, and he set out from Berlin on the fifteenth of November, leaving his secretary of legation, Theodore S. Fay, as chargé d'affaires *ad interim*.[2] About ten days before his departure he had written to Judge Spencer that he understood General Lewis Cass, United States Minister in France, did not intend or expect to retain this commission longer than the spring of 1842. If that were so, Wheaton said that he would have no objection to a transfer to that post.[3] In view of this possibility he went there at this time with the hope that his desire to represent his Government as envoy at Paris might at last be fulfilled.

This winter was to prove one of the most engrossing of his career. The catholicity of his interests brought him into contact with many eminent people. Changes in official positions had produced a group of diplomats in Europe who could discuss frankly with each other controversial questions of international import. In England Lord Aberdeen had succeeded Lord Palmerston in the Foreign Office, and in France Guizot had supplanted Thiers as Louis Philippe's prime minister. Edward Everett, who was traveling with his family in Europe, had received at Naples news of his appointment as United

States minister at London to succeed Andrew Stevenson. Everett immediately started for England, arrived at Paris on the tenth of November, and reached London the eighteenth. He returned to Paris on the twenty-seventh where he remained for about two weeks.[4] On the thirtieth he recorded in his journal that "Mr. Wheaton our Minister at Berlin, Mr. Hodgson our Consul at Tunis, Temple Bowdoin and Governor Cass called." Cass invited him to dinner the following Friday to meet the other American diplomats then in Paris. Besides those mentioned there were William Boulware of Virginia, representing the United States in the Two Sicilies; Ambrose Baber of Georgia, the chargé to Sardinia; and General Washington Barrow of Tennessee, our chargé to Portugal.[5] A week later Everett wrote that he had "passed the evening at Mr. Wheaton's with wife and children. Mr. Boulware our Chargé d'Affaires at Naples was present." [6]

When Everett first arrived in London, there were several matters pending between the United States and England which he had expected to be called upon immediately to discuss. Lord Ashburton's mission to the United States had transferred the more important ones to Washington.[7] The five questions at issue to be covered by his mission were the northeastern boundary, the Oregon boundary, the northwestern (Lake of the Woods to the Rocky Mountains) boundary, the *Caroline* incident, and the right of search for the suppression of the African slave trade.[8] One of those left for discussion in England was the proposal for a new commercial treaty. In his despatches Wheaton had discussed at length the negotiations for a readjustment of commercial arrangements current among the various countries.[9]

The commercial treaties under which trade relations between England and the United States were regulated at that time were the convention of commerce and navigation concluded July 3, 1815, the terms of which were to last for four years with the option of renewal; the convention respecting fisheries, boundary, and the restoration of slaves, concluded October 20, 1818, which extended the former treaty for ten years; and the commercial convention concluded August 6, 1827, indefinitely extending the terms of the former treaties.[10] The provisions were not as favorable to the United States as they might have been, and it was desirable if possible to secure a more advantageous arrangement. Although, in accordance with his instructions from the State Department, Everett had made every effort he could to secure a new commercial treaty, President Tyler and his group distrusted him as a Webster man, supposedly unsympathetic with their policy. For this reason one of the functions of the secret mission of General Duff Green to England in the winter of 1841–42 was to urge the consummation of such a treaty.[11] General Green discussed the subject of reciprocal free trade and the possibility of a new convention between the United States and Great Britain, not only with Sir Robert Peel and members of his ministry, but also with Lord John Russell and leaders of the Whig opposition.[12] Calhoun did not have much hope that anything satisfactory could be done concerning a new treaty, "although," he stated, "I do not doubt the sincerity of the Government on either side. The difficulties are great. . . ." [13]

Coincident with this desire of the United States were the efforts on the part of England to make new commercial arrangements with other countries. Wheaton had written to the State Department about John Macgregor's presence at the Zollverein conference at Munich in 1836 and the signing afterwards of a treaty with Austria on July 3, 1838; [14] he had recounted the activities of Bowring when he had come as British commercial commissioner to the congress in Berlin in September 1839; [15] and he had sent to Webster an analysis of the substance of the convention of commerce and navigation between Great Britain and the Zollverein which had been signed on March 2, 1841.[16]

In view of the arrangements he was endeavoring to make with the Zollverein, Wheaton also had written about the commercial negotiations between England and France.[17] During the period of the Orleans monarchy Great Britain had tried repeatedly to place its commerce with France on a more liberal basis. In 1830, when Palmerston first became secretary of foreign affairs, he told the House of Commons that one of the first things he would endeavor to do would be to negotiate a commercial treaty with France.[18] Such a treaty did not materialize, and from 1840 until March 1844 the commercial relations with France were the subject of much discussion in Parliament. The protracted negotiations caused a great deal of uncertainty in the trade relations between the two countries. In August and September, 1840, following closely the signing of the treaty of July 15, in reference to the affairs of Egypt (described in greater detail on page 194), commercial negotiations had been contemporary with the discussion of a treaty for the repression of the slave trade. Thiers had hesitated to conclude "treaty upon treaty with parties who had behaved so ill to them." [19] The two negotiations thus remained in suspense. On March 26, 1841, Viscount Melbourne had said in the House of Lords that the negotiations which had been interrupted by the events which had taken place at the close of the last year had not been renewed, but that there had been on the part of the British Government a most anxious desire for their resumption, and that he entirely concurred in the belief that nothing could tend more to confirm the good understanding which had existed and, he trusted, did exist between the two countries than a free system of commercial intercourse.[20] Contemporary with these negotiations with France and General Green's visit to England there were discussions in Parliament concerning commercial treaties with Spain, Portugal, and the Brazils. In view of the opinions so vigorously expressed in these debates, the opening of new negotiations with the United States was deemed inadvisable.[21]

Two controversies in which the United States was involved directly with England received Wheaton's special attention while on this visit to Paris—the *Caroline* incident and the affair of the *Creole*. During the insurrection in Canada in 1837 a party of Canadian militia had crossed the Niagara

River to the American shore and destroyed a small steamer, the *Caroline,* which had been hired by the insurgents. In this fray one of the crew, an American named Amos Durfee, had been killed. In 1840 a Canadian, Alexander McLeod, was arrested in New York and imprisoned for trial before the state courts as the murderer of Durfee. Before McLeod's arrest the United States had been unable to obtain an admission from Palmerston that the attack on the *Caroline* had been deliberate and official. After the arrest Palmerston admitted that the ship had been destroyed under orders as a necessary means of defense against American "pirates," and he demanded the immediate release of McLeod. Tension between the two countries was becoming very acute.[22]

Concerning this affair Wheaton wrote to Webster,

I take it for granted that you have provided for every contingency that may arise under the McLeod's case;—that you have taken the necessary precautions to prevent the interference of Lynch-law; that should he be found guilty by the Jury, he will be pardoned by the Governor; and if not, that his counsel will move in arrest of judgment that he was executing the orders of his own government which it has avowed, and taken on itself the consequent responsibility towards the United States Government—it then can be taken to the federal court.[23]

Webster tried unsuccessfully to secure the removal of the case from the state to the Federal Courts. Feeling ran very high against the Federal authorities who were accused of interfering in the internal affairs of a state and of yielding to Great Britain. But in October 1841 when the case came on for trial, McLeod, who was aided by the best legal advice that Webster could obtain, was able to prove an alibi and secure acquittal from the New York Court. The danger of further trouble between England and the United States over this affair thus passed.[24]

"This case," Lawrence stated, "involved two very grave points; the one—the right, on the part of the British authorities, to go into American territory, and to take possession, by force, of a vessel belonging to a citizen of the United States—the other, the right of the tribunals of the country to try, as an offense against the criminal jurisdiction, an act committed under the authority of a foreign government." [25] In order to place the matter fairly before the public opinion of Europe, Wheaton published an article entitled "Affaire de Mac-Leod considérée sous le point de vue du droit des gens" [26] in the *Revue étrangère et française de législation*. Wheaton pointed out that in all free countries governed by representative constitutions the courts are independent of the immediate action of the executive power, though in England, where the prosecution may be terminated in the beginning by the intervention of the Crown, the responsibility of the Government would commence on its refusal to arrest a proceeding against a foreign subject, of which proceeding the Government of the latter had just reason to complain. As to the other point, Wheaton claimed that the United States could not admit that though the *Caroline* might have been a piratical vessel, the whole American nation had become pirates. On the contrary, he maintained that the United States had, as far as possible, fulfilled its duties as a neutral state. Wheaton asserted that all that England could contend for in her contest with the insurgents of Canada was to have the rights that a sovereign might exercise towards his subjects who had rebelled and those rights which are allowed to a belligerent in the time of war with reference to neutral states. It is an incontestable principle that no act of hostility can be exercised by belligerents within the limits of neutral territories. Wheaton contended that the attack on the *Caroline* was not the continuation of a pursuit into an enemy's territory but a premeditated attack, executed during the night, by the military authorities of the Province of Upper Canada against an American vessel at anchor in a harbor of the United States on the shores of the Niagara Strait, which separates the respective territories of the two countries. Such an act of hostility within neutral territory even against an enemy, Wheaton declared, had been proscribed by all the writers on public law.[27] Wheaton's article was afterwards published in pamphlet form.[28]

The northeast boundary question and the McLeod case engendered animosity principally in the northern states, but about this time another case that caused intense irritation against Great Britain throughout the southern states attracted Wheaton's attention. In November 1841, an American planter sailed for New Orleans from Richmond, Virginia, on board an American vessel, the *Creole*, with 135 slaves belonging to him. In the straits between Florida and the Bahama Islands the Negroes revolted, killed their master, put the captain in irons, wounded several of the crew, took possession of the vessel, and carried it into the British port of Nassau in the Bahamas. The governor arrested nineteen of the slaves concerned in the revolt and assassination, and he asked instructions of his Government.[29] He freed the rest of the Negroes in spite of the protests of the Americans in the harbor, who were prepared to resist the process of liberation by using force but were prevented by the appearance of British troops. This case at one time almost disrupted the Webster-Ashburton negotiations entirely, but an agreement was finally reached by an exchange of notes in the beginning of August, 1842.[30]

Wheaton also endeavored to place this case fairly in Europe by another article entitled "Examen des questions de jurisdiction qui se sont élevées entre les gouvernements anglais et américain dans l'affaire de la Creole; suivi d'une analyse du mémoire de l'autem sur le droit de visite en mer" published in the *Revue étrangère et française de législation*.[31] In this article Wheaton set forth the history of laws concerning extradition. He contended that the decision of individual nations on the slavery question must be respected. To allow one nation to change laws recognized by all nations would accord "an immense and unheard of power." The nations had not established "the invariable rule having the force of a moral law" that a slave became free automatically if he touched European soil. Even though that principle had been recognized, it would not have applied to the case of the *Creole*. The question really was whether or not the arrival of the *Creole* in the port of Nassau was such an exception to the general rule that it authorized the United States to seek compensation from England for the damage suffered.

Wheaton regarded the *Creole* affair not as an extradition of offenders by the government of a country in which they had committed a crime, nor as a case in which an asylum had been sought by slaves in a country where slavery was not tolerated. Wheaton contended that it was a "general principle" that vessels in the open seas were under the exclusive jurisdiction of the country from which they came. It was only when they voluntarily entered the port of another country that they came under the jurisdiction of the country to which the port belonged. The *Creole* never ceased to be exclusively the subject of American jurisdiction because it had entered a friendly port against the will of the captain and owner and in consequence of a crime on high seas which was cognizable only in the courts of the United States. Therefore, since the *Creole* "continued to enjoy the rights of the flag, the captain had the right to request the assistance of the local authorities in regaining the possession of his vessel." The slaves had not landed in English territory and had not mixed with the inhabitants of Nassau. Whatever the generality of the expression of the law, Wheaton contended that it did not apply to slaves arriving in a country against the will of the owners and in consequence of the commission of a crime.[32] This article also was published in pamphlet form.[33]

Another controversy which had engaged Wheaton's attention was the one which had arisen between Great Britain and France in their relations to Turco-Egyptian affairs. Soon after arriving in Denmark, Wheaton had included in his despatches some account of affairs in Egypt and Turkey, and had continued to write at length about them in many of the communications which he sent to the State Department. From his despatches a fairly comprehensive contemporary history may be gathered concerning eastern affairs.[34]

Mehemet Ali, the viceroy of Egypt, who had greatly aided the Sultan in the Greek war of independence, becoming dissatisfied with his reward began to extend his possessions by conquest. In 1832 he overran all of Syria and pushed forward into Asia Minor. Having defeated the Turkish generals, he prepared to go still farther, hoping to reach Constantinople. The European powers then began to interfere. Russia succeeded in 1833 in making the treaty of Unkiar Skelessi with the Sultan.[35] Concerning this arrangement Wheaton had written in 1835 that

. . . so long as the treaty of Unkiar Skelessi remains in force,—so long as Russia keeps what the Emperor Alexander called the *keys to his house,*—it is plain that France and England alone, with the utmost exertion of their power and resources, could not prevent the occupation of Constantinople and the Bosphorus by a Russian fleet and army; and it is perhaps even doubtful whether, with the aid of Austria, they could prevent the accomplishment of this design, whenever the favorable moment arrives for its consummation.[36]

England, wishing to maintain its commercial prestige in the East, came to the aid of Turkey. Prussia and Austria took the same side, asserting that the rights of legitimate monarchs must be maintained. On the other hand, France supported Mehemet Ali, for ever since Napoleon's expedition the French had been interested in Egypt. The Egyptian army was organized and drilled by Frenchmen, and France had just conquered Algiers. For this reason a close connection between Mehemet Ali and France would probably result in considerable commercial and political advantage in the Mediterranean. The isolation of France in its support of Mehemet Ali was shown to all the world when the other powers met in conference in London in 1840 and on July fifteenth made a treaty with Turkey pledging themselves to force the Egyptian to terms. The publication of this treaty aroused animosity in France.[37] Thiers urged the adoption of warlike measures to guard the interests of his nation in

Egypt. But King Louis Philippe vigorously opposed such proposals, which would involve France and the July monarchy in the greatest danger. Thiers sent in his resignation October 20, 1840, and Guizot became chief minister nine days later.[38] France adopted a policy of peace, and the danger of a war passed. The final settlement was brought about by a conference at London attended by the representatives of the four powers. This conference on July 10, 1841, signed a protocol and invited the accession of France, the appeal being made "on the invitation and according to the wish of His Highness the Sultan." The protocol was intended to mark the close of the whole incident, and the invitation contained in it was taken in this sense by France. The Four Power Treaty of July 1840 was tacitly suppressed. On July 13 two treaties were signed, the one definitely establishing peace between the Sultan and Mehemet Ali and confirming the latter in the hereditary pashalik of Egypt; the other, known as the "Convention of the Straits," reënacted "the ancient rule of the Ottoman Empire." France subscribed with the other Powers to both these treaties.[39] France simply agreed to facts accomplished in spite of it, and acknowledged the Sultan's right to close the two straits—the Bosphorus and the Dardanelles—to all ships of war.

Lord Palmerston had now achieved his ends. Russia had yielded the privilege given to her navy by the treaty of Unkiar Skelessi, and France had suffered Mehemet Ali to be humbled. The English ministry bought its success at the price of renewed hostility from France, for although the King and Guizot might forget, France would not.[40] This was soon made apparent in subsequent negotiations concerning the slave trade and the right of search, in which Wheaton became actively interested.

Chapter XXV

THE RIGHT OF SEARCH

FROM the time of Wheaton's first trip to Europe, during which he witnessed the boarding of a vessel by British officers, the question of the right of search had received his attention. In his early political articles he had written about it, and he had spoken strongly concerning it in his Fourth of July oration of 1810. Many of his editorials in the *National Advocate* dealt with the matter. The study involved in his *Digest,* his experience as justice of the Marine Court, and the many cases brought under his consideration both as reporter and as counsel before the Supreme Court of the United States had given him a detailed and comprehensive knowledge of the whole subject.

The matter as then under consideration among the nations dated back to 1815. By the tenth article of the Treaty of Ghent it was agreed that both Great Britain and the United States should "use their best endeavors" to promote the entire abolition of the slave trade. The Congress of Vienna denounced the African slave trade "as inconsistent with the principles of humanity and universal morality." At that time England proposed to the other nations that they grant their armed vessels a mutual right of search over merchant vessels in order to detect and prevent the transportation of slaves.[1]

The ministers of the Restoration in France declined the proposition, but as a result of the recognition and support which Great Britain had given to him, Louis Philippe, soon after his accession, accepted it. The first treaty was signed November 30, 1831; new clauses were added two years later. These enlarged the first conditions, extended the right of search indefinitely beyond the thirty-second degree latitude and thus subjected all commerce between Europe and the United States to this maritime inquisition and removed all limits to the number of cruisers of each nation.[2]

Between 1833 and 1839 Great Britain secured treaties by which Hayti, Uruguay, Venezuela, Bolivia, Argentina, Mexico, Texas, Denmark, and the Hanse towns granted her the right of search.[3] As early as the middle of April, 1839, Wheaton had written to Secretary of State Forsyth:

The British Minister here has just received instructions from his government to urge the accession of Prussia to the measures agreed upon in a conference of the Ministers of the five great European Powers, held at the Foreign Office on the 12th December 1838, for the purpose of more effectually suppressing the African slave trade, the Protocol of which was taken *ad referendum* by the Plenipotentiaries of Austria, Prussia and Russia. The Protocol of this Conference has probably been communicated to the Department by our legation in London. It contains the project of a treaty between the five Powers granting a mutual right of search and providing various regulations of its exercise similar to those which were proposed by the British Government to us sometime since.[4]

Guizot, who at this time was the French minister in London, wrote in his *Mémoires* that ten days after the signing of the treaty in reference to the affairs of Egypt on the 15th of July, 1840, Lord Palmerston assembled the representatives of Austria, France, Prussia, and Russia at the Foreign Office and invited them to sign for the repression of the slave trade a treaty by which the three northern powers accepted the conventions which had been concluded on this subject between France and England in 1831 and 1833 and which, moreover, introduced certain modifications into the exercise of the right of search.[5]

Towards the end of August Guizot was informed that Baron de Brunnow had received authority from St. Petersburg to consent to the new limits indicated for the mutual right of search as well as to all the other provisions and to the political character of the treaty. The plenipotentiaries of

Austria and Prussia were furnished with similar powers.[6]

In the meantime at Sierre Leone on March 11, 1840, Commander John S. Paine of the United States Navy, who had been assigned to duty on the African coast to prevent this abuse of the American flag, entered into an agreement with Commander William Tucker of the Royal British Navy binding the two officials to assist each other and to detain all vessels under the American flag employed in the traffic in slaves. If found to be American property, such vessels were to be delivered over to the commander of any American cruiser on the African coast, or, if belonging to other nations, they were to be dealt with according to the treaties of Great Britain with those nations. When, in consequence of the above agreement, British officers became more active in the detention of slave ships sailing under the American flag, a great outcry at once arose in the United States against the search of American vessels in time of peace. The Government was deluged with complaints; but unmistakable evidence was obtained by Great Britain of the misuse of the flag, and this was made the basis of official protests on the part of England. Palmerston conducted the correspondence in a tone of steadily rising temper, and on August 27, 1841, only a few days before he left office, he addressed to Andrew Stevenson, the American minister, a note of a most uncompromising character. The vigor of Palmerston's correspondence on the right of visit had led President Tyler in his annual message to Congress on December 7, 1841, to state emphatically his views concerning the freedom of the seas and to declare that "however desirous the United States may be for the suppression of the slave trade, they cannot consent to interpolations into the maritime code at the mere will and pleasure of other governments. They deny the right of any such interpolation to any one or all the nations of the earth, without their consent." [7] Fortunately Lord Palmerston was succeeded by Lord Aberdeen; and Stevenson, by Everett.

Aberdeen and Guizot resumed the negotiations concerning the slave trade. On December 20, 1841, the Quintuple

Treaty between Great Britain, France, Austria, Prussia, and Russia was consummated. The principal article thereof provided that "the High Contracting Parties agree by common consent that those ships of war which shall be provided with special warrants and orders . . . may search every merchant vessel belonging to any one of the High Contracting Parties which shall on reasonable grounds be suspected of being engaged in the traffic of slaves." This gave a free hand to the British naval officers engaged in the suppression of the trade.[8]

Aberdeen invited the adhesion of the United States to the Quintuple Treaty on the day it was signed. His language was most conciliatory, and he expressly disclaimed any desire to infringe the maritime rights claimed by America.[9] This note was received by Everett just a week after his return to London from Paris. About that time he wrote to Wheaton that since he had expected the right of search to be one of the matters to be discussed by him and since he wanted to have Wheaton's opinion concerning the whole question, he had directed copies of the correspondence to be sent to Paris for him. As Lord Ashburton's mission transferred the discussions to Washington, and the American newspapers furnished nearly all the letters, this was not done, but Everett forwarded one of Aberdeen's letters which had not been published and entered upon a confidential correspondence with Wheaton in an exchange of views concerning the entire matter.[10]

The Quintuple Treaty immediately met with displeasure and with serious opposition in France. The maritime population was incensed to learn that their ships were subject to English inspection on all the African and American coasts. The press became the mouthpiece of popular indignation, and the attitude of France was compared with that of the United States.[11]

A great deal of interest was attracted to the action which France would take concerning the ratification of the Treaty. Its consideration in the French chambers called forth acrimonious discussion. Wheaton regularly attended the Assembly to hear the debates. He saw many deputies and ex-ministers, and endeavored to enlighten them as to the present and future policy of the United States.[12]

In conversation with Wheaton, whom he often saw, Guizot professed the determination of his Government not to abandon the cause of neutral rights, which might be inferred from its accession to the Quintuple Treaty. But by his speeches in the Chamber of Deputies, which Wheaton heard with "a suitable admiration of his talents and courage," he left the United States, Wheaton held, no alternative except to accede to the treaty or to be considered by the rest of mankind as opposing an insurmountable obstacle to the final suppression of the slave trade.

"Disguise it as you will," Wheaton wrote, "the British pretension is the exercise of the right of visitation and search in time of peace, upon vessels of a State which has not consented to its exercise by special compact. The only means of escaping from this consequence is by acceding to the Treaty." Wheaton was confirmed in this view by a short conversation he had with Bulwer, secretary of legation in form, but in fact British ambassador at Paris during the absence of Lord Granville. Bulwer concluded the conversation abruptly by saying, "Your objection is that you are not willing that the character of your vessels, whether American or not should be determined for you by another nation,"—leaving Wheaton to infer that Bulwer had not only considered that to be the real nature of their pretension, but that he did not believe we would submit to such a proposal.[13]

Wheaton informed Webster that the French nation was unanimous in repudiating the treaty, although "all good men in this country as in every other Christian land sincerely desire to suppress the African Slave Trade"; that the Chamber of Deputies would "most certainly have passed M. Billault's amendment, had it not been made a cabinet question, so that the dread of upsetting the ministry carried the milk-and-water substitute of M. Lafebre"; and that Russia, doubtless for reasons of policy deemed sufficient to justify her action, had subscribed to the treaty. America now stood alone in refusing to concede the right of search either under the treaty or independent of the treaty.[14]

Another American interested in the question of the right of search, General Duff Green, had arrived in Paris about the middle of January. According to a note from Webster to his son Fletcher,[15] General Green had left the United States in November with the intention of going first to England and then to France. He was a close friend of Lewis Cass and was invited by him to come to Paris. General Green later claimed that upon his arrival he immediately urged Cass to take active measures of opposition to the Quintuple Treaty.[16] Green himself, in a Paris paper, denounced England's purposes.

Just after Green reached Paris, Cass, in an effort to influence the attitude of France against the treaty, issued a pamphlet anonymously but generally recognized as being written by him, *The Right of Search, an examination of the question, now in discussion, between the American and British Governments, concerning the Right of Search. By an American.* The pamphlet went to press on the seventeenth of January, and on the twenty-eighth of the same month Everett noted in his journal that Cass had sent him a copy.[17] Cass, however, apparently did not send Webster a copy nor officially notify him of his action and the effect it produced. Concerning this publication Everett wrote to Webster confidentially three days after receiving it,

Gen'l Cass has just published a pamphlet at Paris, called "an examination of the question now in discussion between the American and British govts. concerning the right of search." It is anonymous, but his authorship is avowed. A translation into French is in progress, of which a copy is to be given to each member of the Chambers. This publication is of course well meant, but I greatly doubt the expediency of such an interference between the Exec. at home and Lord Ashburton in the discussion of so delicate a question.[18]

The French edition was asserted to be a faithful translation of the original. An interesting statement was appended at the end of the translation as a postscript, to the effect that a similarity of opinions and even of language would be found in the pamphlet to some of the observations of M. Odilon Barrat in the session of the Chamber of Deputies of January 24. It was claimed that the English text had been completed before the opening of the parliamentary debate and that it had come from the press the Monday evening before the reported account of the sessions had appeared. Evidently there was a coincidence of views between two people, strangers to each other, who were occupied with the same subject.[19] Everett wrote to Webster that the "pamphlet did not appear until after the vote of the Chamber which was the real cause for non-ratification. This fact I know in many ways: it is stated in one of Mr. Walsh's letters to the *Intelligencer*." [20]

In writing to Edward Everett, Webster's comment was, "General Cass' pamphlet, however distinguished for ardent American feeling, is nevertheless, as a piece of law logic, quite inconclusive." [21] In a postscript to one of his letters to Wheaton, Everett said,

I believe the government here do not expect us to come into the treaty. I have taken due note of your counsel not to go beyond instructions in encouraging expectations on the subject. I think it also not less expedient to keep within them as to anything which will tend to render more difficult the sufficiently difficult task of the government at home in conducting the negotiations with Lord Ashburton. I think the public wants enlightening rather than stimulating on both sides of the water.[22]

Wheaton also had arrived at the latter conclusion some time before. As always he was particularly interested in creating a sound public opinion in Europe respecting the attitude maintained by the United States. On the twenty-ninth of January he wrote to Webster that it was his intention to publish something on the question, as it was then presented by the documents before the world—its bearing being still very imperfectly understood both in France and in England.

He said further that he would certainly take care not to make any gratuitous concessions and still less presume to anticipate what might be expected in the way of concession on our part with a view to accommodation.[23]

Wheaton was convinced almost from the beginning of the discussions that France would not ratify the treaty. Before the end of January he had so informed Webster. He also said that he had ventured to assure the British diplomats in Paris that the United States would never yield the point for which Lords Palmerston and Aberdeen contended, nor could it accede to the treaty, although he was not sufficiently aware of the intention of the United States Government to say whether or not any new arrangement could be invented by which the same end might be accomplished by less exceptional means.[24] This last suggestion was one which Wheaton considered important, and he later enlarged it and placed greater emphasis upon it.

On February 13, 1842, Cass, in his official capacity as minister, addressed a note to Guizot setting forth a strong remonstrance against the ratification of the Quintuple Treaty, adverting to the President's message, and stating definitely that the United States would go to war if necessary to maintain its principles.[25]

The evening of the same day that this note was delivered, Wheaton had a long conversation with the King at the Château in which the latter expressed very strongly his anxiety and distress of mind at the situation in which his Government might find itself in case of a rupture between the United States and Great Britain. He said it would be the destruction of credit in Europe and might involve the whole world in the conflagration. He conjured us to avoid it by every possible means and was not willing to admit that even resistance to the right of search would furnish a sufficient motive to justify a resort to arms, since it might, in his opinion, be settled by some sort of compromise, such as a relinquishment of impressment on the part of the British. Wheaton doubted if the British Government would connect two subjects so distinct in their nature and relinquish in all time to come their claim of a right to take their seamen out of our vessels as an incident to a right of search in war, for the sake of sustaining our coöperation in suppressing the slave trade by the means proposed. But the King was not willing to listen to objections which might stand in the way of his favorite object of preserving peace according to his own ideas. Wheaton remarked that the principal peril was not in the great questions known or to be anticipated, but in those incidental questions, such as the *Caroline* and the *Creole,* which were constantly arising, and with which diplomacy could not deal very successfully because they arose suddenly and might occasion collision before danger could be averted. "Yes," said the King, "they start up from under the ground when we least expect them, and what can diplomacy do, when its most deliberate acts must pass in review before popular assemblies, and be torn in pieces by a parcel of scoundrelly deputies, and the peace of the world be compromised by men who have nothing to lose." [26]

On February fifteenth, the same day Cass wrote to Webster concerning the Quintuple Treaty and enclosed the letter he had sent to Guizot, Wheaton too wrote to Webster telling him of his interview with the King. Among other things he said he had learned that De Broglie, who was a great partisan of emancipation, had influenced Guizot to sign the treaty by telling him it would give the *coup de grâce* to the slave trade. Wheaton thought that Sir Thomas Fowell Buxton [27] had proved the contrary and that if all the nations of the world were to concede the mutual right of search it would not put an end to the trade. In the last conversation Wheaton had had with him, Guizot had stated in a very strong manner that he should at least insist upon certain alterations before ratifying the treaty.[28]

On the same day Edward Everett wrote to Wheaton concerning arrangements for the publication in London of Wheaton's pamphlet on the right of search which Everett had cordially offered to superintend. The proof sheets, which had been read and corrected by Everett, were sent for publication in the United States on the packet sailing from England on the fourth of March,[29] so that the pamphlet was published both in London and in Philadelphia, in March and April respectively.[30] It was entitled *Enquiry into the Validity of the British Claim to a Right of Visitation and Search of American vessels suspected to be engaged in the African Slave-Trade.*

Wheaton's pamphlet was reviewed in England, France, Germany, and the United States. In some instances his statements were attacked, in others he received commendation. The notice in the *Foreign Quarterly Review* in England, although the reviewer did not agree with Wheaton, stated that the pamphlet was "cleverly written and certainly in a very quiet and gentleman-like spirit." [31]

Wheaton's treatment of the historical side of the slave trade was so excellent that it received General Cass' commendation. In acknowledging the receipt of this essay, Cass wrote to Wheaton:

I have read your work on the right of search with the greatest pleasure, and I may add, with much profit. I thought I knew the whole history of the question, but I find that I had deceived myself, and that I had much to learn, which I have now learned.

Your historical narrative is most satisfactory, and you put the *argumentum ad homines* to our friends the English, on the existence of slavery in the United States, with equal good temper and good sense. How they will get out of the dilemma in which you have placed them as the authors of the evil, I do not see.

Your general deductions are not less convincing; and I think you may safely consider the pretension to search our ships, in time of peace, as a question of right, forever disposed of. I am glad to see you make so good a case of a decision of the Supreme Court.

On the whole, I congratulate you upon the success of your labors. They will do our country good everywhere, and cannot fail to be useful to yourself, and increase the literary reputation you have already so justly acquired.[32]

In his pamphlet Wheaton had endeavored to show that Great Britain was really trying to secure consent to the exercise of "the right of visitation and search, in time of peace upon the high seas, in respect to the vessels of a nation which had not expressly assented to its exercise." He reviewed the history of the slave trade so far as the United States and Great Britain were concerned. He told how the trade, protected by charters of monopoly and public treaties, had been carried on by the British nation for more than two centuries under the patronage of its Government. He cited the memorable treaty of Utrecht, 1713, containing the Assiento contract. He narrated how slavery had been encouraged in the North American colonies by Great Britain even against the protests of the colonists, and he stated the measures immediately taken against the importation of slaves by the American Congress after the colonies had secured their independence. He then traced the history of the proposals, treaties, and measures adopted concerning the slave trade from the Congress of Vienna in 1815 down to the signing of the Quintuple Treaty. He endeavored to set forth clearly the reasons for the attitude of the United States, and showed the weakness inherent in the arguments of Palmerston and Aberdeen to justify the position taken by them. He summed up his arguments on the legal side in the following paragraph:

The United States have never pretended that Great Britain could lawfully be compelled by force to abandon the belligerent right of visitation and search, however anxious they may have been to establish by general compact the maxim, of free ships, free goods, by which the exercise of the right would be limited to the sole cases of contraband and blockade only. On the other hand, it cannot be pretended that the United States may be compelled by force or by that moral duress which is equivalent to the application of force, to abandon the immunity of their flag from the exercise of that right in time of peace. Their conclusive objection to its extension by special compact, in peace or in war, in any form, and under any restrictions, which have heretofore been proposed, is not merely that it may be liable to abuse, as experience has but too well proved; but that such express recognition might involve by implication the establishment of maxims relating to neutral navigation, the reverse of those which they have ever sought to incorporate into the international code by the general concurrence of maritime states.[33]

About the middle of March, it was apparent that the Quintuple Treaty would not be ratified by France. Wheaton therefore brought again to Webster's attention the suggestion of a counter-project made by him several times before, since he felt something should be done in order to justify the attitude of the United States. He wrote to Webster that De Sage, the principal under-secretary of state for foreign affairs, had told him that it would not be sufficient for Webster, in order to satisfy the public opinion of the world, dryly to repel the British pretension of the right of search as a means of suppressing the slave trade under the then existing law of nations; but that the denial of the right assumed by Great Britain or the rejection of any proposal she might make for the mutual concession of the right ought to be accompanied with a counter-project on the part of the United States, showing that it was not obstinately bent on refusing to concur with Europe in regulating this matter by international legislation, although it might not accede to the particular measures which had been adopted or were proposed to be adopted by the European states for that purpose. Guizot had also frequently questioned Wheaton as to the possibility of inventing some plan of mutual coöperation to which the United States might be willing to agree.[34]

Over a month later, Lord Ashburton also suggested to Webster the possibility of a counter-project.[35] Thereupon Webster proposed to Lord Ashburton that England and the United States should each agree to maintain on the coast of Africa for a limited time an independent squadron comprising such a number of vessels and of such force as might be agreed on, with instructions to their commanders respectively to act in concert, so far as might be necessary, in order that no slave ship, under whatever flag it might sail, should be free from visitation and search.[36]

Early in May Wheaton left Paris to return to his post in

Prussia, thus withdrawing from the center of the discussion of this question, but after his arrival in Berlin he communicated to Webster the assurances of Bülow that whatever might have been the views of England, the other contracting parties to the Quintuple Treaty never intended that it should be executed in any other manner than by searching each other's ships; and that the British Government was alone responsible for its application to those of other nations. Bülow also expressed his conviction of the difficulty, if not impossibility, of the American Government's adhering to the principle which formed the basis of the treaty.[37]

Another phase of the matter which had caused mystification in the minds of some people was stated by Jared Sparks in a letter to Wheaton after his return to Berlin. Sparks had written an article for the *North American Review* on the Treaty of Washington, and proposed to add another on the right of search. He had Wheaton's pamphlet which, he said, gave him all the information he could wish as to general principles and facts. The topics on which he wanted more knowledge were the motives and reasons of the three continental powers for entering into the Quintuple Treaty. He stated his inquiry thus:

Why should Russia, Prussia, and Austria be willing to throw themselves by this act into the arms of the gigantic navy of Great Britain? Are they really moved by the disinterested and philanthropic desire of abolishing the slave trade? I ask this question because, looking only upon the surface of things, one cannot imagine what advantage either of these governments can expect from such a union. Moreover, since the days of the Crusades, no nation has been known to measure its policy by a refined philanthropy at the expense of its interests. If a new era has come, in which nations are to study only justice and the good of mankind in their relations to each other, so much the better for the world. The example of Great Britain affords us but slender encouragement to hope for so happy a change, and I cannot explain the conduct of the three powers. Pray unravel the web, and let me know the motives by which they were influenced in this affair of the Quintuple Treaty, in as much detail as your leisure will permit.[38]

In reply Wheaton wrote that, having already detached Great Britain from her close connection with France by the treaty of July 15, 1840, the three countries Russia, Prussia, and Austria, wished to preserve the general harmony of the European alliance. They therefore were very willing to do whatever might be agreeable to the British Government in a matter in which they took no interest but which might gain them some credit, while it could be of no possible injury to their navigation and commerce and was not, at that time, supposed to be disagreeable to the French nation. They had very little navigation in the African, West Indian, and South American seas, and had besides taken very good care in the treaty itself to exempt from its operation the Mediterranean and all ports of the ocean frequented by their merchant vessels. Wheaton further said:

As to the danger of creating a precedent for the right of search, as claimed by Great Britain in time of war, they excuse themselves on the ground that an exceptional right of search, expressly created by treaty, and confined to a specific object, rather confirms the general freedom of navigation than otherwise—*exceptio probat regulam.*[39]

The negotiations between Webster and Lord Ashburton were concluded on August 9, 1842, by the signing of the two treaties, one dealing with the boundary and the other dealing with the suppression of the slave trade and extradition. After the two treaties had been despatched to England for ratification, Webster decided that in order to secure the consent of the Senate it would be better to combine them in one. This was done.[40] Article VIII provided for joint cruising squadrons on the coast of Africa "to enforce, separately and respectively, the laws rights and obligations of each of the two countries, for the suppression of the Slave Trade," under such orders as would "enable them most effectually to act in concert and coöperation, upon mutual consultation, as exigencies may arise, for the attainment of the true object of this article." Article IX pledged the two contracting parties to use their united influence with other powers in bringing about at once and forever the closing of slave markets wherever they existed.[41] The treaty was ratified in the Senate by a vote of thirty-nine to nine within ten days after it was received. It was freely criticized in both countries. In England it was referred to as "Ashburton's capitulation," while many Americans were dissatisfied with the boundary compromise and the failure to secure a renunciation of the British practice of search.[42]

In September, on receipt of the information that the treaty had been consummated between the United States and Great Britain, and before being officially notified of it by Webster, General Cass sent his request for recall.[43] Webster in a letter of August twenty-ninth enclosed a copy of the treaty and explained its provisions.[44]

General Cass immediately responded by a long protest against the treaty, stating that it was the real reason for his resignation, for it did not uphold his conception of the true attitude of the United States concerning the right of search.[45] Concerning this Everett wrote to Webster on the third of November that it was a little curious for Cass to make such an objection to the treaty because it abandoned the American ground on the right of search and for that reason to demand his recall. The ultra-liberal French press which on this point might be expected to be as sharp-sighted as the General considered the self-same articles as an abandonment by England of her pretensions and taunted Guizot for allowing the United States, in her negotiations with Great Britain, to carry a point of such magnitude, which France had been obliged to give up.[46]

Wheaton's attitude, as was to be expected, was entirely different from that of General Cass. He wrote from Berlin to Webster on the sixteenth of November:

Your despatch No. 36, enclosing copy of the treaty recently concluded at Washington, between the United States and Great Britain, has just reached me. I beg leave to congratulate you, sir, on the happy termination of this arduous negotiation, in which the rights, honor, and interests of our country have been so successfully maintained. The arrangement it contains on the subject of the African slave-trade is particularly satisfactory, as adapted to secure the end proposed by the only means consistent with our maritime rights. This arrangement has decided the course of the French Government in respect to this matter. Its ambassador in London notified to the conference of the five great powers the final determination of France not to ratify the treaty of December, 1841, and, at the same time, expressed her disposition to fulfill the stipulations of the separate treaties of 1831 and 1834 between her and Great Britain. The treaty of 1841, therefore, now subsists only between four of the great powers by whom it was originally concluded; and as three of these (Austria, Prussia, and Russia) are very little concerned in the navigation of the ocean and the trade in the African seas, and have, besides, taken precautions in the treaty itself to secure their commerce from interruption by the exercise of the right of search in other parts, this compact may now be considered as almost a dead letter. Indeed it appears to be very doubtful whether Mons. Guizot will be able to maintain the execution of the stipulations contained in the treaties of 1831 and 1834, against the strong current of public opinion in France which will hardly allow their flag to be less favorably treated than that of any other maritime state.

The policy of the United States may consequently be said, on this occasion, perhaps for the first time, to have had a most decisive influence on that of Europe. This will probably more frequently occur hereafter; and it should be an encouragement to us to cultivate our maritime resources, and to strengthen our naval arm, by which alone we are known and felt among the nations of the earth.[47]

Later, in writing to Sparks, Wheaton said that Guizot did not abandon until the last moment, the hope, derived from he knew not what source, that the United States would enter into some stipulation conceding the right of search, on some terms or conditions, as a means of accepting the prohibition of the slave trade. It was only when Guizot "was informed of the provisions contained in the Ashburton-Webster Treaty that he felt himself compelled to close the protocol without ratifying the Quintuple Treaty." [48]

As Cass had written, Wheaton's publications, while in Paris had "increased the literary reputation" he had "already so justly acquired." In addition to these he had written a *mémoire* in answer to a prize question proposed by the Academy of Moral and Political Sciences in the Institute of France. This was published in 1841 and secured for him added honor and distinction. On the thirtieth of April, 1842, he was elected corresponding member of the French Institute.[49] Mr. Lackanal, through whom the appointment was communicated, stated that during the forty-seven years that he had been a member, he had never been at so flattering an election, which had taken place after the report of Bérenger, peer of France, seconded by Rossi, likewise a peer of France, and by De Tocqueville. Lackanal added that Wheaton would undoubtedly be chosen one of the five free academicians on the occurrence of the first vacancy. At the time of his admission Baron Degerando raised the question of whether he should be received in the section of History or of Jurisprudence. It was to the latter that he was attached.[50]

Another expression of esteem was bestowed upon him in 1843 when he was made an honorary member of the Academy of Sciences at Berlin, the membership of which was limited to fifteen. The members at that time were Alexander von Humboldt and Ritter, distinguished in geography, Buch and Lichtenstein in natural history, Encke in astronomy, Rose and Mitscherlich in chemistry, Savigny and Eichhorn in jurisprudence, Raumer and Ranke in history, Schelling and Steffens in philosophy, Boeckh in philology, and Bopp in the Sanskrit language and literature.[51] In announcing this election the *Madisonian* made the comment: "That this is no empty compliment is evinced by the fact that Mr. Wheaton is believed to be the first foreign Minister, certainly he is the first American, on whom this honor has been conferred." [52]

His own country was not entirely lacking in appreciation of his accomplishments, for in the same year Hamilton College conferred upon him the honorary degree of Doctor of Laws.

With his literary and professional reputation steadily growing on the Continent, Wheaton turned away from his beloved Paris to take up actively again his commercial negotiations with the Zollverein.

Chapter XXVI

INTERNATIONAL RELATIONS

ONE of the subjects entrusted to Wheaton was that of procuring the assent of Prussia to act in the arbitration between the United States and Mexico for the adjustment of American claims against the latter republic.

On September 10, 1838, a treaty was signed in Washington by the Mexican Minister Francisco Pizarro Martinez and Secretary of State Forsyth for the adjustment of claims of citizens of the United States against the Mexican Government. It was agreed that the claims should be referred to a mixed commission and that the cases in which the commissioners were unable to agree should be left for the decision of an umpire to be designated by the King of Prussia as the mutual friend of the parties. The treaty was duly ratified by the United States but not by Mexico, as it had assurances from the Prussian chargé d'affaires that his sovereign, apprised in anticipation of the intention of the parties to submit their differences to his arbitration, had declared his unwillingness to accept the invitation.

From information subsequently communicated to Forsyth by Martinez, it appeared that the alleged refusal of the King had its foundation in an unintentional misrepresentation, on the part of the Prussian chargé d'affaires at Mexico, of the contemplated object of the treaty and a consequent misconception by the King of the nature and extent of the mediation to be asked of him.[1]

Since both Mexico and the United States were anxious that the subjects of the claims should no longer be a source of misunderstanding between them, a proposition was made by Mexico for the negotiation of a new treaty, substantially the same as the first, and a convention was signed on April 11, 1839.[2]

This treaty still anticipated the friendly agency of the King of Prussia according to the original intention of the parties, under the belief that their wishes, when accurately made known, would be favorably considered by him. In accordance with one of its provisions a joint note, of which a copy was sent to Wheaton for his information, had been signed by the Mexican minister and Forsyth inviting Baron de Werther to convey to the King of Prussia the request that he would select a person known by him to possess the requisite qualifications to act as arbiter.[3]

The original of the joint note, with a despatch to Wheaton, was committed to the care of Christopher Hughes, the chargé d'affaires of the United States at Stockholm, who, on the eve of his return to his post from a visit to the United States, was instructed to deviate from his direct course and proceed to Berlin for the purpose of handing them to Wheaton in person. A duplicate was forwarded by steam conveyance through England. On the receipt of either, Wheaton was to deliver the joint note to Baron de Werther and verbally to state to him whatever suggestions the former thought would insure the acceptance of their invitation by the King of Prussia.[4]

The despatch was received by Wheaton on May 19, 1839. He immediately called on Baron de Werther and gave him the joint note. He urged in conversation with the minister the various considerations which might induce the King to grant their request such as the interests of humanity, so deeply involved in the maintenance of tranquillity in that part of the world; of commerce, in which Prussia and her commercial allies in Germany had a deep stake in the exportation of their products to Mexico; and of the well-known character of the Prussian King as the patron of peace, to whose Government this contribution would be highly honorable.

Baron de Werther without officially committing himself in his reply promised to prepare his report for the King, after having given the subject that mature examination its importance demanded.[5]

Wheaton also called on Eichhorn, whose opinion in such matters had great weight. The only objection the latter made was a modest doubt if Prussia, a country which had fewer transatlantic relations than the great maritime powers of Europe, could readily find among her subjects a person possessing, together with the other qualifications which would be deemed essential, the requisite knowledge of the laws, customs, and business of that remote country where these disputes originated. From his own personal knowledge of the public men of Prussia Wheaton did not hesitate to assure Eichhorn that there should be no difficulty in selecting a person for the office of arbiter who would do honor to the King's choice and satisfy the expectations of the two republics. Eichhorn promised to give the business very prompt attention.[6]

A prompt answer was not given, and over a month later Wheaton wrote to Forsyth that in reply to his reiterated enquiries on the subject Baron de Werther had always said that they had not yet been able to choose a suitable candidate.[7] After continued effort on Wheaton's part and in fact at his suggestion, the King finally appointed Baron von Roenne as arbiter.[8] Wheaton reported confidentially to Forsyth that, finding another candidate had been proposed to the King for the office in opposition to Roenne, who had been named by Baron de Werther, Wheaton urged his strong conviction that the appointment of Roenne would be more likely to be satisfactory to our Government, to whom he was personally and advantageously known, than that of one who was a stranger to our language, laws, and manner of doing business. In answer to the question whether he was equally sure that the nomination of Roenne would be also satisfactory to the Mexican Government, Wheaton wrote to Forsyth, "I did not hesitate to answer in the affirmative. I have been since informed by Mr. Eichhorn that my assurances had contributed essentially to fix the King's final resolution, whose apparent hesitation probably proceeded from His Majesty's excessive anxiety to satisfy both parties in the choice he should make and, above all, not to lay under the possible imputation of partiality in naming his minister in the United States. This will also, in a great measure, account for the delay which has occurred in bringing this business to a close. I trust that no inconvenience will have occurred from this circumstance which I have done everything in my power to obviate." [9]

Concerning this mission a well-known journal, the *Baltimore American*, on November 7, 1839, stated that among the passengers in the *Great Western* was Baron von Roenne, minister from Prussia to the United States; that one of the duties especially entrusted to him had been mentioned in a recent English paper which had stated that Mr. Wheaton, the American minister at Berlin, had brought to a successful termination the negotiations which had been so long pending respecting the mediation between the United States and the Republic of Mexico; and that the King of Prussia had at last consented to name Roenne to decide as arbiter in case of any difference of opinion which might arise between the members of the mixed commission.[10]

The commission was not organized until August 17, 1840, and did not close its work until February 25, 1842. All the objects contemplated by the convention had not been fully accomplished even then, according to the commission itself.[11]

A troublesome question of proper procedure in connection with a claims case arose as a result of this arbitration. After the cases had been decided and the arbitration closed, a request was made in May 1843 by Secretary of State Webster through Wheaton, for copies of the decisions that had been presented by Roenne as umpire. The papers were asked for confidentially to be used only as useful precedents for the determination of future issues and as clear expositions of the duties of governments in parallel cases.[12] Prussia declined to furnish copies of these reports without the previous consent of Mexico.[13]

In November Secretary of State Abel P. Upshur, who succeeded Webster, instructed Wheaton to request the papers in the case of Aaron Leggett, a United States citizen, who claimed that the decision of the arbiter was based upon forged and false evidence.[14] Again the documents were refused, and it was stated the decision in the case had been made because the proofs presented by Leggett in support of his claim had appeared insufficient. As Prussia was desirous of giving to the United States every explanation which the latter could wish, Baron Gerolt who succeeded Roenne as Prussian Minister to the United States had been instructed that as soon as he arrived in Washington in December 1844, he was to read confidentially to the Secretary of State and also to the Minister of Mexico in the United States the reasons which formed the basis for the decision in the affair of Leggett at the time when it was made.[15]

In the meantime on March 6, 1844, Calhoun had become secretary of state. After a conference with Gerolt, who came to the meeting prepared to execute the instructions which had been given to him by his Government, Calhoun arrived at conclusions very different from those of Upshur. He frankly stated to Gerolt his belief that the whole proceeding had originated in error and misconception. He instructed Wheaton to state to Bülow that as the Government of the United States was entirely satisfied that Roenne had acted in this case, as in all others, "with that love of justice and integrity for which his character was eminently distinguished," it felt constrained, "by duty, as well as by delicacy," to decline the offer made by the Prussian Government. He further said, "The very supposition strikes at the root of all faith in the convention itself, and would, probably, be attended by the evil consequences of making all other claimants unduly dissatisfied with the decisions in their cases."[16]

In reply to these instructions Wheaton reported to Buchanan, who had taken Calhoun's place in the State Department, that Bülow manifested much satisfaction with this decision.[17]

Experiences of this kind render it easy to understand the sentiments expressed some time later by Wheaton to his uncle, "So of the diplomat, his duty is to defend the rights, interests, and honor of his country abroad, whoever may preside over its councils at home. This is a task often rendered sufficiently difficult in the midst of our divided and distracted councils." [18]

On Wheaton's return from his visit to Paris in April 1842, where the discussion of maritime affairs had been so continuously carried on, one of the first duties he had to perform in his diplomatic capacity was connected with the arrest, by the authorities of Hanover, of Captain Rains of the American ship *Maryland*. The captain was charged with harsh and cruel treatment of his crew, as a result of which some of them had become sick, and the cook, a Negro, had died while the vessel was in the River Weser. Wheaton requested that since no injury had been suffered by any subject of Hanover, nor the good order and peace of the country affected in any way, the accused might be delivered to the American consul at Bremen to be sent home to the United States for trial.[19]

In reply to his despatch reporting the affair, Webster wrote that since the event had been made public, the anxious intervention of some of the most respectable citizens of Maryland, and the strong testimonials borne by them to the high character of Captain Rains, had created a strong presumption that the charges were wholly unfounded. Webster approved the course Wheaton had taken and urged him to use every effort for the comfort of the prisoner.[20] The matter was amicably settled by an agreement that in return for the granting of Wheaton's request Hanover should receive the payment of the costs of the criminal proceedings to the time of extradition when the prisoner was to be sent to the United States for trial.[21]

Another case in which Wheaton's help was requested was the claim for indemnity which grew out of three prizes captured during the war of the American Revolution by the squadron under John Paul Jones and carried into a port of Norway, then under the government of Denmark, by which they were delivered up to England. The first demand had been made by Benjamin Franklin without resulting in a settlement, and the claim had been brought forward from time to time, in each case without result.[22]

In 1843 George L. Lowden of Charleston, South Carolina, the legal representative of the heirs of Commodore John Paul Jones, requested Wheaton to present to the State Department such observations as might occur to him upon considering the case [23]; William W. Irwin, the chargé d'affaires at Copenhagen, had been instructed, at the instance of the legal representatives of the claimants, to present the claim for the reconsideration of the Danish court.[24]

Complying with this request, Wheaton wrote a lengthy despatch to Upshur setting forth the principles of public law applicable to the claim in question, in so far as he understood them.[25] A copy of this despatch was sent to Irwin in Copenhagen by Upshur, who called his particular attention to it as entitled to great consideration.[26] Irwin, having been advised that the views of Wheaton had been invited by those interested, waited until he received that opinion before pressing the case, so that he might use the argument thus provided to aid him in advocating the claims.[27]

Wheaton also had occasion to consider a case presenting the question of how far a naturalized citizen of the United States, on his return to the country of his origin, could claim the interposition of the American legation to protect him against the performance of obligations imposed on him as a native subject by the sovereign whose allegiance he had renounced. Johann Philipp Knoche, a naturalized citizen of the United States, on his return to his native country, Prussia, had been required by that Government to perform military duty. To his application for protection Wheaton replied,

Had you remained in the United States or visited any other foreign country (except Prussia) on your lawful business, you would have been protected by the American authorities at home and abroad, in the enjoyment of all your rights and privileges as a naturalized citizen of the United States. But having returned to the country of your birth, your native domicile and national character revert (so long as you remain in the Prussian dominions), and you are bound in all respects to obey the laws, exactly as if you had never emigrated.[28]

Another matter of international interest which involved the commercial relations of the United States was included in the instructions received by Wheaton from the State Department. We have already noticed that during his mission to Denmark, from 1827 to 1835, he called the attention of that Government to the Sound duties with a view to the relief of American navigation. They were discussed by him in several despatches from Copenhagen.[29] He mentioned that great difficulty and inconvenience were experienced by American vessels from the West Indies bound to Russian, Swedish, and Prussian ports in the Baltic, in consequence of the quarantine to which they were subject on passing the Sound; but that as this quarantine was imposed under a compact between Denmark and the other Baltic powers, any general relaxation of its strictness must be looked for in suggestions to be made at the courts of Russia, Sweden, and Prussia. Letters concerning this matter had been interchanged between him and the minister of the United States at St. Petersburg.

Wheaton was informed by Forsyth that, concerning this subject, William Wilkins, who then represented the United States in Russia, would be instructed to correspond with him and with the chargé d'affaires at Stockholm, and to adopt such measures, in concert with them, as might be thought most effectual for procuring the repeal of a regulation which served only as an embarrassment to commerce without affording the least security as a sanitary measure.[30] After his arrival in Berlin, he took the matter up again on December 30, 1835.[31]

The supremacy asserted by the King of Denmark over the Sound and the two Belts which form the outlet of the Baltic Sea into the ocean was rested by the Danish public jurists upon immemorial prescription, sanctioned by a long succession of treaties with other powers.[32] Whether or not Denmark could justly claim the dues in the past was of little importance to the United States, as there was now no adequate reason why it should pay them.[33]

Wheaton recurred to the matter in February 1838.[34] Various circumstances then turned the attention of the commercial world with peculiar interest to the subject of the Danish Sound duties.

By an ordinance published in 1838, Denmark very considerably increased the transit duties on the overland communication between the cities of Hamburg and Lübeck. This new tariff appeared to have been intended to discourage the trade with the Baltic through this channel and to direct it to the Sound, by which act the incidental profits might be secured to the ports of Elsinore and Copenhagen. The Hanseatic towns protested, and a special convention was entered into between them and Denmark. But the agitation of the question had occasioned a more scrutinizing enquiry into the basis on which Denmark claimed to levy this tribute on the navigation and commerce of foreign nations.

For this reason Wheaton brought it to the attention of his Government in 1841.[35] Upon the long memoir on the history of the Sound dues which accompanied this despatch, Daniel Webster, then secretary of state, compiled the part of his report to the President dated May 24, 1841, relating to this subject.[36] This report called the attention of the President to the fact that even though we had comparatively little direct commerce with Denmark, yet we paid a yearly sum of about $100,000 in Sound dues. Besides this, we paid port dues even though we did not enter Danish ports except for the purpose of paying the Sound dues. It was further recommended that our minister to Denmark enter into communication with that Government to have this condition changed.

By the arrangements concluded at London and Elsinore in the same year between Denmark and Great Britain, the tariff of duties levied on the passage of the Sound and Belts was revised; the duties on non-enumerated articles were made specific; others were reduced in amount; while some of the abuses which had crept into the manner of levying the duties in general were corrected. The benefit of this arrangement, which was to subsist for the term of ten years, was extended to all other nations privileged by treaty.[37]

A year later Webster was notified of these revised schedules and regulations in the Sound which had been extended to American commerce by virtue of the most-favored-nation clause in the Convention of 1826. The Secretary of State expressed the satisfaction of the President with these measures, and nothing further was done at the time.[38] In 1843, as a result of his correspondence with Wheaton, Webster's successor, Upshur, advised President Tyler that our treaty with Denmark had extended beyond its original limitation, that we could discontinue it on one year's notice, and that the time had arrived when the United States might properly take some decisive step to relieve its Baltic trade from oppression. "Denmark cannot demand this toll upon any principle of natural or public law, nor upon any other ground than ancient usage, which finds no justification in the existing state of things. She renders no service for this exaction, and has not even the claim of power to enforce it." [39] This was the first official expression of the American contention that the dues had no foundation in law and that we should refuse to pay them.[40]

Calhoun, who succeeded Upshur as secretary of state on February 28, 1844, in requesting information from the Danish Government concerning the collection of the dues at that time, stated that Prussia regarded the dues as the chief obstruction to the direct trade between the German Customs Union and the United States.[41]

In the beginning of 1846 Wheaton wrote to Buchanan, then secretary of state:

The negotiations so long pending between the Prussian and Danish Cabinets respecting the Sound duties, frequently referred to in my former despatches, have at last terminated by an arrangement, in virtue of which the present Treaty of Commerce and Navigation between Prussia and Denmark is renewed, and the Sound duties on certain commodities destined to the Prussian ports in the Baltic, are to be reduced. Among other articles the duty on cotton is to be reduced about one third of its present amount. These reductions are to be extended to the trade of all nations called privileged, as having treaties with Denmark by which they are put on the footing of the most favored nations in respect to the payment of the Sound duties. This arrangement is to last until the year 1851, when the Conventions of 1841, between Great Britain, Sweden and Denmark, regulating the tariff of Sound duties, will expire, and the whole matter will necessarily become subject to revision between Denmark and all other Powers interested in the question.[42]

In 1848, when the matter again came into prominence, Buchanan stated "that there was no basis in international law for the right to levy the dues," and he quoted from Wheaton's work: "Even if such strait be bounded on both sides by the territory of the same sovereign, and is at the same time so narrow as to be commanded by cannon shot from both shores, the exclusive territorial jurisdiction of that sovereign over such strait is controlled by the right of other nations to communicate with the seas thus connected." [43] But Buchanan stated: "The Sound is not bounded on both its shores by Danish territory, nor has it been since the Treaty of Roskilde, in 1658, by which all the Danish provinces beyond the Sound were ceded to Sweden. So that even this pretext for levying the Sound dues has ceased to exist for nearly two centuries." This information he could have found in Wheaton's *International Law,* and also the additional information that the Treaty of Roskilde (1658, confirmed in 1660) stipulated that "Sweden should never lay claim to the Sound tolls in consequence of the cession." [44] He held that the foundations for the dues were laid in a remote and barbarous age even before the discovery of America and that the reasons for their support could have no application to the United States. "They apply exclusively to the nations of Europe." There had been, however, an implied recognition of them by the treaty of 1826 between the United States and Denmark.[45] Wheaton was quoted also by Marcy when the matter was again taken up in 1854.[46] So that throughout the entire discussion the information contained in Wheaton's writings and despatches was quoted and used freely.

The question was finally settled in 1857 when, after quotas of a redemption sum had been assigned to and accepted by the various powers, Denmark agreed to collect no more dues on American commerce, and assumed the obligation of continuing to keep the Sound lighted and buoyed on the Danish side as in the past and of making such additions and improvements in the lights, buoys, and pilot establishments "as circumstances and the increasing trade of the Baltic may require" without charge to American ships and cargoes.[47] Denmark had given up a practice of more than four hundred years, and the United States had added one more contribution to the freedom of the seas, in a large measure as the result of the statements of the case set forth in the writings of Henry Wheaton.

Chapter XXVII

THE TREATY WITH THE ZOLLVEREIN

AFTER Wheaton's return from Paris in April 1842, he was instructed to attend the congress of the Zollverein to be held at Stuttgart, the capital of Württemberg, during the following summer;[1] he arrived there early in July.[2] On the fifteenth he had the pleasure of an interview with William I, the King of Württemberg, who believed in the importance of cultivating commercial relations with the United States. On that occasion Wheaton also visited Munich and had several conferences with Baron de Gise, the Bavarian minister of foreign affairs, in relation to the commercial interests of Germany and of its intercourse with the United States. In the discussion at Stuttgart he found, as had been the case on the former occasion, that the deputies were unwilling to make any changes in the tariff unless accompanied by corresponding reductions in the United States on the productions and manufactures of Germany; and were insisting that the tariffs on tobacco were not higher than those of other countries; while cotton was admitted free of duty, and other American imports were admitted at a moderate rate. It had been early objected that the treaty of 1831 regarding French wines in the United States interfered with the consumption of those from Germany.[3] Concerning the latter Wheaton had been in correspondence with the State Department and at its request with the Government at Berlin.[4]

Since he was unable to give any assurances that the United States would grant the desired equivalents, Wheaton confined himself to a renewal of his protest against the tobacco duties.[5] For this purpose he addressed a note in French to Hartmann, minister of foreign affairs of Württemberg,[6] who brought the matter before the conference and sent a friendly answer.[7] After his return to Berlin Wheaton arranged for an appointment with Bülow, who was then the Prussian minister of foreign affairs, to discuss the negotiations further. In preparation for the interview he wrote to Bülow that he had been for some time in possession of a full power and the necessary instructions to negotiate a treaty of commerce and navigation between the United States and Zollverein, but that circumstances, especially the uncertainty of our own commercial policy growing out of the tariff question which had been so long agitated in the United States and could hardly be said even then to be definitely settled, had prevented his making any overture on that subject. He therefore thought it would be most expedient to reserve the question of a mutual reduction of tariffs to a more convenient season and to endeavor to agree upon the basis of a treaty of commerce and navigation independent of that question. He said further that during his late journey in the south of Germany, he had found a very general desire expressed for such action at Munich, Stuttgart, and Carlsruhe.[8]

A few days later Wheaton outlined for the State Department the terms which he thought would be the most practical and appropriate for a commercial treaty.[9] The embarrassments of making a treaty were increased by the provisions in the American tariff of 1842 which seriously augmented the duties on articles usually imported into the United States from Germany; retaliatory measures had been suggested. Regarding this, Wheaton wrote under the date of the sixteenth of November, 1842:

Baron Bülow has recently stated to me that the Prussian cabinet had been invited, by some of its allies in the Germanic Customs' Association, to concur in measures of retaliation against our tariff, which is much complained of as too fiscal, and even prohibitive, of many German commodities. He intimated that Prussia was not disposed, at present, at least, to take such a step, but would await the result of the deliberations of our Congress, at the ensuing session, to determine the course of policy which the association ought to pursue.[10]

Very little was done about the further negotiations for a treaty until the meeting of the congress of the Customs' Union at Berlin in September 1843.[11] During this session Bülow and Wheaton exchanged notes in which an understanding was reached that a convention could be made for the reduction of the duties on tobacco, and provide for equivalent reductions in the American tariff on German products and manufactures. These might be selected from articles which did not come into competition with the manufactures of the United States.[12] In transmitting these notes to the State Department Wheaton referred to former despatches in which he refuted the idea that any reduction of duties made for equivalent reductions by the Zollverein would accrue gratuitously to the benefit of those countries which had treaties with the United States, stipulating that those countries should be placed on the footing of "the most favored nation." At the same time he stated that there was no obligation on the part of the United States not to make the proposed reductions in duties applicable to imports from other countries as well as Germany.[13]

In connection with this arrangement Wheaton wrote privately to Upshur, then secretary of state, that in order to gain time with a view to the opening of the approaching session of the United States Congress, he had entered into a preliminary agreement with the Prussian Government for a negotiation on the basis of a mutual reduction of tariffs. If this plan met with the President's approbation, the negotiation could be begun as soon as he received instructions for that purpose. This would enable the President to announce in his message to Congress, should he think it expedient, that there was at least one European nation disposed to treat with us on such a basis; it seemed to Wheaton this could have only a favorable effect on the action of Great Britain and other foreign powers in respect to any commercial negotiations which our Government might open with them.[14]

Wheaton further said that though in point of form the preliminaries of the proposed convention appeared to have been adjusted on a proposition originating with him, yet in point of fact they were the result of compromise growing out of oral conferences, and he had seen their answer before his letter was delivered. Indeed the answer was in several respects altered at his suggestion before it was finally drawn up.[15]

The assent of Secretary of State Upshur was immediately given to the proposed course, and Wheaton was directed to proceed with the preliminary arrangements, "bearing always in mind," Upshur said, "that the sanction of Congress, as well as of the Executive, will be indispensably required, before we accomplish the object in contemplation." [16] Three weeks later he wrote to Wheaton that

It gives me pleasure to say that the President entirely approves of the preliminary steps which you have taken, as stated in your communication of the eleventh of October, to make the commercial arrangement with the German Customs' Union; and I now transmit, by his direction, a full power, authorizing you to proceed with the negotiations.[17]

To give further evidence of his approval and prepare the ground for the consideration of the treaty, President Tyler, in his annual message to Congress at the session of 1843–44, referred with satisfaction to those negotiations with the Zollverein, then embracing more than twenty German states and twenty-seven millions of people, and especially to the reduction of the duty on rice and to the strong disposition evinced to reduce the duty on tobacco.

This (he said) being the first intimation of a concession on this interesting subject, ever made by any European power, I cannot but regard it as well calculated to remove the only impediment, which has so far existed to the most liberal commercial intercourse between us and them. In this view our Minister at Berlin, who has heretofore industriously pursued the subject, has been instructed to enter on the negotiation of a commercial treaty, which, while it will open new advantages to the agricultural interests of the United States, and a freer and more expanded field for commercial operations, will affect injuriously no existing interests of the Union.

Accompanying this message was a report of the secretary of state. To this report were annexed the notes of Wheaton and Bülow giving the outline of the proposed arrangement. Upshur stated that the basis of a treaty had been agreed upon and submitted for the consideration and action of the Government; that the contemplated treaty would effect the long-cherished object of procuring the reduction of the duty on our tobacco, secure the continued admission of our cotton free of all duty, and prevent the imposition of any higher duty on rice. For these great advantages the conditional arrangement proposed that the United States should give the Customs' Union proper equivalents by reducing the heavy duties of the existing tariff upon silks, looking-glass plates, toys, linens, and such other articles as were not of the growth or manufacture of the United States.[18]

On the second of January, 1844, Wheaton was further instructed that the President wished him without loss of time to bring the negotiations to a conclusion on the basis of his interchange of notes with Bülow dated the ninth and tenth of October, 1843. As to the mode in which the arrangements were to be carried out, whether by agreement, convention, or treaty, "the President," Upshur wrote, "has such confidence in your judgment, that he leaves it to you to adopt that which, in your opinion, will be likely to effect the object, in a manner most acceptable to both countries; the earnest wish of the President being to place the commerce between the United States and Germany, as speedily as possible, on the most favorable footing for both countries."[19]

On the receipt of these instructions Wheaton immediately resumed the negotiations and strongly urged upon the Department of Foreign Affairs the importance of concluding the arrangement, if the terms could be agreed upon, in time for it to be laid in accordance with the desire of the President before Congress at the session then being held.[20] Concerning the mode in which the arrangements were to be carried out, Wheaton wrote to Upshur that he had become convinced that it would be most expedient to conclude the proposed arrangement with the Zollverein in the form of a convention or treaty to be submitted to the Senate for its advice and consent to the ratification, for he had some doubts whether such a contract with a foreign power could be constitutionally made by the President in any other form, unless indeed it had been previously authorized by a law or joint resolution of the two houses of Congress; [21] that the President might certainly have gone to Congress for this authority, but as he apparently had not thought proper to do so, Wheaton further said:

There are innumerable examples in our diplomatic history of the exercise of the treaty-making power of the President and Senate in respect to conventions of navigation and commerce affecting the existing legislation of Congress in respect to trade and revenue. No doubt has ever been suggested of the constitutional power of the Executive to make such treaties. The question has always been whether a treaty thus made, which the constitution declares to be "the supreme law of the land," binds Congress to pass the laws necessary to carry it into effect, as it binds the other Departments of the Government to execute it; or whether Congress has a discretion, as in the exercise of other legislative powers, to give or withhold its sanction to that which the public is already pledged to carry into effect. On either supposition it will be necessary that the proposed convention, if ratified, should be subsequently laid before the two Houses in order to enable Congress to conform its legislation to the stipulations of the treaty.[22]

In order for Prussia to conclude a convention for the Zollverein it was necessary to obtain the unanimous approval of its members. This required the expenditure of a great deal of time, effort, and diplomacy. Prior to the beginning of March the various states had filed their declarations concerning the proposed treaty with the Department of Foreign Affairs, and had stated their respective wishes for tariff changes on certain of their export articles. As a result of these declarations conferences were held until an agreement was reached.[23]

A treaty was then proposed which the Prussian Government thought was favorable to the interests of the Zollverein, the best they could secure under the circumstances, according to the statements made by them to Wheaton. The different states were notified by the Prussian Department of Foreign Affairs that the ratification would be more easily obtained if it were submitted to the United States Congress then in session, since the election for a new President would be held in the following November, and according to Wheaton's repeated opinion it was very doubtful whether the next Congress would be as much inclined towards concessions as the one then in session, which would end in May; that as the treaty must be sent at the latest on the twenty-sixth of March, the members of the Zollverein were requested to send in their respective replies as soon as possible.[24] After a correspondence with some few states concerning requests for the inclusion of specified articles among the enumerated products or a discussion of some mooted point, the various states one by one sent in their consent to the treaty.[25]

On the twenty-fifth of March, 1844, after eight years of almost continuous effort, Wheaton had the satisfaction of writing to the State Department that he had on that day concluded and signed a convention with the Germanic Association of Commerce and Customs in accordance with his instructions.[26]

"*C'était le premier grand acte de la nouvelle politique commerciale: on s'en réjouissait, on s'en félicitait hautement.*" [27] Thus did the member states of the Zollverein regard the treaty which they had unanimously consented to have signed by their representative, the Prussian minister. It received the approval of the President of the United States and its Secretary of State. Henry Wheaton also had the gratification of knowing that it was well regarded by others who were in a position to understand its significance. He received congratulations from many of his colleagues and friends.

Three days after the treaty had been signed Edward Everett cordially commended Wheaton on the success of his negotiations; [28] and William W. Irwin wrote to him from Copenhagen,

The conventional commercial arrangement made by you with the King of Prussia, on behalf of the Zollverein, has excited deep interest here as well as elsewhere throughout Europe. The achievement being truly regarded as among the most'important of modern times, may naturally be supposed to have aroused the jealousy of those Powers with whose interests it might seem to conflict;— a jealousy that would scarcely be diminished by the announcement in Mr. Upshur's able report of the probable accession to the union of Hanover and the smaller States of the north, by which an addition of more than three millions would be included in your beneficial arrangements.[29]

On the twenty-ninth of April, 1844, the President of the United States transmitted the treaty, accompanied by the appropriate documents, to the Senate, declaring in his message that he could not but anticipate from its ratification benefits to the great agricultural, commercial, and navigation interests of the United States.[30]

Chapter XXVIII

OPPOSITION TO THE TREATY

THAT the treaty would meet opposition in the United States was well recognized by Henry Wheaton. Over a month before its consummation he wrote to his uncle, Dr. Levi Wheaton:

I know well that the arrangement I have proposed with Germany, even if I should be able to carry it through here, will encounter great opposition at home. But I am firmly convinced that it would be of the highest advantage to our commercial and agricultural interests, without the least affecting the great branches of manufacturing industry protected by the existing tariff, and I cannot think it a wise policy on our part to attempt to force into existence manufactures of silk and linen at the expense of every other interest and of the general interest of the consumer.[1]

Six days later, on the twenty-eighth of February, Secretary of State Upshur met his tragic death in the explosion on board the *Princeton*. Thereby Wheaton lost one of his staunchest supporters. The tragedy caused concern in Germany; in writing to one of the Prussian officials, Bülow expressed the hope that the mishap would not interfere with their negotiations.[2]

It was also unfortunate that Roenne, who for ten years had been the Prussian representative in the United States and was cordially liked and respected by everyone, returned to Germany to become head of a new Department of Commerce just about the time the treaty was signed.[3]

Although Wheaton had serious doubts as to whether the treaty would be ratified, he made every effort to insure its success. Less than two weeks after its signature, Eichhorn informed Bülow that Wheaton had come to see him; that he had said he was requesting Marke to go to the United States immediately to urge the importance of the treaty, the ratification of which was by no means sure, as Wheaton himself even at that moment did not know who was at the head of the State Department. Eichhorn further stated it was an unfortunate coincidence that Prussia did not have any representative in Washington—somebody with the experience and knowledge of Roenne—and that Wheaton had said it was even then not too late to despatch a special agent to the United States because the cabinet did not need more than fourteen days to prepare the draft for the Senate.[4] Eichhorn was doubtful whether it would be wise to ask Roenne to go, since he had just returned from the United States.[5]

As will appear later, the lack of an experienced representative in Washington at this time was detrimental to the success of the treaty. That Baron von Roenne was also convinced of this is apparent, since he wrote on the same day to Eichhorn that even though he had so recently returned, he was ready to go to the United States at once, if it were desirable.[6]

The opposition to the treaty was destined to come from at least three sources: from the Hanse towns, from England, and from within the United States. This opposition may be considered in more detail.

The union of Hanover with the German states of the Zollverein, as suggested by Upshur and referred to by Irwin, had been regarded as sooner or later inevitable by Henry Wheaton ever since his arrival in Berlin. It was from this point of view that he had concluded his treaties, first with Hanover and then with the Zollverein. He had negotiated them from the perspective of a statesman rather than from that of a politician. In view of the later activities of the New York newspaper, the *Deutsche Schnellpost,* it is interesting to note an excerpt written by its Frankfort correspondent concerning Wheaton.

The writer thus expressed his high opinion of that gentleman:

If any one is competent to conduct the negotiations for a treaty, on the part of the United States, to a successful issue, Mr. Wheaton is that man. His extent of information, untiring activity, and uniform readiness to oblige, have secured for him the admiration and good will of all classes; while a manly earnestness and un-sullied purity of character have won for him such a degree of confidence, that his word is thought more worthy of reliance than another man's bond. This confidence so amply accorded to him by the representatives of the Zollverein, gives him peculiar facili-ties in respect of the proposed negotiations; and, therefore, it would be very unfortunate, if, as rumor alleges, he is to be re-called.[7]

The Hanse towns were not in accord with the provisions of Wheaton's negotiations. Their attitude regarding their commercial policy with relation both to the United States and the Zollverein was shown in a long article in the *Weser-Zeitung* published at Bremen on the twenty-third of Janu-ary, 1844.[8] Wheaton sent a concise analysis of this article to the State Department. It stressed the great importance of the Hanse towns as the factors, agents, and navigators by whose capital, credit, and industry so great a part of the commercial intercourse between the United States and Ger-many was carried on. It asserted that, if the exact proportion of the exports and imports between the harbors of the United States and those of Holland and Belgium, destined for the con-sumption of or consisting in the products of the Zollverein could be ascertained, the importance of the Hanse towns as an intermediate agency would be still more apparent. The industry and enterprise of Bremen especially, its favorable geographical position with the extreme liberality of its com-mercial system and the very moderate and almost nominal duties imposed by that town, as well as by the republic of Hamburg both upon importation and exportation entitled them to be favorably considered by the United States. The interests of the American planter, by whom the great staples were produced, and of the American consumer, by whom the wines and manufactured commodities of the German Zollverein were purchased, were both essentially promoted by the competition of Bremen's capital, credit, and shipping with those of the United States.

It was the belief of the Hanse towns that in this state of things a party had risen in the United States in opposition to the existing reciprocity treaties with the northern powers of Europe, seeking to revise those treaties as fast as they expired and to substitute other arrangements in their place by which the foreign shipping might be confined to the direct trade between the ports of the country to which they belonged and those of the United States. This new policy they claimed was first disclosed in Wheaton's treaty with Hanover of the twentieth of May, 1840; in John P. Kennedy's report to Congress of the twenty-eighth of May, 1842; and in Webster's "famous speech to his good friends the shipowners of Baltimore, in which the orator indulged his witty propensities at the expense of 'little' Bremen." It had been further developed in the official report of the secretary of state, in which it was recommended, in connection with the subject of Wheaton's current commercial negotiations with the Zollverein, that the existing treaties of navigation with Denmark, Sweden, the Hanse towns, Prussia, Austria, and Russia be simultaneously abolished.[9]

Not only Wheaton but also Dodge, who had been consul at Bremen, had written at length about the great harm that was being done to the American carrying trade through the advantages enjoyed by the shipping of Bremen.

It should be remembered that the Hanse towns had established commercial houses at the principal ports of entry throughout the United States such as Philadelphia, Baltimore, and New Orleans. Through these they could carry on an active campaign against measures in the United States with which they were not in accord. They were, therefore, in a position to offer effective opposition to the Zollverein treaty.

The opposition in England to the treaty also was made apparent even before it was signed. As early as the fifteenth of February, Edward Everett had written to Upshur in connection with the question of a reduction of the tobacco duty by England, that Lord Aberdeen manifested an interest in the negotiation now in progress between the United States and the Zollverein. Everett further said that should the negotiation come to a successful issue and the consequence be a decided effect upon the tobacco trade, it would, he thought, have an important influence on the counsels of the British Government, for the competition of Germany as a manufacturing country was regarded with a good deal of uneasiness in England.[10]

Three days after the treaty was signed Everett wrote to Wheaton that he would be rejoiced if the success of his labors with the Zollverein should pique the English Government to follow the example of Germany; that there was a growing disposition to take hold of the tobacco duty; and that the whole difficulty was in the extent of reduction which was deemed necessary in order to drive the smuggler out of the market. It was supposed that nothing less than a reduction from three shillings to one shilling per pound would have that effect, and this was deemed too bold an experiment. He requested Wheaton, if he had any copies made of the treaty, to let him have one.[11]

Two days later Everett recounted to the State Department a conversation he had had with Lord Aberdeen to the effect that Great Britain would claim the same privileges which the United States expected to grant to Germany by the terms of the treaty just concluded, and that England did not consider that the treaty of commerce of June 3, 1815, required it to give any equivalent. Lord Aberdeen further stated, "In concluding this convention unless you intend at the same time to put an end to that of 1815 between the United States and Great Britain, you violate this stipulation and do what you charge us with doing in reference to admission of rough rice free of duty from Africa.[12]

This controversy had arisen as the result of an act of Parliament of August 13, 1836, which reduced the duty on rough rice "imported from the west coast of Africa," making the ratio of the discrimination between rice of the United States and that of the West African coast of twenty shillings to one penny. This was claimed by the United States to be in violation of the second article of the convention of July 3, 1815. A great deal of correspondence was exchanged between the two Governments, and the Parliament of England by an act of July 9, 1842, again equalized the duty on all foreign rough rice. The United States claimed that a return of duties should be made by Great Britain.

Everett had been pressing these claims, and shortly after the signature of the Zollverein treaty Lord Aberdeen told him, in a conversation at his own house, that they intended to write to Pakenham, the British minister in Washington, remonstrating against the ratification of Wheaton's convention with the German Zollverein as inconsistent with the commercial convention between Great Britain and the United States. Everett felt there was undoubtedly some little embarrassment in the ground the United States would take on this subject in consequence of the strenuous manner in which—in reference to the duties levied on rough rice and exported woolens—it had maintained the principle that as soon as England, for any reason whatever, admitted an article from a third country at a given rate of duty or granted any privilege in exportation from England to any third country, the same relaxation would become *ipso facto* due to the United States in virtue of our convention. In maintaining on the part of the United States the right to conclude a treaty like Wheaton's, and in contesting this right on the part of England, or rather claiming without equivalent the benefit of its provisions, there was on the two sides an apparent, and on England's a real, change of ground, each verging toward the line of arguments hitherto pursued by the other. In our case the change of ground was rather apparent than real; but it would require some care in treating this subject to avoid coming in conflict with several of the measures Everett urged in reference to rough rice and the export duty on woolens.[13]

Over a month later Everett sent to Calhoun a copy of a memorial of the manufacturers of Manchester and its vicinity on the subject of the convention of the Zollverein. This pamphlet, which had been given to him by Mr. H. Ewbank, a partner in one of the houses principally interested in the importation into England of rough rice from the United States, invited the attention of the English Government to the convention recently negotiated by Wheaton.[14]

Everett understood that an unfavorable answer to his request for settlement of the claims of the United States had been prepared, when the news of Wheaton's convention had arrived. It had, therefore, been withheld. In a conversation with Lord Aberdeen on the subject of the claims Everett understood him to say that the further consideration of the rice question would be suspended for the present; that he considered the convention between the United States and the Zollverein to be precisely such a violation of the treaty between the two countries as had been erroneously charged to them in reference to the duties on rough rice, unless the United States were prepared unconditionally to admit British manufactures on the same duties as those on which it had agreed in the new convention to admit the manufactures of the states of the Zollverein; that if it did this, he owned he did not see how they could refuse the reimbursement of the discriminating duties that had been levied on rough rice. Everett wrote to Calhoun:

Lord Aberdeen did not appear to feel, in making this remark, that he indirectly admitted, what he had a moment before denied, for if, as he said, we erroneously charged them with violating the convention, in levying discriminating duties on rough rice, why should they be obliged to reimburse those duties, because we admit them (as they say we are bound to do) to the privileges of the treaty with the Zollverein, without receiving the equivalents on their part?[15]

On April 23, 1844, the matter of the Zollverein treaty was brought before the House of Commons by Dr. Bowring. In reply Sir Robert Peel stated that such a treaty had been signed by Prussia and the United States, but, according to the report in Hansard's *Parliamentary Debates,*

. . . he begged to say that the treaty had not yet been ratified. He believed that, in order to give it effect, it had yet to receive the sanction of the executive government of the United States and of two-thirds of the Senate. . . . As it had not yet been ratified, perhaps it would be better for him not to enter into details, but to content himself with stating, that the matter had not escaped attention. There was a treaty in existence between this country [England] and the United States, by which it was stipulated that England should, in matters of trade, be put upon the same footing as the most favored nation. As the honorable gentlemen were probably aware, there were two kinds of commercial treaties. Under one class of treaties it was agreed by one nation that another should be put on the footing of the most favored nation, without any equivalent being given; and by another description of treaties it was provided, that a country should be placed on the footing of the most favored nations, provided she made certain concessions. It was a treaty of the former kind which existed between this country and the United States.[16]

On April twenty-fifth Everett wrote to John Nelson, secretary of state *ad interim,* conveying the substance of this debate in Parliament.[17] On May first he again wrote verifying the attitude of the English Government and stating that Lord Aberdeen had said that the reduction in reference to cotton and rice might be entertained, but no such reduction as that contemplated on tobacco could be thought of. He had reiterated their right to any reductions which the United States might grant to Germany. At the same time Everett suggested the possibility of the reduction on both cotton and tobacco, in view of the statement made concerning the prosperous condition of the British treasury.[18]

In this connection it should be remembered that by the treaty concluded between Great Britain and the Zollverein in 1841, reciprocity was extended only to the importation of sugar and rice, and did not extend to the import trade generally. Therefore, even if it had been desirable, England could not claim from Germany the privileges which Germany contemplated extending to the United States.[19] Their only recourse was to press their claim against the United States.

Everett had been assured that Westmoreland, the British minister at Berlin, and Pakenham, the British minister in Washington, had already received instructions to start urgent reclamations following the opinions expressed by Sir Robert Peel in Parliament about the consequences of the treaty. When the Prussian representative in London had submitted the article of the *Allgemeine Preussische Zeitung* No. 127, which had been written by a London correspondent, to Everett, the latter had said that Bowring was supposed to be its author, but he (Everett) did not think he was, for Bowring, being a partisan of free trade, was rather positive than otherwise toward the Prussian treaty.[20]

Everett informed Wheaton that Pakenham had been furnished with powers to negotiate with the United States on the subject of tobacco. This circumstance, Everett felt, with Calhoun's ability and zeal and the example of what Wheaton had done at Berlin, constituted a state of things very favorable to an attempt at Washington to revise the commercial relations between Great Britain and the United States. He further said, "If anything should ever be taken up and treated according to its own merits, without disturbing electioneering influence, I should think the moment auspicious." [21]

Everett had previously written to Wheaton that he had had two or three conferences with Lord Aberdeen on the subject of his treaty, and that he thought the English would have no objection to entering into the same stipulations in reference to everything but tobacco.[22]

On the twenty-eighth of May Everett noted in his journal that at half-past three he had had an interview with Lord Aberdeen, the immediate object of which was the duty on tobacco.

He [Aberdeen] said they [England] were clear in the opinion that our new treaty with the Zollverein was inconsistent with the treaty with them. He did not suppose, however, that it could lead to any difficulty since either party could renounce the latter on a year's notice. I told him that we must if we confirmed the treaty take the chance of their doing this and even if they did they would not probably resort to any measures of retaliation which he admitted they could not do without injuring themselves.[23]

On the twenty-ninth of May, Pakenham wrote to Lord Aberdeen:

Previously to the receipt of your Lordship's Despatch No. 17 of the 3rd of this month, I had communicated confidentially with certain members of the Senate upon the subject of the Treaty lately concluded between this country and Prussia as the Head of the German Customs Union, and from the first it was easy to perceive that there was little probability that that Treaty would be ratified.

Further enquiries since the receipt of your Lordship's Despatch have confirmed this impression and I think that I may now venture to assure your Lordship that the treaty will be opposed in the Senate by a number more than sufficient to insure its rejection.

There are several reasons, my Lord, why this should be the case—the first and perhaps the strongest is the spirit of opposition prevailing in the Senate to the Administration of Mr. President Tyler.

The second is the feeling in favor of the protective system which is that of at least one half of the present members of the Senate, and a third reason will be found in the indisposition to concede to England, without an equivalent, what in good faith could scarcely be denied to us, supposing the present Treaty to be ratified, namely, the admission, at an equally low rate of duty of British articles of the same description as those which it is proposed by that Treaty to favor, in consideration of a corresponding reduction in the duties on certain articles of American produce in the Territories included in the German Commercial Union.

Certainly if this object could be accomplished as a permanent arrangement, it would be highly to our advantage that the

Treaty with Prussia should be ratified—but I am convinced my Lord, that with this Country such a result could not rationally be expected.

Supposing the Treaty with Prussia to be ratified, our right to a parity of treatment, by virtue of the 2d Article of the Convention of 1815, might, I dare say, be acknowledged, although it would always be reluctantly and with a bad grace.[24]

Let us turn to the attitude in the United States. The treaty with the Zollverein—transmitted to the Senate accompanied by the appropriate documents on the twenty-ninth of April [25] —was referred to the Committee on Foreign Relations.[26] Notice of the treaty was immediately taken by the periodicals of the day. Among others the *Boston Daily Advertiser,* the *Providence Daily Journal,* and Niles' *Weekly Register* had printed excerpts from foreign newspapers before the arrival of the treaty.[27] The accounts of the treaty were indefinite and in many cases misstatements of fact.

After the treaty had been transmitted to the senate, Niles' *Register* noted:

The treaty which has been recently concluded by Mr. Wheaton, between the Zollverein of Germany and the United States, has not escaped the notice of the British press. The admission of American tobacco into Germany, at a lower duty, to be followed by the admission of the manufactures of Germany into the United States, on favorable terms, is not calculated to prove very palatable to England. As a counteracting measure, it is already talked of, to make a considerable reduction in the duties on American tobacco imported into England, and a similar proposition is talked of in France. "Neither government, however," says the *Times* of the 19th, "would be wise to act hastily, for the high protectionists in this country may defeat the treaty on account of the favorable stipulations it contains in favor of German manufactures." [28]

On the twentieth the *Boston Daily Advertiser* published the entire discussion in the British Parliament as reported by the *London Morning Herald,* which called attention to the doubt entertained by Sir Robert Peel of the ratification of the treaty by the United States Senate.[29]

This same article in the *Morning Herald* was sent by the Prussian representative in London to the Department of Foreign Affairs in Berlin on May second, stating that it represented the opinions of the English Government.[30]

Germany was soon aware of the opposition with which the treaty was meeting. On the last day of May the Prussian representative in London reported to the Department of Foreign Affairs in Berlin that he had been talking the day before with the American ambassador about the news which had come with the last boat from New York, and especially about that concerning the treaty. Everett regretted that there was little hope for its ratification by the Senate, since both political parties were nearly equal in number; that the Government's bill for a new tariff schedule had been defeated with the narrow majority of 105 to 95; and also that the old schedule then valid had been passed with the majority of five votes. It was, therefore, very doubtful that a two-thirds majority could be obtained for the treaty. Everett mentioned also that the British Government was continuing to pay the utmost attention to the treaty and that Lord Aberdeen repeatedly remarked that the United States, through its former treaties with England, was bound to grant it the same privileges as promised to the states of the Zollverein. From another reliable source he heard that Everett had said in this connection, especially relating to the proposed tobacco duties, that if Britain wished to get the same privileges as the Zollverein, it would have to lower its tariff on this article to the level of the Zollverein's grants.[31]

Chapter XXIX

THE TREATY FAILS OF
RATIFICATION

THE treaty, which had been referred by the Senate to its Committee on Foreign Relations, was reported back without amendment on the thirtieth of May.[1] This committee of five members consisted of Archer of Virginia, Berrien of Georgia, Buchanan of Pennsylvania, Tallmadge of New York, and Choate of Massachusetts. On motion of the chairman the treaty was recommitted to the same committee on the first of June. It was returned to the Senate by Choate on the fourteenth, accompanied by a written report against advising its ratification and consenting to it.[2] The next day it was ordered to lie on the table. This was only two days preceding the adjournment of the Senate.[3]

The lack of time for discussion and due deliberation at so late a period of the session was, Calhoun believed, no doubt the motive for laying it on the table, but as the treaty provided that the ratifications should be exchanged at Berlin within four months from its signature, this action was equivalent to a rejection unless the time stipulated for the exchange of ratifications should be prolonged.

In notifying Wheaton of the action of the Senate, Calhoun stated that he felt a final rejection of the treaty would be unfortune, "and no effort on our part should be wanting to prevent it." [4]

The report of the Committee on Foreign Affairs set forth two objections to its ratification; the need of "constitutional competency" to make it, and the "unequal value of the stipulated equivalents," but relied mainly on the former to support the conclusions to which it came, stating it was "upon

247

that single ground" that it advised the treaty should be rejected.[5] In support of its contention of the unconstitutionality of the treaty it held that it was "an innovation on the ancient and uniform practice of the government to change duties laid by law," that "the Constitution in express terms, delegates the power of Congress to regulate commerce and to impose duties and no other, and that the control of trade and the function of taxing belongs without abridgment or participation to Congress and that, therefore, the treaty was unconstitutional and should be rejected." [6]

Calhoun felt that the reasons given by the Senate committee were inadequate and could be refuted on every point, and in writing to Wheaton took them up one at a time with explanations to show their fallacy. He further instructed Wheaton that the President, after due deliberation, could not believe the objections were such as were calculated to present any insuperable or formidable obstacles to the adoption of the treaty, and could not but hope that if the period for the exchange of ratifications should be extended to afford sufficient time for discussion and decision on its merits, that the Senate would take favorable action. He therefore instructed Wheaton to use his best endeavors to have the period so extended as to allow sufficient time for the exchange of ratifications, should the Senate advise and consent to it, during the next session of Congress, which would terminate on the fourth of March, 1845; ". . . unless, indeed," he instructed further, "you should find, as before observed, a decided disinclination on the part of Prussia and the other Zollverein States. In that case, you will not, from motives of delicacy, insist on the extension. Should there be no such disinclination manifested, it is left entirely to your discretion to decide what steps should be taken in order to effect the object." [7]

Concerning the request for an extension of time, Calhoun wrote in a private letter to Wheaton under the same date that if there should be a decided disinclination on the part of Prussia and the other Zollverein states to the extension, which he feared might be the case, it struck him that it would be very indelicate on our part to press it, and that it would, if it should be rejected, be doubly mortifying to us and still more offensive to Prussia and the other states of the league, should we press the extension against their inclination.[8]

In his private letter, after expressing regret for the loss of the treaty on account of the advantages it promised to both parties—advantages which he feared might be lost—and after expressing mortification on account of the effects it might have on the standing of the Government abroad, Calhoun also gave what he believed were the real reasons for the action of the Senate:

The true cause in both cases [the Texas and Zollverein treaties] I believe to be, the bearing which it was feared it would have on the Presidential election. Mr. Clay's friends, who are a decided majority in the Senate, felt confident of his election, under the old issue, as it stood when Congress met; and were adverse to admit any new question to enter the issue. The attempt to prevent it has been in vain; and will prove unwise, even in a party point of view. The Texas question has entered deeply into the issue, and I have no doubt that questions growing out of the Zollverein treaty will also. Nor would I be surprised, if he should be beaten, in consequence of the part which his friends in the Senate have acted, as weak, personally, as the candidate opposed to him is comparatively.

I cannot but hope that the treaty would be sanctioned by the Senate, should the time be prolonged to the next season, when the Presidential election will be over, and the party motives that have led to laying the treaty on the table, shall have passed away. I am strengthened in this opinion from the very inconclusive reasons assigned by the Committee on Foreign Relations for its rejection, and which I feel confident the Senate will never sanction, whatever may be the fate of the treaty.[9]

In acknowledging the receipt of this communication, Wheaton stated to Calhoun that should the convention be ultimately ratified, he anticipated Hanover and other European countries would come forward to negotiate with the United States on the same basis. The Hanoverian chargé d'affaires at Berlin had expressed to Wheaton the desire of Hanover to negotiate with the United States for the admission on the most favorable footing of its tobacco and other agricultural productions into the kingdom. In return for these concessions Hanover would only require a reduction of the duties then levied by the United States on the article of linens, that being the chief article of manufacture exported to it. In reply to this overture, Wheaton merely stated that he would communicate it to the State Department but could not expect to receive any specific instructions upon the subject until the fate of the convention with the Zollverein states was determined by the Senate.

Besides this overture Wheaton was approached by Engelhardt, who was employed by France in the commercial negotiations between that country and the Zollverein. Engelhardt had informed him that he would advise Guizot to open a negotiation with the United States on a similar basis the moment the convention of the twenty-fifth of March was ratified. As the opinion of Engelhardt was known to have great weight with his Government in all commercial questions, Wheaton had no doubt it would be followed in this instance.[10]

"With characteristic shrewdness," it has been commented, "Andrew Jackson, ill at his home in Tennessee, but keenly observing the game of politics, seized on the rejection of the Zollverein treaty as a good campaign issue. He invited Polk's attention to the benefits which the treaty would have secured. 'This conduct of our Senators,' he wrote, 'ought to be kept before the people and this, too, because Great Britain complained of it and would have had to reduce her tariff on those articles or lost this trade. *There never was such treachery to the laborer of the South and West as the rejection of this Treaty!*' "[11]

The same sentiment was expressed in an address of the Democratic Association, published in Washington, which examined in detail the objections stated by the Senate Committee, explaining at length their fallacy, and then showing the connection between the action of the Whig Senate, the pending election, and the rejection of the treaty. It held that the election of Clay would defeat all hope of the adoption of "the tobacco or any similar treaty" in any form whatever, and that "a blind devotion to Mr. Clay, and the ultra tariff policy, and especially to the pledge to preserve unchanged all the duties of the tariff of 1842—preferring, in this case, a mere handful of manufacturers of lace, cologne, etc., to millions of farmers and planters" was responsible for its rejection.[12]

Differences of opinion concerning the rejection of the treaty immediately began to appear in the press throughout the country. *The Madisonian* of Washington published long articles almost daily in favor of the treaty and protesting against the action taken by the Senate. *The National Intelligencer* took exactly the opposite stand. A controversy ensued between the two papers concerning the rejection of the treaty. *Niles' Register* sided with the *Intelligencer*. The *Boston Daily Advertiser* also was opposed to it, as were the *New York Republic* and the *Daily Plebeian;* but the *Richmond Enquirer* was strongly in favor of the treaty, and so were the *Baltimore Sun*, the *Washington Spectator,* and the *St. Louis Evening Gazette.*[13]

The Nashville Union stated that, in further discussion of this subject, it would show that the states of Maryland, Virginia, North Carolina, South Carolina, Georgia, Louisiana, Alabama, Mississippi, Arkansas, Kentucky, Ohio, Missouri, Indiana, Illinois, Michigan, the territories of Florida, Wisconsin, and Iowa, and the state of Tennessee all had a direct and immediate interest in the subject, and that that interest had been shamelessly disregarded by the Whigs of the Senate of the United States; the Whigs by a dead party vote had postponed or rejected the treaty.[14]

Perhaps the paper that had the most active influence and produced the most effective results was the *Deutsche Schnellpost* of New York. A more detailed narrative of its activities will be given later.

The discussions of the treaty by the press were hampered by the fact that the Senate withheld the treaty from publication and refused to make a detailed statement of its provisions, except in so far as they could be gleaned from the reports made upon the treaty by the Committee on Foreign Relations in secret session. These reports were afterwards published.[15]

The submission of the treaty for ratification in Germany was not such a simple matter as turning it over to one body of senators. Just as it had been necessary to send around to the various governments of the states of the Zollverein to obtain their consent to the treaty which had been signed for them by Bülow, the Prussian minister of foreign affairs, so it was necessary to submit it again to each one for ratification.

Nineteen different ratifications had to be secured. These began to be returned as early as April thirtieth when the ratifications from the duchies of Saxony, Schwarzburg, and Reuss were returned.[16] The treaty was ratified by the King of Prussia at Potsdam on May 10, 1844.[17] The next day, since Prussia anticipated its acceptance by the United States, directions concerning the practical handling of the pending treaty stipulations, especially in connection with the tobacco imports, were sent from Berlin to all the Prussian representatives in other German states of the Zollverein.[18] The *Frankfurter Zeitung,* among others of the German press, was in favor of ratification.[19] The official ratifications of the treaty from the various states came in steadily,[20] but on July first the Prussian representative at Darmstadt wrote to the Department of Foreign Affairs that "as it is generally known here, that the treaty was not ratified in this session of the United States Senate, Hesse will not send the official ratification before fall, but assures it then."[21]

After Wheaton had become acquainted with the opposition with which the convention was meeting, he wrote to his uncle:

Before this reaches you the fate of my treaty will have been decided. But whatever may be its doom, I shall never repudiate my share of responsibility for a measure intended, and as I am convinced on the maturest reflection, well adapted to promote the commercial and agricultural interests of the country, without the slightest degree affecting those manufacturing interests meant to be protected by the existing tariff. I can understand the policy of protecting those branches of industry which already exist, and which might perish for want of that protection, but I confess my want of power to comprehend the wisdom of forcing into existence new branches, for which the country has no peculiar aptitude, at the expense of the agricultural and commercial interests and of the general interests of the great body of consumers including the manufacturers themselves. Whatever may be thought of the work on your side of the water, I can assure you it is considered in Europe in a very favorable point of view by competent judges, although John Bull growls his dissatisfaction at discriminating duties, upon the same ground, I suppose, that the Fox exclaimed "sour grapes." [22]

Chapter XXX

THE FINAL FATE OF THE TREATY

On July 26 Wheaton formally notified Bülow of the rejection of the treaty and the reasons which the Senate gave for its decision.[1]

Prussia immediately took action. On the first of August the Department of Foreign Affairs wrote to all the Prussian representatives in the Zollverein notifying them of Wheaton's communciation and stating that it was suggested by him, in the name of his Government, to ask the particular Governments of the Zollverein to extend the time for the treaty ratification, for the United States Congress might in the fall have more time to discuss the treaty and then ratify it. The Department thought it doubtful whether a favorable action would be taken, as the five members of the Committee on Foreign Relations of the United States Senate had opposed it.[2] The Department further stated that it did not think it advisable to extend the time fixed for exchange of ratification notes; it would be against the interest and prestige of the Zollverein should the United States Congress again refuse ratification. It suggested that the different states send a note of regret with the statement that the Zollverein would be ready at any time to enter into similar negotiations under similar circumstances and conditions.[3]

The returns from the states began to come in at once, and they all agreed to consent to Prussia's proposal.[4] An exception was taken by Saxony-Altenburg, which expressed regrets that Wheaton's suggestion of time extension had been rejected, for it certainly set forth the wish of the President of the United States, who, in the Senate Committee, had met with the significant reproach for consummating the treaty— "entreprise trop ambitieuse." [5] Saxony-Altenburg felt that the rejection of Wheaton's proposal seemed to be dangerous for the interests of the Zollverein, since it removed the opportunity for Tyler to try anew for the treaty ratification, and that another occasion on which the United States would approach the German states for a commercial treaty was very unlikely. It wished, therefore, to express the readiness of the Zollverein to uphold the treaty unchanged and conclude it at any time if the United States was ready to do the same.[6] Most of the replies were received by the seventeenth of September.

Taking advantage of the interim between the middle of September and the next session of Congress in December, because it would apparently be a good time for him to be away from his post, Wheaton had gone to Paris to visit his family.[7] Later, however, it became clear that his absence at this time was unfortunate. On the eighteenth of September Theodore S. Fay, chargé d'affaires *ad interim*, during Wheaton's absence wrote to Secretary of State Calhoun that Bülow had just informed him that the time for ratification of the convention of the twenty-fifth of March with the Zollverein would not be prolonged; that Bülow had said all the replies of the states so far received tended the same way, but he had further expressed the assurance that the Zollverein would always be ready to treat with the United States in their mutual interests. This was a verbal message and not a formal notification to the Government. Fay further wrote, "It is plain that Baron von Bülow himself, as well as the States of the Customs' Association, regards our refusal immediately to ratify the Convention, as a slight, and is unwilling to subject himself to the possibility of another one."[8] This sentiment was exactly what Calhoun had anticipated when writing to Wheaton, advising him not to press too strenuously for an extension of time. There is no way of knowing conclusively if Fay had seen Calhoun's private letter to Wheaton, but the action he took during the latter's absence entirely ignored it.

On October third Fay wrote again. After he had communicated the intention of the Prussian Government, acting on behalf of the other states of the Zollverein, not to prolong the time for the exchange of the ratifications, he had conceived the idea that, if the convention were ratified by the United States, the mere fact of the expiration of the very short period named for that purpose need not in reality operate against the conclusion of a mutually advantageous arrangement desired by both parties.[9]

For this reason he made several unsuccessful attempts to see Bülow who was continually engaged in conferences or with the King. Fay, thereupon, drove to Bülow's summer residence, his chateau at Tegel about two hours from Berlin. Here, after some conversation it was agreed that Fay should advise the ratification of the convention by the United States in the hope that an arrangement of such importance would not be laid aside from a consideration of mere form. Bülow stated that without a further consultation with Eichhorn and Michaelis he was not in a position to say whether or not the negative answer of the states of the Customs' Association should be withheld or delayed, but that he would avoid consulting them and did not doubt the ratification would be accepted if it arrived during the winter. He pointed out to Fay that he was acting not only for Prussia; that Saxony, Bavaria, and the other states, if he delayed communicating their refusal to the application for longer time, might say to him, "You are deciding, yourself, a question which you profess to have left to us;" and that there was even a great deal of embarrassment in the least delay on his part to make such a communication. Nevertheless, he knew there were ninety-nine chances out of a hundred of his being able to carry it through were the ratification really in Berlin, and although he could not decide without his colleagues, yet in case of its subsequent arrival he could explain to and reason with them.

Fay further said:

You may judge how far he [Bülow] was serious by his begging me to call your attention to the fact that he had signed the convention without being aware that any other nation was entitled, by existing treaties, to the gratuitous enjoyment of the equivalents granted in it to the states of the Zollverein [10]—and he several times repeated the wish that this point, which had been already too much discussed in the newspapers, might be urged upon your particular consideration.[11]

Whether or not an official reply will now be returned to Mr. Wheaton's late application for time, I have no authority to say, but Baron Bülow went so far as to state that a long delay was to him a delicate matter, and to intimate that a speedy action on the part of our government would relieve him from a certain perplexity.

In all I stated I scrupulously avoided committing either the President or yourself, more than you were already committed by the mere application for a longer time, and I wish, on the other hand, with equal care, to keep before you the unofficial character of my conversation with Baron Bülow, although it has convinced me that no real obstacle exists, here, to the successful termination of the negotiation. The suggestion that I should advise you according to my own judgment I follow with diffidence, but without doubt.[12]

On October twenty-first Fay further wrote that his mediation had been successful and that the convention then stood exactly as it would have stood had it not yet been submitted to the Senate or had the time for the exchange of the ratifications been prolonged by the Zollverein states. Eichhorn had just informed him that in consequence of his conversation with Bülow, the two of them had determined to withhold the negative answer, then on the point of being returned. This course was equivalent to an affirmative, at the same time saving the *amour propre* of the states of the Zollverein and leaving the future plans of the United States Government as to the convention perfectly unobstructed.

He subjoined a copy and translation of a confidential private letter addressed to Bülow, at the latter's suggestion, in which it appeared that Fay had personally assumed the responsibility of his interposition in case the convention should be ultimately rejected.[13] On the original of the letter from Fay to Bülow, which was written in French, appears the following notation in German: "In regard to the contents of this letter, Wheaton's note of July 26 shall not be answered for the present." [14]

So through Fay's endeavors a written refusal for an extension was not given, and Prussia and the German states were ready to have the treaty again brought up for ratification. In the light of later events there is no doubt that it would have been better for all concerned if Fay had not been so active. Wheaton certainly would not have left Berlin if he had felt it was advisable to press urgently for an extension of time.

Another incident also took place in his absence which was unfortunate for him. This occurred in connection with two conventions for the abolition of the *droit d'aubaine* and taxes on emigration, which conventions he had successfully negotiated between the United States and the grand duchy of Hesse and the King of Württemberg respectively, the first on the twenty-sixth of March and the other on the tenth of April. These had been approved and ratified by the President, by and with the advice and consent of the Senate.[15] The part of this transaction which is of interest at this place is that Theophilus Fisk, one of the editors of *The Madisonian*, had been selected as the bearer of the ratified copies of the conventions and of the despatches relating thereto which were to be handed to Wheaton. Special powers authorizing the exchange of ratifications were also sent, and Fisk was to bring back to the United States the copies to be received in exchange.[16] *The Madisonian*, as has been noted, had published long articles vigorously defending Wheaton's treaty with the Zollverein and urging the desirability of its confirmation. Fisk, therefore, naturally was disappointed on his arrival in finding that Wheaton was not in Berlin. He was in accord with Fay's effort to have the time extended by the German states. These circumstances must be remembered when reading the letter which, written by Fisk, was ultimately published in *The Madisonian* a month after the new administration under Polk had been inaugurated.

I found on my arrival at Berlin that the action of the United States Senate, in relation to the Zollverein Treaty, had occasioned serious dissatisfaction and mortification to those most directly concerned in its ratification. They regarded the Treaty so highly important, so vastly beneficial to the United States in all its details, that the delay on the part of the Senate to fulfill its provisions seemed to them a sort of intentional slight—an indirect offense. So seriously were they aggrieved, so deeply were their feelings wounded by this unwise procrastination on our part, that they had come to the positive determination not to prolong the time (which had already expired) for the ratification of the treaty; and but for the remarkable tact and unwearied exertions of our excellent Chargé d'Affaires, Theodore S. Fay, Esq., the whole matter would have been at an end. His immense popularity with the King's Ministers, his commanding talents and indomitable perseverance, were all brought into requisition, and his efforts in prolonging the time were finally successful. Too much credit cannot be bestowed upon this highly accomplished and talented diplomatist, for his unflagging zeal in accomplishing that, which in any other hands, would have been a fruitless undertaking.

I had no opportunity of seeing our Minister, Mr. Wheaton, during my protracted stay in Berlin. His family residing in France, he is necessarily absent a considerable portion of the time. His place is, however, well supplied in his absence by Mr. Fay, who exercises the happiest influence at that polite court—few of the foreign ambassadors are so cordially welcomed, or possess such a commanding influence there as himself. His highly accomplished lady is a universal favorite; Mrs. Wheaton and her daughters living in Paris, the duty of entertaining devolves upon Mr. and Mrs. Fay—and most enviably are the honors of their station performed. Whatever changes it may be thought necessary to make among our diplomatic agents abroad, I most earnestly and confidently hope that Mr. Fay may be permitted to retain his present position. Its duties could not be more satisfactorily performed than they are at present.[17]

After he had become cognizant of this communication, Wheaton informed Buchanan that soon after Fay's arrival in Berlin he had begun to manifest symptoms of insubordination, and a controversy arose about the nature and extent of his official duties. This incident was finally terminated by a written apology from Fay to Wheaton. The latter further said:

I most freely forgave and forgot the past, but was frequently admonished by others that both he and his wife did not manifest the same candour and kindness towards me and my family. I let all this pass as unworthy my notice, until I learnt that Mr. Fisk, on his return home last autumn had made representations as if I were neglecting my public duties in happening to be absent when he arrived here as bearer of Despatches, and until I saw the paragraph in the *Madisonian* of April last signed with the initial F.

These representations, oral and printed, which Mr. Fisk thought himself authorized to make to my disadvantage, could only have originated from information given to him by Mr. Fay and his wife, as Mr. Fisk was a stranger to this Country, its language, and its society; and had he seen any other well-informed persons here, he would have carried home a very different impression of the respective positions of the members of this Legation.

I therefore entirely acquit him of any intention to do me an injury, nor do I wish to have any personal controversy with him or Mr. Fay. I leave the whole matter entirely to your determination, which I am sure will be made with a single eye to the interests of the public service. I have no wish to do Mr. Fay or any other human being, an injury. But my own opinion is that every foreign Minister ought to be consulted in the selection of his Secretary, as it is only in this mode that the proper degree of confidence on the one side, and subordination on the other, can be maintained.[18]

As a result of Fay's successful efforts to secure an extention of time for the ratification of the treaty, the instructions transmitted to the new representative of Prussia in the United States, Baron Gerolt, urged him to devote all his attention to securing the ratification of the treaty. He was given the whole history of the negotiations, with the final objection of the Senate's Committee on Foreign Relations to ratify the treaty. He was informed that Wheaton, in the name and by the order of his Government, proposed that the time should be extended, since the Committee's report had been submitted to the Senate two days before its adjournment and had never been discussed. The members of the Zollverein had expressed their regrets, according to Prussia's formula. But, when they were ready to send such an answer, the American chargé d'affaires had confidentially insisted that they should not send this answer for the present. He had stated that Calhoun was convinced that the Senate Committee at a closer examination of the motives expressed on June fourteenth would change its opinion, and that he would then submit the treaty at once to the Senate and obtain its ratification. For that reason the Zollverein desisted from sending its answer at that time.

Gerolt was told also that it was important that the treaty should soon be brought before the Senate. He was then to insist upon the stipulation that England should not get, without corresponding equivalents, the privileges granted to the Zollverein. Reference was made to the treaties between the United States and England, and the differences in opinion relating thereto were given in detail. It was further stated that during the negotiations Prussia had made the proposition that the Prusso-American treaty of June 1, 1828, which could be withdrawn within a year's notice, should be extended for the same time as the new one and also should include all the members of the Zollverein. But the American representative, Henry Wheaton, declared he did not have proper instructions to do that. In order not to hamper negotiations, the German Government dropped it. "But now," Gerolt was further instructed, "as there is no reason for hurry, we must absolutely try for the extension of the 1828 treaty in regard to time and to all Zollverein members." [19]

In his message to Congress in December President Tyler referred to the Zollverein treaty, regretting that an extension of time for the exchange of ratifications had not been granted.[20] The President must have made this statement in order to avoid, if possible, further public agitation against the treaty, for he sent a secret message to the Senate urging it to reconsider the treaty and act favorably upon it. This was made known to the Prussian Government by Gerolt.[21]

After Gerolt's arrival in the United States in December, he reported to the Department of Foreign Affairs in Prussia that he had presented his credentials to the President, and Calhoun, who had been present, had said the United States Government had had confidential news from Prussia that no objection would be raised if the Senate were to ratify the treaty then even though its time limit had expired, and that he hoped the Senate after closer examination would approve it. On the twenty-seventh of December Gerolt called on Calhoun to ask him what steps the Government had taken to secure the ratification of the treaty. Calhoun told him that the President had already sent a secret message to the Senate strongly recommending it, but he (Calhoun) feared that the opposition of the majority of Whigs for party reasons would obstruct governmental action. He assured Gerolt that the questions raised in the Committee of Foreign Relations as to the authority of the Senate were inessential and also that, if the treaty were ratified, there would be no fear that Congress might invalidate it by other provisions; the United States was unlikely to grant the privileges extended to the Zollverein to England or France without proper reciprocity. He further stated that in the present session of the Senate only the northern states in the United States might raise any opposition to the tariff changes.[22] Gerolt asked Calhoun to recommend also the extension of the 1828 treaty to all members of the Zollverein, since the new treaty seemed very remote.

By this time Fay began to perceive that in his endeavors to save the convention he had undertaken a difficult and delicate task. In a long conversation with Bülow he was informed that circumstances had somewhat changed, that several "important voices" had been raised against the treaty, that some of the states of the Zollverein began to think "the terms not good enough," and that the embarrassment of his position was increasing. Fay called Bülow's attention to the fact that he had given no positive promises on the part of the United States and had made none of an unqualified nature for

Prussia, yet upon the strength of his several interviews with Bülow and Eichhorn he certainly had advised on the part of the United States the measures necessary to carry the convention into effect. Bülow replied that Fay had "done quite right," but that he had since found all was not as smooth as he had then thought. Fay asked if he meant to say the treaty would not be ratified by the Zollverein. Bülow replied that he did not consider the result certain, but only more doubtful. To Fay's enquiry if the claim of England were the principal objection, he said it was one objection, but not the only one.[23]

Gerolt had several interviews with Calhoun and influential members of the Senate concerning the treaty. He tried to show them the great advantages to be derived from commerce between the United States and the Zollverein—that, concessions being granted on German products which competed with those of England and France, the United States would be able to secure for her products privileges which England and France, having their own colonies, could not grant them. He at all times emphasized the fact that both the Zollverein and the United States should break the English monopoly. The fear was expressed from American quarters that Prussia and the rest of the Zollverein might not ratify the treaty after its ratification by the United States. Gerolt reassured them that the Zollverein would ratify it if the grants to the Zollverein were not impaired, and in case all the American tariff was lowered, the Zollverein would get a proportional reduction.[24]

Gerolt reported to the Department of Foreign Affairs that Senator Archer, chairman of the Foreign Relations Committee of the Senate, and several other Whig senators seemed less opposed to the treaty than before. He felt that much depended upon the reception by the Senate of the house bill for the incorporation of Texas. If this bill got through, it would prove that the Whig majority, who were strongly opposing it, were faltering before the Democratic rule. He also expressed the belief that the ratification of the treaty would be more likely in the present session of Congress, though there was strong opposition to any changes which might affect the tariff question. He reported that the influence of foreign embassies, and especially of the English, was not inactive in Congress.

Calhoun advised him to desist for the present from the proposition to extend the 1828 treaty to all members of the Zollverein, since the Senate had again asked the Government for information concerning the results of all reciprocity treaties on American navigation, and a strong party in the Senate wished their cancellation. Calhoun, however, promised to introduce the desired proposition before the end of the session. Gerolt agreed to this. The future Democratic majority would then be more inclined to ratify the treaty. The presidency of Tyler was drawing near its end, for at the November elections James K. Polk had been chosen to succeed him. Whether or not Calhoun would remain in office was doubtful.[25]

Gerolt sent a memoir to Calhoun concerning the advantages of the proposed treaty. As the former came to the conclusion that most of the senators objected to the treaty, not from a constitutional standpoint, but because of the general opinion that the United States did not get privileges in it equivalent to those granted to the Zollverein, he carried the discussion onto the ground of higher politics and succeeded in interesting Senator Archer favorably for the treaty. Moreover, he reported to the Department of Foreign Affairs that Archer had assured him that he would recommend the treaty strongly and bring it to the attention of the committee before the end of the session of Congress. Calhoun told Gerolt that all minds were for the present occupied with the Texas and Oregon questions; that he might even withdraw the treaty from the present Senate, since if the Whig majority refused its ratification, this action would have a very bad effect on the Zollverein; that he would then submit it to the new Senate, which would have a majority friendly to the Government. He would talk over the possibility of such action with

President Tyler and some of his friends in the Senate. Gerolt informed the Department of Foreign Affairs that he had succeeded so far in keeping all these negotiations from the foreign embassies, which with few exceptions were unfriendly toward it, and he had kept it also from the newspapers.[26]

The next day Archer reported against the ratification of the treaty. The reasons given in the previous report were quoted. It was admitted that the treaty, viewed simply as a commercial measure, was a desirable step in advance. Nevertheless, the report ended by recommending, as the previous one had done, that the convention lie on the table of the Senate.[27] This motion prevailed, and the treaty received no further discussion. The press notices of this action were to the effect that the Zollverein treaty had undergone some discussion during the extra session which had just closed, but that it was deemed to involve a question of such vital importance as to require far more deliberation than the Senate could be expected to bestow upon it in the brief space of a session retained for urgent business. It was therefore laid over until Congress should meet again.[28]

The fact that the treaty was again under discussion became known, and Gerolt reported to his Government that all the foreign ambassadors, and especially Pakenham, the English minister, had asked him whether Prussia had extended the time limit for the ratification of the treaty. He did not give a definite answer to any of them. He further reported that there were three English consuls in Washington and that everything was being tried to prevent the ratification of the treaty. By this time he had nearly lost all hope, since Calhoun had told him that Archer had said the committee would not expressly recommend the treaty, but only submit to the Senate its advantages and disadvantages for the United States. Calhoun complained to Gerolt about this behavior of Archer, who, he explained, was a great friend of Pakenham and had probably been intimidated by him, although three weeks ago he had expressed himself in favor of the treaty. Gerolt's opinion was that the defeat Archer and other Whigs had suffered had embittered him against all the propositions coming from Tyler and Calhoun.[29]

Two weeks later he reported that the session of the Senate had closed without definite action on the treaty, and that Caleb Cushing, who had just returned from China, was very much in favor of the idea of a coalition of the Zollverein and the United States to break the English monopoly. Early in February Gerolt had given Calhoun a memoir setting forth the existing relations between the United States and the Zollverein in detail and showing the advantages the former would receive from the treaty. He now reported that the "well known representative," C. J. Ingersoll, had obtained this memoir from Calhoun and had used it in his speech on the diplomatic appropriation bill. The memoir also was given by Cushing to Webster, who used it in his speech in New York on March twenty-fourth. In a conversation with Gerolt, Cushing expressed himself in favor of the former's mercantile opinions, although he was supposed to be a representative of high tariff partisans.

Gerolt also called the attention of Calhoun and Archer to the treaty just concluded between Belgium and the Zollverein, showing its advantages for the direct trade between the Zollverein and the United States through Antwerp.[30] From several of the senators who were in favor of the treaty he got the assurance that nothing stood in the way of its ratification except the objection raised by the Whigs that the President and the Senate had no authority to change entirely or partially the existing tariff, and that this would incur considerable conflict with the House. They seemed to approve in general the grants to the Zollverein but thought that the concurrence of both houses was necessary. Gerolt brought clearly before the Prussian Foreign Office the fact that all this was apparently only party tactics, a fact which had been proved by the ratification of Cushing's treaty with China. This treaty, which contained a complete tariff for both countries, was ratified at the very session the Zollverein treaty was under discussion.[31] The ratification was advised by the Senate on January 16, 1845, and ratified by the President the following day.[32]

Calhoun, who remained in office for several days under the new President, hoped for a favorable result, in spite of the unlikelihood that a two-thirds majority could be secured. After his resignation, when Buchanan became secretary of state, the complexion of affairs changed entirely. Buchanan told Gerolt in a conference on the eighth of March that President Polk was very much in favor of the treaty, but as the necessary majority would not be obtainable, he would advise the present chairman of the Foreign Relations Committee, Allen, to find out during the discussion the exact number of treaty partisans in the Senate, and if it would not suffice, not to bring it to a vote. The treaty had made an effective campaign weapon for Polk, and he naturally would be in favor of it, but a new element for consideration was presented by Gerolt who reported that Buchanan previously had been senator from Pennsylvania and a member of the Committee of Foreign Relations, was naturally a "tariff man" and, until he had assumed the office of secretary of state, had opposed the treaty. In spite of this Gerolt felt the treaty, which had "the mishap to be proposed by President Tyler, so passionately hated by Whigs," might yet succeed in the next Congress to be held in December when the Democrats hoped to secure a two-thirds majority through the new senators from Florida, Iowa, and Texas.[33]

During the session of Congress just closed, Gerolt had hoped for the success of the treaty for two reasons: All its opponents, busy with the question of Texas and Oregon, had no idea that it was being discussed again, since President Tyler in his address had declared that the Prussian Government had refused the extension of the ratification time; therefore Gerolt could work quietly. The second reason was the general feeling against England during the whole session of Congress.

Gerolt further reported that it was doubtful how the treaty would fare in the next Congress in spite of sympathy for it, because other powers, especially England, would exert all their influence to destroy the principle of differential tariffs for manufactured products of the Zollverein, even at the cost of great sacrifices.[34]

As a result of this report the Department of Foreign Affairs sent instructions to all the Prussian representatives in the Zollverein, telling them that Wheaton had proposed to extend the time limit for the exchange of ratifications to March 4, 1845; that the time had expired without any action by the Government of the United States and that it was, therefore, inadvisable to extend longer the period for ratification.[35]

On the same day Bülow sent an official note to Wheaton informing him that the states of the Zollverein, while regretting sincerely that the treaty could not be carried into effect, "would always be disposed, on the request of the United States, and under like circumstances, to sign another treaty adapted to preserve and extend the respective interests in question; but that, under the present conjunction they could not consent to a prolongation of the term fixed for the exchange of ratifications." It was further stated that

. . . the States of the Association, profoundly convinced that the relations between them and the United States of America, combine all the elements for the conclusion of a commercial arrangement satisfactory to both parties, will assuredly not fail, so soon as new propositions shall be made to them, on the part of the government of the United States, to give further proofs of their eagerness to contribute, as much as possible, to the realizing of so useful a project.[36]

The Department of Foreign Affairs also notified Gerolt of the answer sent to Wheaton and instructed him that under existing conditions it was not advisable for the Zollverein to take any steps to reopen negotiations; that it was quite probable the new President would introduce tariff modifications, which would also benefit the Zollverein equally with other nations; that his proposal of slightly preferential tariffs on American imports would hardly be advisable, as the German producers were at that time asking for higher import duties; that he ought to show the growing importance of the Zollverein for the American trade; and that he should express the readiness on the part of the Zollverein for a reciprocal commercial understanding, but the United States would have to address itself to the Prussian Government.[37]

On May seventh Wheaton sent copies of his correspondence with Bülow to Buchanan and informed him that,

. . . though the Zollverein is not disposed further to prolong the time for the ratification of that treaty, the German States composing the Association are perfectly ready to enter into a negotiation for a new commercial arrangement, on a similar basis, as soon as they shall receive propositions from us for that purpose. It is, therefore, desired by the Prussian Cabinet that I should be furnished, as soon as possible, with the President's instructions on this subject, should he deem it expedient to enter into the proposed negotiations. Should that be the case, and should he think fit to confide the business to my care, I have no doubt of being able to conclude, before the next session of Congress, such an arrangement as will prove satisfactory to both countries.[38]

This was to be accomplished by means of an interchange of official notes in which the President should engage to recommend to Congress the passage of a law or joint resolution by which the arrangement might be carried into effect, in return for a promise on the part of the Zollverein states to adapt their legislation to its stipulations.

According to Gerolt, Buchanan had been rather reticent on the question of the treaty. The former wrote to the Department of Foreign Affairs that, after he had received a copy of Prussia's note to Wheaton declining the time extension but expressing readiness to enter a new treaty negotiation, Gerolt had asked Buchanan if it was intended to recommend a commercial treaty with the Zollverein in the next session of Congress. Buchanan then said that he thought not, at least not until the tariff question and the new commercial policy were settled. Buchanan, Gerolt explained, was in favor of the present tariff, and it was improbable that he would take any steps toward a commercial treaty with the Zollverein in the spirit of the treaty of March twenty-fifth, and that "this passive behavior of the present Government in relation to the treaty has changed the whole situation." [39]

Buchanan, it will be remembered, was one of the members of the Committee on Foreign Relations when the treaty was first submitted by the President to the Senate. He was a Democrat, a member of the party which was solidly supporting the measure, and at the same time he was personally opposed to the treaty. When a vote was taken on the proposal to lay the treaty on the table, Buchanan was in a dilemma. He apparently avoided the issue by not casting a ballot; his name is not among those who voted.

Gerolt believed that Buchanan's constituents and neighbors influenced his attitude. Although originally from Franklin County and of Scotch-Irish descent, Buchanan had established his home in Lancaster, a section in which a large percentage of the population were Germans. Some of the newspapers opposed to the treaty made a strong appeal to the Germans throughout the country. The following two excerpts are examples. One cited from *Niles' Register* made the plea:

Let all the German born citizens of the United States, without any respect to any other question whatever, and to whatever party they may belong, exert their influence to convince the government of the United States of the danger in concluding a commercial treaty with Prussia or the Zollverein, on conditions which may force the Hanse Towns and the states bordering on the sea, to bow to the despotism of Prussia, a government in principle hostile to America.[40]

The other excerpt appeared in the *Deutsche Schnellpost*, the editors of which were Eichthal and Bernhard:

All the German citizens in the United States ought to use their influence, that no treaty with the Zollverein be ratified by the Senate, which would not contain the provision, that all German states, which do not belong to the Zollverein, can participate in these privileges as long as their tariffs do not exceed those of the

Zollverein and that the Hanseatic cities would always remain free harbors, where American boats can come freely. That is in the interest of all the Germans, because Prussia would hamper all freedom of emigration, if she gets hold of the Hanseatic cities as members of the Zollverein.[41]

The *Deutsche Schnellpost* not only continuously published long and vigorous articles against the treaty but succeeded in having its articles republished in various papers throughout the country. Gerolt had reported that it was a demagogic paper, revolutionary and opposed fiercely to Prussia in general and her policies in Germany in particular, and that it was strongly attacking the treaty. He added that it was possible that the Hanseatic cities had their hands in this, as they were trying to make the treaty unpopular.[42]

The activities of the Hanseatic cities had been so widely noticed that the *Weser-Zeitung* felt the necessity of publishing an article defending them from the general reproach of having intrigued against the ratification of the treaty by the United States Senate. It emphasized the strong feeling in Germany against these cities, which never tried to interfere with the Zollverein. The article then had recourse to the excuse that the latter did not have at this important moment a proper and influential representative in Washington, such as Prussia's last one (Roenne) whom they (the Hanseatic cities) would have supported in his efforts. It further declared, "To create still more animosity the Hanseatic cities were publicly threatened that the ratification of Wheaton's treaty (as it is generally called) would be followed by the withdrawal of navigation reciprocity-treaties between the United States and the Hanseatic cities." [43]

Wheaton's opinion of this phase of the opposition to his treaty was expressed in a letter to Buchanan.

I have recently noticed in the *German* newspapers published in the U. States several articles against the proposed Treaty with the *Zollverein*. Among these I have been particularly struck with a letter purporting to be dated at Frankfort on the 27 May, which first appeared in the *Deutsche Schnellpost* at New York, and was afterwards transferred to the *Courier* and *Enquirer,* representing the proposed Treaty as both intended and adapted to injure the Hanse towns, and to compel them to enter the *Verein* against their inclination and their interests, and thus to subserve the supposed designs of the King of Prussia against the freedom and independence of these little republics.

Nothing can be more unfounded than this view of the matter. I am the last man in the world who would do anything that might possibly contribute to injure the Hanse towns, for whose citizens I have the highest esteem, and with whose principal statesmen I am on a footing of the most intimate friendship and in constant correspondence. Nor do I believe that these shallow misrepresentations proceed from them. I should think the Hanse towns might be satisfied with the *leonine* share of benefit their shipping derives from our existing Treaty with them, without seeking to prevent our making such arrangements with the *Zollverein* as may secure to our agricultural states a market of 27 millions of consumers, without doing the Hanse towns any injury whatever.

The idea of our refusing the benefits thus proffered to us by the *Zollverein* because the same benefits are already extended to us gratuitously by the Hanse towns, Oldenburg and Mecklenburg, will not bear a moment's examination when the comparative extent and value of the two markets are considered. Unless it can be shown that there is some danger of these small States increasing their existing duties on our tobacco and rice, there can be no reason of policy for extending to them the same concessions we make to the great German *Zollverein* in return for reductions on these articles— And even if this could be shown or if equity might seem to require it, this would only furnish a reason for extending similar concessions to these States by separate arrangements with each of them. How, I ask, are they to be combined in the same treaty of Commerce and Navigation with the *Zollverein* States, whilst they continue perfectly independent of the *Verein* and some of them (e. g. Hanover and Oldenburg) are involved in a separate league with each other?—How can the German Zollverein be made to stipulate for the Hanse Towns, or for the Hanover-Oldenburg league, and vice versa how can the latter be made to stipulate for the former?

These crude notions proceed from the political refugees whose views are always more or less distorted and discoloured by passion and prejudice. They are very unsafe guides to be followed by Statesmen in questions where our national interests alone ought to be considered, without regard to the feelings of men who may have very good reasons for considering themselves as persecuted by the Prussian Government in return. But if we once involve ourselves in the labyrinth of German party politics we shall soon lose sight of our own true national policy in pursuit of phantoms which exist only in the imagination of those by whom they are conjured up.[44]

Senator Duckwitz of Bremen, who in 1846 accompanied A. Dudley Mann on his mission to secure a new treaty with Hanover, laid the responsibility of the refusal to ratify the treaty on the Hanse towns. He asserted that the commercial establishments of the Hanseatic cities in the United States had strongly remonstrated against it in Washington and had started a campaign in the press which had caused the rejection of the treaty by Congress.[45]

Henry Wheaton always considered that great injustice was done him in the taking off of the injunction of secrecy from the proceedings of the Senate, in so far as respected the report of the Committee of Foreign Relations upon the Zollverein treaty, while the injunction was continued as to his despatches of March tenth and twenty-fifth, 1844, accompanying the treaty, which would have anticipated and met, with more or less conclusiveness, the arguments urged by the committee against the ratification.[46]

But the treaty was of value to the United States in an unexpected way, for it was instrumental in helping to secure the settlement of the long pending controversy between the United States and England over the importation of rough rice. When an unfavorable reply was about to be sent to the overtures of Everett, Lord Aberdeen, on learning that the Zollverein treaty had been signed, suppressed his note.[47] After the failure to obtain ratification had been assured, Aberdeen stated to Everett that the rejection of the Zollverein treaty and reimbursement of duties on Portuguese

wines had strengthened the argument of the United States.[48]
The attitude assumed by the English Government against
the Zollverein treaty had really determined that the only
course England could pursue was to pay the claims.

In writing to Calhoun in December of 1845, Wheaton said,

The Zollverein States are not disposed at present, to revive the
negotiation on the basis of the former Treaty, as they expect to
obtain in the revision of our Tariff by Congress, reductions in
favor of their manufactures, without conceding any equivalent reductions in favor of our agricultural staples; and should this be
the result of the deliberations of Congress, it will be seen that a
golden opportunity has been lost, in not obtaining such equivalents for reduction, which we shall have been compelled to make
gratuitously in order to get rid of an exaggerated Tariff.[49]

So the treaty, by a curious combination of forces—the
activity of the Hanse towns, both on the Continent and in
the United States; the absence of a Prussian representative in
Washington at this time; the opposition of England and
other powers; and the conflicting political and mercantile
interests within the United States—was successfully opposed,
and the benefits to be derived from eight years of unceasing
effort were lost, to be followed by a policy of commercial
expediency rather than one which looked forward to ultimate
ends.

Chapter XXXI

TREATIES WITH THE SEPARATE GERMAN STATES

SEVERAL years before the events related in these preceding chapters, Wheaton in accordance with the instructions received from the State Department on April 20, 1835, had made overtures to the diplomatic agents of Bavaria, Saxony, Hesse-Cassel, and Baden respecting stipulations for the abolishment of the *droit d'aubaine* and *droit de détraction*. Ruedorffer, the American consul at Munich, had informed the State Department at Washington that in compliance with the request of a Mr. Ebner of Pennsylvania, he had claimed in behalf of that gentleman the estate of his sister who had died at Munich, but he was compelled before he could obtain it for the purpose of remittance to pay to the police a tax of ten per cent upon the amount because the party interested was a foreigner, resident in the United States. The Consul suggested that there probably would be no difficulty in making a contract with the Government of Bavaria by which such deduction in the future would be abolished. This object the State Department thought could probably be effected most conveniently by Wheaton, in respect not only to Bavaria but also to the other German states, all of which it was presumed had representatives at Berlin through whom the business might be transacted.[1]

Wheaton was to say that there was no law of the United States which placed any obstruction in the way of the disposal to foreigners, or the withdrawal from that country, of the personal estate of any one dying within its jurisdiction. He was to ascertain whether a repeal of the Bavarian regulation and any similar regulations of the other states named above might not be obtained without a formal agreement between the respective countries, and if not, whether or not they would enter into such an agreement. He was also to find out if he could conclude with those states any other arrangement which would afford increased security or accommodation to American citizens in respect to their persons or property in those countries, or which would promote the commercial interests of the United States.[2]

The overtures made by Wheaton were favorably received, and by the middle of December he notified the State Department that the various governments involved were ready to open direct negotiations with him as soon as he was furnished a full power and instructions for that purpose.[3]

A full power was sent for the removal of all obstructions to emigration from the one country to the other, or to the withdrawal from either country by the citizens or subjects of the other of any property which might have been transferred to them by gift, contract, or will, or which they might have inherited; for affording increased security or accommodation in regard to person or property to the citizens or subjects of the one country trading, traveling, or residing in the other; and for securing to each party the right to have consuls resident in the dominions of the other, and establishing the rights and privileges to which they should be entitled.[4]

Wheaton thereupon proceeded with the negotiations and in July 1836 sent to the State Department the project of such a convention.[5] In August, however, he received instructions which informed him that the Senate had just refused its consent to the ratification of a similar treaty concluded in March of 1835 between the United States and Switzerland.[6]

President Jackson, whose term of office had now almost reached its close, had no objection to the conclusion of a treaty for the removal of the restrictions imposed upon the transfer of property from the one country to the other, but he did not wish to authorize an arrangement which, under the circumstances, he had reason to presume the Senate would not ratify. It was not certainly known then upon what grounds that body had withheld its assent to the convention concluded with Switzerland, of which a copy was sent to Wheaton. It had been supposed that the rejection was based on the fact that the treaty was confined to the single point of the withdrawal of property. The secretary of state assured Wheaton that endeavors would be made to ascertain the real reasons for their refusal and if it should be thought expedient to pursue the negotiations which he had commenced, he would be instructed accordingly. In the meantime, his proceedings were to remain suspended in regard to all the subjects upon which it was proposed or intended to treat.[7]

It was not until seven years later, in November of 1843, that Wheaton was authorized by Upshur to renew his efforts to obtain the abolition of the *droit d'aubaine* and *droit de détraction*.[8] A provision covering this matter, similar to the provision contained in article 14 of the treaty of 1828 with Prussia, had been included in article 7 of the treaty with Hanover in 1840. In March of the same year Count Minkewitz, the Saxon minister in Berlin, had approached Wheaton concerning an arrangement for abolishing the *droit d'aubaine* and *droit de détraction* between the United States and Saxony. He had also requested Wheaton to write to the State Department to know whether the same objections still existed.[9] The German states were interested in having the matter adjusted. In reply to a despatch from Wheaton in June 1843, requesting instructions and full powers to conclude conventions from this purpose with Saxony, Bavaria, Württemberg, and Hesse [10] Upshur empowered him to proceed with the negotiations.

On March 26, 1844, the day following the signing of the Zollverein treaty, a convention was concluded by Wheaton with the Grand Duchy of Hesse,[11] and two weeks later, on April 10, one was signed with the Kingdom of Württemberg.[12] The stipulations incorporated in these conventions were principally taken from the treaties then existing with Prussia, Austria, the Hanse towns, and Hanover. The necessity for concluding such arrangements with the different

German states had been fully explained to Congress in Upshur's report of the twenty-fourth of November, 1843.[13]

In an effort to conclude a similar convention with Baden, Wheaton was informed that, since certain of its subjects had vested rights in the taxes on emigrants, Baden declined to enter into a treaty for that purpose. Before such an arrangement could be made with any foreign power these taxes would have to be regulated by municipal legislation.[14]

A convention was concluded by Wheaton with Bavaria on January 21, 1845.[15] In article 3 "real and personal property" was included. The other conventions had referred only to personal property. Ratification of the treaty was refused by the United States Senate until the words "real and" were stricken out.[16] The desired change was made, but due to a misapprehension on Buchanan's part the exchange of ratifications was delayed. This was finally concluded in August 1846.[17]

On May 14, 1845, a convention was concluded with Saxony. This differed in one particular from the others in giving a little more power to the subjects of Saxony as to purchasing and holding funds in the United States in return for the abolition of the taxes on emigrants by which the last named country gained in the amount of capital brought over by the emigrants.[18]

Wheaton believed that the advantages accruing under these arrangements with the different German states were more than equivalent to the concessions made by the United States in respect to the power of taking and holding lands in a limited manner. The tax imposed on the funds removed by emigrants who left Germany amounted in Saxony and most of the other German states to ten per cent on the capital thus transferred. This amount was clear gain in the capital thus brought into America by the rich peasants and others who sold their real property in Germany prior to emigration.[19]

Two other similar conventions were concluded by Wheaton in 1846, one with Hesse-Cassel [20] on May 2, and one with Nassau on May 27.[21] All the treaties were ratified except the one with Hesse-Cassel, the ratification of which was withheld by the Senate for unassigned reasons.[22]

The same thing happened in another phase of international relations which became the subject of negotiation between Wheaton and Prussia and several other German states. This was a convention for the extradition of fugitives from justice, and Prussia had the regrettable experience of meeting again unfavorable action in the United States. Four succeeding secretaries of state were involved in these negotiations. The original instructions were issued by Webster, who enclosed his correspondence with Roenne which had resulted in an agreement for such a convention. If this proved acceptable to Prussia and the other states mentioned, Wheaton was instructed to sign it.[23] Bülow stipulated that the conventions should contain two conditions.[24] Wheaton explained to Calhoun, who had become Secretary, that these conditions provided that, if the accused was a subject of the sovereign of the country wherein he had sought refuge after having committed a criminal offense in the country of the other sovereign, he should not be delivered up, but the sovereign whose subject he was should cause justice to be promptly and strictly administered against him according to the laws of the country. But if any individual had been arrested in the country where he had committed a criminal offense or any misconduct, the sovereign of the country where the arrest took place should cause justice to be administered against him and the punishment he incurred to be inflicted upon him, even if such individual be a subject of the other sovereign.[25]

Calhoun replied by authorizing Wheaton to meet the views of Prussia.[26] The provisions were incorporated in the convention, and it was signed on January 29, 1845.[27] As it was substantially the same arrangement that had been made in Webster's treaty with Lord Ashburton, Wheaton did not anticipate that it would encounter any difficulty in being ratified.[28]

But before this treaty was received in the United States,

Polk had become President; and Buchanan, Secretary of State. When submitting the treaty to the Senate, Polk called attention to the provisions outlined in the preceding paragraph, and recommended that the treaty be amended so that each country would have to surrender its own citizens.[29] The Senate had insisted on this provision in several other extradition treaties, but in this case unanimously agreed to the treaty without making any changes. For this reason apparently Polk refused to ratify the treaty, even though the conditions had been proposed because of the difference between the systems of criminal jurisdiction which prevailed in Europe and in the United States. Yet a treaty with exactly the same provisions was concluded in 1852 between Gerolt, the Prussian minister to the United States, and Webster.

PART FIVE
AN INTERNATIONALIST

Chapter XXXII

INTERNATIONAL INTERESTS

WHEATON's despatches covered, besides the questions which fell strictly within his own diplomatic sphere, many other matters of interest to his Government. He dealt at length with the contemporary relations between all the European countries. He included in his survey not only diplomatic and commercial matters, but also, when they were pertinent, the religious and cultural questions of the day.

Among the affairs of international import which he discussed were the future relations of Europe and America with the Orient. The importance of the treaty of 1842 between Great Britain and China and the probable effect it would have on the commercial and political relations of China with other nations did not escape his notice. His first communications on the subject were sent to the National Institute of Washington in the form of two papers on the geography of Central Asia. His attention had been attracted by the investigations undertaken in Germany to determine the possibilities of intercourse with the Celestial Empire. Shortly after Cushing had left the United States for China, Prussia, in the interests of the Zollverein states, was planning to send a mission of its own to that country.[1]

The survey made in Germany also included the relations of China with the rest of Europe and with America. Wheaton had access to the results of this investigation and to a great deal of other material that was not available in the United States. In a despatch of August 30, 1843, he enclosed a long memoir which gave a comprehensive history of the military and diplomatic activities of other nations in China; the results to be gained from the treaty between Great Britain and that country; and the measures being adopted in Europe to secure the trade of the Orient.[2] In November, Upshur wrote to Wheaton that he had directed this paper to be copied and forwarded to Cushing.[3]

The opening of the Chinese ports to the commerce of the world directed attention to the shortest routes by which they could be reached. Just as statesmen in Europe had given consideration to the restoration of the ancient route between Europe and the East Indies by Egypt and the Red Sea, so scholars and men of affairs investigated the possibility of opening a new route from the United States by way of the Isthmus of Panama. Wheaton studied the material available in Germany, especially the most recent publications of his friend Alexander von Humboldt, with whom he had many consultations. He prepared for the National Institute several papers—two, on the "Panama Canal," one, on the "Ancient Canal across the Isthmus of Suez"; and one on "Impending Revolutions in the Commercial Intercourse of the World." He sent to the State Department the result of his research,[4] and also forwarded a communication received from Humboldt. This was a printed memoir in French, containing several maps.

On February 24, 1846, the United States Senate directed the Secretary of State to submit any information that he had received from the ministers abroad on "the subject of a ship canal across the isthmus of Panama, and of opening new channels of communication with the eastern nations." In compliance with this request the only paper of any consequence that was presented by Buchanan was Wheaton's despatch, which covered thirty-three printed pages of the committee's report. The introduction to this report was based largely on the statements made in Wheaton's communication. The new trade with China had been particularly stressed in it, and the international advantages to be gained by such a canal were fully discussed. In comparing the advantages of the five routes suggested by Humboldt, including the Isthmus of Panama, both Humboldt and Wheaton favored the Nicaraguan waterway.[5]

Wheaton's interest in international affairs, especially those in which his country was directly involved, was not confined merely to written despatches, printed articles, and pamphlets. Both in his official and private intercourse with his contemporaries, he at all times endeavored to create a sound public opinion concerning the attitude and activities of his country. A recognition of the value of the services which he rendered wherever he might be was expressed by Calhoun on December 26, 1844, in writing to him after he had returned to Berlin from Paris. In reference to this absence—during which Fay had been so active in Berlin and Fisk had been disappointed—Calhoun said that Wheaton need make no apology or explanation for his prolonged stay at Paris, as he had no doubt that his time had been efficiently and well employed in "that great centre of diplomatic relations of the civilized world." Calhoun further wrote that to give correct impressions there was all-important in the prevailing state of our relations with England and in reference to Texas, Mexico, and the American continent generally. Calhoun felt that the policy of France at that time was "far from being deep or wise, in reference to the affairs of this continent. It ought to be, on all points, antagonistic to that of Great Britain." [6]

Referring to Texas considered as a question of American policy, Wheaton wrote to his uncle that there might certainly be room for two opinions, yet he did not see what right Great Britain had to interfere with it any more than we had to interfere with her course of aggrandizement in the East Indies. Nor did he think there was any danger of war with England growing out of that affair. From his conversations at Paris, both with King Louis Philippe and Guizot, as well as with the chiefs of the opposition, he had reason to believe that England could not get France to go along with her in any extreme measures to prevent reannexation of Texas. "The British Government," he wrote, "is strongly pressed from without by the powerful party of the abolition which they often find it difficult to resist. Some allowances must therefore be made for the language they are sometimes constrained to use as to the question of abolition, etc." [7]

In February of 1846, Wheaton was in London on a short visit. He attended the debates in Parliament on the Corn Laws, which then engrossed public attention. The Oregon boundary was also one of the foremost topics under consideration. At the invitation of Lord Aberdeen and Sir Robert Peel, Wheaton discussed this matter with these statesmen. He endeavored to impress them with the necessity of making such concessions in the way of compromise, as might enable the moderate party in the United States to keep the peace, and contended this could only be done by a fair division of the disputed territory, with its ports and harbors, between the two countries.[8] Wheaton wrote to Calhoun that he had always let it be distinctly understood "that," to use his own words, "we shall *all* stand upon the parallel of 49 as the boundary most just, equitable and convenient for the partition of the country—without admitting to them the possibility even of some *modification* of this basis although some such appears to be desired here." [9] He believed the British Government sincerely wished to settle the question on what they considered equitable terms. Sir Robert Peel told him that the whole success of his great measure of commercial reform depended upon peace with America. Wheaton also talked with the leaders of the Whig party, the Marquis of Lansdowne, Lord John Russell and Lord Palmerston, and found them disposed to acquiesce in any arrangement the British ministry might make for the settlement of the controversy on the basis of a fair and equitable compromise. Indeed Lord John Russell told Wheaton that he was prepared to support the concession of the 49th parallel as the boundary. He said "let a line be once established, and there is no reason why John Bull and Brother Jonathan should not live in harmony upon the frontier as they do upon the Northeastern." Wheaton assured Calhoun that it was universally regretted in England that Pakenham should have so peremptorily rejected the proposals of the

United States, and it was the hope that some way could be found to correct the error.

Three months later he wrote to his son Robert, "I do not see any reason to doubt that the Oregon question will be amicably arranged notwithstanding the bellicose appearances in Congress. *Si vis pacem, para bellum* is a wise maxim, and we shall negotiate to greater advantage if prepared for war." [10]

One of Wheaton's last official acts was to communicate to the Government of Prussia the circumstances which had led to the declaration of war against Mexico and the blockade instituted in consequence thereof. He stated that the blockade which was to be established would not give any just ground of complaint to neutral powers, since it would not be what is called a "paper blockade," but would be carried into effect by an actual investment of the ports in question by adequate naval forces; that we professed the same principles in respect to neutral rights which had been professed and maintained by Prussia ever since the reign of Frederick the Great, and we should be anxious to preserve our consistency in that respect by meting out to others the same measure of international justice as belligerents which he claimed from them when neutrals.[11]

Chapter XXXIII

PUBLICIST

FROM the time Wheaton, while a student in Europe, had translated the *Code Napoléon* into English, his publications had been numerous, covering a wide range of subjects. There had been the digests of laws, the biography of William Pinkney, the editorials in the *National Advocate*, the twelve volumes of the Supreme Court *Reports*, his work as one of the New York revisers, his articles and books on Scandinavian history and literature, his many reviews of books on varied topics, his several addresses and essays, and the *Elements of International Law*.

In 1838 appeared *Scandinavia, Ancient and Modern: Being a History of Denmark, Sweden and Norway,* by Andrew Crichton, LL.D. and Henry Wheaton, LL.D.[1] In the preface which was signed in Edinburgh, November 1, 1837, apparently by Dr. Crichton, it is stated that

. . . the materials more immediately referred to as the contributions of that learned writer [Wheaton, to the joint work on Scandinavia] consisted of a manuscript of about six hundred and thirty pages, intended as a sequel to the preceding volume [on the Northmen], and bringing down the history of Denmark and Norway from the extinction of the Anglo-Danish dynasty in 1042 to the Revolution of 1660, including the affairs of Sweden under the Union of Calmar.[2]

Wheaton should be remembered, it has been remarked, "for having a hundred years ago with earnestness and persistency, labored to make the achievements of the Northmen in literature and other fields better known to the non-Scandinavian world." [3]

Additional prestige was gained by Wheaton from an entirely different source. The Academy of Moral and Political

Sciences in the Institute of France offered a prize for the best essay on the question, *Quels sont les progrès qu'a fait le droit des gens en Europe depuis la Paix de Westphalie?* Wheaton entered the contest. He wrote a memoir in the French language entitled *Histoire des progrès du droit des gens en Europe, depuis la Paix de Westphalie jusqu'au Congrès de Vienne, avec un précis historique du droit des gens européen avant la Paix de Westphalie.* This was published in book form in 1841 by Brockhaus in Leipzig. Commenting on Wheaton's failure to win the prize, Charles Sumner said,

It was bold and honorable in Mr. Wheaton to venture in a foreign tongue the discussion of so great a subject. . . . [His work] whether in French or English is commended by matter rather than by manner. On this account he was at disadvantage before the polished French tribunal. His effort received what was called Mention Honorable but the prize was awarded to a young Frenchman, whose production has never seen the light. An impartial public opinion has awarded our countryman another prize more than academic.[4]

The review of this work, for the *Revue étrangère et française de législation,* was prepared by Pinheiro Ferreira, an eminent publicist, formerly the minister of foreign affairs of Portugal, who had been the editor both of Vattel and Martens. It declared that Wheaton's work bore evidence of the vast erudition of the author,

. . . showing that nothing which had been done or written that was remarkable was unknown to him; and that if there were defects in it, they were to be ascribed to the circumstances under which it was written, and which had prevented the author from giving it the form that he would have adopted, could he have been allowed to follow the inspirations of his clear and methodical mind.[5]

In the *Edinburgh Review* a paper from the pen of the jurist and political economist, Nassau W. Senior, while it presented the difficulty of reducing to any general rules the practice of nations and, as was to be expected, contested

Wheaton's views on the right of visit and search in time of peace, did justice to his fitness for his task. It remarks:

Few men are better qualified to write a history of the law of nations than Mr. Wheaton. A lawyer, a historian, and a states- man, he unites practical and theoretical knowledge, and is the author of one of the best treatises on the actual state of that law, of which in this essay, the subject of this article, he is the historian. We believe that Mr. Wheaton made as much as was to be made of his materials. We cannot part with him without expressing a hope that he will translate his essay into English. It would form an excellent supplement to his great work on international law. There are many persons in his own country and in ours, to whom it is inaccessible in its present form; and he must be anxious that his field of utility and of fame, should be co-extensive with the English language.[6]

This desire Wheaton fulfilled. A much enlarged edition in English was published in New York in 1845 with the title *History of the Law of Nations in Europe and America, from the Earliest Times to the Treaty of Washington, 1842.* This work traced the progress which the law of nations had made so far and occupied a place never before filled in the litera- ture of the English language. Among the suggested ameliora- tions in the law of nations which Wheaton discussed was that of the establishment of perpetual peace by the settlement of national disputes without resort to hostilities. He outlined in detail the plans of St. Pierre and Rousseau, of Bentham and Kant. In some shape or other they were all referable to the principle of a general council of nations which might serve as a great tribunal whose jurisdiction all states were to acknowledge.[7] In view of the difficulties experienced by the League of Nations since 1918 Wheaton's comment on Bentham's plan is interesting.

The only guarantee which he (Bentham) proposes for the pres- ervation of perpetual peace is the formation of a general league of European states, the laws of which were to be enacted by a common legislature and carried into effect by a common judica- ture, but without providing any means for preventing this league from falling under the exclusive influence and control of its more powerful members. Experience has sufficiently demonstrated the difficulty of reconciling such corporate alliances with the rights and independence of each separate nation, and especially those of states of the second order. The right of perpetual supervision and interference, which these alliances involve as a necessary means of effecting their object, has been hitherto found too liable to abuse to warrant its being incorporated without danger into the international code. The cases where such interference has been allowed in order to preserve the peace of Europe constitute exceptions to a general rule of the most sacred and salutary nature, that by which the independence even of the smallest state ought to be respected by the greatest, as essential to the general security of all and to the maintenance of the balance of power on which that security depends.[8]

In the announcement in the *Revue étrangère et française de législation* of the publication of this edition of Wheaton's *Law of Nations,* the work is said to supply all preceding omissions and to be a necessary complement of the *Elements.*[9]

The German periodicals were not less decided in their commendation of Wheaton's treatises than those of England and France.[10] A German reviewer closed his notice by declaring that

Every student of this important science is bound to acknowledge his deep gratitude to the learned author, who, uniting the accomplishments of a public jurist and of a practical diplomat of the school of Franklin and Jefferson, to those of the scholar, already known by his other literary works, has furnished the best commentary on his *Elements of International Law.*[11]

Wheaton's publications on the Continent continued to cover a wide range of interests. In common with other Americans abroad, he had felt much embarrassment as a result of the repudiation by some of the states of their debts to European creditors. From the beginning of his professional life he had been interested in having the finances of his country put on a firm basis. In 1815 he had actively urged the passage of an adequate federal bankruptcy law. During the widespread crisis of 1837, he had discussed the reorganization of our monetary system and the relation of state and federal finances. Again in 1842, he had written from Paris that the unhappy condition of the finances of the United States, both public and private, was the main obstacle in creating advantageous relations with Europe. His attention had been arrested by the misrepresentations of the attitude of the United States which had been appearing in the German papers, in reference not only to slavery and the slave trade, but also to the repudiation of debts in the individual American states. It is not surprising that in 1843 the *Preussische Staats-Zeitung* contained an essay by him on the "Constitution of the United States," to refute the charges made against his country and to uphold its honor.[12] He showed that there were distinctions between the debts of the various states and those of the Federal Government, and that the latter was not involved in nor responsible for this failure of credit. The Federal Government had always met its obligations, both foreign and domestic, but lacked the constitutional powers to compel the individual states to meet their obligations. A repudiation by some of the states, therefore, was not a *casus belli*.[13] Moreover there were many states which had not repudiated.

Two reviews by Wheaton were published in the *Revue de Droit Français et Étranger* in 1844 and 1845 respectively. Both of these were articles ten pages in length. One entitled "De la Nature du droit des gens en général," on H. Heffter's *Das Europäische Völkerrecht*,[14] and the other, "Du Droit des Gens Maritime," on Ortolan's *Règles internationales et diplomatie de la mer*.[15] Also in the *Monthly Review* of September 1844 there appeared a review of the three volumes on the *History of Modern Art in Germany* by A. Raczynski.[16] Each of these volumes had been reviewed at length by Wheaton as they had appeared.[17]

Wheaton did not, however, devote all his efforts to articles for foreign publication. In December 1842, he undertook to write a series of papers in the form of communications to a new society established in Washington for the promotion of science and letters, a society with, as Henry Wheaton expressed it, "the grand name of National Institute." [18] In the three years from October 1842 to October 1845, he contributed seventeen papers on a variety of subjects ranging from modern art and artists in Germany and the fine arts in Denmark, the revival of Greek tragedy in Prussia and the geography of Central Asia, to the scientific character of Leibnitz. Many of these were published in the *National Intelligencer* and were often republished in other periodicals. In addition to aiding its literary pursuits by sending articles of contemporary interest, he regularly donated periodicals and books which he thought might be of value to the association. [19]

While on a visit to Paris in the winter of 1843–44, Wheaton began the preparation of a much enlarged and, as he hoped, improved edition in French of his *History of the Northmen,* which he intended to publish there. He wrote to Dr. Wheaton that he had given the historical proofs of the discovery and colonization of North America by the Scandinavians in the eleventh century, and fortified the proofs by an interpretation of the celebrated inscription on the Dighton Rock which had so long puzzled Dr. Stiles and other antiquarians and which had a local interest for Rhode Islanders. [20]

In May of the same year he informed Dr. Wheaton that there had just been published at Paris a book entitled *Histoire des peuples du Nord,* which purported to be a translation of his *History of the Northmen,* but was in fact a new work, compiled from his former volume and from Scandinavian and other sources. [21]

In July of 1845 he wrote to his son Robert that he had begun a collection of his miscellaneous writings, but that he had not found all he wished to publish. [22] This undertaking he never completed. An edition of his *History of the Law of Nations* in English was also published about this time in New York.

His attention was now turned to the correction and revision of his *Elements of International Law,* which revision was dated Berlin, November 1845.[23] The author closes his preface to this edition by stating that he has

. . . endeavored to justify the confidence with which he has been so long honored by his country in the different diplomatic missions confided to him, by availing himself of the peculiar opportunities, and the means of information thus afforded, for a closer examination of the different questions of public law which have occurred in the international intercourse of Europe and America since the publication of the first edition of the present work.[24]

Although the introductory "Sketch of the History of International Law" which had been superseded by the separate publication was eliminated from this edition of the *Elements*, the size of the book had almost doubled. Reference is made continually to the new edition of the *History*. The two are really companion volumes which should be read together. If to these are added the cases referred to in the twelve volumes of Wheaton's Supreme Court Reports, the result, it has been said, is "an unrivalled collection of material for the study of international law as understood in 1846." [25] But the value and effect of Wheaton's work has not stopped there. Due to the regard in which the *Elements of International Law* has been held by other countries, subsequent editions have been issued, and it still maintains its place today among the foremost publications on that subject.

A tribute to Wheaton's wide international interests is to be found at his own alma mater, Brown University. A front room on the second floor of the John Hay Library has been named for him, and on the shelves extending from floor to ceiling around the four walls of the room are the volumes forming the nucleus of the extensive library on international law. Wheaton's family presented to the library five hundred or more volumes which had belonged to him. Among them are to be found some of the rarest editions of the first writers on international law, such as Grotius and Pufendorf.[26]

Chapter XXXIV

RECALL

S HOULD I remain where I am," Calhoun while Secretary of State had written to Wheaton, "you may be assured I shall not be indifferent as to what relates to yourself." [1]

Calhoun, however, soon was to be succeeded by James Buchanan, who held very different views about the commercial arrangements which should exist between the United States and the German states from the ones advocated by Wheaton. This is evidenced by the part he had taken in the rejection of the Zollverein treaty, by his subsequent attitude towards it, and by the appointment in March 1846 of A. Dudley Mann as a special agent to make a new treaty with Hanover with much the same purpose that England had so consistently held—the continued separation of Hanover from the Zollverein. Rumors of Wheaton's recall had been afloat as early as April 1844,[2] and they became so definite immediately after the inauguration of Polk that William Beach Lawrence, whose name was afterwards to be closely associated with Wheaton's, wrote to George Bancroft, who had been appointed secretary of the navy by Polk, urging him to use his influence with the President to retain Wheaton in the diplomatic service of the country.[3]

It was months before any definite decision was made, and then Wheaton received an intimation from Buchanan that the name of a new minister to Berlin was to be presented by the President to the session of the Senate of 1845–46. This determination was communicated in such a way that he was left no alternative other than to request his recall.[4]

By this time he apparently had become convinced that in Buchanan could be found the source of the opposition to him. In writing to Calhoun, he said, "I cannot help thinking that if I had been supported in *the proper quarter,* the President would not have taken this step." [5]

Wheaton's real objection was not to the manner in which he had been removed from his post, but to the fact that this decision had not been communicated to him sooner.[6]

In compliance with the request of the President, Wheaton remained in Berlin to await the arrival of his successor, Andrew J. Donelson,[7] who expected to sail from the United States in the Havre packet on the third of June.[8] Gerolt had previously reported to the Foreign Office that Donelson had arrived in Washington with his family; that Gerolt had tried to explain to Donelson the commercial relations between Prussia and the United States, of which he seemed as ignorant and unprepared as about the relations between the United States and Europe; but that his activity and presence in Berlin might prove fruitful for the establishing of a reciprocity system between the United States and the Zollverein, as he enjoyed the favor of the present Government.[9]

The new minister from the United States arrived in Berlin on the fifth of July, but owing to the illness of the Prussian minister of foreign affairs, a delay of several days intervened before he was presented to the King.[10] He finally received a private audience on the eighteenth for the presentation of his credentials,[11] and on the same day Wheaton delivered his letters of recall to the Prussian sovereign at the palace of Charlottenburg. He afterwards had the honor of dining with the King and Queen, and finally took leave, with the repetition on the part of both their majesties, of the kindest sentiments towards him.[12]

Upon being informed by Alexander von Humboldt that a copy of the edition of the *Works of Frederick the Great,* then being published at the King's expense, would have been offered to him if he had been at liberty to accept any present from the King, he requested that a copy might be delivered to him for the use of the Library of Congress at Washington. He afterwards received from the superintendent general of the Royal Museum the first three volumes of the work, to be transmitted to the President.[13]

The King of Prussia not only regretted Wheaton's recall but could not conceive it possible that any Government could make the mistake of voluntarily depriving itself of such a minister. This attitude on the part of the King is apparent not only from his formal acknowledgment to the United States Government, but also from the private note of his confidential friend, Alexander von Humboldt, who, on his part, could not regard Wheaton's removal otherwise than as the prelude to promotion.[14]

Many of the periodicals in Germany expressed surprise at the course of the American government in recalling Wheaton, and it was the subject of a long article in the *Augsburg Gazette*.[15] Later, in a conversation with John C. Stephens, Humboldt inquired what the future career of Wheaton was to be. Humboldt said that it had been understood at Berlin that Wheaton was to be appointed minister to France, and expressed surprise that the United States should be willing to lose the public services of one so long trained in the school of diplomacy and so well acquainted with the political institutions of Europe.[16]

Wheaton did not plan to return to the United States immediately. On July 23, 1846,[17] with the intention of continuing the revision of his principal literary works and with the hope that some other diplomatic mission would be given him, he left Berlin for Paris.

Chapter XXXV

A PRIVATE CITIZEN

HENRY WHEATON arrived in France with his usually sanguine spirit perturbed by the lack of definite plans for the future. Even so, during the time spent in Paris Wheaton prepared and read before the French Institute an *Essay on the Succession to the Crown of Denmark*.[1] From the facts which his long residence in Copenhagen had made familiar to him, he was able to clarify a question which soon thereafter became one of European importance. He was also during this period of uncertainty actively engaged in making amendments to the edition of his *Elements of International Law* which was later published in French by Brockhaus at Leipzig and Paris in 1848.

When rumors of Wheaton's removal had been rife in 1844, the newspapers had stated definitely that Henry Wheaton's nomination for the vacancy of Associate Justice of the Supreme Court had been determined upon.[2] But this report proved to be unfounded. Far more vexatious had been the loss of an opportunity which seemed to present itself at Harvard College. It was concerning this that Wheaton wrote, with very justifiable indignation over the fact that Buchanan had not decided more promptly the matter of the recall:

Had this been done as it might have been immediately on the formation of the present Administration, I should have received the appointment of Professor of Law in the University of Cambridge vacant by the death of Judge Story. But, as my friends could not learn on enquiry at Washington that there was any intention of recalling me, they were not able to answer for my accepting the vacant chair at Cambridge, and as there was a necessity for filling it almost immediately, it was impossible to wait until my determination could be known.[3]

298

A more bitter disappointment, however, was in store for Wheaton. For many years he had hoped for a transfer to Paris, where his family had resided since 1839. His name had been mentioned prominently in connection with the post on several occasions, but in each instance someone else had been appointed. At this time William R. King, who was the United States minister to France, had asked for his recall and expressed the wish that Wheaton should be his successor.[4] So at last it seemed that Wheaton's long-felt desire might be fulfilled. But the next spring brought the news that on March 3, 1847, Richard Rush of Pennsylvania had been appointed Minister to France.[5] The political aspect in the change of ministers becomes apparent when it is considered that the choice of Buchanan for the Secretaryship of State had met with disapproval on the part of a rival faction of Pennsylvania Democrats. For the placating of this group the French mission was employed.

After the news of Richard Rush's appointment reached Paris, Wheaton determined to return to the United States. He and his family embarked at Havre on April 17 and landed in New York on the nineteenth of May, going directly to Rhode Island.

On the tenth of June a public dinner was given in New York to celebrate his return and to express appreciation of his distinguished services during his diplomatic career and of the value of his contributions to the science of international law and to the literature of his country.[6] The invitation to the dinner was headed by the names of James Kent and Albert Gallatin, the most eminent citizens in America in the departments of law and diplomacy respectively. The dinner was presided over by the latter and was attended, without regard to party, by many distinguished men. Gallatin escorted Wheaton to the table, telling the latter that he would not have assisted at a public dinner given to any other man in the world.[7] Gallatin left early, and it proved to be his last public appearance. Buchanan could not be present but at this time sent a tribute which expressed his real opinion. In part, he wrote:

Mr. Wheaton richly merits this token of regard. He has done honor to his country abroad, and deserves to be honored by his countrymen at home. I offer you the following sentiment for the occasion—"The Author of the Elements of International Law"—while we hail with enthusiasm the victorious general engaged in fighting the battles of his country, our gratitude is due to the learned civilian, who, by clearly expounding the rights and duties of nations, contributes to preserve the peace of the world.[8]

According to Robert Wheaton's report of the dinner, the happiest thing in his father's speech on this occasion was the remark,

During my long residence abroad I have seen with sincere pleasure that the State of New York, while so many of her sister states were involved in difficulties, has steered perfectly clear of every imputation of bad faith. You gentlemen have *repudiated repudiation,* and had we not done so our Dutch ancestors would have repudiated us!

He concluded by thanking the company again and proposing the following toast which was received with immense applause: "The City of New Amsterdam, Peace be within thy walls and prosperity within thy palaces!"

It was during his speech at this dinner that he enunciated the doctrine: "The office of a foreign minister is the office of a peacemaker. Diplomacy has been supposed to be a mantle of craft and deceit, but I believe that honor and integrity are the true arts of the diplomatist." [9]

On the first of September Wheaton's last literary discourse was pronounced at Brown University. It was an *Essay on the Progress and Prospects of Germany,* and it was delivered before the Phi Beta Kappa Society. This was received with cordial comment in Germany.[10]

It was Wheaton's intention to bring out a new edition to his *History of the Northmen,* and he had made an arrangement with D. Appleton and Company for that purpose. He had written an introduction of several pages, and he proposed to add a chapter on the Normans of Sicily and some interesting notes which the progress of historical research during the last twenty years had rendered desirable. This work was never completed.

Had a fitting position been opened to Wheaton, in which he could have found adequate scope for his intellectual powers, he might have overcome the disappointment entailed by his recall. But although he possessed such highly esteemed literary and professional attainments, the only opportunity which seemed to be open for him was an arrangement for a course of lectures on international law before the law school of Harvard University, of which Edward Everett was now president.[11] The position was a temporary one with very little promise for the future. It had been offered in an uncomplimentary way, so that Wheaton looked forward to it with a sense of discouragement and with rather a sick heart.

While at Washington, whither he was accompanied by William Beach Lawrence with a view to the discussion in the Supreme Court of the only points connected with his controversy with Peters left open by the previous decision, he became ill but was able to return to his family.[12] By the middle of February it was evident that he could not attempt to give the contemplated lectures. A month later in Dorchester, Massachusetts, his illness proved fatal, and he died at twelve o'clock Saturday night, the eleventh of March 1848. An autopsy determined that he had suffered from a deep-seated disease of the brain.

In announcing his death the *Daily Evening Transcript* of Boston gave the following contemporary opinion of Wheaton:

He stood confessedly at the head of American diplomacy and was regarded more than any other man, as the representative of the American Government. His reputation was even greater in Europe than at home, for there he was better known and more intimately appreciated. Among the friends who esteemed him were the King of Prussia, the King of France, Prince Metternich, Humboldt and Guizot. Perhaps no other American Minister has ever been distinguished by so many despatches upon such a variety of topics and of such universal interest and value.[13]

Frustration, it has been said, is the greatest tragedy in life, and frustration was Wheaton's experience, for his life was harassed by one disappointment following closely upon another. In seeking greater opportunity in New York, he met a barrier to the practice of his profession. His experience in the New York Assembly prevented his election to Congress. His diplomatic career began with a disappointment in the mission entrusted to him. The rewards anticipated from his work as Supreme Court reporter were denied him. The treaty upon which he had spent so much time and effort failed of ratification. Instead of the desired change in his diplomatic post he received his recall, and the only position which was open to him was unworthy of his attainments. Yet, in his writings on the science and history of international law, he reached an eminence from which nothing has detracted, and his influence for peace and good will has extended throughout the entire world.

He translated the ideal dreams of philosophers to a practical science. His work has perhaps had more influence toward maintaining peace than any other one work or circumstance, since it has given to all governments common principles from which and on which to argue. Only a man of genius could have accomplished this.[14]

AN EPILOGUE OF CONTROVERSY

AN EPILOGUE OF CONTROVERSY

THE full appreciation of Wheaton's accomplishments has been denied him in his own country through a litigation in connection with his *Elements of International Law*, a controversy which began almost twenty years after his death.

As a result of the unsuccessful copyright suit against Peters, Wheaton left his family in but moderate circumstances. Several years after his death Mrs. Wheaton tried to secure an increase in her income through the publication of some of his writings. For this purpose William Beach Lawrence, a friend of the family, undertook the preparation of a new edition of the *Elements of International Law*. This edition, published by Little, Brown and Company in 1855, was copyrighted in the name of Mrs. Wheaton. An enlarged edition was brought out in the same way in 1863. Lawrence, besides some introductory remarks and a memoir of Wheaton in both editions, had added to Wheaton's text many comprehensive notes of his own as editor and commentator. He always had been a great admirer of Wheaton and had taken pleasure in aiding in the publication of the work. He refused any compensation for his labor so that Mrs. Wheaton might receive all the profits. Even so a controversy over the arrangement of the title-page had arisen between Lawrence and Charles C. Little, the senior member of the publishing company.[1]

As Little, who had married Wheaton's daughter Abby, and Lawrence were good friends, the latter during the preparation of the work spent some time with the Littles at their home in Cambridge. But when Lawrence wished the title-page of the second edition to appear as "Lawrence's Wheaton," Little did not agree with him. He thought that

Lawrence's name should appear as editor of this seventh edition. Lawrence gained his point, but his friendship with the family was broken. In an effort to protect his claim as editor and the right to his notes, Lawrence tried to secure from Mrs. Wheaton an assignment of the copyright not only to his notes but also to the original text. This Mrs. Wheaton refused to do, but gave her assent to a memorandum which stated that she would make no use of Lawrence's notes in a new edition without his written consent and gave him the right to make any use of his own notes that he might desire. This memorandum was never ratified. In the meantime Wheaton's family had become dissatisfied with the 1863 edition. According to Charles Francis Adams:

This dissatisfaction was due to Mr. Lawrence's very prolix memoir of Mr. Wheaton prefixed to the treatise, rendering it unwieldy in size and costly in publication, while the notes and other matter which the editor insisted, as they alleged, on inserting, were unnecessarily long, and certain of them, it was further alleged, expressed the editor's personal views on current political events, more or less in avowed sympathy with the Southern rebellion. In the judgment of the publishers these facts seriously interfered with the sale of the work, and accordingly Mrs. Wheaton at last made up her mind to have a new edition prepared by another editor.[2]

The new editor, Richard Henry Dana, had been at work nearly two years before Lawrence became aware of the fact. A controversy immediately ensued over the use of the latter's notes. Dana informed Lawrence that his notes and comments would not appear in the new edition. So soon as Dana's edition was published, Lawrence began a comparison of this edition with his own, and in October 1866, brought suit against Dana, the publishers and Martha B. Wheaton, Wheaton's older daughter, who had succeeded to the rights of her mother upon the latter's death in March, 1866.[3] A long litigation resulted which was not settled until November 25, 1893, when the bill was dismissed. In the meantime Lawrence had died in March

1881, and Dana in January 1882.[4] As a result of this controversy no new edition of Henry Wheaton's *Elements of International Law* has been published in the United States since 1866.

There have been five French editions—the first two similar to the American editions of 1848 and 1853, the third and fourth in two volumes each in 1858 and 1864 respectively, and the fifth in one volume in 1874. Besides these, after the controversy began over Dana's edition, Lawrence arranged with F. A. Brockhaus of Leipzig to bring out an edition. When it was ready the publisher found the original work of two volumes had been increased to six volumes. These were afterwards reduced to four and publication started in 1868.[5] A Mexican edition was published in 1854–55, and an Italian edition in 1860. Of special note is the Chinese edition. According to Dana,

The most remarkable proof of the advance of Western civilization in the East is the adoption of this work of Mr. Wheaton, by the Chinese Government, as a textbook for its officials, in international law, and its translation into the language in 1864, under imperial auspices. The translation was made by the Rev. W. A. P. Martin, D.D., an American missionary, assisted by a commission of Chinese scholars appointed by Prince Kung, Minister of Foreign Affairs, at the suggestion of Mr. Burlingame, the United States Minister to whom the translation is dedicated.[6]

This translation was afterwards adapted to the Japanese language and an edition published for use in Japan.[7]

In 1878, as there was no prospect of any further publication of the work in the United States, an edition was brought out in England, and since then five other English editions have been published, the last one appeared in 1929. The introduction to the 1916 edition was written by Sir Frederick Pollock, and gives a recent evaluation of Wheaton's work. He wrote, "In Wheaton's Elements we have an exposition of such principles (accepted and formulated by the wisdom of cool heads in bygone days of peace) delivered on a more spacious historical scene and with more wealth of detailed illustration than can be found in most modern text-books." [8] He commented further on Wheaton's general merits: "They are, to begin with, those of a good scholarly lawyer of the first generation of American independence; but his combination of forensic, judicial and diplomatic experience gave him almost unique advantages in handling this subject." [9]

APPENDICES

I

WRITINGS OF HENRY WHEATON

BOOKS AND PAMPHLETS

Digest of the Law of Maritime Captures and Prizes. New York, 1815.

Considerations on the Establishment of a Uniform System of Bankrupt Laws Throughout the United States. Washington, 1815.

A Digest of the decisions of the Supreme Court of the United States . . . from 1789 to February term 1820, including the cases decided in the Continental Court of Appeals in prize causes, during the War of the Revolution. New York, 1821.

An Abridgment of the Law of Nisi Prius, by William Selwyn, Esq., of Lincoln's Inn, Barrister at Law. Second American, from the Fifth London Edition; with Notes and References to the Decisions of the Courts of this Country. 2 vols. Albany, 1823.

The Case of Gibbons against Ogden, heard and determined in the Supreme Court of the United States, February Term, 1824, on Appeal from the Court of Errors in the State of New York, and involving the Constitutionality of the Laws of the State, granting to Livingston and Fulton the exclusive Navigation of its Waters by Steam Boats. New York, 1824.

Some account of the life, writings, and speeches of William Pinkney. New York, 1826. Reprinted in the Library of American Biography, conducted by Jared Sparks. Boston, 1836. New York, 1856.

Reports of cases, argued and adjudged in the Supreme Court of the United States. 12 vols. Philadelphia, 1816–1827. 12 vols. New York, 1883.

History of the Northmen, or Danes and Normans, from the earliest times to the Conquest of England by William of Normandy. Philadelphia, 1831. London, 1831.

Elements of International Law.

Editions issued by Wheaton or his family:

1st   Edition, London, 1836 (with a sketch of the history of the science).

2nd Edition, Philadelphia, 1836.

3rd   Edition, Rev. and cor., Philadelphia, 1846. Omitted history of the science.

4th   Edition (in French), Leipzig and Paris, 1848.

5th   Edition (in French), Leipzig and Paris, 1853.

6th   Edition. Edited by William Beach Lawrence, Boston, 1855. London, 1857.

7th   Edition. Edited by William Beach Lawrence, Boston, 1863. London, 1864.

8th   Edition. Edited by Richard Henry Dana, Jr., Boston, 1866.

Editions issued in French:

1st Edition, 2 vols. in 1. Same as 4th Edition listed above, Leipzig and Paris, 1848.

2nd Edition, 2 vols. in 1. Same as 5th Edition listed above, Leipzig and Paris, 1852.

3rd   Edition, 2 vols., Leipzig, 1858.

4th   Edition, 2 vols., Leipzig, 1864.

5th   Edition, 2 vols. in 1, Leipzig, 1874.

Extra Edition, 4 vols., Leipzig, 1868–1880. Brought out by Lawrence after the controversy began over Dana's Edition.

Editions issued in England after publication had ceased in the United States:

1st   Edition. Edited by A. C. Boyd, London, 1878.

2nd Edition. Edited by A. C. Boyd, London, 1880.

3rd   Edition. Edited by A. C. Boyd, London, 1889.

4th   Edition. Edited by J. Beresford Atlay, London, 1904.

5th   Edition. Edited by Coleman Phillipson, with an Introduction by Sir Frederick Pollock, London, 1916.

6th   Edition. Edited by A. Berriedale Keith, 2 vols., London, 1929.

Edition issued in Italy. Translated by Constantino Arlia, 1 vol., Naples, 1860.

Edition issued in Mexico. Translated by José Maria Barros, 2 vols., 1854–55.

Edition issued in China:
  The translation into Chinese was made by the Rev.
  W. A. P. Martin, D.D., an American missionary, as-
  sisted by a commission of Chinese scholars appointed
  by Prince Kung, Minister of Foreign Affairs, at the sug-
  gestion of the United States Minister to China, Anson
  Burlingame, to whom the translation is dedicated,
  Pekin, 1864.
Edition issued in Japan, Tokio, 1867.

*Scandinavia, Ancient and Modern; being a History of Denmark,
Sweden, and Norway, etc.* By Andrew Crichton, LL.D. and
Henry Wheaton, LL.D., 1838. (Harper's Family Library) 1841.
New York, 1846–50.

*Histoire des progrès du droit des gens en Europe depuis la paix
de Westphalie jusqu'au congrès de Vienne. Avec un précis
historique du droit des gens européen avant la paix de Westphalie.* Leipzig, 1841. (Written as a *mémoire* in answer to the
following prize question proposed by the Academy of Moral
and Political Sciences in the Institute of France: "Quels sont
les progrès qu'a fait le droit des gens en Europe depuis la
paix de Westphalie?")

*Histoire des progrès du droit des gens en Europe et en Amérique
depuis la paix de Westphalie jusqu'à nos jours, avec une introduction sur les progrès du droit des gens en Europe avant
la paix de Westphalie, par Henry Wheaton.*
  2. éd., rev., cor. et augm. par l'auteur. 2 vols., Leipzig, 1846.
  3. éd., 2 vols. in 1, Leipzig, 1853.
  4. éd., 2 vols., Leipzig, 1865.

*History of the law of nations in Europe and America; from the
earliest times to the Treaty of Washington, 1842.* New York,
1845.

*Historia de los progresos del derecho de gentes, en Europa y en
América, desde la paz de Westfalia hasta nuestros dias. Tr.
y aum . . . por Cárlos Calvo.* 2 vols., Besanzon, 1861.

*Enquiry into the Validity of the British Claim to a Right of Visi-
tation and Search of American Vessels suspected to be engaged in the African Slave Trade.* London, 1842. Philadelphia, 1842. New Edition, London, 1858.

*Affaire de Mac-Leod considérée sous le point de vue du droit des
gens, par M. Henri Wheaton.* Paris, 1842. Extrait de la Revue

étrangère et française de législation, de jurisprudence, et d'économie politique . . . 9e année, cahier 1.

Examen des questions de jurisdiction qui se sont élevées entre les gouvernements anglais et américain dans l'affaire de la Créole; suivi d'une analyse du mémoire de l'auteur sur le droit de visite en mer. Paris, 1842. Extrait de la Revue étrangère et française de législation, de jurisprudence, et d'économie politique. tome IX. 1842.

Histoire des peuples du Nord, ou des Danois et des Normands, depuis les temps les plus reculés jusqu'à la conquête de l'Angleterre par Guillaume de Normandie, et du royaume des Deux-Siciles par les fils de Tancrède de Hauteville. Édition revue et augmentée par l'auteur, avec cartes, inscriptions et alphabet runiques, etc. Traduit de l'anglais par Paul Guillot. Paris, 1844.

ADDRESSES, ESSAYS, ETC.

An Oration delivered before the Tammany Society or Columbian Order, and the Republican Citizens of Providence and its Vicinity at the Town-House, on the Anniversary of American Independence, July 4th, 1810. Providence, 1810.

An Oration delivered before the different Republican Societies at the theatre, Anthony St., New York, on the Anniversary of American Independence, July 4th, 1814. New York, 1814.

Essay on the Means of Maintaining the Commercial and Naval Interests of the United States. 1817.

An anniversary discourse, the *History of the Science of Public or International Law,* delivered before the New York Historical Society, December 28, 1820. New York, 1821. New York Historical Society Collections, Vol. 3, pp. 281–320. New York, 1821.

An Address on literature and science in America, pronounced at the opening of the New York Athenaeum, December 14, 1824. New York, 1825.

Discourse, intended to have been delivered before the New York Law Institute on its Anniversary celebration, May 14, 1834. New York, 1834.

Législation et institutions judiciaires de l'Islande, pendant le

Moyen Âge. Revue de Droit Français et Étranger, Vol. 1, pp. 182–198. 1844.

Essay on the Succession to the Crown of Denmark. Read before the French Institute.

Constitution of the United States. *Preussisches Staats-Zeitung.* March 27, 1843.

The progress and prospects of Germany: a discourse before the Phi Beta Kappa Society of Brown University, at Providence, R. I., September 1, 1847. Boston, 1847.

NATIONAL INSTITUTE PAPERS

On Modern Art and Artists in Germany. October 1842.

On the Geography of Central Asia (with a map). December 1, 1842.

On the National Institute. State of the Fine Arts in Denmark. Karsten and Thorwaldsen. January 15, 1843.

Description of the Canal which unites the river Mayn with the Danube (with a plan). Works of Art in the Bavarian Capital (Munich). Description of Walhalla. January 25, 1843.

Character of Frederick the Great. February 1, 1843.

On the Errors of Dr. Robinson's Account of the last days of the Emperor Charles V. April 26, 1843.

On Baron Von Humboldt's Work on the Physical Geography of Central Asia. June 1, 1843.

Impending Revolutions in the Commercial Intercourse of the World. On the Panama Canal. June 15, 1843.

An addition to his paper on the Panama Canal, and recommendation of Professor Von Raumer, Rector of the University of Berlin, as a corresponding member. July 1843.

On the Scientific Character of Leibnitz. Proceedings of the Berlin Academy of Sciences, in honor of the memory of Leibnitz. His genius and labors, etc. August 1, 1843.

Labors of Professor Lepsius, of Berlin, in Egypt; Antiquities; Ancient Canal across the Isthmus of Suez. August 14, 1843.

Life and Writings of Diderot, the Coryphaeus of the French Encyclopedists, etc. August 15, 1843.

On the Revival of Greek Tragedy in Prussia. September 14, 1843.

On the History of the Reformation in Germany. Review of Professor Ranke's History of Germany during the time of the Reformation. "1st Vol. appeared in 1839 and the fifth has just been published." October 15, 1843.

Musical Celebration given by the Academy of Arts in Berlin, in honor of the memory of Thorwaldsen, etc. July 3, 1844.

Continuation of the subject of former letters on the junction of the Atlantic and Pacific Oceans, etc. September 25, 1844.

On the Destruction of the Liberties of Aragon by Philip II. October 5, 1845.

REVIEWS

The United States and England, being a reply to the criticism on Inchiquin's Letters, contained in the Quarterly Review for January 1814. *North American Review*, Vol. 1, pp. 61–91. New York, May 1815.

Reports of Cases Argued and Determined in the Circuit Court of the United States, for the First Circuit. Vol. 1. Containing the Cases determined in the Districts of New Hampshire, Massachusetts and Rhode Island, in the years 1816, 1817, and 1818. By William P. Mason, Counsellor at Law. Boston, 1819. *North American Review*, Vol. 8, pp. 253–276. March 1819.

A Biographical Memoir of Hugh Williamson, M.D. LL.D. etc., by David Hosack, M.D. LL.D., etc. New York, 1820. *North American Review*, Vol. 11, pp. 31–37. July 1820.

Trial of Robert M. Goodwin, on an indictment of manslaughter, for killing James Stoughton, Esq., in Broadway, in the City of New York, etc. Taken in short hand by William Sampson, Counsellor at Law. New York, 1820. *North American Review*, Vol. 11, pp. 114–124. July 1820.

A Treatise on Maritime Contracts of Letting to Hire, by Robert Joseph Pothier; translated from the French, with notes and a life of the author, by Caleb Cushing. Boston. *North American Review*, Vol. 13, pp. 1–20. July 1821.

Yelverton's Reports. First American from the fourth English edition, with notes and references to prior and subsequent decisions, by Theron Metcalf. Andover, 1820. *North American Review*, Vol. 16, pp. 196–199. 1823.

1. Code Civil, suivi de l'Exposé des Motifs sur Chaques Loi présentée par les Orateurs du Gouvernement, etc. 11 Tomes. Paris, 1809.

2. Conférence du Code Civil avec la Discussion particulière du Conseil d'État et du Tribunat. 8 Tomes. Paris, 1805.

3. Code de Procédure Civile. 2 Tomes. Paris, 1808.

4. Code Pénal, suivi des Motifs présentés par les Orateurs du Gouvernement etc. 2 Tomes. Paris, 1812.

5. Code d'Instruction Criminelle, suivi des Motifs, etc. Paris, 1809.

6. Code de Commerce. 2 Tomes. Paris, 1812.

7. Les cinq Codes avec Notes et Traités pour servir à un Cours complet de Droit Français à l'Usage des Étudiants en Droit, et de toutes les Classes de Citoyens cultivés. Par J. B. Sirey, Avocat aux Conseils du Roi, et à la Cour de Cassation. Paris, 1819.

North American Review, Vol. 20, pp. 393–417. April 1825.

An Essay on the Doctrine of Contracts; being an Inquiry how Contracts are affected in Law and Morals, by Concealment, Error, or Inadequate Price. By Gulean C. Verplanck. New York, 1825. *North American Review*, Vol. 22, p. 253. April 1826.

Précis du Système Hiéroglyphique des anciens Egyptiens, ou Recherches sur les Elémens premiere de cette Ecriture Sacrée, etc. Par M. Champollion le jeune. Paris, 1824. *American Quarterly Review*, Vol. 1, pp. 438–458. June, 1827.

1. Edda Saemunder hins fróda, Collectio Carminum veterum Scaldorum, saemundiana dicta, ex recensione Erasmi Rask curavit A. A. Afzelius, Holmiae, 1818.

2. Snorra-Edda ásamt Skáldu ok parmed fylgjandi ritgjördum, útgefin af Rasmúsi Rask, Stockhólmi, 1818.

3. R. Rask om Zendsprogets og Zendavestas Ælde og Ægthed, Köbenhavn, 1826.

4. Den Gamle Ægytiske Tidsregning efter kilderne på ny bearbejdet af R. Rask, Köbenhavn, 1827.

This review appeared under the title of "Scandinavian Literature." *American Quarterly Review*, Vol. 3, pp. 481–490. It was subsequently translated into French:

De la littérature scandinave. Traduit de l'anglais, avec notes, par Edouard Frere. Rouen, 1835.

Danmarks og Hertugdommenes Statsret med Stadigt Hensyn til dens alldere horfstning ved Joh. Fred. Wilhelm Schlegel, etc. The Present Public Law of Denmark, and of the Duchies, in connexion with its Past State. By J. F. W. Schlegel, Counsellor of Conferences, Doctor and Professor of Law in the Royal University of Copenhagen. Assessor to the Supreme Court, Knight of Dannebrog, etc. Vol. I, Copenhagen, 1827. *North American Review*, Vol. 27, pp. 285–299. October 1828. (Really an Article on the Public Law of Denmark though purporting to be a review of Schlegel. Explained not only the constitution of that realm, but its political connection with the Duchies of Schleswig, Holstein, and Lauenburg, which in 1850 became the subject of a controversy that threatened the peace of Europe.)

Histoire des Expéditions Maritimes des Normands, et de leur établissement en France au dixième siècle; par G. B. Depping. Ouvrage couronné en 1822 par l'Académie Royale des Inscriptions et Belles Lettres. 2 vols. Paris, 1826. History of the Maritime Expeditions of the Normans, and of their establishment in France in the tenth century; by G. B. Depping. A work which obtained the palm in 1822 from the Royal Academy of Inscriptions and Belles Lettres. Paris, 1826. *American Quarterly Review*, Vol. 4, pp. 350–366. December 1828.

1. Edda Saemundar hins Fróda, Edda Rhythmica sive Antiquior, vulgo Saemundina dicta, Pars III. continens Carmina Voluspá, Hávamál, et Rigsmál. Accedit Magnüssen (Finni) Priscae veterum Borealium Mythological Lexicon, etc. Havniae, 1828.

2. Svea—Rikes Häfder af E. G. Geijer. 1 sta Delen. Upsala, 1825. (This is really an Essay on Scandinavian Mythology, Poetry and History, in which the sources of the materials for the early history of the Gothic or Teutonic kingdoms of Norway, Sweden and Denmark are indicated.)
North American Review, Vol. 28, pp. 18–37. January 1829.

Histoire de la Louisiane et de la Cession de cette Colonie par la France aux États-Unis de l'Amérique Septentrionale; précédée d'un Discours sur la Constitution et le Gouvernement des États-Unis. Par M. Barbé-Marbois. Paris, 1829. *North American Review*, Vol. 28, pp. 389–418. April 1829.

1. Analysis of the Egyptian Mythology; to which is subjoined a Critical Examination of the Remains of Egyptian Chronology. By J. C. Prichard, M.D. London, 1819.

2. Aperçu des Résultats Historiques de la Découverte de l'Alphabet Hiéroglyphique Égyptien, par M. Champollion. Paris, 1827.

3. Den Gamle Aegyptiske Tidsrefning, efter Kilderne paa ny bearbejdet, af R. Rask, etc., Copenhagen, 1827.
North American Review, Vol. 29, pp. 361–388. October 1829.

The History of Louisiana, particularly of the Cession of that Colony to the United States of America; with an Introductory Essay on the Constitution and Government of the United States. By Barbé-Marbois. Translated from the French, by an American Citizen. Philadelphia, 1830. *North American Review*, Vol. 30, pp. 551–556. April 1830.

Hin forna Lögbok Islendinga sem nefnist Grágás, i. c. Codex Juris Islandorum antiquissimus, qui nominatur Grágás, ex duobus manuscriptis pergamensis (quae sola supersunt) Bibliothecae Regiae et Legati Arnae-Magnaeani, nunc primum editus; cum Interpretatione Latinâ, Lectionibus Variis, Indicibus Vocum et Rerum, praemissâ Commentatione historicâ et criticâ de hujus Juris Origine et Indole, ab J. F. Schlegel conscriptâ. Havniae, 1829. (This appeared under the title of "Ancient Laws of Iceland.") *North American Review*, Vol. 30, pp. 556–558. April 1830.

Danish Grammar, adapted to the use of Englishmen, with Extracts and Dialogues, etc. By Professor Erasmus Rask. Copenhagen, 1830. *North American Review*, Vol. 30, pp. 558–559. April 1830.

1. A Grammar of the Anglo-Saxon Tongue, with a Praxis. By Erasmus Rask, Professor of Literary History in, and Librarian to, the University of Copenhagen. A new edition, enlarged and improved by the Author, translated from the Danish. By B. Thorpe, Honorary Member of the Icelandic Literary Society, etc. Copenhagen, 1830.

2. Illustrations of Anglo-Saxon Poetry, by John Josias Conybeare, M.A., etc. Professor of Anglo-Saxon and of Poetry in the University of Oxford. Edited with additional notes, etc., by his brother, William Daniel Conybeare. London, 1826. (The review of these two volumes appeared under the title of Anglo-Saxon Language and Literature.)
North American Review, Vol. 33, pp. 325–350. October 1831.

Iceland: or the Journal of a Residence in that Island, during the years 1814 and 1815, containing observations on the Natural Phenomena, History, Literature and Antiquities of the Island; and the Religion, Manners and Customs of its Inhabitants. By Ebenezer Henderson, Doctor in Philosophy, etc. Abridged from the Second Edinburgh Edition. Boston, 1831. *North American Review,* Vol. 35, pp. 75–92. July 1832.

Critisk Undersögelse af Saxos Histories sys Sidster Böger. Ved Dr. Peter Erasmus Müller, Bishop i Sioelland. Kiöbenhavn, 1830. (This is really an Essay on the Danish Constitution.) *Foreign Quarterly Review,* Vol. 11, pp. 128–140. January 1833.

De l'Art Moderne en Allemagne, par M. le Comte A. de Raczynski. Tome 1. Paris, 1836.
Die neuere deutsche Kunst. Berlin, 1836.
(Really an Article on Modern Painting in Germany.)
Foreign Quarterly Review, Vol. 18, pp. 109–118. 1836.

1. Antiquitates Americanae; sive Scriptores Septentrionales rerum ante-Columbianarum in America. (American Antiquities; or accounts from Northern Writers respecting America before the Time of Columbus.) Copenhagen, 1837.
2. Samling af de i Nordens Oldskrifter indeholdhe Efterretninger om de gamle Nordboers Opdagelsesreiser til America, fra det 10de til det 14de Aarhundrede. (Collection of the Evidence contained in Old Writings, respecting the Voyages of Discovery made to America by the Ancient Inhabitants of the North from the 10th to the 14th Century.) Published by the Royal Society of Northern Antiquarians. Copenhagen, 1837. (Really an Essay on the Discovery of America by the Northmen, before Columbus.)
Foreign Quarterly Review, Vol. 21, pp. 89–118. April 1838.

Histoire de l'Art moderne in Allemagne, par le Comte A. Raczynski. Tome III. Paris. *Foreign Quarterly Review,* Vol. 28, p. 455. January 1842.

De la Nature du droit des gens en général, et de l'ouvrage intitulé: "Droit des Gens Actuel de l'Europe" (Das europäeische Völkerrecht der Gegenwart); par M. Heffter, conseiller à la cour de cassation pour la Prusse rhénane, et professeur à la faculté de droit de l'université de Berlin. *Revue de Droit Français et Étranger,* Vol. 1, pp. 955–966. 1844.

Du Droit des Gens Maritime, et de l'ouvrage de M. Théodore

Ortolan, lieutenant de vaisseau, intitulé; Règles internationales et diplomatie de la mer. Tome I, Paris. *Revue de Droit Français et Étranger,* Vol. 2, pp. 199–211. 1845.

Histoire de l'Art Moderne en Allemagne, par le Comte A. Raczynski. 3 vols. Paris, 1836–1841. (Essay on Modern Art in Germany.) *Monthly Review,* Vol. III, N. & I. Series 2, Vol. 166. London, September 1844.

TRANSLATIONS

Carnot, Lazare Nicolas Marguerite, Comte, 1753–1823. An exposition of the political conduct of Lieutenant General Carnot, since the first of July, 1814. By himself. Containing the secret history of the events which happened at Paris, from the return of Napoleon from Elba, until his final abdication. To which is added, Carnot's speeech in the Tribunate, in 1804, against the elevation of Bonaparte to the imperial throne. New York, 1815.

Articles in *National Advocate* from French.

Buenos Aires and Chile Prize Codes.

Code Napoléon (unpublished).

MISCELLANEOUS

Articles in *National Intelligencer, Rhode Island Patriot,* and many other papers and periodicals.

Editorials in *National Advocate.*

"Progress of the Mathematical and Physical Sciences during the Eighteenth Century," (Commencement Address) unpublished.

II

CASES BEFORE THE SUPREME COURT IN WHICH HENRY WHEATON APPEARED AS COUNSEL

1816–1827

The Antonia Johanna. Mr. Wheaton for the appellants. Mr. Gaston contra. Wheaton's Reports, Vol. I, p. 159.

The Friendschaft—Winn et al, Claimants. Mr. Wheaton for appellants and captors. Mr. Gaston for respondents and claimants. *Ibid.,* Vol. III, pp. 14–52.

The United States v. Bevans. Mr. Webster for the defendant. Mr. Wheaton for the United States. *Ibid.,* Vol. III, pp. 336–391.

The Aeolus—Wood, Claimant. Mr. D. B. Ogden and Mr. Wheaton for appellants and claimants. The Attorney General and Mr. Preble contra. *Ibid.,* Vol. III, pp. 392–408.

The Langdon Cheves—Lamb, Claimant. Mr. Hunter and Mr. Wheaton for appellant and claimant. The Attorney General for the United States. *Ibid.,* Vol. IV, pp. 103–104.

The Friendschaft—Moreira, Claimant. Mr. Hopkinson for the claimant. Mr. D. B. Ogden and Mr. Wheaton, contra. *Ibid.,* Vol. IV, pp. 105–107.

The Amiable Isabella—Munos, Claimant. Mr. Gaston and Mr. Harper for appellant and claimant. Mr. Wheaton, Mr. Pinkney and the Attorney General for the captors and respondents. *Ibid.,* Vol. VI, pp. 1–101.

The Bello Corrunes—The Spanish Consul, Claimant. The Attorney General for the United States, Mr. Winder, for the appellants and captors. Mr. Webster and Mr. Wheaton for the respondent and claimant, the Spanish Consul. *Ibid.,* Vol. VI, pp. 152–176.

The Collector—Wilmot, Claimant. Mr. Mitchell for the appellant and claimant. Mr. Pinkney and Mr. Wheaton, contra. *Ibid.,* Vol. VI, pp. 194–203.

The Jonquille. An Admiralty suit. Mr. Wheaton for the respondents. *Ibid.,* Vol. VI, p. 452.

Spring et al. v. The South Carolina Insurance Company. Mr. Hunt for the respondents. Mr. Wheaton for the appellants. *Ibid.*, Vol. VI, pp. 519–520.

The United States v. Six Packages of Goods—Toler, Claimant. The Attorney General and Mr. Pinkney for the United States. Mr. D. B. Ogden and Mr. Wheaton for the claimant. *Ibid.*, Vol. VI, pp. 520–528.

Otis v. Walter. The Attorney General for the plaintiff in error. Mr. Webster and Mr. Wheaton for the defendant in error. *Ibid.*, Vol. VI, pp. 583–592.

Hunt v. Rousmanier's Administrators. Mr. Wheaton for the appellant. Mr. Hunter for the respondents. *Ibid.*, Vol. VIII, pp. 174–217.

Dailey's Lessee v. James. Mr. Wheaton and Mr. D. B. Ogden for the plaintiff. Mr. Sergeant, contra. *Ibid.*, Vol. VIII, pp. 495–542.

Baites v. Peters and Stebbins. Mr. Wheaton for the plaintiff. No counsel appearing for defendants. *Ibid.*, Vol. IX, pp. 556–557.

The United States v. Morris, Marshal of the Southern district of New York. Mr. Wheaton, for the plaintiffs in error. Mr. Webster, Mr. Emmet and Mr. D. B. Ogden for the defendant. *Ibid.*, Vol. X, pp. 246–305.

Stephen Harding & Others, Appellants, v. Asa Handy & Caleb Wheaton, Respondents. Asa Handy & Caleb Wheaton, Appellants v. Stephen Harding & Others, Respondents. Mr. Wheaton for the original plaintiffs. Mr. Coxe (with whom was Mr. Webster) for the defendant, Handy. *Ibid.*, Vol. XI, pp. 103–134.

Armstrong, Plaintiff in Error *against* Toler, Defendant in Error. Mr. Webster and Mr. Wheaton for the plaintiff in error. Mr. C. J. Ingersoll, contra. *Ibid.*, Vol. XI, pp. 258–279.

The Post Master General of the United States *against* Early and others. The Attorney General and Mr. Wheaton, for the plaintiff. Mr. Webster and Mr. Berrien, for the defendants. *Ibid.*, Vol. XII, pp. 136–152.

Jackson, *ex dem,* St. John, *against* Chew. The Attorney General and Mr. D. B. Ogden for the plaintiffs. Mr. Webster and Mr. Wheaton for the defendant. *Ibid.*, Vol. XII, pp. 153–169.

Armstrong *against* Lear, Administrator (with the will annexed) of

Kosciuszko. Mr. E. Livingston and Mr. Wheaton, for the appellant. The Attorney General and Mr. Lear for the respondent. *Ibid.*, Vol. XII, pp. 169–176.

The United States *against* Tillotson and another. The Attorney General and Mr. Coxe for the plaintiffs. Mr. Webster and Mr. Wheaton for the defendants. *Ibid.*, Vol. XII, pp. 180–183.

Ogden, Plaintiff in Error *against* Saunders, Defendant in Error. Mr. Clay, Mr. D. B. Ogden, and Mr. Haines, for the plaintiff in error. Mr. Webster and Mr. Wheaton for the defendant in error. Mr. Webster and Mr. Wheaton against validity. The Attorney General, Mr. E. Livingston, Mr. D. B. Ogden, Mr. Jones, and Mr. Sampson, for the validity. *Ibid.*, Vol. XII, pp. 213–369.

Mason *against* Haile. Mr. Webster and Mr. Bliss, for the plaintiff. Mr. Whipple and Mr. Wheaton, for the defendant. *Ibid.*, Vol. XII, pp. 370–383.

The General Interest Insurance Company, Plaintiffs in Error, *against* Ruggles, Defendant in Error. Mr. D. B. Ogden and Mr. Wheaton for the plaintiffs in error. Mr. Webster and Mr. Bliss for the defendant in error. *Ibid.*, Vol. XII, pp. 408–419.

III

THE COMMERCIAL TREATY BETWEEN THE UNITED STATES AND THE GERMAN CUSTOMS ASSOCIATION

(Taken from the manuscript copy in Henry Wheaton's handwriting. Wheaton MSS)

The United States of America on the one part, & His Majesty the King of Prussia, as well for himself & as representing other sovereign States & parts thereof included in the Prussian system of Customs & Impost, namely, &c. on the other part, being equally animated with the desire of extending, as much as possible, the commercial relations & the mutual exchange of productions between their respective States have agreed with this view, to enter into negotiations, & have named their Plenipotentiaries, that is to say to be who, after having communicated their full Powers, have agreed upon & signed the following articles:

Article I.

The United States of America agree not to impose duties on the importation of the following articles, the growth, produce, & manufacture of the States of the Germanic Association of Customs & Commerce, exceeding

I. Twenty per centum ad valorem on the importation of

1. All woolen, worsted, & cotton mits, caps & bindings, & woolen, worsted, & cotton hosiery, that is to say, stockings, socks, drawers, shirts & all other similar manufactures made on frames.

2. On all musical instruments of every kind, except pianofortes.

II. Fifteen per centum ad valorem on the importation of

1. All articles manufactured of flax or hemp, or of which flax

or hemp shall be the component part of chief value, except cotton-bagging, or any other manufacture suitable to the uses to which cotton-bagging is applied.

2. All manufactures of silk, or of which silk shall be the component part of chief value.

3. Thibet, merinos, merino shawls, & all manufactures of combed wool, or of worsted & silk combined.

4. Polished plate-glass, silvered or not silvered, small pocket-looking glasses from three to ten inches long, & from one & a half to six inches broad, toys of every description, snuff-boxes of papier mâché, lead pencils, lithographic stones, & wooden clocks known under the name of Schwarzwalder clocks.

5. Cologne water, needles, bronze wares of all kinds, planes, scissors, scythes, files, saws, & fish-hooks, gold, silver, & copper wire, tinfoil, & musical strings of all kinds.

6. Leather pocket-books and etuis & all sorts of similar fine leather manufactures known under the name of Offenbacher fine leather fabrics.

III. Ten per centum ad valorem on the importation of

1. All thread-laces & insertings, laces, galoons, tresses, tassels, knots, stars of gold & silver, fine and half fine.

2. Mineral waters, spelter, & hare's wool dressed.

Article II.

The United States of America agree not to increase the present duties of importation upon the wines of Prussia, & not to impose any higher duties upon the wines produced in the other States of the Germanic Association than are, or shall be, imposed upon the wines of Prussia.

Article III.

The States of the Germanic Association of Customs & Commerce agree not to impose duties on the importation of the following articles, the growth & produce of the United States of America exceeding

1. On unmanufactured tobacco leaves four thalers per centner, & on stems three thalers per centner.

2. On lard, two thalers per centner.

Article IV.

The States of the Germanic Association of Customs & Commerce agree not to increase the present duty on the importation of Rice, the growth & produce of the United States of America, & not to impose any duty upon Cotton the growth & produce of the same.

Article V.

The diminutions of, & exemptions from, duties of importation stipulated in the preceding 1, 2, 3, & 4th articles, shall only be applied to the productions & manufactures therein mentioned when laden on board the vessels of one or the other contracting Party, or on board the vessels of those States which are placed on the footing of national vessels by the laws & treaties of one or the other contracting Party, & imported directly from the ports of one Party into the ports of the other.

The States of the Germanic Association of Customs & Commerce reserve the right of considering the ports between the mouths of the Elbe & the Scheldt, both rivers included, or any of them, in this respect, as ports of the Germanic Association of Customs & Commerce.

Article VI.

The productions & manufactures mentioned in this Convention shall be accompanied, on their importation into the respective States, with certificates of origin granted by the competent authorities of the Country, or by the Consuls-General, Consuls, Vice Consuls, or commercial Agents of the contracting Parties resident at the place where the goods are expedited or shipped.

Article VII.

The Contracting Parties reserve the right of extending to other States the advantages respectively granted by the present Convention.

General reductions of duties on importation which may be made by the legislative Acts of either Party, in respect to the articles mentioned in the present Convention shall always be applied to the importation of such articles from the other Party.

If either Party shall, hereafter, grant to any other nation any particular favour in respect to its importations such favour shall immediately become common to the other Party, freely, where it is freely granted, to such other nation, or on yielding the same equivalent when the grant is conditional.

Article VIII.

The stipulations of the present Convention shall be extended to such other States of Germany as may accede to the Germanic Association of Customs & Commerce during the continuance of this Convention.

Article IX.

The stipulations of this Convention shall be carried into execution on the first day of August next.

The present Convention shall remain in force until the first day of August, 1847, & if, twelve months before that day, one of the contracting Parties shall not have given official notice to the other of its intention to terminate the same, this Convention shall remain in force until the first day of August, 1848, and so on until the expiration of twelve months from the day on which one of the contracting Parties shall have received the notice from the other.

Article X.

The present Convention shall be ratified, & the ratifications shall be exchanged at the City of Berlin, within four months from the signature thereof, or sooner if possible.

Signed 25 March, 1844.

NOTES

ABBREVIATIONS OF REFERENCES MOST FREQUENTLY CITED

(The full titles of all works cited will be found in the Bibliography)

Lawrence—William Beach Lawrence, "Introductory Remarks" in *Elements of International Law*, by Henry Wheaton, 1855 Edition.

Wheaton, *Elements*—Wheaton, Henry, *Elements of International Law*, 1855 Edition.

Wheaton MSS.—Copies kept by Wheaton of the despatches sent by him to the United States Department of State when he represented the United States at Berlin. Two volumes. These were given to the Massachusetts Historical Society by Wheaton's daughters. In these volumes may be found copies of several of the despatches missing from the volumes in the State Department.

Wheaton Papers—This refers to the collection of Wheaton's personal papers in the John Hay Library, Brown University.

Wheaton's *Reports*—*Reports of Cases Argued and Adjudged in the Supreme Court of the United States*, 1816–1827.

Preussisches Geheimes Staatsarchiv—The photostatic copies of the German archives now in the Library of Congress. The ones cited are to be found in Preussisches Geheimes Staatsarchiv, Berlin, Auswärtiges Amt, Abteilung II. Rep. 6, Handel, Nordamerika, volumes V to XIV inclusive, Acta betreffend die Handelsverhältnisse mit den Nordamerikanischen Freistaaten. These cover the period from January, 1834, to December, 1847.

Hansard—*Hansard's Parliamentary Debates*, Third Series, 1830–1859.

In the archives of the State Department the Instructions to United States Ministers to all countries are contained in the first thirteen volumes, with the exception of Great Britain. The Instructions to the separate countries start with Volume 14.

NOTES

CHAPTER I

1. Foster Rhea Dulles, *The Old China Trade,* Chapter III, pp. 26–49.
2. *The Book of Rhode Island* (Rhode Island State publication), pp. 43 and 45.
3. Gilbert Chinard, *Thomas Jefferson,* p. 232.
4. Seth Wheaton was born on Friday, November 15, 1759. See William Ensign Lincoln, *Some descendants of . . . Robert Wheaton of Wales, . . . and notes of Related Families,* p. 35.
5. Lawrence, p. xiv.
6. Henry R. Chace, *Owners and Occupants of the Lots, Houses and Shops in the Town of Providence, Rhode Island, in 1798,* Plates I, III, and VI.
7. Lawrence, p. xiv.
8. Among the Wheaton Papers is a document which contains the following: "A Record of the family of Seth Wheaton. The within recorded in Book No. 2, Page 190 of the Records of the Town of Providence for the Recording of births and marriages in said Town, January 19, 1807, Nathan W. Jackson, Clerk. Seth Wheaton was married by the Rev. James Manning on Sunday the 29th day of August 1784, to Abigail Wheaton daughter of Ephraim Wheaton. Their Offspring,

Henry	Wheaton	born	Nov. 28,	1785	died	Mar. 11, 1848.
Sally Marsh	"	"	Sep. 12,	1788	"	Nov. 23, 1816.
Eliza	"	"	June 10,	1790	"	Feb. 24, 1876.
Mary	"	"	May 27,	1793	"	Feb. 1871.
Ann	"	"	Dec. 19,	1794	"	Feb. 1876.
Abigail	"	"	Jan. 5,	1797	"	June 24, 1872.
Ruth	"	"	July 18,	1799	"	same day.
Thomas Jefferson	"	"	Nov. 25,	1800	"	Mar. 14, 1806."

9. Lawrence, p. xiv.
10. Lincoln, *op. cit.,* p. 41. See also the *Biographical Cyclopedia of Representative Men of Rhode Island.*
11. Henry Wheaton to Levi Wheaton, Berlin, May 10, 1843, Wheaton Papers.
12. *Memories of Brown. Traditions and Recollections gathered from many sources.* Editors, Robert Perkins Brown, Henry Robinson Palmer, Henry Lyman Koopman, Librarian, and Clarence Saunders Brigham (hereinafter cited as *Memories of Brown*), pp. 32–37.
13. The early catalogues of Rhode Island College were written in Latin; when possible even the names of the students were so written. Wheaton's name appears in them as *Henricus Wheaton.*
14. *Memories of Brown,* pp. 32–37.

15. Henry M. King, D.D., *Historical Statement*. Folder issued by The First Baptist Church, Providence, R. I.

16. *Ibid.*, p. 4.

17. *Historical Catalogue of Brown University, Providence, Rhode Island, 1764–1894,* pp. 45–47.

18. *Ibid.*

19. Letter from John Whipple to William Beach Lawrence, February 1854, Wheaton Papers.

20. According to Edward Everett Hale in "A Fossil from the Tertiary," *Atlantic Monthly,* Vol. XLIV, p. 106, July, 1879, the refusal was simply on the ground that the Providence college had admitted as "Sophimores" persons who would not rank as Freshmen at Cambridge.

21. Whipple to Lawrence, February 1854, Wheaton Papers.

22. Walter C. Bronson, *The History of Brown University, 1764–1914,* pp. 139–141; *Memories of Brown,* pp. 35–36.

23. Program of Commencement, 1802, Brown University.

24. Bronson, *op. cit.,* p. 154.

CHAPTER II

1. The Alumni records of Brown University were used, and the career of each member of the class of 1802 was checked from them.

2. Anonymous. "Henry Wheaton." *Homes of American Statesmen: with Anecdotical, Personal, and Descriptive Sketches, by various Members* (hereinafter cited as *Homes of American Statesmen,* p. 449.

3. Whipple to Lawrence, February 1854, Wheaton Papers.

4. Lawrence, p. xv.

5. Letter from Wheaton to his father, Paimboeuf, July 11, 1805, Wheaton Papers. The letters of Wheaton to his father for the years 1805–1806 have been printed in the *Proceedings Mass. Hist. Soc.,* Vol. XVIII, pp. 20–22 and Vol. XIX, pp. 361–367.

6. Wheaton to his father, Nantes, July 16, 1805, Wheaton Papers.

7. *Ibid.*, Bordeaux, July 30, 1805.

8. *Ibid.*

9. *Ibid.*, Poitiers, August 18, 1805.

10. *Homes of American Statesmen,* p. 450.

11. *Ibid.*

12. Wheaton to his father, Paris, October 10, 1805, Wheaton Papers.

13. *Ibid.*, London, November 7, 1805.

14. *Ibid.*

15. *Ibid.*, London, January 6, 1806.

16. *Ibid.*

17. *Ibid.*, London, January 30, 1806.

18. *Homes of American Statesmen,* p. 453.

19. Wheaton to his father, London, March 2, 1806, Wheaton Papers.

20. *Ibid.*, London, May 12, 1806.

21. Note in Wheaton Papers.

22. Papers in Rhode Island Historical Society, Providence.

23. Lawrence, p. xxiii.

24. Papers of James Madison, Library of Congress.

25. Jabez D. Hammond, *History of Political Parties in the State of New York, from the ratification of the Federal Constitution to Dec. 1840 in 2 vols.* (hereinafter cited as Hammond), Vol. 1, Chap. XVIII, p. 340.

26. John S. Jenkins, *History of Political Parties in the State of New York, from the Acknowledgment of the Independence of the United States to the Inauguration of the twelfth President, March, 1849* (hereinafter cited as Jenkins), pp. 155–156.

27. This oration was published in pamphlet form, Providence, 1810.

28. Lawrence, p. xxiv.

29. Wheaton's oration, pamphlet, p. 16.

CHAPTER III

1. Lawrence, p. xxiv.

2. Frederic Hudson, *Journalism in the United States, from 1690 to 1872*, p. 225; Lawrence, p. xxv.

3. *The National Advocate*, Dec. 15, 1812.

4. Henry Wheaton to Levi Wheaton, January 2, 1813, Wheaton Papers.

5. *Ibid.*, March 9, 1813.

6. *The National Advocate*, March 11, 1813.

7. Edward Everett, "Life, Services and Works of Henry Wheaton," *North American Review*, Vol. LXXXII, p. 11, January 1856.

8. *The National Advocate*, March 6, 1813.

9. *Ibid.*, July 19, 20 and 21, 1813.

10. *Ibid.*, July 30, 1813.

11. Lawrence, p. xxix.

12. *Ibid.*

13. *The National Advocate;* Lawrence, p. xxxi.

14. Lawrence, p. xxviii.

15. *The National Advocate*, August 2, 1813.

16. *Ibid.*, August 13, 1813.

17. *Ibid.*, November 30, 1813.

18. Henry Wheaton to Levi Wheaton, February 23, 1814, Wheaton Papers.

19. *Ibid.*, May 11, 1813.

20. *Ibid.*, July 21, 1813.

21. Mrs. Henry Wheaton to Levi Wheaton, August 22, 1814, Wheaton Papers.

22. Henry Wheaton to Levi Wheaton, September 15, 1814, Wheaton Papers.

23. *Ibid.*, December 1, 1814.

24. *Ibid.*, April 16, 1814.

25. This oration was published in pamphlet form, New York, 1814.

26. Catherine Wheaton to Levi Wheaton, Baltimore, July 5, 1814, Wheaton Papers. This reference was to Peter S. Du Ponceau, linguist, ethnologist and international lawyer.

27. Lawrence, p. xxx.

28. *The National Intelligencer*, Jan. 6, 1815.

29. *North American Review,* Vol. I, May, 1815.

30. F. L. Mott, "One Hundred and Twenty Years," *North American Review,* Vol. CCXL, No. 1, pp. 144–145, June 1935.

31. Lawrence, p. lvii.

32. George Douglass to Henry Wheaton, November 21, 1815, Wheaton Papers.

33. Lawrence, p. xxxii.

34. Richard Rush, *American Jurisprudence: Written and published at Washington, being a few reflections suggested on reading "Wheaton on Captures,"* Washington City, 1815. Presented Dec. 6, 1816, to the American Philosophical Society by the Author. A pamphlet of 52 pages which is in the library of the Society among their "Pamphlets on Law," Vol. 8, No. 8.

35. Comte Lazare Nicholas Marguerite Carnot, 1753–1823. *An exposition of the political conduct of Lieutenant General Carnot, since the first of July, 1814.* By himself. Translation published in New York, 1815.

36. Henry Wheaton to Levi Wheaton, April 9, 1815, Wheaton Papers.

37. Lawrence, p. xxix.

CHAPTER IV

1. Albert J. Beveridge, *Life of John Marshall,* Vol. III, pp. 1–10.

2. Frederick C. Hicks, *Men and Books Famous in the Law* (hereinafter cited as Hicks), p. 199.

3. *Writings and Speeches of Daniel Webster,* Vol. XV, pp. 51–52.

4. Wheaton's *Reports,* Vol. I, p. 1.

5. *Report of the Copyright Case of Wheaton vs. Peters,* p. 6.

6. Henry Wheaton to Edward Wheaton, Sept. 23, 1818, Wheaton Papers.

7. *Daily National Intelligencer,* Feb. 13, 1817.

8. Wheaton's *Reports,* Vol. I, pp. 1–10.

9. Edward Channing, *History of the United States,* Vol. V, p. 309.

10. Wheaton's *Reports,* Vol. I, Preface.

11. *Writings and Speeches of Daniel Webster,* Vol. XV, pp. 44–54.

12. *Daily National Intelligencer,* Feb. 13, 1817.

13. Henry Wheaton to Edward Wheaton, Feb. 13, 1817, Wheaton Papers.

14. *United States Statutes at Large,* Ch. 63; Warren, Vol. I, p. 455.

15. Hicks, p. 201.

16. Published in pamphlet form, 1817; Lawrence, p. xxxiii.

17. Henry Wheaton to Levi Wheaton, Oct. 18, 1817, Wheaton Papers.

18. Wheaton's *Reports,* Vol. I, p. 159.

19. *The Friendschaft*—Winn, et al., Claimants, Wheaton's *Reports,* Vol. III, pp. 14–52. *The United States* v. *Bevans, ibid.,* pp. 336–391. *The Aeolus*—Wood, Claimant, *ibid.,* pp. 392–409.

20. Henry Wheaton to John Bailey, Feb. 1818, Washburn Papers, Vol. XX.

21. Webster to Justice Story, Sept. 9, 1818, *Writings and Speeches of Daniel Webster,* Vol. XVII, p. 287.

22. Henry Wheaton to Edward Wheaton, Sept. 21, 1818, Wheaton Papers.

23. Wheaton's *Reports,* Vol. IV, p. 316.

24. *Ibid.,* p. 518.

25. *The Langdon Cheves*—Lamb, Claimant, Wheaton's *Reports,* Vol. IV, pp. 103–104. *The Friendschaft*—Moreira, Claimant, *ibid.,* pp. 105–107.

26. *Ibid.,* Note 2.

27. Henry Wheaton to John Bailey, March 8, 1819, Washburn Papers, Vol. XX.

28. *Ibid.,* March 28, 1819.

29. *Ibid.,* June 14, 1819.

30. *North American Review,* Vol. VIII, pp. 253–276, March 1819.

31. Edward Everett in *North American Review,* Vol. LXXXII, p. 14, January 1856.

32. Henry Wheaton to John Bailey, July 10, 1819, Washburn Papers, Vol. XX.

33. *Ibid.*

34. Henry Wheaton to Levi Wheaton, Nov. 11, 1820, Wheaton Papers.

35. *Ibid.*

36. Published in New York, 1821.

37. *North American Review,* July 1820, Vol. II, pp. 31–37.

38. *Ibid.,* pp. 114–124.

39. Lawrence, p. lviii.

40. Published in New York Historical Society *Proceedings.* Reviewed by Edward Everett in *North American Review,* Vol. XIII, p. 154.

41. Lawrence, p. liv.

42. *Ibid.,* p. lv.

43. *Ibid.,* p. lvii.

44. Postscript by Mrs. Wheaton to letter from Henry Wheaton to Levi Wheaton, March 11, 1817, Wheaton Papers.

45. Letter from Theophilus Parsons to Mrs. Charles C. Little, Cambridge, May 23, 1853, Wheaton Papers.

46. *Homes of American Statesmen,* pp. 449–469.

47. *Ibid.*

48. Letter from The First Congregational Church in New York to the Church in Chelsea, also sent to twenty other churches, Nov. 26, 1821, Wheaton Papers.

CHAPTER V

1. Dixon Ryan Fox, *The Decline of Aristocracy in the Politics of New York,* pp. 229–237 (hereinafter cited as Fox); Hammond, Vol. 2, pp. 1–2.

2. Fox, p. 236, Note 5; Lawrence, p. xlvii.

3. Fox, p. 240, refers to letter of Van Buren to J. A. King, Oct. 28, 1821, *King Correspondence;* Jenkins, p. 241.

4. Fox, pp. 237–239; Jenkins, p. 241; Lawrence, p. xlvii.

5. Stone and Carter, *Proceedings of New York State Constitutional Convention;* Fox, pp. 239–243; Jenkins, pp. 242–244.

6. Fox, p. 244; Hammond, Vol. 2, p. 7.

7. Jenkins, p. 243.

8. Fox, p. 244.

9. *Ibid.*, p. 264; Hammond, Vol. 2, p. 55.

10. Jenkins, p. 252.

11. Hammond, Vol. 2, pp. 57, 61.

12. *Ibid.*, p. 63.

13. Jenkins, p. 257.

14. Edward Everett, *North American Review*, Vol. LXXXII, pp. 14–15; Lawrence, p. xlviii.

15. Fox, p. 268.

16. Everett, *op. cit.;* Lawrence, p. xlviii.

17. Fox, p. 268, quotes from John Fiske, "Thomas Jefferson, Conservative Reformer," *Essays, Historical and Literary*, New York, 1902, p. 145 *et seq.*

18. Jenkins, p. 259.

CHAPTER VI

1. Hammond, Vol. 2, p. 126.

2. Wheaton to Levi Wheaton, April 11, 1823, Wheaton Papers.

3. Thomas Robson Hay, "John C. Calhoun and the Presidential Campaign of 1824," *The North Carolina Historical Review*, Vol. XII, p. 30, January 1935; Jenkins, p. 279.

4. Hammond, Vol. 2, pp. 130–131.

5. Calhoun to M. Stanly, July 20, 1823, Calhoun Correspondence, pp. 210–211.

6. Wheaton to Levi Wheaton, Oct. 19, 1823, Wheaton Papers.

7. C. H. Rammelkamp, "The Campaign of 1824 in New York," *American Historical Association Annual Report, 1904* (hereinafter cited as Rammelkamp), p. 186.

8. Hammond, Vol. 2, p. 132.

9. Rammelkamp, p. 190.

10. Henry Wheaton to Theophilus Parsons, Sept. 6, 1823, Wheaton Papers.

11. Wheaton to Levi Wheaton, Sept. 27, 1823, Wheaton Papers.

12. Wheaton to Daniel Webster, Nov. 30, 1823, Webster Papers, Vol. 1, Library of Congress.

13. Wheaton to Webster, Dec. 1, 1823, Webster Papers, Vol. 2, New Hampshire Historical Society.

14. Wheaton to Levi Wheaton, Dec. 13, 1823, Wheaton Papers.

15. *Ibid.*, Dec. 24, 1823.

16. Jenkins, pp. 281–282.

17. Hammond, Vol. 2, pp. 140–142.

18. Journal of the Assembly of the State of New York of the 47th Session, Jan. 6, 1824, p. 7.

19. *Ibid.*

20. Journal of the New York Assembly, Jan. 7, 1824, p. 17; Jenkins, p. 282.

21. Journal of the New York Assembly, Jan. 7, 1824, p. 18.

22. *Ibid.*, Jan. 8, 1824, p. 18.

23. *Ibid.*, pp. 23–24.

24. *Ibid.*, p. 24.

25. *Albany Daily Advertiser,* Jan. 10, 1824.

26. Henry Wheaton to Levi Wheaton, Jan. 15, 1824, Wheaton Papers. The same thought is expressed in a letter from Wheaton to Samuel L. Gouvernour, February 3, 1824, Gouvernour Papers. Wheaton was appointed a member of various committees, Journal of the Assembly, Jan. 8, 1824, p. 23; Jan. 9, 1824, p. 29; Jan. 9, 1824, p. 30; Jan. 10, 1824, p. 33; Jan. 10, 1824, p. 35; Jan. 13, 1824, p. 51.

27. Journal of the Assembly, Jan. 22, 1824, pp. 146–148.

28. Journal of the Assembly, Feb. 4, 1824, pp. 291–298.

29. *Ibid.*, Feb. 7, 1824, p. 381.

30. Jenkins, p. 286.

31. *Memoirs of John Quincy Adams,* Vol. VI, March 13, 1824.

CHAPTER VII

1. *Memoirs of John Quincy Adams,* April 6, 1824, Vol. VI, p. 282.

2. Jenkins, p. 290.

3. *Ibid.*, p. 291.

4. *Ibid.*

5. Hammond, Vol. 2, p. 159.

6. Rammelkamp, p. 190.

7. Jenkins, p. 292.

8. Henry Wheaton to Rufus King, April 12, 1824, *Life and Correspondence of Rufus King,* Vol. VI, pp. 564–565.

9. Hammond, Vol. 2, p. 163.

10. *Ibid.*

11. *Autobiography of Martin Van Buren,* p. 143.

12. Rammelkamp, p. 192.

13. *Ibid.*, p. 194.

14. Fox, pp. 289–290; Rammelkamp, p. 195.

15. Henry Wheaton to Levi Wheaton, Aug. 21, 1824, Wheaton Papers.

16. Rammelkamp, p. 193.

17. Hammond, Vol. 2, p. 169.

18. Rammelkamp, p. 196.

19. Hammond, Vol. 2, pp. 170–171.

20. *Ibid.*, p. 170.

21. John Bigelow, "DeWitt Clinton as a Politician," Extracts of letters of DeWitt Clinton, published in *Harper's Monthly Magazine,* Vol. L, p. 569.

22. Hammond, Vol. 2, p. 172.

23. *Ibid.*

24. *Ibid.*, p. 173.

25. Rammelkamp, p. 195.

26. Hammond, Vol. 2, p. 175.

27. Rammelkamp, p. 196.

28. *Ibid.*, p. 198.

29. *Ibid.*

30. Adams to Wheaton, Nov., 1824, Lawrence, p. l.

31. Calhoun to Wheaton, Nov. 20, 1824, Lawrence, p. li.

CHAPTER VIII

1. Henry Wheaton to Levi Wheaton, March 5, 1824, Wheaton Papers.

2. *Hunt* v. *Rousmanier's Administrators, Wheaton Reports,* 1823, Vol. VIII, pp. 174–217. *Dailey's Lessee* v. *James, ibid.,* pp. 495–542.

3. Henry Wheaton, *An Abridgment of the Law of Nisi Prius, by William Selwyn, Esq., of Lincoln's Inn, Barrister at Law,* Second American, from the Fifth London Edition; with Notes and References to the Decisions of the Courts of this Country, 2 vols.

4. *North American Review,* Vol. XIX, pp. 155–158, July 1824.

5. Hicks, p. 198.

6. *North American Review,* Vol. XVI, pp. 196–199, January 1823.

7. Henry Wheaton to John Bailey, March 24, 1823, Washburn Papers, Vol. XX. There are also two other letters in this collection from Wheaton to Bailey concerning this vacancy; one with no date, which was received by Bailey on May 2, 1823; the other, dated June 9 or 10, 1823. The fact that Wheaton was a candidate as was also Chief Justice Spencer is stated both in Jenkins, p. 278 and in Hammond, Vol. 2, pp. 136–137.

8. John C. Calhoun to M. Stanly, July 20, 1823, Calhoun Corresp., pp. 210–211. See also Warren, Vol. II, pp. 47–48.

9. Wheaton's *Reports,* Feb. Term, 1824, Vol. IX, p. 1.

10. Henry Wheaton to Daniel Webster, Nov. 30, 1823, Daniel Webster Papers, Vol. 1, Library of Congress. The three cases mentioned were *Baits* v. *Peters & Stebbins; Ogden* v. *Saunders; J. Green Pearson* v. *Lewis & Carter.*

11. *Baits* v. *Peters & Stebbins,* Wheaton's *Reports,* Vol. IX, pp. 556–557.

12. Wheaton's *Reports,* Vol. XII, p. 213; Claude M. Fuess, *Daniel Webster,* Vol. I, p. 263. Warren, Vol. II, pp. 147–148.

13. Wheaton's *Reports,* Vol. IX, p. 738.

14. Fuess, *Daniel Webster,* Vol. I, pp. 262–263.

15. Wheaton's *Reports,* Vol. IX, p. 1.

16. *The Case of Gibbons against Ogden;* heard and determined in the Supreme Court of the United States, Feb. Term, 1824, on appeal from the Court of Errors in the State of New York, and involving the Constitutionality of the laws of that State, granting to Livingston and Fulton the exclusive navigation of its Waters by Steam Boats, New York, 1824.

17. Charles Warren, *Congress, the Constitution, and the Supreme Court,* p. 268.

18. An address pronounced at the opening of the New York Athenaeum, December 14, 1824, published in pamphlet form in New York, 1825.

19. Lawrence, p. lvi.

20. *Ibid.*

21. Wheaton's *Reports,* Feb. Term 1825, Vol. X, pp. 246–305. Memorandum, *ibid.,* p. 1. *Stephen Harding and others,* v. *Asa Handy and Caleb Wheaton,*

Wheaton's *Reports,* Feb. Term, 1826, Vol. XI, pp. 103–134. *Armstrong* v. *Toler, ibid.,* pp. 258–279.

22. Wheaton's *Reports,* Jan. Term, 1827, Vol. XII, pp. 169–176, *Armstrong* v. *Lear, Administrator.*

23. *Ibid.*

24. *Ogden* v. *Saunders, ibid.,* pp. 213–369. *Jackson* v. *Chew, ibid.,* pp. 153–169. *The United States* v. *Tillotson, ibid.,* pp. 180–183.

25. *Ogden* v. *Saunders, ibid.,* pp. 213–369.

26. *The Postmaster General of the United States* v. *Early and others, ibid.,* pp. 136–152.

27. *Mason* v. *Haile, ibid.,* pp. 370–383.

28. *The General Interest Insurance Co.* v. *Ruggles, ibid.,* pp. 408–419.

29. Henry Wheaton to Theophilus Parsons, Sept. 6, 1823, Wheaton Papers.

30. Henry Wheaton to James Madison, Sept. 29, 1823, Papers of James Madison, Library of Congress.

31. Madison to Wheaton, Oct. 15, 1823, *ibid.*

32. Wheaton to Madison, Jan. 1, 1824, *ibid.*

33. *Ibid.,* Feb. 27, 1825.

34. Madison to Wheaton, April 1, 1825, *ibid.*

35. Madison to Wheaton, July 18, 1824, and Feb. 26, 1827, Lawrence, pp. lviii-lix.

36. *Ibid.*

37. Henry Wheaton to James Monroe, Nov. 25, 1825, Papers of James Monroe, Vol. XXI, No. 2752, Library of Congress.

38. *Ibid.,* Dec. 1, 1825 and Dec. 14, 1825, Vol. XXI, Nos. 2753 and 2754; April 16, 1827, Vol. XXII, No. 2787. Also letters of Monroe to Wheaton, 1827, *ibid.,* Vol. VI, Nos. 732 and 749.

39. Henry Wheaton, *Life of William Pinkney,* pp. 193–372.

40. *Ibid.,* pp. 517–549.

41. Henry Wheaton to James Madison, July 26, 1826, Madison Papers.

42. *North American Review,* Vol. XXIV, p. 68.

CHAPTER IX

1. William Allen Butler, *The Revision of the Statutes of the State of New York and Revisers,* pp. 5 and 25; Hicks, *op. cit.,* pp. 195–196.

2. Butler, *op. cit.,* p. 30.

3. *Ibid.,* p. 31.

4. The following were reviewed in the *North American Review,* Vol. XX, pp. 393–417, April 1825:

    1. Code Civil, suivi de l'Exposé des Motifs sur Chaque Loi preséntée par les Orateurs du Gouvernement, etc. 11 Tomes. Paris, 1809.

    2. Conférence du Code Civil avec la Discussion particulière du Conseil d'État et du Tribunat. 8 Tomes. Paris, 1805.

    3. Code de Procédure Civile. 2 Tomes. Paris, 1808.

    4. Code Pénal, suivi des Motifs présentés par les Orateurs du Gouvernement, etc. 2 Tomes. Paris, 1812.

    5. Code d'Instruction Criminelle, suivi des Motifs, etc. Paris, 1809.

6. Code de Commerce. 2 Tomes. Paris, 1812.

7. Les cinq Codes avec Notes et Traités pour servir à un Cours complet de Droit Français à l'Usage des Étudians en Droit, et de toutes les Classes de Citoyens cultivés. Par J. B. Sirey, Avocat aux Conseils du Roi, et à la Cour de Cassation. Paris, 1819.

5. The review of "An Essay on the Doctrine of Contracts; being an Inquiry how Contracts are affected in Law and Morals, by Concealment, Error, or Inadequate Price." By Gulean C. Verplanck. New York, 1825. *North American Review*, Vol. XXII, April, 1826.

6. Lawrence, p. lvii.

7. *Memoirs of John Quincy Adams*, March 13, 1827, Vol. VII, p. 238.

8. Lawrence, p. lxi.

9. Butler, *op. cit.*, p. 30.

10. *Ibid.*

11. Lawrence, p. liii; Wheaton to Governor Clinton, June 1827.

CHAPTER X

1. *Memoirs of John Quincy Adams*, Vol. VI, p. 472.

2. *Ibid.*, Feb. 28, 1825, p. 514.

3. *Ibid.*, pp. 413–415, 484–524.

4. Henry Wheaton to Mrs. Wheaton, 1825, Wheaton Papers.

5. Henry Wheaton to Daniel Webster, Webster Papers, Library of Congress.

6. Lawrence, p. lx.

7. Wheaton's *Reports*, Vol. X, Feb. Term, 1825, p. 1; Vol. XI, Feb. Term, 1826, p. 1; Vol. XII, Feb. Term, 1827, p. 1.

8. Edward Everett to Henry Wheaton (Confidential), Oct. 9, 1826, Everett Papers, Vol. 58, p. 26, Massachusetts Hist. Soc.

9. John Quincy Adams to Henry Wheaton, March 3, 1827, Credences, Vol. 2, Dept. of State MSS.

10. *Memoirs of John Quincy Adams*, March 13, 1827, Vol. VII, p. 238.

11. *Ibid.*, March 18, 1827, Vol. VII, p. 242.

12. Jonathan Russell to Henry Wheaton, June 6, 1827, Russell Papers, Brown University.

13. Henry Wheaton to James Monroe, April 16, 1827, Monroe Papers, Vol. XXII, No. 2787.

14. *American Quarterly Review*, Vol. I, pp. 438–458, June 1827.

CHAPTER XI

1. Henry Wheaton to Seth Wheaton, July 28, 1827, Wheaton Papers.

2. G. P. Gooch, *History and Historians in the Nineteenth Century*, pp. 1–283.

3. Wheaton to Story, Nov. 20, 1827.

4. Lawrence, pp. lx-lxi.

5. Herbert B. Adams, *The Life and Writings of Jared Sparks*, 1893, Vol. II, p. 63.

6. Lawrence, p. lxi.

7. Henry Wheaton to Seth Wheaton, Sept. 25, 1827, Wheaton Papers.

8. Henry Wheaton to Henry Clay, Secretary of State, Sept. 29, 1827, Despatches, Denmark, Vol. 1B, No. 1, Dept. of State MSS.

9. Henry Clay to the Minister of Foreign Affairs, Denmark, May 21, 1827, Credences, Vol. 2, Dept. of State MSS.

10. Wheaton to Clay, Despatch No. 1, Sept. 29, 1827, Dept. of State MSS.

11. Lawrence, p. lxii.

12. Wheaton to Clay, Despatch No. 1, Sept. 29, 1827, Dept. of State MSS.

13. Lawrence, p. lxii.

14. Wheaton to Clay, Despatch No. 1, Sept. 29, 1827, Dept. of State MSS.

15. Diary of Henry Wheaton, Entry under date of Sept. 27, 1827, Wheaton Papers.

16. *Ibid.*, Sept. 29, 1827.

17. Henry Wheaton to Seth Wheaton, Sept. 25, 1827, Wheaton Papers.

18. *Homes of American Statesmen*, pp. 449–469.

19. Diary of Henry Wheaton, Entry under date of Oct. 28, 1827, Wheaton Papers.

20. *Ibid.*, Nov. 11, 1827.

21. *Ibid.*, Nov. 17, 1827.

22. *Ibid.*, Nov. 22, 1827.

23. *Ibid.*, Jan. 22, 1827. He was buried on the 25th of January in the "Burying Ground out of the Walls."

24. Diary of Henry Wheaton, Dec. 7, 1827, Wheaton Papers.

25. *Ibid.*, Feb. 23, 1827.

26. Wheaton to Clay, Nov. 20, 1827, Despatches, Denmark, Vol. 1B (marked "Private"), Dept. of State MSS.

27. Jonathan Russell to Henry Wheaton, June 30, 1827, Russell Papers.

CHAPTER XII

1. Diary of Henry Wheaton, Oct. 10, 1827, Wheaton Papers.

2. Lawrence, pp. lxii, lxiii.

3. Herbert B. Adams, *op. cit.*, Vol. II, p. 84.

4. Diary of Henry Wheaton, Oct. 12, 1827, Wheaton Papers.

5. Lawrence, pp. lxii, lxiii.

6. *American Quarterly Review*, Vol. III, pp. 481–490, June 1828.

7. *Ibid.*, p. 481.

8. *Ibid.*, pp. 485–489. *See also* Adolph B. Benson, "Henry Wheaton's Writings on Scandinavia," (hereinafter cited as Benson) *Journal of English and Germanic Philology*, Vol. XXIX, p. 548, October 1930.

9. *North American Review*, Vol. XXVII, pp. 285–299, October 1828.

10. Lawrence, p. lxiv. Also Edward Everett in article on Wheaton in *North American Review*, Vol. LXXXII, p. 19, January 1856.

11. *American Quarterly Review*, Vol. IV, pp. 350–366, December 1828.

12. *Ibid.*, p. 350.

13. *North American Review*, Vol. XXVIII, pp. 18–37, January 1829.

14. Everett, *North American Review*, Vol. LXXXII, p. 19.

15. Benson, p. 551.

16. *North American Review*, Vol. XXIX, pp. 361–388, October 1829.

17. *Ibid.*, Vol. XXX, pp. 556–559, April 1830.

18. Benson, pp. 547–548.

19. Proposal submitted Nov. 7, 1829, Minutes of American Philosophical Society.

20. Minutes of American Philosophical Society.

21. Records of Alpha of Phi Beta Kappa Society, Brown University.

22. Lawrence, p. lxiii.

23. *Ibid.*

24. *North American Review*, Vol. XXXIII, pp. 325–350, October 1831.

25. Wheaton to Levi Wheaton, June 1831, Wheaton Papers.

26. Wheaton, *History of the Northmen*, Preface p. vi.

27. *Ibid.*, p. v.

28. Wheaton to Levi Wheaton, Berlin, Feb. 22, 1844, Wheaton Papers.

29. *Revue de Droit Français et Étranger*, Tome I, p. 633.

30. *The London Athenaeum*, 1831, p. 453.

31. *The Westminster Review*, Vol. XV, pp. 442–457, October 1831.

32. *The Monthly Review*, New and Improved Series, Vol. III, pp. 1–12, September 1831.

33. *Ibid.*, p. 12.

34. *American Quarterly Review*, Vol. X, pp. 311–334, December 1831.

35. *American Monthly Review*, Vol. III, pp. 245–256, March 1832.

36. *North American Review*, Vol. XXXV, pp. 342–371, October 1832. This review also was published in Vol. 8, of his works, 1883. Discussions of Irving's review appear in Everett, *North American Review*, Vol. LXXXII, p. 20, and in Benson, "Scandinavians in the Works of Washington Irving." *Scandinavian Studies and Notes*, Vol. IX, pp. 207–223.

37. *Foreign Quarterly Review*, Vol. XI, pp. 128–140, January 1833.

CHAPTER XIII

1. Clay to Wheaton, Instructions, U. S. Ministers, Vol. 11, p. 339, No. 1, Dept. of State MSS. Also H. Ex. Doc. 249, 22 Cong., 1 Sess., p. 2.

2. Wheaton to Van Buren, Nov. 24, 1829, enclosing Protocol of last conference with Danish Commissioners, Despatches, Denmark, Vol. 1B, No. 11, Dept. of State MSS. Also H. Ex. Doc. No. 249, *op. cit.*, pp. 22–39.

3. Clay to Wheaton, Instructions, U. S. Ministers, Vol. 11, p. 339, No. 1, Dept. of State MSS. Also H. Ex. Doc. No. 249, *op. cit.*, pp. 2–10.

4. *Ibid.* The official note of de Rosenkrantz to Erving was dated May 8, 1812.

5. *Ibid.*

6. *Ibid.* The despatch of Hughes was dated August 19, 1825.

7. Miller, *Treaties etc., of the United States*, Doc. No. 51, April 26, 1826, Vol. 3, pp. 239–248.

8. Instructions, U. S. Ministers, Vol. 11, p. 354, No. 1, Dept. of State MSS.

9. Clay to Chevalier Pederson, April 25, 1826, Instructions, U. S. Ministers, Vol. 11, p. 339, No. 1, Dept. of State MSS. Also H. Ex. Doc. No. 249, *op. cit.,* pp. 2–10.

10. Clay to Wheaton, May 31, 1827, Instructions, U. S. Ministers, Vol. 11, pp. 339–354, No. 1, Dept. of State MSS. Also H. Ex. Doc. No. 249, *op. cit.,* pp. 2–10.

11. *Ibid.,* August 3, 1827, Vol. 11, p. 370, No. 3, and August 13, 1827, Vol. 11, p. 371, No. 4.

12. Wheaton to Clay, December 22, 1827, Despatches, Denmark, Vol. 1B, No. 2, Dept. of State MSS.

13. *Ibid.*

14. *Ibid.,* Despatch No. 3, March 4, 1828.

15. *Ibid.,* Despatch No. 2, December 22, 1827.

16. *Ibid.,* (marked "Private"), July 28, 1828.

17. *Ibid.,* Despatch No. 5, December 31, 1828.

18. *Ibid. Elements,* pp. 460, 594–606.

19. Count Schimmelmann to Wheaton, January 12, 1829, Dept. of State MSS. Also II. Ex. Doc. 249, *op. cit.,* pp. 15–16.

20. Wheaton to Clay, January 31, 1829, Despatches, Denmark, Vol. 1B, No. 6, Dept. of State MSS. Also H. Ex. Doc. No. 249, *op. cit.,* p. 14.

21. Wheaton to Van Buren, October 17, 1829, Despatches, Denmark, Vol. 1B, No. 9, Dept. of State MSS. Also H. Ex. Doc. No. 249, *op. cit.,* p. 18.

22. Van Buren to Wheaton, May 11, 1829, Instructions, U. S. Ministers, Vol. 13, pp. 4–6, No. 6, Dept. of State MSS.

23. Wheaton to Van Buren, Oct. 17, 1829, Despatch No. 9, enclosing protocol dated August 27, 1829, and results of meeting of Sept. 10, 1829. The State Dept. was further informed of the state of the negotiations by Despatches Nos. 10 and 11, dated respectively Dec. 5, 1829 and Jan. 9, 1830, enclosing an extensive protocol of a conference on Nov. 24, 1829, Despatches, Denmark, Vol. 1B, Dept. of State MSS.

24. Van Buren to Wheaton, January 13, 1830, Instructions, U. S. Ministers, Vol. 13, pp. 81–82, No. 8, Dept. of State MSS. Also H. Ex. Doc. No. 249, *op. cit.,* pp. 39–40.

25. Wheaton to Van Buren, March 27, 1830, Despatches, Denmark, Vol. 1B (marked "Private"), Dept. of State MSS.

26. *Ibid.,* March 29, 1830, No. 14. The text of the treaty is given in Miller, *Treaties, etc., of the United States,* Doc. No. 68, Vol. 3, pp. 531–540. See also Martens, *Nouveau Recueil,* tom. viii, p. 350; Elliot's *American Diplomatic Code,* Vol. 1, p. 453. A Report of the passing of the Convention was quoted from the *Washington Telegraph* in *Niles' Weekly Register* on June 12, 1830, Vol. 38, p. 292, and the treaty was printed in full in the same paper on June 19, 1830, Vol. 38, pp. 307–308.

27. Miller, *Treaties, etc., of the United States,* Doc. No. 68, Article V, Vol. 3, p. 537. *Elements,* p. 603.

28. Wheaton to Van Buren, March 29, 1830, Despatches, Denmark, Vol. 1B, No. 14, Dept. of State MSS.

29. Lawrence, p. lxxiv. *Elements,* p. 606.

30. Wheaton to Van Buren, April 3, 1830, Despatches, Denmark, Vol. 1B, No. 15, Dept. of State MSS. In his Despatch No. 16 to Van Buren, dated April

9, 1830, Wheaton enclosed a Memoir written by de Reedtz, which contained a full view of the basis upon which the condemnations in the Prize Courts of Denmark were justified or extenuated by the Danish Government. This is a long memoir of 129 pages in French with a chronological table of the vessels condemned. See also Wheaton's *Elements of International Law*, 1855 Ed., p. 603, n. 3a.

31. Livingston to Wheaton, June 29, 1832, Instructions, U. S. Ministers, Vol. 13, p. 317, No. 15, Dept. of State MSS.

32. *Niles' Weekly Register*, May 25, 1833, Vol. 44, p. 198. See also Miller, *Treaties, etc., of the United States*, Doc. No. 68, Vol. 3, p. 540. For full discussion of subject *see* Moore, *International Arbitrations*, Vol. V, pp. 4549–4573.

33. Lawrence, p. lxxiv.

34. Wheaton to Van Buren, Jan. 9, 1830, Despatches, Denmark, Vol. 1B, No. 11, Dept. of State MSS.

35. *Ibid.* (marked "Private"), March 27, 1830.

36. Note from Pichon to Rives, dated Paris, Jan. 15, 1831, enclosed in Rives Despatch No. 60, Paris, Jan. 18, 1831, Despatches, France, Vol. 25, Dept. of State MSS.

37. Edward Livingston to John Nelson, Oct. 27, 1831, enclosing copy of treaty with France, July 4, 1831, and extracts of Rives correspondence, Instructions, U. S. Ministers, Vol. 13, No. 2, Dept. of State MSS.

38. Lawrence, pp. lxxiv, lxxv.

CHAPTER XIV

1. Wheaton to Van Buren, June 1, 1829, Despatches, Denmark, Vol. 1B (marked "Private"), Dept. of State MSS.

2. *Ibid.*, Despatch No. 10, Dec. 5, 1829; Despatch No. 15, April 3, 1830.

3. *Ibid.*, Despatch marked "Private," May 30, 1830.

4. *Ibid.*

5. Lawrence, pp. lxxviii, lxxix.

6. *North American Review*, Vol. XXVIII, pp. 389–418, April 1829, and Vol. XXX, pp. 551–556, April 1830.

7. Lawrence, p. lxxix.

8. Mrs. Wheaton to Levi Wheaton, Boston, Oct. 20, 1830, Wheaton Papers.

9. Wheaton to Niles, Oct. 1, 1830, Papers of Nathaniel Niles, Vol. 1, Library of Congress.

10. Christopher Hughes to Samuel Smith, of Baltimore, Brussels, Dec. 1, 1829, Van Buren Papers, Vol. 10, Library of Congress.

11. Wheaton to Van Buren, Copenhagen, Sept. 30, 1830, Despatches, Denmark, Vol. 1B (marked "Private"), Dept. of State MSS.

12. William Cabell Rives to Martin Van Buren (marked "Private"), Paris, Sept. 8, 1830, Van Buren Papers, Vol. 11, Library of Congress.

13. Wheaton to Levi Wheaton, Nov. 9, 1830, Wheaton Papers.

14. Miller, *Treaties, etc., of the United States*, Doc. No. 68, Vol. 3, p. 533; Martens, *Nouveau Recueil*, tom. viii, p. 350; Elliot's *American Diplomatic Code*, Vol. 1, pp. 453–458; H. Ex. Doc. No. 264, 28 Cong., 1 Sess., pp. 9–10.

15. Van Buren to Wheaton, Dec. 23, 1830, Instructions, U. S. Ministers, Vol. 13, p. 198, No. 9, Dept. of State MSS.

16. Wheaton to Van Buren, Despatches (marked "Private"), Feb. 19, 1831; London, April 29, 1831. The power to receive the Danish bills was acknowledged by Wheaton to Van Buren, March 12, 1831 and May 23, 1831, Despatches, Denmark, Vol. 1B (marked "Private"), Dept. of State MSS.

17. Lawrence, pp. lxxix, lxxx.

18. Lawrence, p. lxxx.

19. Wheaton to Levi Wheaton, London, June 6, 1831, Wheaton Papers. *History of the Northmen or Danes and Normans, from the earliest times to the Conquest of England by William of Normandy.* Philadelphia, 1831. London, 1831. Described in more detail in Chapter XI.

20. Lawrence, p. lxxx.

21. Wheaton to Levi Wheaton, London, June 6, 1831, Wheaton Papers.

22. *Ibid.*

23. Wheaton to his sister, Mrs. Eliza Lyman, London, June 29, 1831, Wheaton Papers.

24. Wheaton to Levi Wheaton, London, July 13, 1831, Wheaton Papers.

25. Livingston to Wheaton, June 25, 1831, Instructions, U. S. Ministers, Vol. 13, pp. 229–231, No. 13, Dept. of State MSS.

26. Wheaton to Livingston, Sept. 30, 1831, Despatches, Denmark, Vol. 1B (marked "Private"), Dept. of State MSS. The negotiation of the bill amounted to £46,945. 12.7 Sterling. Wheaton to Livingston, Nov. 4, 1831, *ibid.*

27. Livingston to Wheaton, June 29, 1832, Instructions, U. S. Ministers, Vol. 13, p. 317, No. 15, Dept. of State MSS.

28. Wheaton to Martha Wheaton, Hamburg, Sept. 17, 1832, Wheaton Papers.

29. Wheaton to Livingston, Oct. 28, 1832, Despatches, Denmark, Vol. 2, No. 38, Dept. of State MSS.

30. *Ibid.*

31. Wheaton to Eliza Lyman, Copenhagen, Feb. 5, 1833, Wheaton Papers.

32. Wheaton to Livingston, Dec. 8, 1832, Despatches, Denmark, Vol. 2, No. 39, Dept. of State MSS.

CHAPTER XV

1. Lawrence, p. lxxvi.

2. Wheaton to Clay, Nov. 20, 1827, Despatches, Denmark, Vol. 1B (marked "Private"), Dept. of State MSS.

3. Wheaton to Van Buren, Jan. 16, 1830, *ibid.*

4. *Ibid.*, April 9, 1830.

5. Count Schimmelmann to Wheaton, April 9, 1830, *ibid.*

6. Van Buren to Wheaton, Jan. 7, 1831, Instructions, U. S. Ministers, Vol. 13, pp. 199–201, No. 10, Dept. of State MSS.

7. Wheaton to Van Buren, March 12, 1831, Despatches, Denmark, Vol. 1B (marked "Private"), Dept. of State MSS.

8. Wheaton to McLane, June 18, 1833, *ibid.*, Vol. 2, No. 44.

9. *Ibid.,* Notation made by Dept. of State on Despatch.

10. Wheaton to Forsyth, Nov. 29, 1834, No. 52, *ibid.*

11. *Ibid.*

12. *Ibid.*

13. Lawrence, p. lxxvii. An incident similar to this occurred a decade later. Lord William Russell, the British minister at Berlin, urged Wheaton, who was in Paris at that time, to go to London on his way back to Berlin. He offered to give Wheaton a letter to his brother, Lord John Russell, with the hope Wheaton might be able to bring about an adjustment. Wheaton declined to do this on the ground that he had no authority to meddle in the business officially and to interfere unofficially would be not only "indelicate" towards his colleague but also useless. Thereafter Lord William Russell often expressed his regret at Wheaton's refusal. In July of 1840 Stevenson, United States minister at London, requested Wheaton to find out whether the King of Prussia would accept the office of Arbiter of the boundary controversy. Wheaton applied to Alexander von Humboldt, who at that time was residing with the King at Potsdam in the summer palace of Sans Souci. Stevenson also communicated with Bülow, the Prussian minister in London, who was a relative and intimate friend of Humboldt. The conclusion was that the King of Prussia would accept if chosen as Arbiter, and in Wheaton's judgment the cause of the United States would be "perfectly safe in his hands." Wheaton to Van Buren, Berlin, July 15, 1840 (marked "Private and most Confidential"), Van Buren Papers, Vol. 39.

14. Wheaton to Van Buren, Feb. 19, 1831, Despatches, Denmark, Vol. 1B (marked "Private"), Dept. of State MSS.

15. *The Washington Globe,* Aug. 1, 1831.

16. Notation of insertion of extract in *Globe* made by Dept. of State on Despatch marked "Private," Wheaton to Livingston, from London, June 14, 1831.

17. Lawrence, p. lxxv.

18. Soren J. M. P. Fogdall, *Danish American Diplomacy, 1776–1920,* p. 66, University of Iowa Studies in the Social Sciences, Vol. 8, No. 2.

19. Wheaton to Livingston, January 23, 1832, Despatches, Denmark, Vol. 2, No. 25, Dept. of State MSS.

20. *Ibid.,* Despatch No. 30, May 26, 1832.

21. *Ibid.,* Despatch No. 31, June 20, 1832.

22. *Ibid.,* Despatch No. 34, September 1, 1832.

23. *Ibid.,* Despatch No. 36, September 16, 1832.

24. *Ibid.,* Despatch No. 54, February 18, 1835.

25. *Ibid.,* Despatch No. 55, March 12, 1835.

26. *Ibid.*

27. *Ibid.*

CHAPTER XVI

1. Rives to Van Buren, Paris, Sept. 8, 1830 (marked "Private"), Van Buren Papers, Vol. 11.

2. Wheaton to Van Buren, August 10, 1829, Despatches, Denmark, Vol. 1B, No. 8, Dept. of State MSS.

3. Wheaton to Clay, Nov. 20, 1827 (marked "Private"), *ibid.*

4. Wheaton to Van Buren, Feb. 19, 1831, *ibid.*

5. *Ibid.*, Nov. 23, 1830; Dec. 18, 1830; Feb. 19, 1831. Wheaton to Livingston, Despatches No. 33, July 13, 1832; No. 40, Jan. 29, 1833; No. 42, April 15, 1833; *ibid.*, Vol. 2.

6. Wheaton to Clay, Despatch No. 2, December 22, 1827, *ibid.*, Vol. 1B.

7. *Ibid.*

8. Wheaton to Livingston, Despatch No. 21, Dec. 20, 1831; Despatch No. 22, Dec. 31, 1831, *ibid.*

9. *Ibid.*, Despatches No. 20, Dec. 15, 1831; No. 21, Dec. 20, 1831; No. 22, Dec. 31, 1831; No. 26, Feb. 4, 1832; No. 28, April 10, 1832; No. 32, July 1, 1832; No. 33, July 13, 1832; No. 35, Sept. 15, 1832; No. 40, Jan. 29, 1833; No. 42, April 15, 1833. Wheaton to McLane, Despatch No. 48, Sept. 7, 1833.

10. Wheaton to Livingston, Despatch No. 33, July 13, 1832, *ibid.*

11. *Ibid.*

12. *Ibid.*, Despatch No. 42, April 15, 1833.

CHAPTER XVII

1. Report of the Copyright case of *Wheaton vs. Peters*, p. 9.

2. Hicks, p. 207 and p. 208.

3. Wheaton to Webster, Nov. 25, 1828, Daniel Webster Papers, Vol. 2, Library of Congress.

4. Hicks, pp. 208–209.

5. Wheaton to Webster, July 22, 1831, Daniel Webster Papers, Vol. 3, Lib. of Cong. In December Paine, the former partner of Wheaton wrote to Webster: "Mr. Wheaton has been obliged to institute a suit in Chancery in the Circuit Court of Pennsylvania against Mr. Peters for a violation of the copyright of the former in his reports. This suit will be brought to a hearing in the Circuit Court next spring and will without any doubt be carried to Washington. Mr. Wheaton has written me desiring me to retain you to argue the case on his behalf at Washington. I should have called on you for that purpose when you were in this city had I known of your being in town. But I hope and trust that no engagement will prevent your undertaking for Mr. Wheaton. His fortune is at stake in this suit. If Mr. Peters has spoken to you since you left this city, I can only say that Mr. Wheaton's application to you would still be prior, as I received it some time since. Messrs. Binney and Channey are engaged for Mr. Wheaton in the Circuit Court and you may rely on the cause being well prepared. It will be more interesting than any reported case on copyrights, and I believe the future interest of all authors in this country will be greatly affected by its decision. Will you be good enough to inform me soon whether you can be engaged for Mr. Wheaton." Paine to Webster, Dec. 6, 1831, Daniel Webster Papers, Vol. V, New Hampshire Hist. Soc.

6. Hicks, p. 209.

7. *Ibid.*

8. Wheaton to Mrs. Lyman, May 22, 1837, Wheaton Papers.

9. Wheaton to McLane, June 1, 1833, Despatches, Denmark, Vol. 2, No. 43,

Dept. of State MSS. Also Despatch, June 1, 1833 (marked "Private"), *ibid.*

10. McLane to Wheaton, August 8, 1833, Instructions, Denmark, Vol. 14, p. 5, No. 24, Dept. of State MSS.

11. Wheaton to McLane, London, Oct. 14, 1833, Despatches, Denmark, Vol. 2 (marked "Private"), Dept. of State MSS.

12. *Ibid.*, New York, Nov. 26, 1833.

13. Hicks, pp. 209–210. Of the six volumes, Volume III contained Wheaton's Volume I; Volume IV, Wheaton's Volumes II, III, IV and V; Volume V, Wheaton's Volumes VI, VII, VIII and IX; and Volume VI, Wheaton's Volumes X, XI and XII.

14. Hicks, p. 210. The cases cited were *Miller* v. *Taylor*, 4 Burr. 2303; *Donaldson* v. *Becket*, 4 Burr. 2408; *Roper* v. *Streater*, Skinner's Report, 234.

15. *Ibid.*

16. *Ibid.*, p. 211.

17. Lawrence, p. lxxxiii.

18. 8 Peters, 591.

19. Report of the copyright case *Wheaton* v. *Peters* decided in the Supreme Court of the United States. With an appendix, containing the acts of Congress regulating the copyright. New York, 1834.

20. Lawrence, p. lxxxiii.

21. Kellen, Appreciation, pp. 27–28. The letter was dated January 15, 1834.

22. Lawrence, pp. lxxxi, lxxxii.

23. John Pitman to Henry Wheaton, Providence, March 16, 1829, Wheaton Papers.

"Legacy from Father's estate	$9,000
Accrued interest	690
	9,690
Paid Gen'l Carrington	1,495
Balance	$8,195

Placed with Mr. Wild."

24. Wheaton to Mrs. Lyman, May 22, 1837, Wheaton Papers.

25. Story to Kent, May 17, 1834, Story, Vol. II, p. 181; Warren I, pp. 786–787.

26. Wheaton to Mrs. Lyman, May 14, 1837, Wheaton Papers.

27. Wheaton to Chancellor Kent, London, July 26, 1834, Papers of James Kent, Vol. VII, Lib. of Cong. See also Warren, Vol. II, pp. 245–247.

28. Wheaton to Mrs. Lyman, May 22, 1837, Wheaton Papers.

29. *The London Westminster Review*, American Edition, January 1836, Vol. III and XXV, pp. 97–102.

30. Wheaton to Niles, October 28, 1834, Papers of Nathaniel Niles, Vol. 1, Lib. of Cong.

31. Lawrence, p. lxxxi.

32. Discourse, intended to have been delivered before the New York Law Institute on its Anniversary celebration, May 14, 1834; New York, 1834.

33. American Antiquarian Society, *Proceedings*, 1812–1849, Worcester, 1912, p. 227.

34. Wheaton's request for an extension of his leave of absence for three or four months was contained in a letter from him to McLane dated March 22,

1834. His request was granted and his leave extended for four months. March 27, 1834, Instructions, Denmark, Vol. 14, p. 6, No. 26, Dept. of State MSS.

35. Wheaton to Forsyth, Aug. 15, 1834, Despatches, Denmark, Vol. 2, No. 50, Dept. of State MSS.

36. Wheaton to McLane, June 19, 1833 (marked "Private"), *ibid.*, containing translation of a letter from Count Raczynski. The correspondence concerning Wheaton's transfer began in June 1833. Wheaton to Livingston, June 22, 1833, No. 45, *ibid.* Wheaton to Buchanan, Dec. 3, 1834, *The Works of James Buchanan*, Vol. II, pp. 401–402.

37. Lawrence, p. lxxxvi. Buchanan to President Jackson, March 13, 1834.

38. Forsyth to Wheaton, March 23, 1835, Instructions, Denmark, Vol. 14, p. 8 and p. 9, Dept. of State MSS.

CHAPTER XVIII

1. Wheaton to Forsyth, Despatch No. 13, Berlin, Dec. 16, 1835, Wheaton MSS., Vol. 1, Mass. Hist. Soc.

2. *Homes of American Statesmen*, pp. 449–469.

3. Wheaton to Forsyth, Sept. 20, 1835, Despatches, Prussia, Vol. 1, No. 5, Dept. of State MSS.

4. Wheaton to Forsyth, Despatch No. 1, Berlin, June 12, 1835, Wheaton MSS., Vol. 1, Mass. Hist. Soc.

5. *Ibid.*, Berlin, Oct. 17, 1835, No. 6.

6. Wheaton to Forsyth, Despatch No. 1, Berlin, June 12, 1835, Wheaton MSS., Vol. 1, Mass. Hist. Soc.

7. Wheaton to Forsyth, Carlsruhe, August 2, 1835, Despatches, Prussia, Vol. 1, No. 4, Dept. of State MSS.

8. *Ibid.*

9. *Ibid.*, Hamburg, Sept. 20, 1835, No. 5.

10. *Ibid.*

11. *Ibid.*

12. Forsyth to Wheaton, April 20, 1835, Instructions, Prussia, Vol. 14, pp. 3–6, No. 2, Dept. of State MSS.

13. In May 1834 Hanover, Oldenburg, and Brunswick, in opposition to the Prussian Association, joined in a union known as the Steuerverein. This new league, although conceived in a spirit of opposition to the Prussian commercial confederation, had borrowed its leading features from that system. The tariff was less prohibitive, especially the duties upon foreign manufactures and colonial produce, which were much less than in Prussia. The net amount of duties collected in both States was to be divided between them in the ratio of their respective population, and the articles of salt and playing-cards, which were government monopolies almost throughout Germany, were excepted from the operation of the treaty. This compact was to last until the year 1841, the year previous to that in which the Treaties of the German Zollverein might be revised. It also contained a provision for the accession of other states. By the terms of this convention, Hanover expressly reserved the right of making separate treaties of navigation and commerce with any foreign state. Hano-

ver was bound in a personal union to England. While this lasted it refused to join the Zollverein. Although the internal administration of the kingdom was entirely separate from that of Great Britain, yet there was no doubt this treaty might be considered as made under the influence of the British cabinet with a view of counteracting the policy of Prussia in matters of trade. Wheaton to Forsyth, Despatch No. 9, Berlin, Nov. 11, 1835, Wheaton MSS., Vol. 1, Mass. Hist. Soc.

14. Wheaton to Forsyth, Carlsruhe, Aug. 2, 1835, Despatches, Prussia, Vol. 1, No. 4, Dept. of State MSS. The following were the States of Germany which had not yet acceded to the Union, with the respective population of each state.

STATES	POPULATION
Hanover	1,700,000
Brunswick	250,000
Oldenburg	270,000
Mecklenburg	560,000
Holstein and Lauenburg	200,000
The Hanse Towns	260,000
	3,250,000

15. This map with the border lines of the Zollverein inked in by Wheaton and the notations in Wheaton's handwriting, was enclosed in Despatch No. 4, supra.

16. Wheaton to Forsyth, Nov. 25, 1835, Despatches, Prussia, Vol. 1, No. 11, Dept. of State MSS.

17. To the Dept. of Foreign Affairs, Sub-division of Commerce, from Rother, Dec. 23, 1835, Preussisches Geheimes Staatsarchiv, Vol. V.

18. Dept. of Foreign Affairs to Rother, Jan. 17, 1836; Dept. of Foreign Affairs to Roenne, Jan. 24, 1836; *ibid.*

19. Wheaton to Forsyth, Dec. 23, 1835, Despatches, Prussia, Vol. 1, No. 14 (marked "confidential"), Dept. of State MSS.

20. Dept. of Foreign Affairs, Div. of Commerce, to Roenne, Jan. 28, 1836, Preussisches Geheimes Staatsarchiv, Vol. 5.

21. *Washington Globe,* July 20, 1836.

CHAPTER XIX

1. Henry Wheaton, *Elements of International Law,* Ed. 1855, pp. cxcv–cxcvi, Advertisement to the First Edition, January 1, 1836.

2. *Ibid.*

3. Henry Wheaton, *Elements of International Law,* the first edition was published in two volumes by Fellowes at London, 1836, and a second edition in the same year by Carey in Philadelphia.

4. *Ibid.,* Preface.

5. *Ibid.*

6. Henry Wheaton, *Elements of International Law,* Ed. 1855, p. 22. In a note Wheaton refers to Madison, *Examination of the British Doctrine,* which

subjects to capture a neutral trade not open in Time of Peace, p. 41, London Ed., 1806.

7. Wheaton, *Elements of International Law*, Ed. 1855, pp. 22–26.

8. Amos S. Hershey, *The Essentials of International Public Law*, New York, 1919, pp. 56–89. L. Oppenheim, *International Law*, 4th Edition, edited by Arnold D. McNair, New York, 1928, Vol. 1, pp. 103–129.

9. *Monthly Review*, Series 2, Vol. 142, pp. 428–442, November 1836.

10. *Revue étrangère et française de Legislation et d'Economic Politique*, Vol. 4, 1837, pp. 161–179. The review was by M. Foelix, the editor of the periodical and an advocate of the Royal Court of Paris.

11. *North American Review*, Vol. XLIV, pp. 16–29, January 1837.

12. Lawrence, pp. cxlv, cxlvi.

13. *Ibid.*, p. clii.

14. Francis R. Jones, "Henry Wheaton," *The Green Bag*, Vol. XVI, No. 12, pp. 781–785.

15. L. Oppenheim, *International Law*, 4th Edition, edited by Arnold D. McNair, Vol. 1, p. 121, note 2.

16. *The Library of American Biography* conducted by Jared Sparks, Vol. VI.

17. *North American Review*, Vol. XLIII, p. 516, October 1836.

18. *Foreign Quarterly Review*, Vol. XVIII, 1836.

19. Mrs. Wheaton to Levi Wheaton, Berlin, April 26, 1835, Wheaton Papers.

CHAPTER XX

1. Lawrence, p. lxxxix.

2. *Ibid.*, p. xc.

3. Wheaton to Van Buren, Berlin, April 25, 1837, Van Buren Papers, Vol. 27, April 8, 1837–June 1, 1837.

4. Wheaton to Forsyth, Aix-la-Chapelle, July 20, 1837, Despatches, Prussia, Vol. 1, Dept. of State MSS.

5. Wheaton to Van Buren, Aix-la-Chapelle, July 20, 1837, Van Buren Papers, Vol. 28.

6. *Ibid.*

7. *Ibid.*

8. Forsyth to Wheaton, March 25, 1837, Instructions, Prussia, Vol. 14, pp. 14–15, No. 11.

9. Lawrence, p. xci.

10. Wheaton to Van Buren, Aix-la-Chapelle, July 20, 1837, Van Buren Papers, Vol. 28.

CHAPTER XXI

1. Wheaton to Forsyth, Despatch No. 9, Berlin, Nov. 11, 1835. Wheaton MSS., Vol. I, Mass. Hist. Soc.

2. Wheaton to Ancillon, Berlin, May 27, 1836. Preussisches Geheimes Staatsarchiv, Vol. V, pp. 243–245.

3. Ancillon to Wheaton, Berlin, May 30, 1836. Preussisches Geheimes Staatsarchiv, Vol. V, pp. 249–250.

The commercial relations between the United States and Germany rested on the basis of three treaties—the treaty concluded May 1, 1828, between the United States and Prussia [a] which referred back to two previous treaties—one concluded on Sept. 10, 1785,[b] and the other on July 11, 1799.[c] The treaty of 1828 was never formally abrogated. According to the report of the tariff commission of 1918, the question whether it called for unconditional or for conditional most-favored-nation treatment was never settled officially.[d]

Article IV provided for indirect trade.[e] This was a feature to the advantage of Prussia, which, therefore, Prussia was loathe to surrender and the fear that this trade would not be included in a new treaty rendered her wary to enter negotiations for a new treaty.[f]

    a. Miller, *Treaties, etc., of the United States*, Doc. No. 62, Vol. 3, pp. 427–445.

    Malloy, *Treaties, Conventions, International Acts, Protocols and Agreements between the U. S. and other Powers, 1776–1909*, p. 1496.

    Scott, J. B., *Treaties of 1785, 1799 and 1828 between the United States and Prussia*, pp. 50–63.

    U. S. Statutes at Large, Vol. 8, p. 378 and Vol. 18, pt. 2, p. 656.

    b. Miller, *Treaties, etc., of the United States*, Doc. No. 13, Vol. 2, pp. 162–184.

    Malloy, p. 1477. Scott, pp. 3–25.

    U. S. Statutes at Large, Vol. 8, p. 84 and Vol. 18, pt. 2, p. 641.

    c. Miller, *Treaties, etc., of the United States*, Doc. No. 24, Vol. 2, pp. 433–456.

    Malloy, p. 1486. Scott, pp. 26–49.

    U. S. Statutes at Large, Vol. 8, p. 162 and Vol. 18, pt. 2, p. 648.

    d. Tariff Commission, *Reciprocity and Commercial Treaties*, p. 432.

    e. Miller, *Treaties, etc., of the United States*, Doc. No. 62, Vol. 3, p. 430.

    f. Wheaton to Harrison (Private), January 27, 1841. Despatches, Prussia, Vol. 2, Dept. of State MSS.

4. Preussisches Geheimes Staatsarchiv, Vol. V, pp. 251–260.

5. *Ibid.*, p. 261.

6. Roenne to Dept. of Foreign Affairs, Baltimore, July 20, 1836, *ibid.*, p. 262.

7. *Ibid.*, Baltimore, Sept. 5, 1836, Vol. VI, pp. 139–144.

8. *Ibid.*

9. Preussisches Geheimes Staatsarchiv, Vol. VI.

10. February 18, 1837, 24 Cong., 2d. Sess., House of Representatives Report No. 239. Tobacco.

11. Forsyth to Wheaton, June 1, 1837, Instructions, Prussia, Vol. 14, pp. 16–20, No. 12, Dept. of State MSS.

12. Wheaton to Forsyth, Frankfort-on-the-Main, August 9, 1837. Also H. Exec. Doc. No. 229, 26 Cong., 1 Sess., p. 64, Vol. VI.

13. Wheaton to Dodge, Berlin, Sept. 30, 1837. Also *ibid.*, p. 66.

14. *Ibid.*

15. Wheaton to Forsyth, Berlin, October 25, 1837, Despatches, Prussia, Vol. 1, No. 51, Dept. of State MSS. Also H. Ex. Doc. No. 229, *op. cit.*, p. 67.

16. Clipping under "Foreign News," Wheaton MSS., Mass. Hist. Soc.

17. *Berliner Spernicher Gazette*, December 23, 1837. A translation of this article appears in H. Ex. Doc. No. 229, *op. cit.*, pp. 60–63.

18. Wheaton to Forsyth, Berlin, December 27, 1837, Despatches, Prussia, Vol. 1, No. 58. Dept. of State MSS. Also H. Ex. Doc. No. 229, *op. cit.*, p. 58.

19. *Ibid.*

20. Wheaton to Forsyth, March 21, 1838, Despatches, Prussia, Vol. 1, No. 68, Dept. of State MSS. Also in H. Ex. Doc. No. 229, *op. cit.*, p. 68.

21. Forsyth to Wheaton, Feb. 13, 1838, Instructions, Prussia, Vol. 14, No. 15, Dept. of State MSS.

22. Wheaton to Baron de Werther, March 24, 1838, Preussisches Geheimes Staatsarchiv, Vol. VII, pp. 31–32.

23. Wheaton to Forsyth, April 22, 1838, Despatches, Prussia, Vol. 1, No. 72, Dept. of State MSS. Also H. Ex. Doc. No. 229, *op. cit.*, pp. 68–70.

24. Wheaton to Buchanan, Berlin, July 23, 1843 (marked "Private and Most Confidential"), Buchanan Papers. Fay had acknowledged receipt of his commission as Secretary of Legation at Berlin, on November 14, 1837, Despatches, Prussia, Vol. 1.

25. Wheaton to Forsyth, Dresden, July 20, 1838, Despatches, Prussia, Vol. 1, No. 76, Dept. of State MSS.

26. *Ibid.*

27. Lawrence, p. xcv.

28. Wheaton to Forsyth (Confidential), Toplitz, July 19, 1838, Despatches, Prussia, Vol. 1, No. 77, Dept. of State MSS. Also H. Ex. Doc. No. 229, *op. cit.*, pp. 70–71.

29. *Ibid.*

30. Clapham, J. H., "Zollverein Negotiations, 1828–1865," *Cambridge History of British Foreign Policy*, Vol. II, p. 468.

31. Wheaton to Forsyth (confidential), July 22, 1838, Despatches, Prussia, Vol. 1, No. 78, Dept. of State MSS.

32. *Ibid.*, Aug. 7, 1838, No. 80.

33. *Ibid.*, Aug. 10, 1838, No. 82.

34. *Ibid.*, Aug. 12, 1838, No. 85.

35. Lawrence, p. xciv.

36. Cong. Doc. H. R., 25 Cong., 3 Sess., Rep. Com., p. 310.

37. Wheaton to Forsyth, Berlin, Dec. 12, 1838, Despatches, Prussia, Vol. 1, No. 89, Dept. of State MSS.

38. Wheaton to Baron de Werther, Berlin, July 11, 1839, enclosing copies of correspondence between Wheaton and Baron de Werther, Despatches, Prussia, Vol. 2, No. 122, Dept. of State MSS. Also H. Ex. Doc., No. 229, *op. cit.*, pp. 81–84.

39. Wheaton to Forsyth, Berlin, Dec. 12, 1838, Despatches, Prussia, Vol. 1, No. 89, Dept. of State MSS. Also in H. Ex. Doc. No. 229, *op. cit.*, pp. 78–79.

CHAPTER XXII

1. Wheaton to Forsyth, Despatch No. 9, Berlin, Nov. 11, 1835, Wheaton MSS., Vol. I, Mass. Hist. Soc.

2. Wheaton to Forsyth, Carlsruhe, August 2, 1835, Despatches, Prussia, Vol. 1, No. 4, Dept. of State MSS.

3. Wheaton to Forsyth, Despatch No. 148, Berlin, May 20, 1840, Wheaton MSS., Vol. II, Mass. Hist. Soc.

4. Wheaton to Webster, Berlin, Sept. 24, 1841, Despatches, Prussia, Vol. 2, No. 188, Dept. of State MSS.

5. *Ibid.*

6. Wheaton to Forsyth, Despatch No. 9, Berlin, Nov. 11, 1835, Wheaton MSS., Vol. I, Mass. Hist. Soc.

7. Wheaton to Forsyth, June 1, 1836, Despatches, Prussia, Vol. 1, No. 25, Dept. of State MSS.; *ibid.*, Berlin, March 6, 1836, No. 100; *ibid.*, Sept. 8, 1841, No. 187.

8. Wheaton to Forsyth, Despatch No. 21, Berlin, March 16, 1836, Wheaton MSS., Vol. 1, Mass. Hist. Soc.

9. *Ibid.*, Despatch No. 22, May 18, 1836; Despatch No. 25, June 1, 1836.

10. Forsyth to Wheaton, Dec. 15, 1837, Instructions, Prussia, Vol. 14, No. 14, Dept. of State MSS.

11. Wheaton to Forsyth, Feb. 28, 1838, Despatches, Prussia, Vol. 1, No. 65, Dept. of State MSS.; *ibid.*, Despatch No. 68, March 21, 1838.

12. Forsyth to Wheaton, May 10, 1838, Instructions, Prussia, Vol. 14, pp. 26–27, No. 17, Dept. of State MSS.

13. Wheaton to Forsyth, Berlin, June 31, 1839, Despatches, Prussia, Vol. 2, No. 124, Dept. of State MSS.

14. *Ibid.*, Despatch No. 130, Sept. 11, 1839.

15. *Ibid.*, Despatch No. 138, Oct. 12, 1839.

16. Forsyth to Wheaton, Dec. 12, 1839, Instructions, Prussia, Vol. 14, pp. 32–34, No. 23, Dept. of State MSS.

17. Wheaton to Forsyth, Berlin, Oct. 12, 1839, Despatches, Prussia, Vol. 2, No. 138, Dept. of State MSS. The Stade toll was further discussed in Wheaton's despatches No. 192, Oct. 27, 1841; No. 217, March 8, 1843, and No. 260, March 18, 1845.

18. Wheaton to Forsyth, Berlin, May 20, 1840, Despatch No. 148, Wheaton MSS., Vol. 2, Mass. Hist. Soc.

19. Miller, *Treaties, etc., of the United States*, Doc. No. 92, Vol. 3, pp. 257–274.

20. Wheaton to Forsyth, Berlin, May 20, 1840, Despatch No. 148, Wheaton MSS., Vol. 2, Mass. Hist. Soc.

21. *Ibid.*

CHAPTER XXIII

1. Wheaton to Baron de Werther, Berlin, July 11, 1839, enclosing copies of correspondence between Wheaton and Baron de Werther, Despatches, Prus-

sia, Vol. 2, No. 122, Dept. of State MSS. Also H. Ex. Doc., 26 Cong., 1 Sess., Vol. VI, No. 229, Tobacco Trade, pp. 81–84.

2. Wheaton to Forsyth, Berlin, August 7, 1839, Despatches, Prussia, Vol. 2, No. 125, Dept. of State MSS. Also H. Ex. Doc. No. 229, *op. cit.,* pp. 84–85.

3. *Ibid.*

4. Forsyth to Dodge, May 14, 1839, Instructions, Prussia, Vol. 1, p. 30, Dept. of State MSS.

5. Wheaton to Forsyth, Berlin, Sept. 17, 1839, enclosing letter from Bowring to Wheaton of the same date, Despatches, Prussia, Vol. 2, No. 132, Dept. of State MSS.

6. *Ibid.,* Despatch No. 135, Oct. 2, 1839, Bowring afterwards published a famous report on the Zollverein.

7. *Ibid.,* Despatch No. 140, Paris, Nov. 11, 1839.

8. *Ibid.,* Sept. 11, 1839.

9. Wheaton to President Harrison, Berlin, Jan. 27, 1841 (marked "Private"), Despatches, Prussia, Vol. 2, Dept. of State MSS.

10. Forsyth to Wheaton, Sept. 24, 1840, Instructions, Prussia, Vol. 14, No. 26, pp. 37–38, Dept. of State MSS.

11. Wheaton to Webster, Berlin, May 30, 1841, Despatches, Prussia, Vol. 2, No. 181 (marked "Private and Confidential"), Dept. of State MSS.

12. *Ibid.,* Wheaton to Forsyth, Berlin, Feb. 10, 1841, Despatch No. 170.

13. *Ibid.*

14. *Ibid.,* Wheaton to Baron de Werther, Berlin, Jan. 31, 1841, enclosed in Wheaton's Despatch No. 170. Also Sen. Doc. No. 55, 27 Cong., 1 Sess., pp. 16–18.

15. Dodge to Wheaton, Berlin, Jan. 14, 1841; *ibid.,* pp. 18–25.

16. Wheaton to Webster, Berlin, March 25, 1841, Despatches, Prussia, Vol. 2, No. 175, Dept. of State MSS.

17. Clapham, "Zollverein Negotiations," 1828–1865, *Cambridge History of British Foreign Policy,* Vol. II, p. 469.

18. *Ibid.,* p. 470. See also Wheaton to Webster, June 15, 1841, Despatches, Prussia, Vol. 2, No. 183, Dept. of State MSS.

19. *Ibid.,* Despatch No. 183, *supra.*

20. *Ibid.,* Despatch No. 186, August 24, 1841.

21. *Ibid.,* April 21, 1841. (Private.)

22. Senate Document, No. 55, 27 Cong., 1 Sess. Also *Webster's Works,* Vol. VI, p. 407.

23. Wheaton to Webster (Private), July 15, 1841, Despatches, Prussia, Vol. 2, Dept. of State MSS.

24. Wheaton to Webster, May 30, 1841, Despatches, Prussia, Vol. 2, No. 181 (marked "Private and Confidential"), Dept. of State MSS.

25. Webster to Wheaton, July 6, 1841, Instructions, Prussia, pp. 40–41, No. 33, Dept. of State MSS.

26. *Ibid.,* p. 42.

27. Roenne to the Foreign Office, Berlin, Washington, May 28, 1842, Preussisches Geheimes Staatsarchiv, Vol. X, pp. 27–33.

CHAPTER XXIV

1. Wheaton to Webster (Private), July 15, 1841, Despatches, Prussia, Vol. 2, Dept. of State MSS.

2. Webster to Wheaton, Aug. 27, 1841, Instructions, Prussia, Vol. 14, No. 34; Fay to Webster, Nov. 17, 1841, Despatches, Prussia, Vol. 2, No. 1, Dept. of State MSS.

3. Wheaton to John C. Spencer, after the latter had been appointed Secretary of War in 1841, letter (marked "Confidential"), dated Berlin, Nov. 3, 1841. MSS letter in Library of Historical Society of Penna.

4. Everett to Webster, Paris, Nov. 15, 1841, Everett Papers, Vol. 44, p. 1.

5. *Ibid.*, Vol. 157, p. 167, Tuesday, Nov. 30, 1841.

6. Everett's Journal, Monday, Dec. 6, 1841, Everett Papers, Vol. 157, p. 172.

7. Everett to Wheaton (confidential), London, Jan. 15, 1842, *ibid.*, Vol. 72, pp. 113–114.

8. John H. Latané, *American Foreign Policy*, pp. 210–211.

9. Wheaton to Forsyth, Paris, Dec. 27, 1839, Despatches, Prussia, Vol. 2, No. 141, Dept. of State MSS.

10. Miller, *Treaties, etc., of the United States*, Vol. 2, pp. 595–599; 660; *ibid.*, No. 57, Aug. 6, 1827, Vol. 3, pp. 315–317.

11. St. George L. Sioussat, *Duff Green's "England and the United States,"* p. 7, reprint from American Antiquarian Society *Proceedings.*

12. Green to Calhoun, Aug. 2, 1842(?) *Correspondence of John C. Calhoun* (hereinafter cited as *Calhoun Cor.*), pp. 846–848.

13. Calhoun to Green, Fort Hill, June 7, 1843, *ibid.*, p. 537.

14. Wheaton to Forsyth, Toplitz, July 19, 1838, Despatches, Prussia, Vol. 1, No. 77 (marked "Confidential"), Dept. of State MSS. Also H. Ex. Doc. No. 229, *op. cit.*, pp. 70–71.

15. Wheaton to Forsyth, Berlin, Sept. 17, 1839, enclosing letter from Bowring to Wheaton of the same date, Despatches, Prussia, Vol. 2, No. 132, Dept. of State MSS.

16. Wheaton to Webster, Berlin, March 25, 1841, *ibid.*, Despatch No. 175.

17. Wheaton to Forsyth, Paris, Dec. 27, 1839, *ibid.*, No. 141.

18. Hansard, Vol. 55, June 23, 1840 to Aug. 11, 1841, pp. 881–902; July 22, 1840, pp. 900–902.

19. Guizot, *An Embassy to the Court of St. James's in 1840*, p. 284.

20. Hansard, Vol. 57, March 8, 1841 to May 6, 1841, pp. 609–610, March 26, 1841.

21. Besides the above references to Hansard, interest in pending commercial negotiations was manifested almost continuously for several years in the debates of the House of Commons. Among these may be mentioned Hansard, third series, Vol. 52, p. 179; Vol. 56, pp. 625–626; Vol. 63, pp. 1018–1020; Vol. 68, pp. 678–687; Vol. 72, pp. 276–277; Vol. 73, pp. 602–603.

22. John H. Latané, *American Foreign Policy*, pp. 210–211. A. P. Newton, "United States and Colonial Developments, 1815–1846," *Cambridge History of British Foreign Policy*, Vol. II, pp. 240–241.

23. Private letter Wheaton to Webster, Berlin, Oct. 28, 1841, Despatches, Prussia, Vol. 2, Dept. of State MSS.

24. Newton, *op. cit.*, pp. 241–242.

25. Lawrence, p. cxxvi.

26. Henry Wheaton, "De la question de juridiction qui s'est presentée devant les cours des États-Unis dans l'affaire de MacLeod," *Revue étrangère et française de législation, de jurisprudence, et d'economie politique.* tom. ix, p. 81, 1842.

27. *Ibid.* Lawrence, pp. cxxvi–cxxix. A discussion of this case in connection with the Webster-Ashburton negotiations with detailed references to official documents and correspondence is given in Miller, *Treaties, etc., of the United States,* Vol. 4, pp. 443–457.

28. Henry Wheaton, *Affaire de Mac-Leod considérée sous le point de vue du droit des gens.* Extrait de la *Revue étrangère et française de législation, de jurisprudence, et d'economie politique,* entitled "De la qustion de juridiction qui s'est presentée devant les cours des États-Unis dans l'affaire de MacLeod," tom. ix, p. 81, 1842.

29. Lawrence, p. cxxix.

30. A detailed discussion of this case with references to official documents and correspondence is also given in Miller, *Treaties, etc., of the United States,* Vol. 4, pp. 457–469.

31. *Revue étrangère et française de législation, de jurisprudence et d'economie politique,* . . . tom. ix, p. 345, 1842.

32. *Ibid.* Lawrence, pp. cxxix–cxxxi.

33. Henry Wheaton, *Examen des questions de jurisdiction qui se sont élevées entre les gouvernements anglais et américain dans l'affaire de la Creole; suivi d'une analyse du mémoire de l'auteur sur le droit de visite en mer.* Paris, 1842. "Extrait de la Revue étrangère et française de législation, de jurisprudence et d'economie politique," . . . tom. ix, p. 345, 1842.

34. Prior to the fall of 1841, Wheaton had written to the State Department about Eastern affairs in his Despatches No. 86, Nov. 21, 1838; No. 87, Dec. 5, 1838; No. 94, Jan. 23, 1839; No. 110, June 5, 1839; No. 114, June 19, 1839; No. 117, June 26, 1839; No. 118, July 3, 1839; No. 119, July 10, 1839; No. 120, July 27, 1839; No. 123, July 24, 1839; No. 124, July 31, 1839; No. 127, August 14, 1839; No. 128, August 21, 1839; No. 130, Sept. 11, 1839; No. 137, Oct. 8, 1839; No. 139, Oct. 16, 1839; No. 146, April 29, 1840; No. 153, July 1, 1840; No. 156, July 22, 1840; No. 158, August 5, 1840; No. 159, August 9, 1840; No. 164, Nov. 25, 1840; No. 165, Dec. 2, 1840; No. 169, Feb. 3, 1841; No. 175, March 25, 1841; No. 177, March 31, 1841; No. 180, May 5, 1841; No. 182, June 3, 1841; No. 184, July 7, 1841; No. 185, July 14, 1841; No. 186, August 24, 1841; Despatches, Prussia, Vols. 1 and 2, Dept. of State MSS.

35. C. D. Hazen, *Europe since 1815,* pp. 131–132.

36. Berlin, Dec. 9, 1835, Despatches, Prussia, Vol. 1, No. 12, Dept. of State MSS.

37. Hazen, *op. cit.*, pp. 131–132.

38. Henri Martin, *History of France from the First Revolution to the Present Time,* p. 86.

39. R. B. Mowat, "The Near East and France," Chap. IV, *Cambridge History of British Foreign Policy,* Vol. II, p. 180.

40. Martin, *op. cit.*, p. 80.

CHAPTER XXV

1. Miller, *Treaties, etc., of the United States,* Doc. No. 35, July 3, 1815, Vol. 2, pp. 595–599. See also Hugh G. Soulsby, *The Right of Search and the Slave Trade in Anglo-American Relations, 1814–1862,* Chap. I, pp. 13–38.

2. Martin, *op. cit.,* p. 85.

3. A. P. Newton, "United States and Colonial Developments, 1815–1846," *Cambridge Hist. of Brit. For. Policy,* Vol. II, p. 244.

4. Wheaton to Forsyth, Berlin, April 17, 1839, Despatches, Prussia, Vol. 2, No. 106, Dept. of State MSS.

5. Guizot, *Memoirs of Sir Robert Peel,* p. 151.

6. Guizot, *English Embassy,* pp. 282–284.

7. President Tyler's Message to Congress, Dec. 7, 1841, Richardson, *Messages of the Presidents,* Vol. IV, p. 77.

8. A. P. Newton, *op. cit.,* p. 244.

9. Aberdeen to Everett, Dec. 20, 1841, Webster's *Diplomatic and Official Papers,* p. 145.

10. Everett's Journal, Monday, Dec. 6, 1841, Everett Papers, Vol. 157, p. 172.

11. Martin, *op. cit.,* p. 85.

12. Wheaton to Webster, Paris, Jan. 26, 1842 (Private), Webster Papers, Vol. 8, New Hampshire Hist. Soc.

13. *Ibid.*

14. *Ibid.*

15. Webster to Fletcher Webster, Oct. 16, 1841, Webster Papers, Vol. 8, New Hampshire Hist. Soc.

16. St. George L. Sioussat, *Duff Green's "England and the United States,"* pp. 8–10.

17. Everett's Journal, Friday, Jan. 28, 1842, Everett Papers, Vol. 157, p. 217.

18. Everett to Webster (Private and Confidential), London, Jan. 31, 1842, Everett Papers, Vol. 44, p. 55.

19. Examen de la question aujourd'hui pendante entre le Gouvernement des États-Unis et celui de la Grande-Bretagne, concernant le Droit de Visite; Par un Américain. (Lewis Cass) Paris, 1842, *The London Times,* Jan. 1842. The statement appended at the end reads:
"On trouvera une similitude d'opinions et même de langage entre la portion de cet écrit où il s'agit de la suppression de la traite par la suppression des marchés à esclaves, et quelques observations de M. Odilon Barrot dans la séance de la Chambre des Députés de janvier. L'auteur croit donc devoir déclarer que l'original Anglais de la brochure, dont l'exemplaire Français est une fidèle traduction, était complètement rédigé avant l'ouverture des débats parlementaires sur le droit de visite, et qu'il était sorti de la presse lundi soir, avant que le compte rendu de cette séance eut paru. Evidemment la similitude n'est pas un plagiat, mais une coincidence de vues entre deux personnes étrangères l'une à l'autre, s'occupant, du même sujet." See also, Sioussat, *Duff Green, op. cit.,* pp. 22–23.

20. Everett to Webster (Private and Confidential for yourself alone), Everett Papers, Vol. 73, pp. 130–132.

21. Webster to Everett, April 26, 1842, *Writings and Speeches of Daniel Webster*, Vol. XVIII, pp. 124–125.

22. Everett to Wheaton, London, Feb. 10, 1842, Everett Papers, Vol. 72, pp. 185–187.

23. Wheaton to Webster, Paris, January 29, 1842, Webster Papers, Vol. 8, N. H. Hist. Soc.

24. *Ibid.*

25. Correspondence in relation to the Quintuple Treaty, Senate Doc., 27 Cong., 3d Sess., Vol. 4, Doc. 223, pp. 25–28. See also Sioussat, *Duff Green*, pp. 26–27.

26. Wheaton to Webster (Private), Paris, Feb. 15, 1842, Webster Papers, Vol. 9, New Hampshire Hist. Soc.

27. Sir Thomas Fowell Buxton, *The African Slave Trade and its Remedy*, Phila., 1839.

28. Wheaton to Webster (Private), Paris, Feb. 15, 1842, Webster Papers, Vol. 9, N. H. Hist. Soc.

29. Everett had written to Wheaton, Feb. 23, 1842,
"Your parcel arrived safe at 2 o'clock P. M. and was in Miller's hands by 4. I shall daily stimulate him but I do not think him very energetic. I shall with pleasure correct the proofs. If I hear anything about the ratification, you shall certainly have it. Lord Aberdeen told me when we first got news of the Creole, that we must have an understanding for extradition of murderers. I write these few lines to you with tired fingers and aching eyes to relieve your anxiety about your MSS."
On March 4, Everett wrote,
"Your proof sheets were sent off with the despatches yesterday. I had to alter two sentences in which you speak of Lord Aberdeen's notes. One note only from him forms a part of the printed correspondence."
Everett Papers, Vol. 72, p. 215, and p. 244.

30. On April 23rd. a notice appeared in *Niles' Register*, Vol. 62, p. 128—
"Right of Search—An essay from the pen of Henry Wheaton, LLD., Minister of the U. S. at the Court of Berlin, entitled 'enquiry into the validity of the British claim to the right of visitation, and search of American vessels suspected to be engaged in the African slave trade,' has just been published from the Philadelphia press."

31. *Foreign Quarterly Review*, Vol. XXIX, London, 1842, pp. 246–247.

32. Despatches, Prussia, Vol. 3, No. 195, enclosed in Wheaton's Despatch to State Dept., May 18, 1842, Dept. of State MSS. Also Lawrence, p. cxxii.

33. Henry Wheaton, *Enquiry into the Validity of the British Claim to a Right of Visitation and Search of American Vessels suspected to be engaged in the African Slave Trade*. Philadelphia, 1842.

34. Wheaton to Webster, Paris, March 12, 1842, Webster Papers, Vol. 9, N. H. Hist. Soc.

35. Lord Ashburton to Earl of Aberdeen, Washington, April 25, 1842, Foreign Office 84, Vol. 423; Photostats from Public Record Office, London,

Manuscript Division of Library of Congress. In this communication Ashburton wrote in part ". . . considering this state of things, I put it to several persons of influence and of honest feeling what remedy they could suggest and whether America could remain in the notorious and scandalous position of refusing all remedy against crimes which they had been the most vehement to denounce, and of the existence of which they could not doubt. This view of the case has brought Mr. Webster to the consideration of a scheme of joint cruising on the coast of Africa, on the plan suggested by the Commissioners at Sierra Leone in their report to Lord Palmerston of the 31 Jan. 1839, and by his Lordship's order communicated by Mr. Fox to Mr. Forsyth in his note of the 29th October of the same year. . . ."

36. Webster to Everett, April 26, 1842, *Writings and Speeches of Daniel Webster*, Vol. XVIII, pp. 124–125.

37. Wheaton to Webster, May 18, 1842, Despatches, Prussia, Vol. 3, No. 195, Dept. of State MSS.

Wheaton was also informed by Bülow pending the discussions in the French Chamber of Deputies, in a conversation respecting the ukase of the twenty-sixth of March (seventh April), 1842, for carrying it into effect, that it was not the intention of the Prussian government to adopt, at that time, any similar measure, or to publish the treaty as a public law of the kingdom, as they did not consider it existing, so far as France was concerned, until ratified by that power.

Ibid., Despatch No. 200, June 18, 1842.

38. Sparks to Wheaton, March 29, 1843, Herbert B. Adams, *The Life and Writings of Jared Sparks*, Vol. II, pp. 414–415.

39. Wheaton to Sparks, May 8, 1843, *ibid.*, pp. 415–418. See also Lawrence, p. cxxv, note 1.

40. Miller, *Treaties, etc., of the United States*, Document 99, Vol. 4, pp. 363–477.

Miller gives here a detailed description of the Webster-Ashburton negotiations with valuable references to official documents and correspondence.

41. Miller, *Treaties, etc., of the United States*, Doc. 99, Vol. 4, pp. 369.

42. Latané, *op. cit.*, pp. 221–222.

43. Cass to Webster, Paris, Sept. 17, 1842, Senate Docs. 27 Cong., 3 Sess., Vol. 4, No. 223, p. 34.

44. Webster to Cass, Washington, Aug. 29, 1842, *ibid.*, pp. 4–5.

45. Cass to Webster, Paris, Oct. 3, 1842, *ibid.*, pp. 34–37.

46. Everett to Webster, Nov. 3, 1842, Everett Papers, Vol. 45, p. 189.

47. Wheaton to Webster, Berlin, Nov. 16, 1842, Despatches, Prussia, Vol. 3, No. 206, Dept. of State MSS. Also Senate Doc. 27 Cong., 3 Sess., Vol. 4, No. 223, pp. 47–48, with the exception that the last sentence of the next to last paragraph is consistently omitted in printing Wheaton's letter.

48. Adams, *Life and Writings of Jared Sparks*, Vol. II, p. 47.

49. In the *Revue étrangère et française de Legislation de Jurisprudence et d'Economie Politique*, Vol. 9, 1842, p. 600, appears the following: "Dans sa séance du 30 avril, l'Académie des sciences morales et politiques de l'Institut a nommé correspondant étranger M. Henri Wheaton, ministre des États-Unis à Berlin."

50. Lawrence, p. clxiii.

51. *Ibid.*, p. clvii.

52. *Niles' Weekly Register*, Sept. 16, 1843, Vol. 65, p. 34, prints excerpt from *The Madisonian.*

CHAPTER XXVI

1. Forsyth to Wheaton, April 17, 1839, Instructions, Prussia, Vol. 14, No. 20, Dept. of State MSS.

2. Miller, *Treaties, etc., of the United States*, Doc. 89, Vol. 4, pp. 189–206.

3. Forsyth to Wheaton, April 17, 1839, Instructions, Prussia, Vol. 14, No. 20, Dept. of State MSS.

4. *Ibid.*

5. Wheaton to Forsyth, May 22, 1839, Despatches, Prussia, Vol. 2, No. 109, Dept. of State MSS.

6. *Ibid.*

7. *Ibid.*, Despatch No. 115, June 25, 1839.

8. *Ibid.*, Despatch No. 133, Sept. 20, 1839.

9. *Ibid.*, Despatch No. 134, Sept. 20, 1839.

10. *Niles' Weekly Register*, Nov. 9, 1839, Vol. LVII, p. 165.

11. *Register of Department of State in Four Parts*, corrected to March 1, 1874, Part II. *Historical Register*, p. 126. A description of the activities of this commission is given in Miller, *Treaties, etc., of the United States*, Doc. No. 89, Vol. 4, pp. 204–206.

12. Wheaton to Bülow, May 12, 1843, enclosed in Wheaton's Despatch No. 227, to Legaré, June 27, 1843, Despatches, Prussia, Vol. 3, Dept. of State MSS.

13. Bülow to Wheaton, June 20, 1843, enclosed as above.

14. Upshur to Wheaton, Nov. 13, 1843, Instructions, Prussia, Vol. 14, No. 48, Dept. of State MSS.

15. Bülow to Wheaton, April 10, 1844, enclosed in Wheaton's Despatch No. 247 to Nelson, Secretary *ad interim*, April 12, 1844, Despatches, Prussia, Vol. 3, Dept. of State MSS.

16. Calhoun to Wheaton, March 3, 1845, Instructions, Prussia, Vol. 14, No. 66, Dept. of State MSS.

17. Wheaton to Buchanan, April 23, 1845, Despatches, Prussia, Vol. 3, No. 264, Dept. of State MSS.

18. Wheaton to Levi Wheaton, Berlin, Jan. 29, 1845, Wheaton Papers.

19. Wheaton to Webster, June 1, 1842, enclosing correspondence with Grund, Consul of Bremen, Despatches, Prussia, Vol. 3, No. 198, Dept. of State MSS.

20. Webster to Wheaton, August 16, 1842, Instructions, Prussia, Vol. 14, No. 35, p. 44, Dept. of State MSS. Wheaton acknowledged receipt of these instructions in his Despatch No. 204, Oct. 17, 1842. Before receiving Webster's Instructions No. 37, Nov. 15, 1842, the case had been brought to a conclusion.

21. Wheaton to Webster, Dec. 5, 1842, enclosing correspondence with the Hanoverian minister at Berlin, Despatches, Prussia, Vol. 3, No. 209, Dept. of State MSS.

22. Wheaton, *International Law,* 2d Edition, pp. 41–42.

23. Wheaton to Upshur, August 23, 1843, Despatches, Prussia, Vol. 3, No. 233, Dept. of State MSS. Also in Exec. Doc. 28 Cong., 1 Sess., Doc. No. 264.

24. Upshur to Irwin, Nov. 21, 1843. Exec. Doc. No. 264, *op. cit.*

25. Wheaton to Upshur, August 23, 1843, Despatches, Prussia, Vol. 3, No. 233, Dept. of State MSS.

26. Upshur to Irwin, Nov. 21, 1843. Exec. Doc. No. 264, *op. cit.*

27. Irwin to Upshur, Feb. 10, 1844, *ibid.*

28. Wheaton to Forsyth, Berlin, July 29, 1840, Despatches, Prussia, Vol. 3, No. 157, Dept. of State MSS. Wheaton to Johann Philipp Knoche, Berlin, July 24, 1840. Senate Documents, 36 Cong., 1 Sess., Vol. XI, pp. 6–7.

29. Especially Despatches No. 16, April 9, 1830 and No. 41, Feb. 20, 1833.

30. Forsyth to Wheaton, April 20, 1835, Instructions, Prussia, Vol. 14, No. 2, pp. 3–6, Dept. of State MSS.

31. Despatches, Prussia, Vol. 1, No. 14, Dec. 30, 1835, Dept of State MSS. This subject was again referred to by Wheaton in his Despatches No. 191, Feb. 10, 1836, No. 21, March 16, 1836 and No. 27, June 18, 1836, *ibid.*

32. Henry Wheaton, Memoir attached to his Despatch No. 173, Berlin, March 10, 1841. This long memoir is a detailed history of the Sound dues from the beginning of the fourteenth century, Wheaton MSS., Mass. Hist. Soc.

33. Soren J. M. P. Fogdall, *Danish-American Diplomacy, 1776–1920,* p. 66. On pp. 69 and 70 Fogdall refers to the expression of the first popular discontent in the United States through an article by Caleb Cushing published in the *Boston Monthly Magazine,* January 1826. The article is reprinted in the *North American Review,* April 1826, Vol. XXII, pp. 456–459.

34. Despatches, Prussia, Vol. 1, No. 64, Berlin, Feb. 14, 1838, Dept. of State MSS.

35. Wheaton to Webster, Berlin, March 10, 1841, Despatches, Prussia, Vol. 2, No. 173, Dept. of State MSS.

36. Executive Documents and Reports of Committees, 27 Cong., 1 Sess., Doc. 1, pp. 26–28.

37. Henry Wheaton, *Elements of International Law,* pp. 244–245.

38. Charles E. Hill, *The Danish Sound Dues and the Command of the Baltic,* p. 274.

39. Besides the Despatches cited, Wheaton had written to the Dept. of State on this subject in two Despatches (marked "Private"), dated Jan. 27, 1841 and July 15, 1841, and in his Despatches No. 186, Aug. 24, 1841 and No. 208, Nov. 30, 1842, Dept. of State MSS.

40. Hill, *op. cit.,* p. 275.

41. Wheaton wrote to Calhoun about the Sound dues in his Despatch No. 253, June 30, 1844. This was followed later by his Despatches No. 259, Feb. 15, 1845 and No. 273, Sept. 17, 1845. See also Hill, *op. cit.,* p. 276; Dept. of State Instructions, Denmark, Vol. 14, No. 42; *Calhoun Cor.,* pp. 590–591; Executive Documents, 33 Cong., 1 Sess., Doc. 108, pp. 28–30.

42. Wheaton to Buchanan, Jan. 21, 1846, Despatches, Prussia, Vol. 3, No. 281, Dept. of State MSS.

43. Wheaton, *Elements of International Law,* p. 241.

44. *Ibid.*, p. 243.

45. *Ibid.*, p. 244, note *a*. See also Hill, *op. cit.*, pp. 278–279.

46. *Ibid.* Also House Exec. Docs., 33 Cong., 1 Sess., Vol. 13, Doc. 108, pp. 53–57.

47. Hill, *op. cit.*, pp. 285–286.

CHAPTER XXVII

1. Wheaton to Webster, April 1, 1842, Despatches, Prussia, Vol. 2 (Private), Dept. of State MSS.

2. *Ibid.*, Stuttgard, July 22, 1842, Vol. 3, No. 201.

3. Lawrence, p. c.

4. There is a great deal of correspondence concerning efforts to have the duties on German wines reduced by the United States, in the archives of both countries.

5. Wheaton to Webster, July 22, 1842, Despatches, Prussia, Vol. 3, No. 202, Dept. of State MSS.

6. Wheaton to Hartmann, Sept. 1842, Preussisches Geheimes Staatsarchiv, Vol. X, pp. 86–89.

7. Report of Michaelis to Dept. of Foreign Affairs, Berlin, Sept. 14, 1842, Preussisches Geheimes Staatsarchiv, Vol. X, p. 85.

8. Wheaton to Bülow (Private and Confidential), Berlin, Oct. 18, 1842, Preussisches Geheimes Staatsarchiv, Vol. X, pp. 120–123.

9. Wheaton to Webster, Oct. 26, 1842, Despatches, Prussia, Vol. 3, No. 205, Dept. of State MSS.

10. *Ibid.*, Nov. 16, 1842, No. 206.

11. Richelot, *op. cit.*, p. 487.

12. Wheaton to Bülow, and Bülow to Wheaton, Oct. 9 and 10, 1843, respectively, enclosed in Wheaton's Despatch No. 237, Despatches, Prussia, Vol. 3, Dept. of State MSS.

13. Wheaton to Upshur, Oct. 11, 1843, Despatches, Prussia, Vol. 3, No. 237, Dept. of State MSS.

14. *Ibid.*, Oct. 11, 1843. (Private.)

15. *Ibid.*

16. Upshur to Wheaton, Nov. 10, 1843, Instructions, Prussia, Vol. 14, No. 47, Dept. of State MSS.

17. *Ibid.*, Dec. 1, 1843, Instructions No. 51, pp. 71–72.

18. House Exec. Doc., 28 Cong., 1 Sess., Doc. No. 2.

19. Upshur to Wheaton, Jan. 2, 1844, Instructions, Prussia, Vol. 14, pp. 72–73, No. 52, Dept. of State MSS.

20. Wheaton to Upshur, Feb. 21, 1844, Despatches, Prussia, Vol. 3, No. 239, Dept. of State MSS.

21. *Ibid.* (Private), March 10, 1844, No. 241. In this connection Wheaton further stated:

"The only examples, which I recollect, of contracts being entered into by the President with foreign nations in any other form than that of a treaty or convention submitted to the Senate for ratification, are the following:

"1st. The arrangement made between the United States and Great Britain in 1809, by which the British Orders in Council relative to neutral trade were to have been repealed so far as respects American commerce, on certain conditions. This arrangement was made in consequence of a previous authority vested in the President by Act of Congress, authorizing him in case the orders and decrees of either of the belligerent Powers should be thus repealed, to declare the renewal of commercial intercourse with that Power which had been suspended by the Non-Intercourse Act.

"2nd. The second instance of such an arrangement was that made by Mr. McLane with the British Government in 1830 relating to the Colonial trade. This was also made under a previous Act of Congress passed in May of that year, authorizing the President, whenever he should receive satisfactory evidence that the British Government would open its ports in the West Indies, etc., to the vessels of the United States, on certain specified terms, to issue his Proclamation declaring that the ports of the United States were opened to British vessels coming from the Colonies on similar terms.

"It will be perceived that these two cases are to be considered as examples of the exercise of the ordinary power, made to depend upon the contingent action of a foreign government rather than as instance of the exercise of the treaty-making power properly so called."

22. *Ibid.*

23. The details of these communications and conferences are given in Preussisches Geheimes Staatsarchiv, Berlin, Vol. XI, from pages 1 to 200, inclusive.

24. Instructions addressed to Prussia's ambassadors in the different Zollverein States. Berlin, March 11, 1844; *ibid.*, Vol. XI, pp. 74–81.

25. *Ibid.*, pp. 5–200.

26. Wheaton to Calhoun, Berlin, March 25, 1844, Despatches, Prussia, Vol. 3, No. 242, Dept. of State MSS.

27. Richelot, *op. cit.*, p. 189.

28. Everett to Wheaton, March 28, 1844, Everett Papers, Vol. 48, pp. 368–370.

29. Lawrence, p. civ.

30. Richardson, *Messages and Papers*, Vol. IV, p. 314; Sen. Jol., 28 Cong., 1 Sess., p. 444.

CHAPTER XXVIII

1. Wheaton to Levi Wheaton, Feb. 22, 1844, Wheaton Papers.

2. Bülow, March 16, 1844, Preussisches Geheimes Staatsarchiv, Vol. XI, p. 158.

3. Wheaton to Calhoun, June 30, 1844, Despatches, Prussia, Vol. 3, No. 253, Dept. of State MSS.

4. Eichhorn to Bülow, April 7, 1844, Preussisches Geheimes Staatsarchiv, Vol. XI, pp. 311–314.

5. *Ibid.*

6. Roenne to Eichhorn, Potsdam, April 7, 1844, Preussisches Geheimes Staatsarchiv, Vol. XI, pp. 315–316.

7. *Boston Daily Advertiser*, Vol. LXIII, No. 93, April 18, 1844, contained excerpt from the *Deutsche Schnellpost*.

8. Wheaton to Upshur, Despatch No. 239, Feb. 21, 1844, contained a concise analysis of a very elaborate article in the *Weser-Zeitung*, which Wheaton believed was written' by, or under the immediate inspection of Dr. Smidt. Concerning it he said, "It may be considered as containing an authentic statement of the present views of the Hanse Towns, in respect to their commercial policy, with relation both to the United States and the German Customs Association." Despatches, Prussia, Vol. 3, Dept. of State MSS.

9. *Ibid.* From the analysis mentioned above.

10. Everett to Upshur, Feb. 15, 1844, Despatches, Great Britain, Vol. 52, No. 87, Dept. of State MSS. Also in Everett Papers, Vol. 48, pp. 237–238.

11. Everett to Wheaton, March 28, 1844, Everett Papers, Vol. 48, pp. 368–370. On April second, Everett noted in his Journal that Fay, Secretary of Legation at Berlin, who had been sent by Wheaton with the treaty concluded with the Zollverein, called upon him with Heath and both were invited to dine for Thursday. Everett's Journal, Tuesday, April 2, 1844, Everett Papers, Vol. 161, p. 177.

12. Everett to Nelson, April 3, 1844, Despatches, Great Britain, Vol. 52, No. 109, Dept. of State MSS. Also Everett Papers, Vol. 48, pp. 415–419.

13. Everett to Calhoun (Private), May 3, 1844, Everett Papers, Vol. 49, pp. 27–30.

14. *Ibid.*, Despatch No. 142, June 14, 1844, Vol. 49, pp. 221–226.

15. *Ibid.*

16. Hansard's Parliamentary Debates, Third Series, Vol. 74, April 15, 1844 to May 24, 1844, pp. 212–214. Discussion took place in House of Commons, Tuesday, April 23, 1844.

17. Everett to Nelson, April 25, 1844, Despatches, Great Britain, Vol. 52, No. 115, Dept. of State MSS. Also Everett Papers, Vol. 48, pp. 502–506.

18. *Ibid.*, Despatch No. 117, May 1, 1844. Also Vol. 49, pp. 10–14.

19. Treaty signed March 2, 1841. In Wheaton's despatch to Webster, No. 175, March 25, 1841, he gives an analysis of this treaty. Despatches, Prussia, Vol. 2, Dept. of State MSS.

20. Prussian Representative to Dept. of Foreign Affairs, London, May 31, 1844, Preussisches Geheimes Staatsarchiv, Vol. XI, pp. 388–390.

21. Everett to Wheaton, May 13, 1844, Everett Papers, Vol. 49, pp. 55–56.

22. *Ibid.*, April 29, 1844, Vol. 48, pp. 509–511.

23. Everett's Journal, Tuesday, May 28, 1844, Everett Papers, Vol. 161, p. 234.

24. Pakenham to Aberdeen, May 29, 1844, F. O. No. 51, Photostats in Library of Cong.

25. Richardson, *Messages and Papers*, Vol. IV, p. 314; Sen. Jol., 28 Cong., 1 Sess., p. 444.

26. Senate Ex. Jol., 28 Cong., 1 Sess., Vol. VI, p. 262.

27. One example of many was in the *Providence Daily Journal*, Wednes-

day, April 24, 1844, Vol. XV, No. 99, p. 2. Here is printed a column from the *Boston Daily Advertiser* headed German Treaty and in this appear quotations from both Prussia and Hamburg March 29. Paris *Journal des Debats,* copied from the *Gazette de Cologne* of March 24.

28. *Niles' Weekly Register,* Vol. 66, p. 176, May 11, 1844, headed "The German Treaty."

29. *Boston Daily Advertiser,* May 20, 1844, headed "The German and American Treaty."

30. Prussian Representative in London to the Department of Foreign Affairs, London, May 2, 1844. Preussisches Geheimes Staatsarchiv, Vol. XI, pp. 356–359.

31. Prussian Representative to Dept. of Foreign Affairs, London, May 31, 1844, Preussisches Geheimes Staatsarchiv, Vol. XI, pp. 388–390.

CHAPTER XXIX

1. Senate Journal, 28 Cong., 1 Sess., p. 445.

2. *Ibid.*

3. The action of the Senate was reported by *Niles' Register* on June 22, 1844, Vol. 66, p. 257, as follows: "The treaty with Prussia, hastily negotiated under instruction from President Tyler by Mr. Wheaton, and communicated to the Senate some time since for their advice thereon, was on the last day of their session, on motion of Mr. Morehead, ordered to lie on the table by the following vote: YEAS:—Messrs. *Archer,* Barrow, Bates, Bayard, *Berrien, Choate,* Clayton, Crittenden, Dayton, Evans, Foster, Francis, Henderson, Huntingdon, Jarnigan, Johnson, Mangum, Merrick, Miller, Morehead, Pearce, Phelps, Simmons, Sturgeon, *Tallmadge,* Upham, White—27. NAYS:—Messrs. Atchison, Atherton, Bagby, Benton, Breese, Colquitt, Fairfield, Fulton, Haywood, Huger, Lewis, McDuffie, Niles, Semple, Sevier, Tappam, Walker, Woodbury—18." NOTE:—The names in italics were members of the committee on Foreign Relations. The other member was Buchanan, who apparently was absent when the vote was taken.

4. Calhoun to Wheaton, June 28, 1844, Instructions, Prussia, Vol. 14, No. 57, pp. 75–83, Dept. of State MSS.

5. Senate Documents, Vol. 26, pp. 36–38, Executive Journal, Vol. VI, p. 333.

6. *Ibid.*

7. *Ibid.*

8. Calhoun to Wheaton, June 28, 1844. Lawrence, pp. cvi–cviii.

9. *Ibid.*

10. Wheaton to Calhoun, Aug. 7, 1844, Despatches, Prussia, Vol. 3, No. 256, Dept. of State MSS.

11. St. George L. Sioussat, "John Caldwell Calhoun," *American Secretaries of State,* Vol. V, p. 226.

12. Address of Democratic Association signed by James Towels, Chairman, and C. P. Sengstack, Secretary, dated Washington City, Sept. 20, 1844. Also included in Preussisches Geheimes Staatsarchiv, Vol. XII, pp. 191–194.

13. *The Madisonian*—June 10, 1844, Vol. III, No. 766; June 19, 1844, Vol.

III, No. 774; June 22, 1844, Vol. III, No. 776; June 24, 1844, Vol. III, No. 778; June 25, 1844, Vol. III, No. 779; June 27, 1844, Vol. III, No. 781; July 5, 1844, Vol. III, No. 787; July 12, 1844, Vol. III, No. 793; July 16, 1844, Vol. III, No. 796; July 19, 1844, Vol. III, No. 799; July 26, 1844, Vol. III, No. 805; July 27, 1844, Vol. III, No. 866.

The National Intelligencer, June 25, 1844, published the report of the Committee on Foreign Relations as justification of its action in rejecting the treaty, stating it had been "rough handled" in consequence; July 16, 1844, published long article in defense of the action of the Senate in rejecting the treaty.

Niles' Register, June 29, 1844, Vol. 66, p. 287, republished article in *National Intelligencer* of June 25, 1844.

Boston Daily Advertiser, June 17, 1844, Vol. LXIII, No. 144; June 19, 1844, Vol. LXIII, No. 146; June 20, 1844, Vol. LXIII; June 29, 1844, Vol. LXIII, No. 155.

14. Republished in the *Madisonian Daily,* Sept. 30, 1844, Vol. III, No. 861.

15. On June 17, 1844, on motion of Hayward of North Carolina it was agreed to remove the injunction of secrecy from the proceedings of the Senate in relation to the Convention with the Germanic Customs Union. Senate Jol., 28 Cong., 1 Sess., p. 448.

16. Dated Weimar, April 30, 1844, Preussisches Geheimes Staatsarchiv, Vol. XI, pp. 385–386.

17. Potsdam, May 10, 1844, *ibid.,* p. 366.

18. Dept. of Foreign Affairs to Prussian Representatives, May 11, 1844, *ibid.,* pp. 376–383.

19. The following excerpt was reprinted from the *Frankfort Zeitung* by the *Morning Courier* of Montreal, Vol. X, No. 75, June 22, 1844. "The commercial treaty concluded between the Zollverein States and the N. A. Union, and which beyond doubt will be ratified, is most important and advantageous to Germany. The conditions on which it is grounded are such that no sacrifice will be made of home industry, and no particular article of German manufacture will be brought into very disadvantageous competition with North American products; for these objects of American commerce which will be admitted on the payment of a moderate duty will be either such as we do not produce, or as produced so badly and in such small quantities that their prices cannot be much affected. This is especially the case with tobacco. The principal disadvantage will, doubtless, be sustained, but for the moment only, by the coffee of the Zollverein States."

20. Ratifications subsequent to April 30 in Preussisches Geheimes Staatsarchiv, Vol. XI, pp. 385, ff., and Vol. XII, p. 15, ff.

21. Prussian Representatives to Dept. of Foreign Affairs, Darmstadt, July 1, 1844, Preussisches Geheimes Staatsarchiv, Vol. XII, p. 40.

22. Wheaton to Levi Wheaton, May 1, 1844, Wheaton Papers.

CHAPTER XXX

1. Wheaton to Bülow, letter in French, July 26, 1844, Preussisches Geheimes Staatsarchiv, Vol. XII, pp. 41–46. Also in Despatches, Prussian, Vol. 3,

enclosed with Wheaton's Despatch No. 265 to Buchanan, May 7, 1845, Dept. of State MSS.

2. Dept. of Foreign Affairs to one of Prussia's Representatives, Berlin, July 31, 1844, Preussisches Geheimes Staatsarchiv, Vol. XII, pp. 64–68.

3. Dept. of Foreign Affairs to von Kuster, Prussian Representative in Munich, Berlin, August 1, 1844, *ibid.*, Vol. XII, pp. 69–70. The same was sent to all other Prussian Representatives in the Zollverein, *ibid.*, Vol. XII, pp. 71–75.

4. Preussisches Geheimes Staatsarchiv, Vol. XII, pp. 96–132.

5. The sentence quoting this phrase is given in Sioussat, "John Caldwell Calhoun," *American Secretaries of State*, Vol. V, p. 225.

6. Altenburg, August 28, 1844, Preussisches Geheimes Staatsarchiv, Vol. XII, pp. 122–123.

7. Fay to Calhoun, Sept. 18, 1844, Despatches, Prussia, Vol. 3, No. 21, Dept. of State MSS.

8. *Ibid.*

9. *Ibid.* (Private and Confidential), Oct. 3, 1844.

10. *Ibid.*

11. *Ibid.*, short note of explanation supplementing letter of same date, Oct. 3, 1844.

12. *Ibid.*, letter of Oct. 3, 1844.

13. *Ibid.*, Fay to Calhoun, Oct. 21, 1844.

14. Fay to Bülow (Confidential), Oct. 21, 1844, Preussisches Geheimes Staatsarchiv, Vol. XII, pp. 133–134. A copy of the above letter is also enclosed in Fay's letter to Calhoun of same date.

15. Calhoun to Wheaton, July 8, 1844, Instructions, Prussia, Vol. 14, No. 58, Dept. of State MSS.

16. *Ibid.*

17. *The Madisonian*, April 8, 1845, Vol. IV, No. 1021.

18. Wheaton to Buchanan ("Private and Most Confidential"), dated July 23, 1845, Buchanan Papers.

19. Instructions dated Berlin, Nov. 4, 1844, Preussisches Geheimes Staatsarchiv, Vol. XII, pp. 135–154.

20. Richardson, *Messages and Papers*. Also published in newspapers and periodicals. Excerpt in *Niles' Register* (weekly), dated Dec. 7, 1844.

21. Gerolt to Dept. of Foreign Affairs, Washington, Dec. 28, 1844, Preussisches Geheimes Staatsarchiv, Vol. XII, pp. 183–190.

22. *Ibid.*

23. Fay to Calhoun, Dec. 4, 1844, Despatches, Prussia, Vol. 3, Dept. of State MSS.

24. Gerolt to Dept. of Foreign Affairs, Washington, Jan. 29, 1845, Preussisches Geheimes Staatsarchiv, Vol. XII, pp. 195–200.

25. *Ibid.*

26. *Ibid.*, Washington, Feb. 25, 1845, Vol. XII, pp. 201–204.

27. Senate Doc., Vol. 26, No. 231, 56 Cong., 2 Sess., p. 38, ff.

28. *Niles' Weekly Register*, March 22, 1845, Vol. 68, p. 36.

29. Gerolt to the Dept. of Foreign Affairs, March 6, 1845, Preussisches Geheimes Staatsarchiv, Vol. XII, pp. 216–219.

30. *Ibid.,* March 20, 1845, Preussisches Geheimes Staatsarchiv, Vol. XII, pp. 220–227.

31. *Ibid.*

32. Miller, *Treaties, etc., of the United States,* Doc. No. 109, July 3, 1844, Vol. 4, pp. 559–662; Malloy, *Treaties, Conventions, International Acts, Protocols and Agreements between The United States and other Powers,* Vol. 1, pp. 196–211.

33. Gerolt to the Dept. of Foreign Affairs, March 20, 1845, Preussisches Geheimes Staatsarchiv, Vol. XII, pp. 220–227.

34. *Ibid.*

35. Dept. of Foreign Affairs to the Prussian Representatives in the Zollverein, May 3, 1845, Preussisches Geheimes Staatsarchiv, Vol. XII, pp. 228–244.

36. Bülow to Wheaton, May 3, 1845.

37. Dept. of Foreign Affairs to Gerolt, May 3, 1845, Preussisches Geheimes Staatsarchiv, Vol. XII, pp. 245–247.

38. Wheaton to Buchanan, May 7, 1845, Despatches, Prussia, Vol. 3, No. 265, Dept. of State MSS.

39. Gerolt to the Dept. of Foreign Affairs, June 27, 1845, Preussisches Geheimes Staatsarchiv, Vol. XII, pp. 272–275.

40. *Niles' Weekly Register,* August 23, 1845, Vol. 68, pp. 397–399.

41. *Deutsche Schnellpost,* April 23, 1845, letter received from Main, middle of March.

42. Gerolt to Dept. of Foreign Affairs, July 14, 1845, Preussisches Geheimes Staatsarchiv, Vol. XII, pp. 286–292.

43. Articles from the *Weser-Zeitung,* Aug. 6, 1844, Preussisches Geheimes Staatsarchiv, Vol. XII, pp. 105–106.

44. Wheaton to Buchanan, Berlin, Aug. 23, 1845, marked "Private," Buchanan Papers.

45. A. Duckwitz, *Denkwürdigkeiten aus meinem öffentlichen Leben von 1841–1866,* p. 37.

46. Wheaton to Calhoun, Berlin, Dec. 24, 1845, *Calhoun Cor.,* pp. 1063–1065.

47. Everett to Nelson, April 3, 1844, Despatches, Great Britain, Vol. 52, No. 109, Dept. of State MSS. Also Everett Papers, Vol. 48, pp. 415–419.

48. Conversation between Lord Aberdeen and Everett, noted in Everett's Journal, Aug. 16, 1844, Everett Papers, Vol. 162, p. 63.

49. Wheaton to Calhoun, Berlin, Dec. 24, 1845, *Calhoun Cor.,* pp. 1063–1065.

CHAPTER XXXI

1. Forsyth to Wheaton, April 20, 1835, Instructions, Prussia, Vol. 14, pp. 3–6, No. 2, Dept. of State MSS.

2. *Ibid.*

3. Wheaton to Forsyth, Dec. 16, 1835, Despatches, Prussia, Vol. 1, No. 13, Dept. of State MSS.

4. Forsyth to Wheaton, March 14, 1836, Instructions, Prussia, Vol. 14, pp. 7–10, No. 3, Dept. of State MSS.

5. Wheaton to Forsyth, Berlin, July 11, 1836, Despatches, Prussia, Vol. 1, No. 28, Dept. of State MSS.

6. Forsyth to Wheaton, June 14, 1836, Instructions, Prussia, Vol. 14, p. 10, No. 4, Dept. of State MSS.

7. *Ibid.*, Sept. 26, 1836, No. 7, pp. 12–13.

8. *Ibid.*, Upshur to Wheaton, Nov. 18, 1843, No. 50.

9. Wheaton to Forsyth, Berlin, March 31, 1840, Despatches, Prussia, Vol. 2, No. 143, Dept. of State MSS.

10. June 14, 1843, Despatches, Prussia, Vol. 3, No. 226, Dept. of State MSS.

11. Miller, *Treaties, etc., of the United States*, Doc. 106, Vol. 4, pp. 539–548.

12. *Ibid.*, Doc. 107, Vol. 4, pp. 549–554. The two conventions, with Württemberg and Hesse were enclosed in Despatch No. 244, Wheaton to Nelson, Secretary *ad interim*, April 10, 1844.

13. Senate Doc., 28 Cong., 1 Sess., pp. 18–19, No. 1. Wheaton had also entered fully into the subject in his Despatch to Legaré No. 226, dated June 14, 1843. These treaties also are briefly discussed by St. George L. Sioussat in Vol. V of *The American Secretaries of State and Their Diplomacy*, in connection first with his sketch of John C. Calhoun on p. 225 and again in the one on James Buchanan, p. 325.

14. Wheaton to Calhoun, June 12, 1844, Despatches, Prussia, Vol. 3, No. 252, Dept. of State MSS.

15. Miller, *Treaties, etc., of the United States*, Doc. 111, Vol. 4, pp. 671–683. This convention was enclosed in Despatch No. 257, Jan. 21, 1845, Despatches, Prussia, Vol. 3, Dept. of State MSS.

16. Wheaton to Buchanan, Despatch No. 290, July 11, 1846; also Despatch No. 291, July 20, 1846, Despatches, Prussia, Vol. 3, Dept. of State MSS.

17. Miller, *Treaties, etc., of the United States*, Vol. 4, pp. 671–683.

18. Miller, *Treaties, etc., of the United States*, Doc. 115, Vol. 4, pp. 751–760. Wheaton to Buchanan, May 14, 1845, Despatches, Prussia, Vol. 3, No. 267, Dept. of State MSS.

19. *Ibid.*, No. 267.

20. Wheaton to Buchanan, May 2, 1846, Despatches, Prussia, Vol. 3, No. 284, Dept. of State MSS.

21. *Ibid.*, Despatch No. 285 (should be No. 286), May 27, 1846.
Miller, *Treaties, etc., of the United States*, Doc. 120, Vol. 4, pp. 817–823.

22. W. Stull Holt, *Treaties Defeated by the Senate*, p. 88.
Ralston Hayden, "The States Rights' Doctrine and the Treaty-making Power," *American Historical Review*, Vol. XXII, pp. 566–585. See in this connection St. George L. Sioussat's note No. 152 to his writing on James Buchanan, *American Secretaries of State*, Vol. V, pp. 413–414.

23. Webster to Wheaton, March 16, 1843, Instructions, Prussia, Vol. 14, No. 39, pp. 46–50, Dept. of State MSS.

24. Bülow to Wheaton, Feb. 17, 1844.

25. Wheaton to Calhoun, July 17, 1844, Despatches, Prussia, Vol. 3, No. 255, Dept. of State MSS.

26. Calhoun to Wheaton, August 23, 1844, Instructions, Prussia, Vol. 14, No. 59, Dept. of State MSS.

27. Wheaton to Calhoun, Jan. 29, 1845, Despatches, Prussia, Vol. 2, No. 258, Wheaton MSS., Mass. Hist. Soc.

28. Wheaton to Webster, Nov. 26, 1845, Webster Papers, Vol. 10.

29. President Polk's message to the Senate, Dec. 15, 1845.

CHAPTER XXXII

1. Wheaton to Webster, May 17, 1843, Despatches, Prussia, Vol. 3, No. 223, Dept. of State MSS.

2. Wheaton to Upshur, August 30, 1843, *ibid.*, Despatch No. 234.

3. Upshur to Wheaton, Nov. 10, 1843, Instructions, Prussia, Vol. 14, No. 47, Dept. of State MSS.

4. Wheaton to Buchanan, Berlin, Dec. 17, 1845, Memoir enclosed with Despatch No. 278, Despatches, Prussia, Vol. 3, Dept. of State MSS.

5. James Buchanan to the Senate, May 7, 1846, 29 Cong., 1 Sess., Senate Doc. No. 339. Also in *Works of James Buchanan*, Vol. VI, pp. 474–475.

6. Calhoun to Wheaton, Dec. 26, 1844, Instructions, Prussia, Vol. 14, Dept. of State MSS. Lawrence, pp. lxxiii, lxxiv.

7. Wheaton to Levi Wheaton, Berlin, Jan. 29, 1845, Wheaton Papers.

8. *Ibid.*, May 27, 1846.

9. Wheaton to Calhoun, London, Feb. 10, 1846, *Calhoun Cor.*, Vol. II, pp. 1071–1074.

10. Wheaton to his son Robert Wheaton, April 22, 1846, Wheaton Papers.

11. Wheaton to Buchanan, May 27, 1846, Despatches, Prussia, Vol. 3, No. 286, Dept. of State MSS. Lawrence, pp. cxix, cxx.

CHAPTER XXXIII

1. *Scandinavia, Ancient and Modern:* Being a History of Denmark, Sweden, and Norway, by Andrew Crichton, LL.D. and Henry Wheaton, LL.D. London, 1838. An American edition was published in Philadelphia the same year and in 1841 the work was republished in two small-typed volumes in *Harper's Family Library*.

2. *Ibid.*, Preface, pp. 9–10.

3. Benson, p. 561.

4. Charles Sumner, *Works*, Vol. 2, p. 67.

5. Lawrence, pp. cxlvi, cxlvii. Also Rev. fr. et etr., tom. ix, p. 70.

6. *Edinburgh Review*, Vol. LXXVII, p. 161, Am. Ed.

7. Lawrence, pp. cxlvi, cxlvii.

8. Wheaton, *History of the Law of Nations*, 1845 ed., pp. 343–344.

9. Lawrence, p. cxlviii.

10. *Ibid.*, p. cxlix.

11. *Ibid.*

12. *Preussisches Staats-Zeitung*, March 27, 1843. Lawrence, p. cxxxii.

13. *Ibid.*

14. *Revue de Droit français et étrangère*, Vol. 1, pp. 955–966, 1844.

15. *Ibid.*, Vol. 2, pp. 199–211, 1845.

16. *Monthly Review,* Vol. III, N. & I., Series 2, Vol. 166, September 1844.

17. *Foreign Quarterly Review,* Vol. XVIII, p. 109; *ibid.,* Vol. 21, p. 89; *ibid.,* Vol. XXVIII, p. 455.

18. Letter from Henry Wheaton, Berlin, Dec. 21, 1842, Wheaton Papers.

19. National Institute *Proceedings,* February 1842 to February 1845.

20. Wheaton to Levi Wheaton, Berlin, Feb. 22, 1844, Wheaton Papers.

21. *Ibid.,* May 1, 1844.

22. Wheaton to Robert, July 17, 1845, Wheaton Papers.

23. Wheaton, *Elements of International Law,* 1846.

24. *Ibid.*

25. Hicks, p. 221.

26. The Librarian of the John Hay Library, Brown University, reported in April, 1896, that the books given to the Library by the Wheaton Estate comprised 567 volumes.

The Wheaton Collection of International Law was founded in 1902 as a memorial to Henry Wheaton on the occasion of the hundredth anniversary of his graduation. It was originally established and subsequently developed largely through the efforts of the Honorable William V. Kellen of Boston and Professor George Grafton Wilson of Harvard University, then at Brown. At the present time there are about 4,000 volumes in the Collection. This includes, in addition to the editions of Wheaton's works, one of the best American collections of editions of Grotius' *De Jure Belli et Pacis* (including a first edition, second issue); an unusually complete collection of general treatises on international law; fairly complete documentation for international arbitrations, the League of Nations, and the Permanent Court of International Justice; and complete files of the more important international law periodicals. At present efforts are being made to develop the Collection in the direction of source materials and general treatises.

CHAPTER XXXIV

1. Calhoun to Wheaton, Dec. 26, 1844, Instructions, Prussia, Vol. 14, Dept. of State MSS.

2. *Boston Daily Advertiser,* Vol. LXIII, No. 93, April 18, 1844, contained excerpt from the *Deutsche Schnellpost.*

3. Lawrence to Bancroft, New York, March 26, 1845, Bancroft Papers, Mass. Hist. Soc.

4. Wheaton to Calhoun, Berlin, January 26, 1846, *Calhoun Cor.,* Vol. II, pp. 1069–1071.

5. *Ibid.*

6. *Ibid.*

7. Buchanan to Wheaton, April 25, 1846, Instructions, Prussia, Vol. 14, No. 71, pp. 95–97, Dept. of State MSS.

8. Donelson to Buchanan, New York, May 31, 1846, Despatches, Prussia, Vol. 3, Dept. of State MSS.

9. Gerolt to Dept. of Foreign Affairs, Preussisches Geheimes Staatsarchiv, Vol. XII.

10. Donelson to Buchanan, Berlin, July 7, 1846, Despatches, Prussia, Vol. 3, Despatch No. 1, Dept. of State MSS.

11. *Ibid.,* Despatch No. 3, Berlin, July 19, 1846.

12. *Ibid.,* Despatch No. 291, July 20, 1846. (Wheaton's last official despatch.)

13. *Ibid.*

14. Alexander von Humboldt to Wheaton, Potsdam, June 18, 1846. Lawrence, p. clix.

15. Lawrence, p. clviii.

16. *Ibid.,* pp. clix, clx.

17. Wheaton to Buchanan, Berlin, July 20, 1846, Despatches, Prussia, Vol. 3, Despatch No. 291, Dept. of State MSS.

CHAPTER XXXV

1. Lawrence, p. clxiv.

2. Warren, Vol. II, p. 388.

3. Wheaton to Calhoun, Berlin, Jan. 26, 1846. *Calhoun Cor.,* Vol. II, pp. 1069–1071.

4. King to Tyler, Paris, Sept. 13, 1844, Tyler, Lyon G., *Life and Times of the Tylers,* pp. 328–329.

5. Wheaton to Levi Wheaton, May 1847, Wheaton Papers.

6. Invitation, June 10, 1847, Wheaton Papers.

7. Letter of Robert Wheaton, New York, June 11, 1847, Wheaton Papers.

8. Lawrence, pp. clxiv, clxv.

9. *Ibid.*

10. Lawrence, pp. clxv, clxvi.

11. Everett to Wheaton, March 31, 1846, Everett Papers, Vol. 78, pp. 153–156; Oct. 14, 1847, Everett Papers, Vol. 82, pp. 255–256; Oct. 29, 1847, Everett Papers, Vol. 83, p. 2; Nov. 13, 1847, Everett Papers, Vol. 83, p. 34.

The arrangement was temporary, only for one year. Wheaton was to give two or three lectures a week for two terms, of twenty weeks each. The compensation was to be $2,000 per annum.

12. Lawrence, p. clxvii.

13. *Daily Evening Transcript,* Boston, Tuesday evening, March 14, 1848.

14. Francis R. Jones, in *The Green Bag,* Vol. XVI, No. 12.

EPILOGUE

1. Charles Francis Adams, *Richard Henry Dana, a Biography,* Vol. II, pp. 282–285.

2. *Ibid.,* p. 284.

3. *Ibid.,* p. 305.

4. For the effect upon Dana, see the pamphlet entitled *The Lawrence-Wheaton Controversy,* printed for private circulation, pp. 1–16; also Adams, *op. cit.,* Vol. II, pp. 283–327.

5. *Commentaire sur les Éléments du droit international, et sur l'Histoire*

des progrès du droit des gens de Henry Wheaton. Précédé d'une notice sur la carrière diplomatique de M. Wheaton. Par William B. Lawrence. 4 vols. Leipzig, 1868–1880.

Volume 4 has added title page: "Études sur la juridiction consulaire et pays chrétiens et en pays non chrétiens et sur l'extradition. par W. B. Lawrence."

6. Richard Henry Dana, Wheaton's *Elements of International Law,* p. 22, Note 8.

7. Harvard University has a separate Chinese Library. In this may be found both the Chinese edition of Wheaton's *Elements of International Law,* and the edition adapted to Japanese use.

8. *Wheaton's Elements of International Law,* 5th English Edition by Coleman Phillipson, with an Introduction by Sir Frederick Pollock, London, 1916, p. xli.

9. *Ibid.,* p. xlii.

BIBLIOGRAPHY

BIBLIOGRAPHY

MANUSCRIPT MATERIAL

UNITED STATES—DEPARTMENT OF STATE ARCHIVES

The following volumes were consulted for the period of Wheaton's diplomatic activities, 1827–1847.

Instructions, United States Ministers—Denmark, Prussia, England and France.

Instructions, Denmark, Prussia, England and France.

Despatches—Denmark, Prussia, England and France.

Notes to Foreign Legations.

Notes from Legations of Denmark and Prussia.

Report Books.

Credences.

The manuscript Index of the despatches from Prussia for this period was useful for checking through special topics of interest.

LIBRARY OF CONGRESS—DIVISION OF MANUSCRIPTS

Reproductions of official documents in foreign archives relating to the United States. These are usually either photostatic copies or films. Here are gathered together into one place a large collection of archives relating to this period which makes possible not only a detailed study of official documents not previously available, but also in some instances a more comprehensive survey than formerly could be obtained in Europe.

Prussia:

Preussisches Geheimes Staatsarchiv, Berlin-Dahlem

Auswärtiges Amt, Abteilung II, Rep. 6, Handel, Nordamerika, Acta betreffend die Handelsverhältnisse mit den Nordamerikanischen Freistaaten, Volumes V to XIV inclusive, comprising some 3,400 pages, which cover the period from January, 1834 to December, 1847, were consulted in detail. They consist of photostatic reproductions of German official correspondence, written in German script with a quill pen, and are difficult to decipher. These documents are described in Learned's *Guide to German State Archives,* pp. 43–45, *see infra.*

Volumes for this period relating to the commercial relations and navigation of the German States with the United States may also be found among the photostatic copies listed under: Preussisches Geheimes Staatsarchiv, Berlin-Dahlem. Auswärtiges Amt. Under different series and descriptions, over 20 volumes. A few of these are listed in Learned, pp. 40, 41, 47, 54–55.

Preussisches Staatsarchiv, Marburg. Kurfürstlich Hessisches Ministerium der Auswärtigen Angelegenheiten. Several volumes under different series and descriptions.

Preussisches Staatsarchiv, Stettin, Regierung, Abteilung, Tit. 19, Sect. 1, Commercien Sachen Gen. No. 26, Acta der Koniglichen Regierung von Pommern die Handels Verhältnisse zwischen den Preussischen und Nordamerikanischen Staaten betreffend.

Staatsarchiv, Breslau, Rep. 14, P. A. VIII, Acta der Königlichen Regierung zu Reichenbach, bezwischen zu Breslau, betreffend den Handel mit den Nord-Amerikanischen Frei-Staaten. Also several other volumes under different series and descriptions.

Staatsarchiv, Bremen, B 13 a, Verschiedene Papiere betreffend Handels-polit., auswanderung, Schiffahrt dipl. Korresp. Listed in Learned, pp. 238–239.

Films have been made for several groups which are not listed in Learned. Among these are:

Preussisches Staatsarchiv, Hannover, Ha. Des. 115, A. I. C. 4, Handels-und Schiffahrts-Vertrag.

Sächsisches Hauptstaats Archiv, Dresden, Loc. 8745, 488, 30046, 30347, Verschiedene Papiere.

Staatsarchiv, Bremen, C 76 a, Handel mit den Vereinigten Staaten—3 films.

Oldenburgisches, Landesarchiv, Aa Kabinetts-Registr. Oldenburg, Reciprozitat wegen Handels- und Schiffahrtsabgaben.

M. D. Learned's *Guide to the manuscript materials relating to American history in the German state archives,* Carnegie Institution of Washington, 1912, has been supplemented by two volumes of a written report entitled *Supplements, corrections and new inventory-lists to be added to M. D. Learned's*

Guide, etc. This supplement was made by the German staff of the European Historical Mission of the Library of Congress, 1929–1932, and may be consulted in the Division of Manuscripts of the Library.

Great Britain:

Public Record Office, London.

Volumes for this period may also be found listed under: Foreign Office Records—America, usually designated as F. O. Series 5. Various volumes and dates. A photostatic reproduction of the instructions to and despatches from the British representatives and ministers in the United States.

These are described on pages 30–31 of *Guide to the materials in London archives for the history of the United States since 1783,* by C. O. Paullin and F. L. Paxson, published by the Carnegie Institution of Washington in 1914.

Manuscript Collections

Papers of Sylvanus Bourne.

Valuable principally as a background for the period. Only a few letters relating to Henry Wheaton.

Papers of James Kent.

Due in part to their community of interests a continuous friendship existed between Chancellor Kent and Wheaton from the time of the latter's arrival in New York until the former's death and many items of interest are to be found among these papers. They consist of

11 volumes mounted and bound, 1779–1847.

15 volumes of journals and diaries, 1792–1846.

Papers of James Madison.

In this collection is the correspondence relating to Wheaton's biography of William Pinkney. These papers consist of:

12 volumes of writings by Madison, 1723–1845.

63 volumes of letters to Madison, 1723–1845.

The section transferred to the Library by the State Department is covered by a printed calendar, the remainder by a manuscript calendar. The printed calendar appears as:

Calendar of the Correspondence of James Madison. Department of State. Washington, 1894–95. Reprinted 1902.

Papers of James Monroe.

Contains at least part of Monroe's correspondence with William Pinkney, and with Wheaton concerning Pinkney besides other letters of interest relating to Wheaton's activities. There is a printed calendar of these papers:

Calendar of the Correspondence of James Monroe. New edition with corrections and additions covering the years 1783–1831. Department of State, Washington, 1893. Reprinted 1902.

As a complement to this calendar, which is arranged alphabetically, there is a list published by the Library of Congress which presents the entire collection in chronological order:

Papers of James Monroe, listed in chronological order from the original manuscripts in the Library of Congress. Edited by Worthington C. Ford. Washington, 1904.

Papers of Nathaniel Niles.

Nathaniel Niles was sent to Austria in June, 1837, as tobacco agent similar to the mission of Joshua Dodge to Berlin. Among other items of interest relating to this period were various references to Wheaton. The Papers consist of 2 volumes in which are contained 7 letters from Wheaton, dated as follows: Vol. 1, Copenhagen, Oct. 1, 1830, June 9, 1832 (second page of this letter is at the end of Volume 2), April 27, 1833, Oct. 28, 1834, Dec. 26, 1834 (marked confidential); Vol. 2, Berlin, Oct. 14, 1837, and Aug. 20, 1839.

Papers of Andrew Stevenson.

The papers consist of 26 volumes of mounted correspondence covering the years 1810 to 1859. From 1836 to 1841 Stevenson was United States Minister to England. Some of the letters during this period are of interest, especially Letterbooks, April 1839 to Oct. 1841, since they are contemporary with Wheaton's mission to Berlin. Stevenson left England just prior to Wheaton's visit to Paris during the winter 1841–1842.

Papers of Martin Van Buren.

This collection of 72 bound volumes besides other papers is an extensive one and contains many letters of direct and indirect interest. There is a calendar covering most of them.

Calendar of the Papers of Martin Van Buren. Edited by Elizabeth Howard West. Library of Congress, Washington, 1910.

Papers of Daniel Webster.

This collection comprises 4 volumes of mounted papers, 1804–1853, and 2 portfolios of unbound papers, 1826–1852. There are many letters of contemporary interest. There is also a larger collection of Webster papers in the New Hampshire Historical Society at Concord, New Hampshire.

Several other collections were of value in this study. Among these should be mentioned the Papers of John C. Calhoun, Henry Clay, Andrew J. Donelson, Duff Green, Andrew Jackson, William L. Marcy, James K. Polk and Virgil Maxcy, the last are part of the collection generally known as the Galloway-Maxcy-Markoe Papers.

JOHN HAY LIBRARY—BROWN UNIVERSITY

Papers of Henry Wheaton.

This collection is comprised mainly of letters between Wheaton and the various members of his family. With the exception of the letters written to Levi Wheaton which discuss questions of national import, most of the correspondence deals with personal affairs. The diary which Wheaton kept for a short time after his arrival in Copenhagen is with these papers, but the entries are short and the information contained in it rather meager. From letters received by Brown University, it would seem that the main part of his papers were taken to Europe by his daughters who presented them to a friend.

Papers of Jonathan Russell.

When the first attempt was made to consult these papers it was found that they had been sent from Brown University to the Massachusetts Historical Society to be classified by Mr. Worthington C. Ford, and it was in the Library of that Society that they were used for this study. Since then they have been returned to the John Hay Library where they have been catalogued.

MASSACHUSETTS HISTORICAL SOCIETY

Letters of John Bailey—Washburn Papers—Vol. XX.

These are of interest principally in throwing light upon the early activities of Wheaton as reporter and counsellor before the Supreme Court.

Papers of George Bancroft.

Contain only a few letters concerning Wheaton directly but much that is interesting indirectly.

Papers of Edward Everett.
> A valuable and unusually large collection. The copies of official, confidential, and personal correspondence and a carefully kept journal or diary are written in Everett's clear handwriting and indexed by him.

Manuscript copy of *Despatches* to the State Department from Henry Wheaton while representing the United States at Berlin given to the Massachusetts Historical Society by Wheaton's daughters. In these may be found copies of several of the despatches missing from the volumes in the State Department.

NEW HAMPSHIRE HISTORICAL SOCIETY

Papers of Daniel Webster.
> The most important collection of Webster Papers. Several important letters which have never appeared in print were found in this collection. Most of the letters relating to the period under discussion were located in the first 10 volumes covering the years from July 1807 to June 1846.

HISTORICAL SOCIETY OF PENNSYLVANIA

Papers of James Buchanan.
> A large collection, important for the period covered.

In addition to the foregoing, letters from Henry Wheaton and concerning Henry Wheaton relating to diverse matters are to be found in various places, some in collections, some as single entries. Among the former may be mentioned the Papers of Azariah C. Flagg, of George Bancroft, of Jared Sparks, and of Samuel L. Gouvernour, who was President Monroe's son-in-law and private secretary, in the New York Public Library; the Papers of DeWitt Clinton in the Columbia University Library; the Papers of Albert Gallatin and of Richard Rush in the New York Historical Society; and the Papers of General Joseph G. Swift in the United States Military Academy Library at West Point, New York. Among the single entries are several letters from Wheaton in the Boston Public Library, the Harvard University Library, the Harvard Law Library, and the Rhode Island Historical Society.

PRINTED MATERIAL

OFFICIAL PUBLICATIONS

Congressional Documents. Washington, various dates.

These include Journals, Reports, Executive and Miscellaneous Documents of both the Senate and House of Representatives during the period under consideration. Among those of especial interest to this study are the following:

"Instructions, correspondence, etc., under which the treaty of indemnity with Denmark was negotiated. Report of Secretary of State," *22:1 House Executive Document 249.*

"Report on Tobacco Trade," *24:2 House of Representatives Report 239.*

"Report on Tobacco Trade," *25:3 House of Representatives Report 310.*

"The Tobacco Trade between the United States and foreign countries. Report of the Secretary of State, April 1840," *26:1 House Executive Document, VI, 229.* Contains part of Wheaton's official correspondence, 1837–1840.

"Commercial relations of the United States with the Zollverein and discussion of Sound Dues. Report of Secretary of State Daniel Webster to President Tyler, May 24, 1841," *27:1 Senate Document 1*, pp. 28–32. Materials from which this report was compiled were furnished by the Despatches of Wheaton from Berlin and Copenhagen.

"Report of the Secretary of the Treasury on the subject of the Commerce and Navigation with France, August 2, 1841," *27:1 House Executive Document 46.*

"Correspondence with the Prussian Government, in relation to the duties levied on tobacco in the German States of the Customs Union. Report of Secretary of State Daniel Webster, June 29, 1841," *27:1 Senate Document 55.* This was based on Wheaton's correspondence with German officials and with the State Department.

"Report of the Commercial Relations of the United States with Foreign Nations; Comparative Tariffs, etc. Report of the Secretary of State, Daniel Webster, March 29, 1842," *27:2 House Executive Document, IV, 163.*

"Laws and Regulations of France as to the Importation of Tobacco. Report of the Secretary of State, Daniel Web-

ster, July 16, 1842," *27:2 House Executive Document,
V, 5, 272.*

"Copies of the Correspondence between the government of
the United States and that of Great Britain, on the subject of the right of search, with copies of the protest of
the American minister at Paris against the Quintuple
Treaty, and the correspondence relating thereto," *27:3
Senate Document 223;* also *29:1 Senate Document 377.*

"Relations of the United States with the German Customs
Union. Report of Secretary of State Upshur to President Tyler," *28:1 Senate Document 1;* also in *28:1 House
Executive Document 2;* Report Book—State Department,
6, April 2, 1842–March 21, 1853, pp. 77–85; *Niles' Register,* Sept. 1843–March 1844, LXV or XV, 5th Series,
Dec. 23, 1843, pp. 263–264.

"Message transmitting commercial treaty with Germanic
Customs Union, President Tyler to United States Senate,
April 29, 1844," *28:1 Senate Jol. 444;* also in *Messages
and Papers,* IV, 314.

"Ship canal across the Isthmus of Panama and the opening
of new channels of communication with the Eastern
nations," Report Book—State Department, VI, p. 198;
also in *29:1 Senate Document 339; 30:2 House of Representatives Report of Committee 145.* Feb. 20, 1849; *The
Works of James Buchanan,* Moore, VI, pp. 474–475.

"Report of Department of State," *32:2 Senate Executive
Document 52,* pp. 9–16.

"Compilation of Reports of the Committee on Foreign Relations, United States Senate, 1789–1901," 1 Cong., 1 Sess.
to 56 Cong., 2 Sess. Treaties and Legislation respecting
them, *56:2 Senate Document 231,* Part 8.

"Tariff Acts passed by the Congress of the United States
from 1789 to 1909, including all acts, resolutions, and
proclamations modifying or changing those acts." *61:2
House of Representatives Document 671.*

Messages and Papers of the Presidents, 1789–1897. 10 volumes.
Published by the authority of Congress. Compiled by James
D. Richardson. Washington, 1896–1899. This collection also
appears as *53:2 House Miscellaneous Document 210.*

Special Report of the Customs-Tariff Legislation of the United

States. Edward Young, Chief of the Bureau of Statistics. Washington, 1847.

Treaties, Conventions, International Acts, Protocols and Agreements between the United States of America and other Powers, 1776–1909. Compiled by William M. Malloy. 2 vols. Washington, 1910. Supplement, 1910–1923. Compiled by Charles Garfield. Washington, 1923.

This collection was prepared under the direction of the Committee on Foreign Relations, United States Senate, pursuant to a resolution of the Senate, January 18, 1909, and appears also as *61:2 Senate Document 357.* Malloy's was the standard compilation of treaties until it was superseded by the following publication.

Treaties and other International Acts of the United States of America. Edited by Hunter Miller, 4 vols., covering period from 1776 to 1846, Washington, 1931–1934.

This definitive edition is compiled from original texts or facsimiles thereof and contains valuable historical notes concerning each entry. It is so arranged that it can be carried on indefinitely. It supersedes all previous compilations.

Opinions of Attorneys General, Decisions of Courts and Diplomatic Correspondence. Edited by James Brown Scott. New York, 1918. Published by the Carnegie Endowment for International Peace. Interprets the treaties of 1785, 1799, and 1828 between the United States and Prussia.

Reciprocity and Commercial Treaties. Report of Tariff Commission dated December 4, 1918.

This is a study of the commercial agreements between the United States and foreign countries. It contains a discussion of the conditional and unconditional forms of the most-favored-nation clause and the practice of the United States in regard to these principles. It also gives an account of the relations and discussions with Germany on the subjects of the most-favored-nation clause as a basis of the commercial relations between the two countries.

The Public Statutes at Large of the United States, from the Organization of the Government in 1789 to March 3, 1845, arranged in Chronological order. 8 vols. Boston, 1845–1856.

Reports of cases, argued and adjudged in the Supreme Court of the United States, 1816–1869:

Wheaton's *Reports,* 1816–1827. 12 vols.

Peters' *Reports,* 1827–1835.

Clifford's *Reports,* 1869.

Register of Department of State in Four Parts, corrected to March 1, 1874, Part II, "Historical Register," Washington, 1874.

This is valuable as giving for the century 1774 to 1874 a list with a fair amount of detail of the diplomatic representatives or agents both to and from the United States. It is a rare edition not entirely accurate. A more detailed card catalogue is available in the Department of State.

Journal of the Assembly of the State of New York at their Forty-seventh Session begun and held at the Capitol, in the City of Albany, the 6th day of January, 1824. Albany, 1824.

British and Foreign State Papers, 1812–1860. 51 vols. London, 1841–1868.

Commercial Tariffs and Regulations of the Several States of Europe and America, together with the Commercial Treaties between England and Foreign Countries. Report of John MacGregor, Secretary of the Board of Trade, to the Lords of the Committee of Privy Council of Trade and Plantations, 7 vols., London, 1841–1849.

A series of valuable comprehensive reports, which are important for a study of this period.

Tables showing the Trade of the United Kingdom with different Foreign Countries and British Possessions in each of ten years.

    I. From 1831 to 1840. London, 1842.

    II. From 1841 to 1850. London, 1855.

Hansard's Parliamentary Debates. Third Series, 1830–1859, 155 vols. London, 1831–1859.

A Complete Collection of the Treaties and Conventions and Reciprocal Regulations at present subsisting between Great Britain and Foreign Powers, and of the Laws, Decrees and Orders in Council concerning the same, etc. Edited by Lewis Herstlet, 31 vols. London, 1820.

The Great European Treaties of the Nineteenth Century. Edited by Sir Augustus Oakes and Robert B. Mowat. Oxford, 1918.

Financial Statement of Sir Robert Peel in the House of Commons, Friday, March 11, 1842. London, 1842.

Recueil des Traités de la France publié sous les auspices de M. Charles L. de Freycinet, President de Conseil, Ministre des Affaires Étrangères, 1713–1904. 22 vols. Paris, 1880–1907.

Recueil des Principaux Traités d'Alliance, de Paix, de Trève, de Neutralité, de Commerce, de Limites, d'Échange, etc., conclus par les Puissances de l'Europe tante entre elles qu'avec les Puissances et États dans d'autres parties du Monde depuis 1761 jusqu'à present. Par M. de Martens. Göttingen, 1791– Leipzig, 1894.

MEMOIRS, ETC.

Memoirs of John Quincy Adams comprising portions of his Diary from 1795 to 1848. Edited by Charles Francis Adams. 12 vols. Philadelphia, 1874–1877.

The Works of James Buchanan. Comprising his speeches, state papers and private correspondence, 1813–1868. Collected and edited by James Bassett Moore. 12 vols. London and Philadelphia, 1908–1911.

"Correspondence of John C. Calhoun." Edited by J. Franklin Jameson. Fourth Annual Report of the Historical Manuscripts Com. in Vol. II of the *Annual Report of the American Historical Association* for the year 1899. 2 vols. Washington, 1900.

The Works of John C. Calhoun. Edited by R. K. Cralle. 6 vols. New York, 1851–1856.

The Works of Henry Clay, comprising his Life, Correspondence, and Speeches. Edited by Calvin Colton. 6 vols. New York, 1863.

"DeWitt Clinton as a Politician." By John Bigelow. *Harper's New Monthly Magazine*, Vol. L, Dec. 1874 to May 1875. New York, 1875.

> With the exception of a few paragraphs of commentary this is composed entirely of excerpts of letters from Clinton to his friend Henry Post of New York.

An Embassy to the Court of St. James's, in 1840. By F. Guizot (Francois Pierre Guillaume) Ambassador from his Majesty Louis-Phillippe. London, 1862.

The Life and Correspondence of Rufus King, comprising his letters, private and official, his public documents, and his speeches. Edited by Charles R. King. 6 vols. New York, 1894–1900.

The Writings of James Madison, comprising his public papers and his private correspondence, including numerous letters and documents now for the first time printed. Edited by Gaillard Hunt. 9 vols. New York, 1900–1910.

The Writings of James Monroe, including a collection of his public and private papers and correspondence now for the first time printed. Edited by S. M. Hamilton. 7 vols. New York, 1898–1903.

Memoirs of Sir Robert Peel. By M. Guizot. (Francois Pierre Guillaume.) London, 1857.

Private Letters of Sir Robert Peel. Compiled by George Peel. London, 1920.

Memoirs of Sir Robert Peel. 2 vols. London, 1856–1857.

"Letters of James K. Polk to Andrew J. Donelson, 1843–48." Edited and with Introduction by St. George L. Sioussat. *Tennessee Historical Magazine,* Vol. III, pp. 51–73. Nashville, 1917.

"Selected Letters, 1844–1845, from the Donelson Papers." Edited with Introduction by St. George L. Sioussat. *Tennessee Historical Magazine.* Vol. III, pp. 134–162. Nashville, 1917.

The Diary of James K. Polk during his Presidency, 1845 to 1849, now first printed from the original manuscript in the collections of the Chicago Historical Society. Edited by Miles Milton Quaife. 4 vols. Chicago, 1910.

The Later Correspondence of Lord John Russell, 1840–78. Edited by G. P. Gooch. London, 1925.

The Letters and Times of the Tylers. By Lyon G. Tyler. 2 vols. Richmond, 1884–1885.

"The Autobiography of Martin Van Buren." Edited by John Clement Fitzpatrick. *Annual Report of the American Historical Association,* 1918. Vol. II. Washington, 1920.

Speech delivered at the Dinner given to Mr. Webster by the Merchants of Baltimore, on Thursday, May 18, 1843. New York, 1843.

Diplomatic and Official Papers of Daniel Webster, while Secretary of State. New York, 1848.

The Works of Daniel Webster. 6 vols. Boston, 1851.

Great Speeches and Orations of Daniel Webster. Edited by E. P. Whipple. Boston, 1879.

The Letters of Daniel Webster, from documents owned principally by the New Hampshire Historical Society. Edited by C. H. VanTyne. New York, 1902.

The Writings and Speeches of Daniel Webster. Edited by J. W. McIntire. 18 vols. Boston, 1903.

The most complete printed edition of Webster's writings.

"Letters of Henry Wheaton to his Father, 1805–1806." *Proceedings* of the Massachusetts Historical Society.

Vol. XVIII, 1880–1881, pp. 20–22. Boston, 1881.

Vol. XIX, 1881–1882, pp. 361–376. Boston, 1882.

PERIODICALS AND NEWSPAPERS

1. *Periodicals.*

American Historical Review.

American Monthly Review.

American Quarterly Review.

Blackwood's Magazine.

Boston Monthly Magazine.

Edinburgh Review.

English Historical Review.

Foreign Quarterly Review.

Fraser's Magazine for Town and Country.

Harper's Monthly Magazine.

Hunt's Magazine.

London Athenaeum.

Monthly Review–London.

North American Review.

The Boston Public Library contains the set of the *North American Review* formerly owned by Edward Everett. In many instances in the margin opposite the review appears the name of the reviewer in Everett's handwriting. These notations proved to be valuable in verifying the authorship of the various reviews attributed to Henry Wheaton.

Political Science Quarterly.

Revue des Deux Mondes.

Revue de Droit Français et Étranger.

Revue étrangère et française de Legislation et d'Économie
  Politique.
Southern Literary Messenger.
Westminster Review—London.
2. *Newspapers.*
Albany Daily Advertiser.
Albany Daily Register.
American Commercial Advertiser.
Baltimore Sun.
Boston Daily Advertiser.
Congressional Globe—Washington.
Daily Evening Transcript—Boston.
Daily National Intelligencer—Washington.
Daily Union—Washington.
Deutsche Schnellpost—New York.
London Times.
The Madisonian—Washington.
Morning Chronicle—London.
Morning Herald—London.
Nashville Union.
National Advocate—New York.
New York American.
New York Commercial Advertiser.
New York Herald.
New York Patriot.
New Yorker Staats-Zeitung.
New York Sun.
Niles' Register (Weekly).
Providence Daily Journal.
Rhode Island Patriot—Providence.
Rhode Island Phoenix—Providence.
Richmond Enquirer.
Washington Telegraph.

ESSAYS ON HENRY WHEATON

Benson, Adolph B. "Henry Wheaton's Writings on Scandinavia." *The Journal of English and Germanic Philology.*
Vol. XXIX, pp. 546–561, October 1930.
  An excellent article limited to this phase of Wheaton's activities.

Carson, Hampton L. "Henry Wheaton." *The Supreme Court of the United States: its History.* 2 vols., pp. 563–565. Philadelphia, 1891.

Everett, Edward. "Life, Services and Works of Henry Wheaton." *North American Review,* Vol. LXXXII, pp. 1–32. January 1856.

A fairly stated tribute to Wheaton by one who had known him well in his diplomatic life.

Hall, Edward B. "The Value of a Man." A Discourse occasioned by the death of Hon. Henry Wheaton; delivered Sunday Evening, March 19, 1848, in the First Congregational Church, Providence, R. I. Providence, 1848.

Hicks, Frederick C. "Henry Wheaton." *Men and Books Famous in the Law,* pp. 190–235. New York, 1921.

The best discussion of Wheaton as a lawyer and Supreme Court Reporter.

Jones, Francis R. "Henry Wheaton." *The Green Bag,* Vol. XVI, No. 12, pp. 781–785. Boston, 1904.

A short but appreciative article.

Kellen, William Vail. "Henry Wheaton." An appreciation; being the address delivered before the alumni of Brown University on the occasion of the one hundredth anniversary of his Graduation, June 17, 1902. Boston, 1902.

A well-written appreciation by one who has done a great deal to pay tribute to Henry Wheaton, especially by his activity in aiding in the establishment of the Henry Wheaton room on International Law in the John Hay Library, Brown University.

Lawrence, William Beach. "Notice of the Author (Wheaton) by the Editor." *Elements of International Law,* by Henry Wheaton. Edited by W. B. Lawrence. 2d. anno. ed. pp. xix–lxxvii. London, 1863.

The comprehensive and authoritative account of Wheaton.

Lincoln, William Ensign. *Some descendents of . . . Robert Wheaton of Swansea, Wales . . . and notes of Related Families.* New York, 1930.

Scott, James Brown. "Henry Wheaton, 1785–1848." *Great American Lawyers,* Vol. 3, pp. 243–285. Edited by W. D. Lewis.

Shea, George. "Some thoughts on Henry Wheaton and the

epoch to which he belonged." New York State Bar Association. *Reports,* Vol. 2, pp. 95–103.

Sumner, Charles. "The Late Henry Wheaton." Article in the *Boston Daily Advertiser,* March 16, 1848. Also in *Charles Sumner, his Complete Works,* Vol. 2, pp. 63–73. Boston, 1870.

Anonymous. "Henry Wheaton." *Homes of American Statesmen: with Anecdotical, Personal, and Descriptive Sketches, by Various Writers,* pp. 449–469. New York, 1860.

This article, although anonymous, was undoubtedly written by Wheaton's daughter and can, therefore, be considered authentic. The original of the letter from Theophilus Parsons quoted in the article is among the Wheaton Papers in the John Hay Library, Brown University.

Anonymous. ("Old Lady 31") *Henry Wheaton, Diplomatist and Publicist.* An Essay submitted in competition for the Gaspee Chapter, Daughters of the American Revolution Prize. May 14, 1920.

This is unimportant. Some of the statements therein are incorrect. The manuscript is in the Rhode Island Historical Society.

BIOGRAPHY

Adams, Charles Francis. *Richard Henry Dana, A Biography.* 2 vols. Boston and New York, 1890.

Adams, Herbert B. *The Life and Writings of Jared Sparks.* 2 vols. Boston and New York, 1893.

Adams, Randolph G. "Abel P. Upshur." *The American Secretaries of State and their Diplomacy.* Edited by Samuel Flagg Bemis. 10 vols. New York, 1928. Vol. V.

(Hereinafter designated as American Secretaries of State)

Ashley, Evelyn. *The Life of Henry John Temple, Viscount Palmerston, 1846–65, with selections from his Speeches and Correspondence.* 2 vols. London, 1876.

Bancroft, George. *Martin Van Buren to the End of his Public Career.* New York, 1889.

Beveridge, Albert J. *The Life of John Marshall.* 4 vols. Boston and New York, 1916–1919.

Bigham, Clive. *The Prime Ministers of Britain, 1721–1921.* New York, 1923.

Bulwer, Sir Henry. (Lord Dalling) *The Life of Henry John*

Temple, Viscount Palmerston, with selections from his Correspondence. 3 vols. London, 1874.

Chinard, Gilbert. *Thomas Jefferson. The Apostle of Americanism.* Boston, 1929.

Colton, Calvin. *Life and Times of Henry Clay.* 3 vols. New York, 1846.

Curtis, George T. *Life of James Buchanan.* 2 vols. New York, 1883.

Duniway, Clyde Augustus. "Daniel Webster," *American Secretaries of State,* Vol. V. New York, 1928.

Fuess, Claude Moore. *The Life of Caleb Cushing.* 2 vols. New York, 1923.

———.*Daniel Webster.* 2 vols. Boston, 1930.

Gordon, Sir Arthur. G. C. M. Q. (Lord Stanmore) *The Earl of Aberdeen.* London, 1893.

McCormac, Eugene I. "John Forsyth." *American Secretaries of State,* Vol. IV. New York, 1927.

———. *James K. Polk—A Political Biography.* Berkeley, 1922.

McLaughlin, A. C. *Lewis Cass.* Boston, 1891.

Parker, Charles Stuart. *Sir Robert Peel. From his Private Papers.* 3 vols. London, 1891–1899.

Sioussat, St. George Leakin. "James Buchanan." *American Secretaries of State,* Vol. V. New York, 1928.

———. "John Caldwell Calhoun." *American Secretaries of State,* Vol. V. New York, 1928.

Walpole, Sir Spencer. *Life of Lord John Russell.* 2 vols. London, 1889.

———. *Studies in Biography.* New York, 1907.

GENERAL WORKS

Allison, John M. S. *Thiers and the French Monarchy.* Boston, 1926.

Ame, Léon. *Étude sur Les Tarifs de Douanes et sur Les Traités de Commerce.* 2 vols. Paris, 1876.

American Antiquarian Society. *Proceedings of the Society, 1812–1849.* Worcester, 1912.

Ashley, Percy. *Modern Tariff History. Germany—United States —France.* New York, 1905.

Bastable, C. F. *The Commerce of Nations.* London, 1891. Ninth Edition revised by T. E. Gregory. London, 1925.

Brown, Everett S. "The Presidential Election of 1824–1825." *Political Science Quarterly,* September 1925, Vol. XL, pp. 384–403. New York, 1925.

Brown University. *Historical Catalogue of Brown University, Providence, Rhode Island, 1764–1894.* Providence, 1895.
Alumni Records.
Phi Beta Kappa Society Records.
Program of Commencement, 1802.

Bronson, Walter C. *The History of Brown University, 1764–1914.* Providence, 1914.

Butler, William Allen. *The Revision of the Statutes of the State of New York and the Revisers.* New York, 1889.
An address delivered before the Association of the Bar of the City of New York, January 22, 1889.

Buxton, Sir Thomas Fowell. *The African Slave Trade and its Remedy.* Philadelphia, 1839.

Chace, Henry R. *Owners and Occupants of the Lots, Houses and Shops in the Town of Providence, Rhode Island in 1798.* Providence, 1914.

Channing, Edward. *A History of the United States.* 6 vols. New York, 1905–1925.
This is the best general history of the United States from 1492 to 1865. A *General Index* has been compiled by Eva G. Moore (New York, 1932) as a supplementary volume to this history.

Clapham, J. H. "The Last Years of the Navigation Acts." *The English Historical Review,* Vol. XXV, pp. 480–501, 687–707. New York, 1910.

Cushing, Caleb. "Claims of the United States on Denmark." *Boston Monthly Magazine,* Vol. I, p. 401.
This article was reprinted from the *Boston Monthly Magazine* in the *North American Review,* April, 1826. Vol. XXII, pp. 456–459.

Dawson, William Harbutt. *Protection in Germany. A History of German Fiscal Policy during the Nineteenth Century.* London, 1904.

Dewey, Davis Rich. *Financial History of the United States.* New York, 1924.

Duckwitz, A. *Denkwürdigkeiten aus meinen öffentlichen Leben von 1841–1866: ein Beitrag zur bremischen und deutschen Geschichte.* Bremen, 1877.

Dulles, Foster Rhea. *The Old China Trade.* Boston and New York, 1930.

Fisk, George M. *Die handelspolitischen und sonstigen völkerrechtlichen Beziehungen zwischen Deutschland und den Vereinigten Staaten von Amerika: ein historisch-statistische Studie.* Stuttgart, 1897.

This is a history of the political and commercial relations between the United States and Germany from colonial days, when the chief relations were with Prussia, until 1894. The study was based on the archives of the American Embassy at Berlin. Fisk had access to them while he was secretary to the embassy but he did not have access to the archives of the German Government.

Fogdall, Soren J. M. P. *Danish-American Diplomacy, 1776–1920.* University of Iowa Studies in Social Science, Vol. VIII, 1921–1922, No. 2. Iowa City, 1922.

This is based principally on printed sources for the United States and on Danish archives.

Fox, Dixon Ryan. *The Decline of Aristocracy in the Politics of New York in Studies in History, Economics and Public Law, Columbia University.* Vol. LXXXVI. Whole Number 198. New York, 1919.

Gooch, G. P. *History and Historians in the Nineteenth Century.* London, 1920.

Guild, Reuben Aldridge. *History of Brown University, with illustrated Documents.* Providence, 1867.

Hale, Edward Everett. "A Fossil from the Tertiary." *Atlantic Monthly,* Vol. XLIV, pp. 98–106. July, 1879. Boston, 1879.

This is a brief history of the Phi Beta Kappa Society.

Hammond, Jabez D. *The History of Political Parties in the State of New York from the ratification of the Federal Constitution to December, 1840.* 2 vols. 4th Edition, corrected and enlarged. Buffalo, 1850.

Hay, Thomas Robson. "John C. Calhoun and the Presidential Campaign of 1824." *The North Carolina Historical Review,* Vol. XII, No. 1, pp. 20–44, January, 1935. Raleigh, N. C., 1935.

Hayden, Ralston. "The States' Rights Doctrine and the Treaty-

Making Power." *American Historical Review,* Vol. XXII. Richmond, Va., 1917.

Hazen, Charles Downer. *Europe Since 1815.* New York, 1910.

Heatley, D. P. *Diplomacy and the Study of International Relations.* Oxford, 1919.

Hershey, Amos S. *The Essentials of International Public Law.* New York, 1919.

Hessenland, F. *On Sound Dues and their Relations with General Commerce, translated from the German.* Stettin, 1854.

Hill, Charles E. *The Danish Sound Dues and the Command of the Baltic: a Study of International Relations.* Durham, N. C., 1926.
A scholarly study based on Danish source material.

Holt, W. Stull. *Treaties defeated by the Senate: a Study of the Struggle between President and Senate over the conduct of Foreign Relations.* Baltimore, 1933.
An analysis of the reasons for the defeat of the treaties based on a study of the documents.

Hudson, Frederic. *Journalism in the United States, from 1690 to 1872.* New York, 1873.

Jenkins, John S. *History of Political Parties in the State of New York: From the acknowledgment of the Independence of the United States, to the Inauguration of the Twelfth President, March, 1849.* Second Edition. Auburn, N. Y., 1849.

King, Henry, D. D. *Historical Statement.* Folder issued by the First Baptist Church. Providence, R. I. No Date.

Latané, John H. *American Foreign Policy.* New York, 1927.

Lingelbach, William E. "England and Neutral Trade." *The Military Historian and Economist.* Vol. II, No. 2. April, 1917. Reprint, 1917.

Martin, Henri. *History of France from the First Revolution to the Present Time.* Translated by Mary L. Booth and A. L. Alger. 3 vols. Boston, 1882.

Moore, John Bassett. *History and Digest of the International Arbitrations to which the United States has been a Party.* 6 vols. Washington, 1898.

Mott, F. L. "One Hundred and Twenty Years." *North American Review,* Vol. 240, No. 1, pp. 144–174. June, 1935. Concord, N. H., 1935.

Mowat, R. B. *The Diplomatic Relations of Great Britain and the United States.* London, 1925.

> This has to be checked with care. Intended for the general reader.

Nash, E. Gee. *The Hansa.* New York, 1929.

National Institute for the Promotion of Science. *Bulletins of the Proceedings.* Washington, 1842–1846.

Newton, A. P. "United States and Colonial Developments, 1815–1846." *The Cambridge History of British Foreign Policy,* Vol. II, 1783–1919. Edited by Sir A. W. Ward and G. P. Gooch. 3 vols. Cambridge, 1922–1923.

Ogg, Frederic Austin. *Economic Development of Modern Europe.* New York, 1926.

Oppenheim, L. *International Law, 4th Edition.* Edited by Arnold D. McNair. 2 vols. New York, 1928.

Paullin, C. O. *Diplomatic Negotiations of American Naval Officers, 1778–1883.* Baltimore, 1912.

> Contains extracts from Commanders' Letters and is based on research in the Navy and State Departments.

Rammelkamp, C. H. "The Campaign of 1824 in New York." *American Historical Association Annual Report, 1904.* Washington, 1905.

Reeves, Jesse S. *American Diplomacy under Tyler and Polk.* Baltimore, 1907.

> A scholarly study based on materials available in the United States.

Reddie, James. *Inquiries in International Law, Public and Private.* 2nd Edition enlarged. Edinburgh, 1851.

Rhode Island—A State Publication. *The Book of Rhode Island.* Providence, 1930.

> "An illustrated description of the advantages and opportunities of the state of Rhode Island and the progress that has been achieved, with historical sketches of many leading industries and a biographical record of citizens who have helped to produce the superb structure—historical, commercial, industrial, agricultural and recreational—which comprises the strength of this charming state."

Richelot, Henri. *L'Association Douaniere Allemande ou Le Zollverein son Histoire, son Organisation, ses Relations avec L'Autriche, ses Resultats.* Deuxième Edition. Paris, 1859.

One of the best histories of the organization and activities of the Zollverein from 1815 to 1859.

Rush, Richard. *American Jurisprudence.* Washington, 1815.
Written and published at Washington, being a few reflections suggested on reading "Wheaton on Captures," Presented Dec. 6, 1816, to the American Philosophical Society by the Author. A pamphlet of 52 pages which is in the library of the Society among their "Pamphlets on Law," Vol. 8, No. 8.

Sioussat, St. George Leakin. "Duff Green's 'England and the United States': with an Introductory Study of American opposition to the Quintuple Treaty of 1841." American Antiquarian Society *Proceedings* for October, 1930. Worcester, 1931. Reprinted by the Society, Worcester, 1931.

Soulsby, Hugh G. *The Right of Search and the Slave Trade in Anglo-American Relations, 1814–1862.* The Johns Hopkins University Studies in Historical and Political Science. Series LI, No. 2. Baltimore, 1933.

Stanwood, Edward. *American Tariff Controversies in the Nineteenth Century.* 2 vols. Boston, 1903–1904.

Taussig, F. W. *A Tariff History of the United States.* New York, 1914.

—— *International Trade.* New York, 1927.

Sybel, Heinrich von. *The Founding of the German Empire.* Translated by Helene Schimmelfannig White. 7 vols. New York, 1898.

Warren, Charles. *Congress, the Constitution, and the Supreme Court.* Boston, 1925.

—— *The Supreme Court in United States History.* 3 vols. Boston, 1922.

Weber, W. *Der Deutsche Zollverein.* Leipzig, 1871.

Wriston, Henry Merritt. *Executive Agents in American Foreign Relations.* London and Baltimore, 1929.
A valuable work as a guide for this phase of the diplomacy of the United States, but must be used carefully.

Zimmermann, Alfred. *Geschichte der preussisch-deutschen handelspolitik aktenmaszig dargestellt.* Oldenburg and Leipzig, 1892.
This is an important account and gives both the German and the English texts of Wheaton's treaty with the Zollverein, dated March 25, 1844.

INDEX

INDEX